1I0864912

GREAT BRITAIN

TOP SIGHTS, AUTHENTIC EXPERIENCES

Date: 2/2/22

914.1 GRE 2021
Harper, Damian,
Great Britain : top sights,
authentic experiences /

PALM BEACH COUNTY
LIBRARY SYSTEM
3650 Summit Boulevard
West Palm Beach, FL 33406-4198

Damian Harper, Isabel Albiston, Oliver Berry,
Joe Bindloss, Fionn Davenport, Belinda Dixon,
Anna Kaminski, Catherine Le Nevez,
Tasmin Waby, Neil Wilson

Contents

Northern Islands inset
Northern Islands
0 100 km
0 50 miles
Unst
Yell
Fetlar
Ulsta
Toft
Hillswick
Shetland
Lerwick
Foula
Mousa
Orkney
Fair Isle
Westray
North Ronaldsay
Sanday
Rousay
Stronsay
NORTH SEA
Kirkwall
Stromness
Hoy
South Ronaldsay
John O'Groats
Fraserburgh
Aberdeen
Stonehaven
RGH p217
Berwick-upon-Tweed
Newcastle-upon-Tyne
Durham
Middlesbrough
Darlington
Scarborough
York
YORK p173
Leeds
Hull
ENGLAND
Sheffield
Lincoln
Skegness
Nottingham
Leicester
Norwich
CAMBRIDGE p159
Birmingham
Northampton
Ipswich
Cheltenham
Luton
Colchester
Oxford
Southend-on-Sea
Windsor
LONDON
LONDON p35
Reading
Canterbury
Strait of Dover
Dover
Salisbury
Southampton
Brighton
Eastbourne
Portsmouth
ENGLISH CHANNEL
STONEHENGE p101
Dieppe
NORTH SEA
NETHERLANDS
AMSTERDAM
Den Haag (The Hague)
Rotterdam
Antwerp
Ghent
BRUSSELS
Liège
Calais
Lille
Charleroi
BELGIUM
FRANCE
Amiens
Islands inset

Welcome to Great Britain

The Tower of London, Oxford colleges, Stonehenge: Great Britain is such a roll call of crucial visitor viewing it's hard to know where to start. But that's not a problem: it's a compact nation, so you're never far from the next highlight.

From the soaring ramparts of Edinburgh Castle, via the mountains of North Wales and the picture-postcard landscape of the Cotswolds, Britain's extraordinary diversity is reason enough to visit. Urban Great Britain tempts with some of the world's finest museums, shops and restaurants, while cutting-edge clubs and world-famous theatres provide endless nocturnal excitement. Next morning, you can find yourself deep in the countryside, high in the hills or lounging by the seaside.

A journey through Britain is also a journey through history, culture and the unexpected. Stroll alongside the megaliths of a 5000-year-old stone circle, punt a boat past dreamy Cambridge colleges or see the school room where Shakespeare first learned to spell. Bath is a city flush with gorgeous Georgian architecture, but put time aside for the aristocratic ostentation of Blenheim Palace or the royal splendour of Windsor Castle. Scotland's Highlands and islands beckon you to the big outdoors, along with English lakes rich in literary heritage and Welsh mountains alive with adventure sports.

Variety is the name of the game – the countless castles, pubs and stately homes are ringed by lush farmland, snow-covered slopes or wind-whipped moors. Few countries pack so much into such a small space.

> *“Few countries pack so much into such a small space”*

Tower of London (p42)
IAKOV KALININ/SHUTTERSTOCK ©

0 200 km
0 100 miles
ATLANTIC
OCEAN
Lewis
Stornoway
Tarbert
St Kilda
Harris
North Uist
Lochmaddy
Uig
SKYE p267
Portree
South Uist
Lochboisdale
Barra
Sea of the Hebrides
The Minch
Durness
Thurso
John
Wick
Helmsdale
Ullapool
Dornoch
Gairloch
Elgin
Kyle of Lochalsh
Inverness
Nairn
Fort Augustus
Loch Ness
Aviemore
Newtonmore
Mallaig
Fort William
Ben Nevis (1345m)
SCOTLAND
THE SCOTTISH HIGHLANDS p249
Glencoe
Mull
Oban
Perth
Inveraray
Stirling
Loch Lomond
Jura
Dumbarton
Glasgow
Islay
Kilmarnock
Peebles
Arran
Melrose
Ayr
Campbeltown
Dumfries
Derry
NORTHERN IRELAND
Stranraer
Carlisle
Donegal
Omagh
BELFAST
Whitehaven
Sligo
Armagh
Isle of Man
Douglas
THE LAKE DISTRICT
Dundalk
Irish Sea
Blackpool
IRELAND
Liverpool
Galway
DUBLIN
Llandudno
Caernarfon
Betws-y-Coed
SNOWDONIA p207
Limerick
Kilkenny
Wexford
Aberystwyth
Killarney
Waterford
St George's Channel
Llanwrtyd Wells
WALES
Cork
OXFORD & THE COTSWOLDS p125
Pembroke
Abergavenny
Swansea
CARDIFF
Bristol Channel
BATH
Ilfracombe
Barnstaple
Exeter
Torquay
Plymouth
Penzance
Land's End
Isles of Scilly
Channel Islands
0 50 km
Alderney
Guernsey
St-Peter Port
Jersey
St Helier
FRANCE

In Focus

Survival Guide

COVID-19

We have re-checked every business in this book before publication to ensure that it is still open after the COVID-19 outbreak. However, the economic and social impacts of COVID-19 will continue to be felt long after the outbreak has been contained, and many businesses, services and events referenced in this guide may experience ongoing restrictions. Some businesses may be temporarily closed, have changed their opening hours and services, or require bookings; some unfortunately could have closed permanently. We suggest you check with venues before visiting for the latest information.

Plan Your Trip
Great Britain's Top 12

MARCO SIMONI/GETTY IMAGES ©

London

Truly one of the world's greatest cities

Mercurial and endlessly fascinating, London (p35) is a city you could spend a lifetime getting to know, then realise it's gone and changed again. Stretching back from the mighty River Thames, its lush parks and historic districts are crammed with extraordinary sights: royal palaces, grand cathedrals and remarkable museums and galleries. Add the pick of the world's theatres, restaurants, sports venues and shops, and you could be reluctant to leave.

1

PIO3/SHUTTERSTOCK ©

GIMAS/SHUTTERSTOCK ©

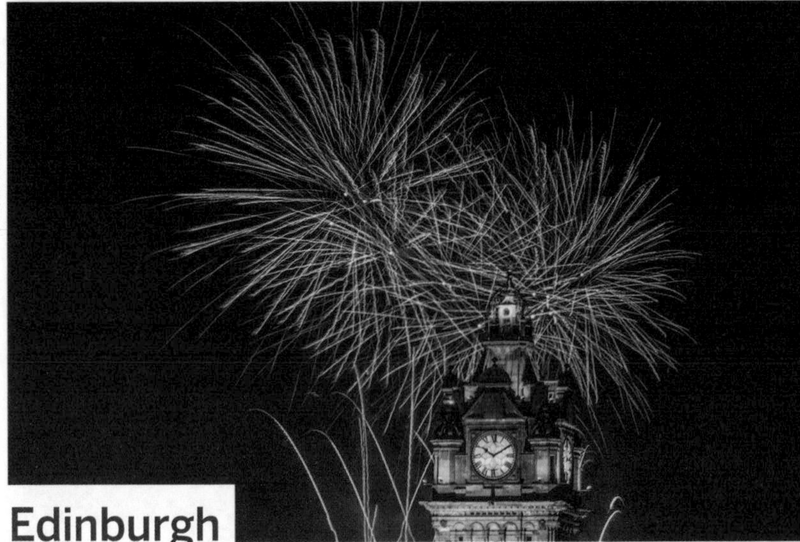

BRETT MCCALDIN/SHUTTERSTOCK ©

Edinburgh

Ancient, atmospheric and rich in lively pubs

Edinburgh (p217) is a city of many moods – famous for its festivals and for being particularly vibrant in the summer. But spring sees the castle silhouetted against a vivid blue sky, while chill winter mornings have the fog blurring the spires of the Old Town and steeping the ancient alleyways in more mystery than ever, with rain on shining cobbles and a warm glow emanating from pubs.

2

TRAVELLIGHT/SHUTTERSTOCK ©

Bath

Sublime architecture and chic city streets

Britain boasts many great cities, but Bath (p111) is the belle of the ball. The Romans built a health resort here, thanks to the natural hot springs that bubble to the surface. The waters were rediscovered in the 18th century, and Bath became the place to be seen. Today the stunning Georgian architecture of grand town houses and sweeping crescents means Bath would demand your undivided attention even without its Roman remains and swish 21st-century spa.

3

4

The Scottish Highlands

Scenic grandeur and echoes of the past

The Highlands (p249) abound in magnificent views. From the regal charm of Royal Deeside, via the brooding majesty of Glen Coe, to the mysterious waters of sweeping Loch Ness – these are landscapes that inspire awe. The region is scattered with fairy-tale castles and the hiking is suitably glorious. Add the nooks of warm Highland hospitality found in classic rural pubs and romantic hotels, and you have an unforgettable corner of the country.

Stonehenge

Massive, mysterious and utterly compelling

Stonehenge (p101) is Britain's most iconic ancient site. People have been drawn to this myth-laden ring of bluestones for 5000 years, and we still don't know why it was built. Most visitors gaze at the megaliths from the path, but with enough planning you can book an early-morning or evening tour and walk around the inner ring. Experiencing this ethereal place, in the slanting sunlight and away from the crowds, is unforgettable.

JOOST VAN UFFELEN/SHUTTERSTOCK ©

FUNKYFOOD LONDON - PAUL WILLIAMS/ALAMY STOCK PHOTO ©

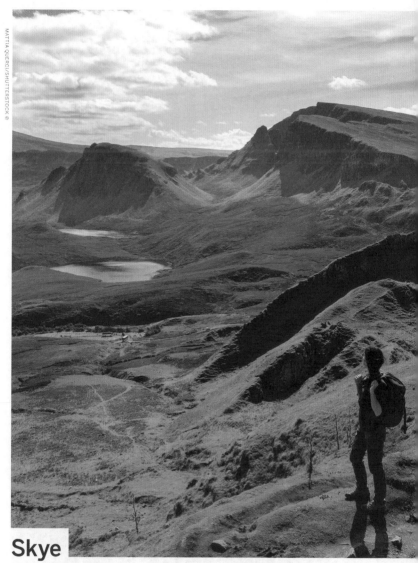

MATTIA QUERCI/SHUTTERSTOCK ©

Skye

The Scottish island of your imagination

Among Scotland's many islands, Skye (p267) is the most famous and best loved, thanks to a mix of history (Bonnie Prince Charlie and the 'Skye Boat Song'), accessibility (a bridge links to the mainland) and sheer, uninterrupted beauty. With jagged mountains, velvet moors and towering sea cliffs, Skye's scenery never fails to impress. And for those days when the mist comes in, there are plenty of castles, local museums and cosy pubs.

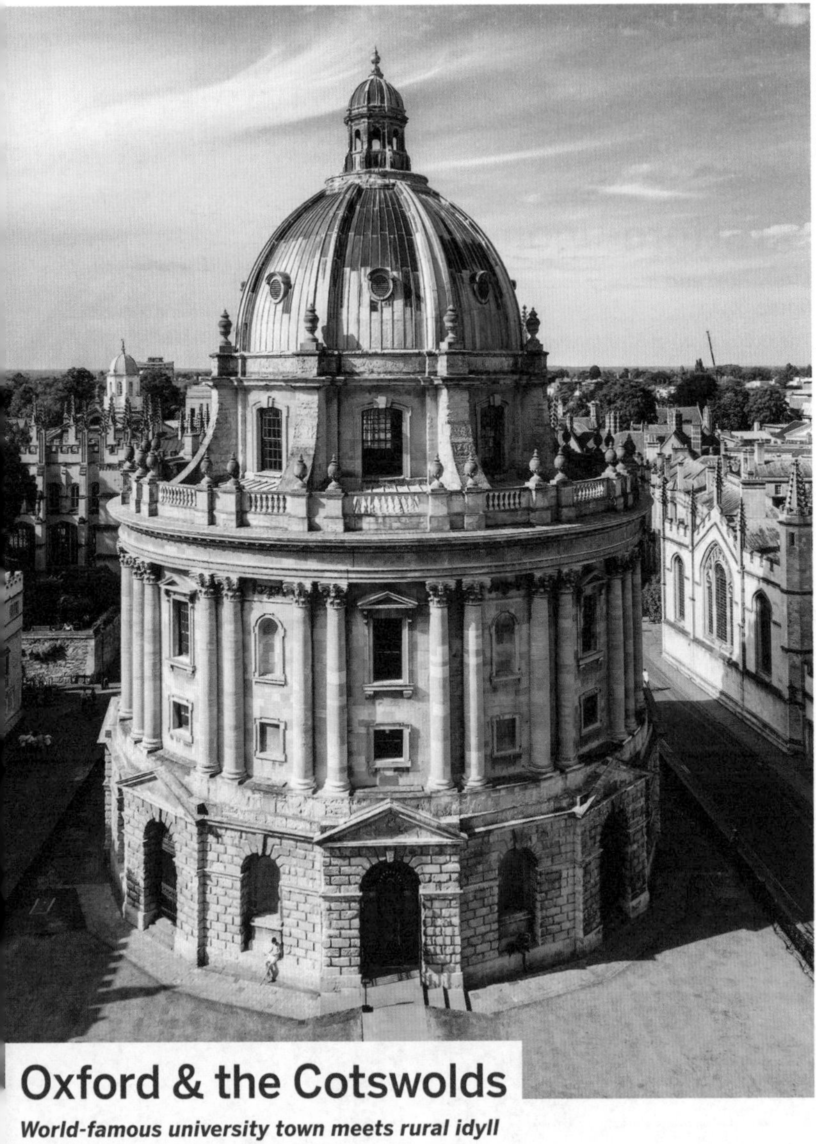

S-F/SHUTTERSTOCK ©

Oxford & the Cotswolds

World-famous university town meets rural idyll

For centuries, the brilliant minds and august institutions of Oxford University (p128) have made the city famous. It's a revered world you'll encounter as you stroll hushed college quads and cobbled lanes, discovering archaic traditions and stunning architecture. A short drive away lie the Cotswolds, where impossibly picturesque villages feature rose-clad cottages, honey-coloured churches, and pubs with fine ales and views of the lush green hills.

7

Stratford-upon-Avon

Literature and history in Shakespeare's home town

The pretty town of Stratford-upon-Avon (p147) is the birthplace of the nation's best-known dramatist, William Shakespeare. Today the town's tight knot of Tudor streets form a living map of Shakespeare's life and times, while crowds of fans and would-be thespians come to enjoy a play at the theatre or visit the historic houses owned by Shakespeare and his relatives, with a respectful detour to the old stone church where the Bard was laid to rest.

DANIEL_KAY/SHUTTERSTOCK ©

OVERSNAP/GETTY IMAGES ©

MONKEY BUSINESS IMAGES/SHUTTERSTOCK ©

9

The Lake District

Lyrical landscapes replete with literary links

William Wordsworth and his Romantic friends were the first to champion the charms of the Lake District (p193), and it's not hard to see why. The soaring mountains, whaleback fells, razor-edge valleys and – of course – glistening lakes make this craggy corner of the country the spiritual home of English hiking. Strap on the boots, stock up on mint cake and drink in the views: inspiration is sure to follow.

PHILMACDPHOTO/SHUTTERSTOCK ©

ROOTSSHOOTS/SHUTTERSTOCK ©

ANDREW MONTGOMERY/LONELY PLANET ©

Yorkshire

Dramatic moorland views; Roman and Viking history

Yorkshire (p173) lays claim to some of Britain's finest and wildest landscapes, with brooding moors and green dales rolling down to the shore. The historic county capital, York, is rich in Roman remains and Viking heritage. With ancient city walls and a maze of medieval streets, it's a living showcase for the highlights of English history and is also home to York Minster – the biggest medieval cathedral in all of northern Europe.

10

JUSTIN FOULKES/LONELY PLANET ©

Snowdonia

An adrenaline junkie's outdoor delight

The rugged northwest corner of Wales (p207) has rocky mountain peaks, glacier-hewn valleys, sparkling lakes and rivers, and charm-infused villages. The busiest part is around Snowdon itself, where many people hike to the summit, and many more take the jolly rack-and-pinion railway to the top. And all around, activity providers are just itching to set up adrenaline thrills ranging from zip lining and inland surfing to learning snow-craft skills.

CHRIS LAWRENCE TRAVEL/SHUTTERSTOCK ©

Cambridge

Extraordinary architecture and rich traditions

University town extraordinaire, Cambridge (p159) – with its tightly packed core of ancient colleges, picturesque riverside 'Backs' (college gardens) and surrounding green meadows – has a more tranquil appeal than its historic rival Oxford. Highlights include the intricate vaulting of King's College Chapel, while no visit is complete without an attempt to steer a punt along the river, or even better, find someone else to do it for you.

12

Plan Your Trip
Need to Know

When to Go

High Season (Jun–Aug)

- The best weather. Accommodation rates peak around August school holidays.
- Busy roads, especially in coastal areas, national parks and big-draw cities.

Shoulder (Mar–May, Sep & Oct)

- Crowds reduce; prices fall.
- Weather often good. March to May: sunny spells and sudden showers. September to October: chance of balmy Indian summer. For many Scottish outdoor activities, May and September are the best months.

Low Season (Nov–Feb)

- Wet and cold. Expect snow falls especially in mountain areas and the north.

Currency

Pound sterling (£)

Language

English; also Welsh and Scottish Gaelic

Visas

Generally not needed for stays of up to six months. Not a member of the Schengen Zone.

Money

Change bureaux and ATMs widely available, especially in cities and major towns.

Mobile Phones

The UK uses the GSM 900/1800 network, which covers the rest of Europe, Australia and New Zealand, but isn't compatible with the North American GSM 1900.

Time

Britain is on GMT/UTC. The clocks go forward for 'summer time' one hour at the end of March, and go back at the end of October. The 24-hour clock is used for transport timetables.

Daily Costs

Budget: **Less than £55**

- Dorm beds: £15–30
- Cheap meals in cafes and pubs: £8–12
- Long-distance coach: £15–40 (200 miles)

Midrange: **£55–120**

- Double room in a midrange hotel or B&B: £65–130 (London £100–200)
- Main course in a midrange restaurant: £10–20
- Long-distance train: £20–80 (200 miles)

Top End: **More than £120**

- Four-star hotel room: from £130 (London from £200)
- Three-course meal in a good restaurant: around £40
- Car rental per day: from £35

Useful Websites

BBC (www.bbc.co.uk) News and entertainment from the national broadcaster.
Visit Britain (www.visitbritain.com) Comprehensive official tourism website.
Lonely Planet (www.lonelyplanet.com/great-britain) Destination information, hotel bookings, traveller forum and more.
Traveline (www.traveline.info) Great portal site for public transport in all parts of Britain.
British Arts Festivals (www.artsfestivals.co.uk) Lists hundreds of festivals – art, literature, dance, folk and more.

Opening Hours

Expect shorter winter hours in rural areas; some places close completely from October to April.
Banks 9.30am–4pm or 5pm Monday to Friday; some open 9.30am–1pm Saturday
Pubs and bars Noon–11pm Monday to Saturday (many till midnight or 1am Friday and Saturday, especially in Scotland) and 12.30–11pm Sunday
Shops 9am–5.30pm (or 6pm in cities) Monday to Saturday, and often 11am– 5pm Sunday; big-city convenience stores open 24/7
Restaurants Lunch is noon–3pm, dinner 6–9pm (later in cities)

Arriving in Great Britain

Heathrow Airport (London) Trains, the London Underground and buses to central London run from just after 5am to before midnight (night buses run later); fares from £6 to £25.
Gatwick Airport (London) Trains to central London run from 4.30am to 1.35am (£17.80 to £19.90); hourly buses to central London around the clock from £9.
St Pancras International Station (central London) Receives Eurostar trains from Paris or Brussels; linked by London-wide Underground lines.
Victoria Coach Station (central London) Buses from Europe arrive here; frequent Underground links.
Edinburgh Airport (Edinburgh) Frequent trams (£6) and buses (£4.50) to Edinburgh city centre. Night buses every 30 minutes from 12am to 4am (£4.50).

Getting Around

Transport can be expensive compared to continental Europe. Bus and rail services are sparse in remote regions. For timetables, see www.traveline.info.

Car Set your own pace, especially in far-flung parts. Widespread car hire.

Train Relatively expensive. Extensive, frequent coverage country-wide.

Bus Cheaper and slower than trains; useful in more remote regions.

For more on **getting around**, see p312 

Plan Your Trip
Hotspots for...

DONSIMON/SHUTTERSTOCK ©

History

In Great Britain the past is ubiquitous, brought vividly to life by countless headline sights. It's a magical history tour.

London (p34)
With superlative parks, unique royal palaces and magnificent museums, London is a heritage-lover's dream.

Tower of London (p42)
Executions, royal intrigue and the splendiferous Crown Jewels.

Edinburgh (p217)
Crag-top castles, symbol-rich chapels and a maze of medieval alleys: Edinburgh is permeated with history.

Rosslyn Chapel (p226)
The dimly lit, densely decorated chapel in *The Da Vinci Code*.

Stonehenge (p101)
The mysterious monument exudes an almost hypnotic allure, amid a landscape rich in ritual and lore.

Stone Circle Experience (p106)
Book months in advance to walk between the stones.

MARMALADE PHOTOS/SHUTTERSTOCK ©

The Great Outdoors

From Scotland's wind-whipped isles, via adventure-packed Wales to the sublime Lake District, Britain offers an extraordinarily diverse landscape.

Skye (p267)
Scotland's wild isle is a patchwork of velvet moors, jagged mountains, sparkling lochs and towering sea cliffs.

Skye Wilderness Safaris (p273)
Hike into the Quiraing or through the Cuillin Hills.

Snowdonia (p207)
Adrenaline-pumping activities include heart-in-the mouth hiking, caving and white-water sports.

Surf Snowdonia (p211)
An adventure park centred on a vast artificial wave pool.

Lake District (p193)
All natural splendour: deep valleys, plunging passes, glittering lakes and barren hills.

Windermere Lake (p205)
Cruise the lake aboard a modern or period vessel.

CLAUDIO DIVIZIA/SHUTTERSTOCK©

Arts & Architecture

Thriving theatres, galleries packed with world-class art, fairly-tale castles, Georgian cityscapes and stately homes.

London (p34)
Blockbuster theatre shows, exquisite ballet and opera, iconic architecture and thought-provoking art.

Tate Modern (p46)
Free guided highlights tour of the modern art powerhouse.

Bath (p111)
Grand Georgian architecture, a Roman bathhouse and a cultured, sophisticated air.

No 1 Royal Crescent (p116)
A glimpse into the genteel splendour of Georgian life.

Stratford-upon-Avon (p147)
Few places are as steeped in Shakespeare as the birthplace of the Bard. Don't miss a performance.

RSC Guided Tours (p157)
A behind-the-scenes view of one of the world's grand stages.

LUCYDPHOTO/GETTY IMAGES ©

Food

Across the nation, stylish eateries and gourmet gastropubs vie for your attention.

Oxford & the Cotswolds (p125)
From zingy tapas to modern-British degustations, discover globetrotting restaurants and seasonal produce.

Two One Five (p142)
Relaxed, comfortable, contemporary and top-notch dining.

London (p34)
A dining destination of head-spinning culinary diversity, from Michelin-starred restaurants to global street food.

Foyer & Reading Room at Claridge's (p85)
Afternoon tea? Do it in style.

Skye (p267)
A small Scottish island offering a surprising wealth of superb culinary choice.

Scorrybreac (p275)
An intimate eatery serving Skye's local produce.

Plan Your Trip
Essential Great Britain

MICHAEL ROBERTS/GETTY IMAGES ©

Activities

The British love the great outdoors, and every weekend sees a mass exodus from the towns and cities to the mountains, hills, moors and shores. Hiking and biking are the most popular pursuits, but there's a huge range of activities available – from fishing and horse riding to skiing, climbing, kayaking and sailing. The Scottish Highlands, North Wales, Yorkshire and the Lake District are focal points for many activities. Stop off there and you might find getting wet and muddy is the highlight of your trip.

Shopping

From charity-shop finds to bespoke suits, Great Britain offers thousands of ways to spend your hard-earned cash. London boasts many big-name shopping attractions, including Harrods, Hamleys and Camden Market. In Edinburgh, Princes St's department stores are augmented by shops selling everything from designer threads and handmade jewellery to tartan goods. Oxford, Cambridge and York are dotted with antiques and secondhand bookshops. And everywhere there's a resurgence in farmers markets championing local produce. Get ready to spend.

Eating

Britain has enjoyed a culinary revolution over the past two decades. London is recognised as having one of the best restaurant scenes in the world, but the rest of Britain is also scattered with fine eateries making the most of superb local produce – you'll find happy feeding grounds in Edinburgh, the Highlands, the Cotswolds, Oxford, Cambridge, York and Bath, to name just a few. And everywhere in between all kinds of dining options – from swish restaurants to rural inns – are championing the culinary mantra: local, seasonal, organic.

BARMALINI/SHUTTERSTOCK ©

Drinking & Nightlife

Despite the growth of stylish clubs and designer bars, the traditional neighbourhood or village pub is still the centre of social life, and a visit can lead you right under the nation's skin. In these 'locals' the welcome is genuine, the fire is real and that tankard has perhaps hung on that hook for centuries. So now is the time to try the alcoholic beverages most associated with England (beer) and Scotland (whisky). Sampling them and appreciating their complexities – as well as visiting breweries and distilleries – could keep you occupied the whole trip.

Entertainment

As you'd expect, London offers theatre, dance and classical-music scenes that are among the best in the world. However you budget your time and money in the capital, make sure you take in a show. Edinburgh also has a thriving cultural scene, typified by its annual feast of performance: the Edinburgh Festival Fringe. The university cities of Cambridge and Oxford, and to a lesser extent Bath, are cultural hot spots too, with a wealth of new theatre works and classical concerts.

★ Best Restaurants

Clove Club (p89)
Menu Gordon Jones (p122)
Mason's Arms (p204)
Cochon Aveugle (p189)
Timberyard (p242)

From left: Hiker climbing Snowdon (p212); Scotch whisky

Plan Your Trip
Month by Month

OSCAR GARRIGA ESTRADA/SHUTTERSTOCK

January

London Parade
A ray of light in the gloom, the New Year's Day Parade in London (to use its official title; www.londonparade.co.uk) is one of the biggest events of its kind in the world, featuring marching bands, street performers, classic cars, floats and displays winding their way through the streets.

February

Jorvik Viking Festival
The ancient Viking capital of York becomes home once again to invaders and horned helmets galore, with the intriguing addition of longship races (www.jorvik-viking-festival.co.uk).

Fort William Mountain Festival
Britain's capital of the outdoors celebrates the peak of the winter season with ski workshops, mountaineering films and talks by big names in climbing (www.mountainfestival.co.uk).

March

University Boat Race
Annual race (www.theboatrace.org) down the River Thames in London between the rowing teams from Cambridge and Oxford universities; an institution since 1829 that still enthrals the country.

Six Nations Rugby Championship
The highlight of the rugby calendar (www.sixnationsrugby.com) runs from late January to March, with the home nations playing at London's Twickenham, Edinburgh's Murrayfield and Cardiff's Principality stadiums.

April

London Marathon
More than 35,000 runners take to the streets; super-fit athletes cover the 26.22 miles in just over two hours, while others dress up in daft costumes and take considerably longer (www.virginmoneylondonmarathon.com).

THEASIS/GETTY IMAGES ©

Beltane
Thousands of revellers climb Edinburgh's Calton Hill for this modern revival of a pagan fire festival (www.beltane.org) marking the end of winter.

Spirit of Speyside
Based in Dufftown, a Scottish festival (www.spiritofspeyside.com) of whisky, food and music, with five days of art, cooking, distillery tours and outdoor activities.

May

☆ FA Cup Final
Grand finale of the football (soccer) season for almost 150 years. Teams from across England battle it out over the winter months, culminating in this heady spectacle at Wembley Stadium – the home of English football.

Chelsea Flower Show
The Royal Horticultural Society flower show (www.rhs.org.uk/chelsea) at Chelsea is the highlight of the gardener's year.

★ Best Festivals
Glastonbury Festival, June

Edinburgh International Festival and Fringe, August

Trooping the Colour, June

Braemar Gathering, September

Guy Fawkes Night, November

June

☆ Cotswolds Olimpicks
Welly-wanging, pole-climbing and shin-kicking are the key disciplines at this traditional Gloucestershire sports day (www.olimpickgames.co.uk), held every year since 1612.

Trooping the Colour
Military bands and bear-skinned grenadiers march down London's Whitehall in this

From left: Trooping the Colour; Beltane

martial pageant (www.trooping-the-colour.co.uk) to mark the monarch's birthday.

☆ Wimbledon Tennis
The world's best-known tennis tournament (www.wimbledon.com), attracting all the big names, while crowds cheer and eat tons of strawberries and cream.

Glastonbury Festival
One of Britain's favourite pop and rock gatherings (www.glastonburyfestivals.co.uk) is invariably muddy, and still a rite of passage for every self-respecting British music fan.

July

Great Yorkshire Show
Harrogate plays host to one of Britain's largest county shows (www.greatyorkshireshow.co.uk). This is the place for Yorkshire grit, Yorkshire tykes, Yorkshire puddings, Yorkshire beef…

International Musical Eisteddfod
Festival of international folk music (www.international-eisteddfod.co.uk) at Llangollen, with eclectic fringe and big-name evening concerts.

Cowes Week
Britain's biggest yachting spectacular (www.cowesweek.co.uk) on the choppy seas around the Isle of Wight.

Womad
Roots and world music take centre stage at this festival (www.womad.org) in a country park in the south Cotswolds.

August

☆ Edinburgh's Festivals
Edinburgh's most famous August happenings are the International Festival and Fringe, but this month the city also has an event (www.edinburghfestivalcity.com) for anything you care to name – books, art, theatre, music, comedy, marching bands…

Notting Hill Carnival
London's famous multicultural Caribbean-style street carnival (www.nhcarnival.org) in the district of Notting Hill. Steel drums, dancers, outrageous costumes.

September

☆ Braemar Gathering
The biggest and most famous Highland Games (www.braemargathering.org) in the Scottish calendar, traditionally attended by members of the royal family. Highland dancing, caber tossing and bagpipe playing.

October

Falmouth Oyster Festival
The West Country port of Falmouth marks the start of the traditional oyster-catching season (www.falmouthoysterfestival.co.uk) with a celebration of local food from the sea and fields of Cornwall.

November

Guy Fawkes Night
Fireworks fill Britain's skies on 5 November for Bonfire Night (www.bonfirenight.net) in commemoration of a failed attempt to blow up parliament, way back in 1605.

Remembrance Day
Red poppies are worn and wreaths are laid in towns and cities around the country on 11 November in commemoration (www.britishlegion.org.uk) of fallen military personnel.

December

New Year Celebrations
The last night of December sees fireworks and street parties in town squares across the country. London's Trafalgar Sq is where the city's largest crowds gather to welcome the New Year.

Plan Your Trip
Get Inspired

Read

Notes from a Small Island (Bill Bryson; 1995) An American's fond and astute take on Britain.

Raw Spirit (Iain Banks; 2003) An enjoyable jaunt around Scotland in search of the perfect whisky.

Slow Coast Home (Josie Drew; 2003) The chatty tale of a 5000-mile cycle tour through England and Wales.

The Remains of the Day (Kazuo Ishiguro; 1989) Hypnotising first-person narration by a dignified English butler, penned by a master novelist.

On the Slow Train (Michael Williams; 2011) A paean to the pleasure of British rail travel.

Watch

Brief Encounter (1945) Classic tale of a buttoned-up English love affair.

An American Werewolf in London (1981) Superb lycanthropic horror-comedy set between the Yorkshire moors and London.

Trainspotting (1996) The gritty underbelly of life among Edinburgh drug addicts.

Withnail & I (1987) Cult comedy about two out-of-work actors on a disastrous Lake District holiday.

Submarine (2010) Scabrous coming-of-age tale set in 1980s-era Swansea.

Listen

Warwick Avenue (Duffy; 2008) Song of heartbreak and break-up from the beautifully voiced Welsh starlet.

You Know I'm No Good (Amy Winehouse; 2006) Classic song from the deceased North London chanteuse.

Ghost Town (The Specials; 1981) Classic track from the maestros of two-tone.

Hometown Glory (Adele; 2007) London soulstress muses fondly on West Norwood.

Parklife (Blur; 1994) Britpop-meets-Barnet courtesy of Damon Albarn and co.

Common People (Pulp; 1994) Jarvis Cocker's wry commentary on British class.

Above: Statue of Amy Winehouse by Scott Eaton

Plan Your Trip
Five-Day Itineraries

Capitals & Colleges

On this trip you'll experience Britain's best cities and oldest universities. Start with a day in Oxford for a taste of prestigious college life, then it's two days in London and Edinburgh discovering your favourite parts of these two irresistible cities.

FROM LEFT: A.B.G/ SHUTTERSTOCK © ; ALEX SEGRE/SHUTTERSTOCK ©

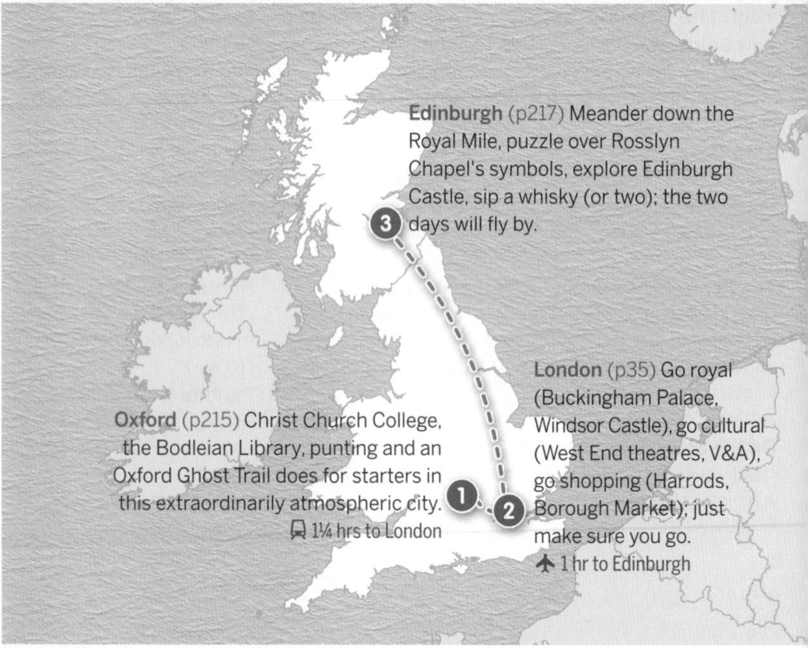

Edinburgh (p217) Meander down the Royal Mile, puzzle over Rosslyn Chapel's symbols, explore Edinburgh Castle, sip a whisky (or two); the two days will fly by.

London (p35) Go royal (Buckingham Palace, Windsor Castle), go cultural (West End theatres, V&A), go shopping (Harrods, Borough Market); just make sure you go.

✈ 1 hr to Edinburgh

Oxford (p215) Christ Church College, the Bodleian Library, punting and an Oxford Ghost Trail does for starters in this extraordinarily atmospheric city.

1¼ hrs to London

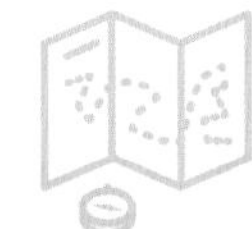

Glorious Scotland

Scotland, they say, stays with you. This trip ensures it does, leading from Edinburgh's blockbuster sights and cultural venues into the Highlands, to find scenery, wildlife and distilleries. It ends with a jaunt to the hauntingly beautiful Isle of Skye.

1 **Edinburgh** (p217) Historic Holyroodhouse, Edinburgh's winding medieval alleyways and (some of) the city's 700 pubs and bars can be squeezed into a day. 🚗 3 hrs to Fort William

2 **The Highlands** (p249) Time for a Highland fling: towering Ben Nevis, glowering Glen Coe and glittering Loch Ness. Prepare for spectacular views. 🚗 2½ hrs to Portree

3 **Isle of Skye** (p267) Hike the slopes of the Cuillin Hills beneath knife-edge ridges, sea-kayak around sheltered coves and fall in love with pretty harbour-town Portree.

FROM LEFT: ILAN SHACHAM/GETTY IMAGES ©; IAMINUT/SHUTTERSTOCK ©

Plan Your Trip
10-Day Itinerary

Mountains & Moors

Pack your hiking boots and your waterproofs: this outdoor extravaganza winds through some of Wales' and England's best wild spaces. Start by increasing your heart rate in activity-central Snowdonia, then peel off north to hike the Lake District and Yorkshire's dales and moors.

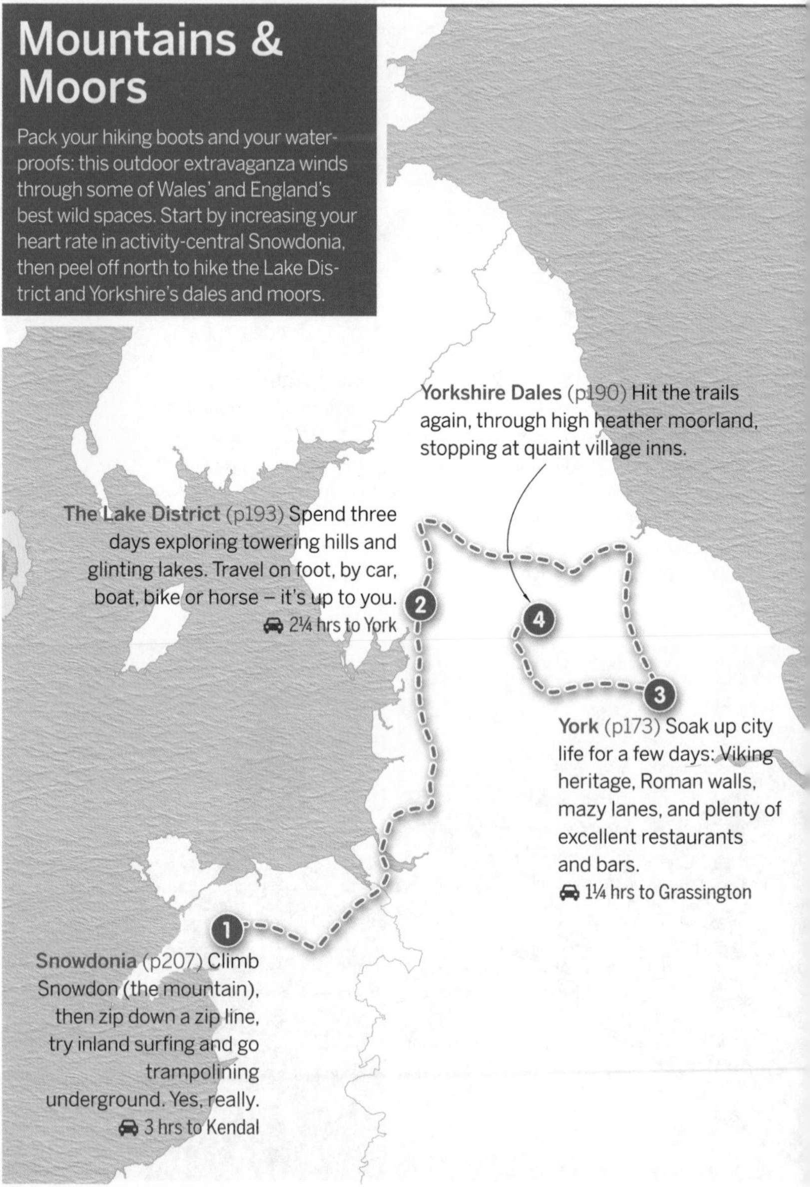

1 Snowdonia (p207) Climb Snowdon (the mountain), then zip down a zip line, try inland surfing and go trampolining underground. Yes, really.
🚗 3 hrs to Kendal

2 The Lake District (p193) Spend three days exploring towering hills and glinting lakes. Travel on foot, by car, boat, bike or horse – it's up to you.
🚗 2¼ hrs to York

3 York (p173) Soak up city life for a few days: Viking heritage, Roman walls, mazy lanes, and plenty of excellent restaurants and bars.
🚗 1¼ hrs to Grassington

4 Yorkshire Dales (p190) Hit the trails again, through high heather moorland, stopping at quaint village inns.

CLOCKWISE FROM LEFT: KEVIN EAVES/SHUTTERSTOCK ©; STEVE ALLEN/SHUTTERSTOCK ©; UNDIVIDED/SHUTTERSTOCK ©

Plan Your Trip
Two-Week Itinerary

Historic South

Energising cities, must-see ancient sites and two world-class universities – this is a tour of Britain's big heritage drawcards. After three leisurely London days, meander west to take in Stonehenge, Georgian Bath and the bucolic Cotswolds before heading off to prestigious seats of literature and learning.

Stratford-upon-Avon (p147) Strolling from sight to sight in Shakespeare's home town means you'll walk a veritable map of his life. Finish with a show at the RSC. 🚗 1 hr to Oxford

The Cotswolds (p125) Cruise rolling hills, stopping at honey-coloured villages for afternoon tea. Burford, the Slaughters and Chipping Campden are highlights. 🚗 ¼ hr to Stratford-upon-Avon

Bath (p111) Take two days to drink in Bath's Roman and Georgian beauty. Don't miss an alfresco, roof-top dip in the swish spa. 🚗 1 hr to Bibury

DAVID HUGHES/SHUTTERSTOCK ©

Cambridge (p159) King's College Chapel and Trinity College are must-dos, as is a chauffeur-driven punt. The Fitzwilliam and Polar museums are tempting, too.

Oxford (p125) Two days sees you touring college quads, atmospheric libraries and eclectic museums, plus stopping by ancient pubs and Harry Potter sights. 🚗 2 hrs to Cambridge

London (p35) Explore the Tower of London, the Tate Modern and the British Museum, plus hip eateries and pubs. 🚌 1½ hr to Salisbury, then 🚌 ½ hr to Stonehenge

Stonehenge (p101) Learn about Stonehenge's construction at the high-tech, on-site museum, then visit the vast stones themselves. 🚌 ½ hr to Salisbury, then 🚌 1hr to Bath

FROM LEFT: ARIADNA DE RAADT/SHUTTERSTOCK ©; ALEXKOZLOV/GETTY IMAGES ©

Plan Your Trip
Family Travel

ELROCE/SHUTTERSTOCK ©

Britain is ideal for travelling with children because of its compact size, packing numerous attractions into a small area. Many places of interest cater for kids as much as adults. At historic castles, for example, mum and dad can admire the medieval architecture, while the kids can stride around the battlements or watch jousting tournaments and falconry displays. In the same way, many national parks and holiday resorts organise specific activities for children. Everything ramps up in the school holidays.

When to Go

The best time for families to visit Britain is from April/May to the end of September. It's worth avoiding August – the heart of school summer holidays – when prices go up and roads are busy, especially near the coast. Other school holidays are the two weeks around Easter Sunday, and mid-December to early January, plus three week-long 'half-term' breaks – usually late February (or early March), late May and late October.

Accommodation

Some hotels welcome kids (with their parents) and provide cots, toys and babysitting services; others maintain an adult atmosphere. Many B&Bs offer 'family suites' of two adjoining bedrooms with one bathroom, and an increasing number of hostels have family rooms. If you want to stay in one place for a while, renting a holiday cottage is ideal and camping is very popular with British families.

Baby-Changing Facilities

Most museums and other attractions in Britain usually have good baby-changing facilities. Elsewhere, some city-centre public toilets have baby-changing areas, although these can be a bit grimy; your best bet for clean facilities is an upmarket department store. On the road, baby-changing facilities are generally bearable at motorway service stations.

KEV GREGORY/SHUTTERSTOCK ©

Best Regions for Kids

London Children's attractions galore, with many free. Ample green space.

The Lake District Kayaks for teenagers; boat rides and Beatrix Potter for youngsters.

Oxford & the Cotswolds Oxford has Harry Potter connections; the Cotswolds is ideal for little-leg strolls.

Snowdonia Zip wires, artificial surf lagoons and vast, subterranean trampolines.

Edinburgh Tons of kid-friendly museums and castles.

The Scottish Highlands Hardy teenagers plunge into outdoor activities; Nessie-spotting at Loch Ness is fun for the whole family.

Useful Resources

Lonely Planet Kids (www.lonelyplanetkids.com) Loads of activities and great family-travel blog content.

City Trails London (shop.lonelyplanet.com) Discover London's best-kept secrets, amazing stories and loads of other cool stuff.

★ Best Experiences for the Family

Science Museum (p75), London

Ghost Hunt of York (p185), York

Roman Baths (p115), Bath

Natural History Museum (p75), London

National Railway Museum (p182), York

MumsNet (www.mumsnet.com) No-nonsense advice from a vast network of UK mums.

Baby Goes 2 (www.babygoes2.com) Advice, tips and information for families on tour.

Kids Rule! (www.english-heritage.org.uk/members-area/kids) Engaging historical facts for UK sites.

Geocaching UK (www.geocaching.co.uk) Treasure-hunting for the digital age.

From left: Natural History Museum (p75), London; National Railway Museum (p182), York

London Eye

LONDON
Big Ben

The Shard
Westminster Abbey

St. Thomas' Hospital

Camden Market
Clerkenwell, Shoreditch & Spitalfields
A regenerated, creative area of excellent markets and a lively nightlife.
Euston
Paddington
The West End
Bursting with life and packed with blockbuster sights, shops, theatres and bars.
(18mi)
Windsor Castle
Buckingham Palace
Natural History Museum
Victoria & Albert Museum
Victoria
Kensington & Hyde Park
London's museum central: the extraordinary V&A, Natural History and Science Museums.

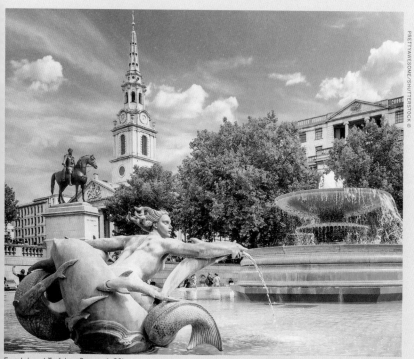

PRETTYAWESOME/SHUTTERSTOCK ©

Fountains at Trafalgar Square (p66)

Arriving in London

Heathrow Airport Trains, the Tube and buses to the centre (£5.10 to £25). Taxi £50 to £100.

Gatwick Airport Train (£10 to £20), bus (from £10) or taxi (£100) to the centre.

Stansted Airport Train (£19.40), bus (£7 to £10) or taxi (from £130) to the centre.

St Pancras International Train Station In central London (for Eurostar train arrivals); connected to the Tube.

Where to Stay

Hanging your hat (or anything else you care to remove) in London can be expensive, and you'll almost always need to book well in advance. London's hostels have improved in standard in recent years. Hotels range from no-frills chains through to the world's most ritzy establishments, such as the Ritz itself. For more information on the best neighbourhoods to stay in, see p99.

JAROSLAV MORAVCIK/SHUTTERSTOCK ©

British Museum

One of the oldest and finest in the world, this famous museum boasts vast Egyptian, Etruscan, Greek, Roman, European and Middle Eastern galleries, among others. It is frequently London's most visited attraction, drawing 5.8 million visitors annually.

Great For...

☑ Don't Miss

The Rosetta Stone. This sizeable jagged fragment was the key to deciphering Egyptian hieroglyphics.

Great Court

Covered with a spectacular glass-and-steel roof designed by Norman Foster in 2000, the Great Court is the largest covered public square in Europe. In its centre is the world-famous Reading Room.

Ancient Egypt, Middle East & Greece

The Ancient Egypt collection is the star of the show. It comprises sculptures, fine jewellery, papyrus texts, coffins and mummies, including the beautiful and intriguing Mummy of Katebet (room 63). The most prized item in the collection is the Rosetta Stone (room 4), discovered in 1799. In the same room, look out for the enormous bust of the pharaoh Ramesses II.

KIEVVICTOR/SHUTTERSTOCK ©

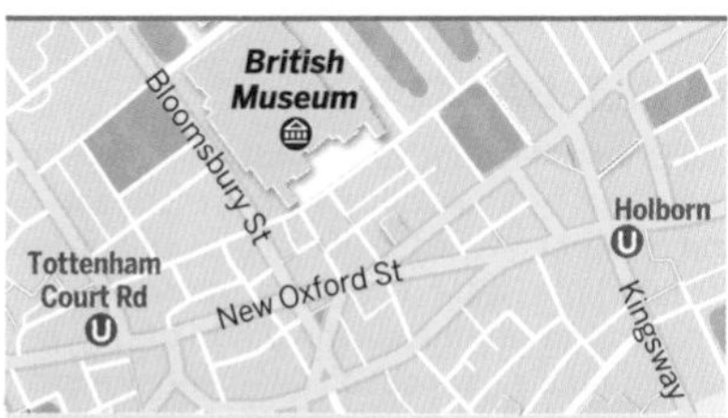

Need to Know

Map p64; 020-7323 8000; www.britishmuseum.org; Great Russell St, WC1; 10am-5pm (last entry 3.30pm); Tottenham Court Rd or Russell Sq; FREE

Take a Break

Enjoy a cake and browse at **London Review Bookshop** (020-7269 9030; www.londonreviewbookshop.co.uk; 14 Bury Pl, WC1; 10am-6.30pm Mon-Sat, noon-6pm Sun; Holborn) around the corner.

★ Top Tip

Pre-book your visit at least a month in advance.

Assyrian treasures from ancient Mesopotamia include the 16-tonne Winged Bulls from Khorsabad (room 10).

Another major highlight is the controversial Parthenon sculptures (room 18), which were taken from the Parthenon in Athens by Lord Elgin (the British ambassador to the Ottoman Empire).

Roman & Medieval Britain

The Mildenhall Treasure (room 49) is a collection of pieces of 4th-century CE Roman silverware from Suffolk with both pagan and early Christian motifs.

Don't miss Lindow Man in room 50 – the preserved remains of a 1st-century man, discovered in a bog in northern England in 1984. Equally fascinating are artefacts from the Sutton Hoo Ship Burial, an elaborate 7th-century Anglo-Saxon burial site from Suffolk.

Perennial favourites are the Lewis Chessmen (room 40), 12th-century game pieces carved from walrus tusk and whale teeth that were found on a remote Scottish island.

Enlightenment Gallery

Formerly known as the King's Library, this neoclassical space (room 1) contains collections tracing how biology, archaeology, linguistics and geography emerged during the 18th-century Enlightenment.

History of the World in 100 Objects

For a more digestible way to absorb the museum, download the free podcast *History of the World in 100 Objects*, a 100-part BBC series from the British Museum's former director. It truly spans human history, from a two-million-year-old stone tool to a Sharia-law-compliant credit card. Not all objects are always on display; check the museum website to see what's there.

The British Museum

A HALF-DAY TOUR

The British Museum, with almost eight million items in its permanent collection, is so vast and comprehensive that it can be daunting for the first-time visitor. To avoid a frustrating trip – and getting lost on the way to the Egyptian mummies – set out on this half-day exploration, which takes in some of the museum's most important sights. If you want to see and learn more, download the British Museum audio guide app to your phone pre-arrival.

A good starting point is the **1 Rosetta Stone**, the key that cracked the code to ancient Egypt's writing system. Nearby treasures from Assyria – an ancient civilisation centred in Mesopotamia between the Tigris and Euphrates Rivers – including the colossal **2 Winged Bulls from Khorsabad**, give way to the **3 Parthenon Sculptures**, high points of classical Greek art that continue to influence us today. Be sure to see both the sculptures and the

Winged Bulls from Khorsabad
This awesome pair of alabaster winged bulls with human heads once guarded the entrance to the palace of Assyrian King Sargon II at Khorsabad in Mesopotamia, a cradle of civilisation in present-day Iraq.

Parthenon Sculptures
The Parthenon, a white marble temple dedicated to Athena, was part of a fortified citadel on the Acropolis in Athens. There are dozens of sculpture and friezes with models and interactive displays explaining how they all once fitted together.

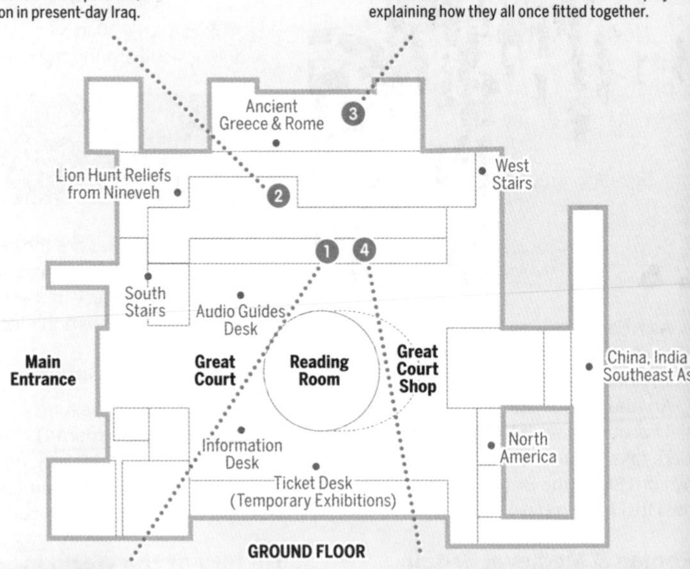

Bust of Pharaoh Ramesses II
The most impressive sculpture in the Egyptian galleries, this 725kg bust portrays Ramesses the Great, scourge of the Israelites in the Book of Exodus, as great benefactor.

Rosetta Stone
Written in hieroglyphic, demotic (cursive ancient Egyptian script used for everyday) and Greek, the 762kg stone contains a decree exempting priests from tax on the first anniversary of young Ptolemy V's coronation.

PHOTOS.COM / GETTY IMAGES ©

ıonumental frieze celebrating the birth of .thena. En route to the West Stairs is a huge 4 **Bust of Pharaoh Ramesses II**, just a int of the large collection of 5 **Egyptian ıummies** upstairs. (The earliest, affection- tely called Ginger because of wispy reddish air, was preserved simply by hot sand.) he Romans introduce visitors to the early ritain galleries via the rich 6 **Mildenhall reasure**. The Anglo-Saxon 7 **Sutton Hoo hip Burial** and the medieval 8 **Lewis hessmen** follow.

EATING OPTIONS

Court Cafe At the northern end of the Great Court; takeaway counters with salads and sandwiches; communal tables.

Gallery Pizzeria Out of the way off Room 12; quieter; children's menu available.

Great Court Restaurant Upstairs overlooking the former Reading Room; sit-down meals.

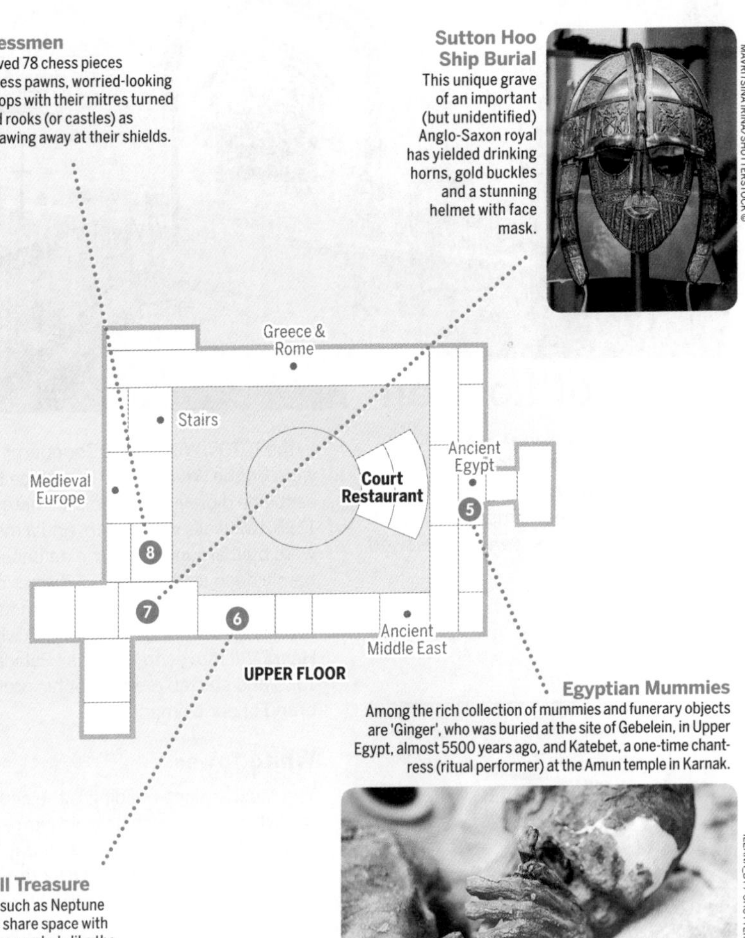

ewis Chessmen
he much-loved 78 chess pieces ortray faceless pawns, worried-looking ueens, bishops with their mitres turned deways and rooks (or castles) as arders', gnawing away at their shields.

Sutton Hoo Ship Burial
This unique grave of an important (but unidentified) Anglo-Saxon royal has yielded drinking horns, gold buckles and a stunning helmet with face mask.

MAVRITSINA IRINA/SHUTTERSTOCK ©

Egyptian Mummies
Among the rich collection of mummies and funerary objects are 'Ginger', who was buried at the site of Gebelein, in Upper Egypt, almost 5500 years ago, and Katebet, a one-time chantress (ritual performer) at the Amun temple in Karnak.

ILEANA_BT / SHUTTERSTOCK ©

ildenhall Treasure
oman gods such as Neptune nd Bacchus share space with rly Christian symbols like the *i-rho* (short for 'Christ') on e find's almost three dozen

ANDREY ALDONIN/SHUTTERSTOCK ©

Tower of London

The unmissable Tower of London offers a window into a gruesome and compelling history. This was where a king and three queens met their death and countless others were imprisoned.

Great For...

☑ Don't Miss

The spectacular Crown Jewels, including the Imperial State Crown, set with 2868 diamonds.

In the 1070s, William the Conqueror started work on the White Tower to replace the castle he'd previously had built here. By 1285, two walls with towers and a moat were built around it and the defences have barely been altered since. A former royal residence, treasury, mint and armoury, it became most famous as a prison when Henry VIII moved to Whitehall Palace in 1529 and started meting out his preferred brand of punishment.

White Tower

The most striking building is the central White Tower, with its solid Norman architecture and four turrets. Today on the entrance floor it houses a collection from the Royal Armouries, including Henry VIII's commodious suit of armour. On the middle floor is St John's Chapel, dating from 1080

Yeoman Warders

WILL RODRIGUES/SHUTTERSTOCK ©

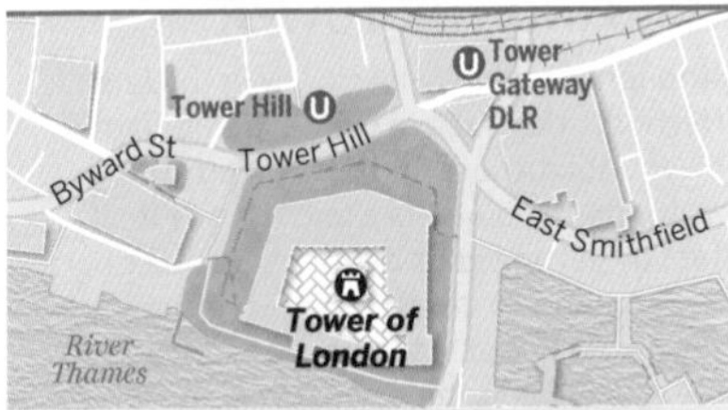

Need to Know

Map p72; 020-3166 6000; www.hrp.org.uk/tower-of-london; Petty Wales, EC3; adult/child £25/12.50; 9am-4.30pm, from 10am Sun & Mon; Tower Hill

Take a Break

The **New Armouries Cafe** in the south-eastern corner of the inner courtyard offers hot meals and sandwiches.

★ Top Tip

Book online for cheaper rates for the Tower.

and therefore the oldest place of Christian worship in London.

Crown Jewels

Waterloo Barracks now contains the glittering Crown Jewels, including the platinum crown of the late Queen Mother, set with the 106-carat Koh-i-Nûr (Mountain of Light) diamond and the Imperial State Crown, worn by the Queen at the State Opening of Parliament. Slow-moving travelators shunt wide-eyed visitors past the collection.

The Bloody Tower

On the far side of the White Tower is the Bloody Tower, where 12-year-old Edward V and his little brother Richard were held 'for their own safety' and later murdered, perhaps by their uncle, the future Richard III. Sir Walter Raleigh did a 13-year stretch here, too, under James I, when he wrote his *Historie of the World*.

Executions & Ravens

In front of the Chapel Royal of St Peter ad Vincula stood Henry VIII's scaffold, where nobles such as Anne Boleyn and Catherine Howard (Henry's second and fifth wives) were beheaded. Look out for the latest in the Tower's long line of famous ravens, which legend says could cause the White Tower to collapse should they leave (their wing feathers are clipped in case they get any ideas).

Guided Tours

To get your bearings, take the entertaining (and free) guided tour with any of the Beefeaters. The 45-minute-long tours leave every 30 minutes from the bridge near the main entrance; the last tour is an hour before closing.

Tower of London

TACKLING THE TOWER

Although it's usually less busy in the late afternoon, don't leave your assault on the Tower until too late in the day. You could easily spend hours here and not see it all. Start by getting your bearings on one of the Yeoman Warder (beefeater) tours; they are included in the cost of admission, entertaining and the easiest way to access the 1 **Chapel Royal of St Peter ad Vincula**, which is where they finish up.

When you leave the chapel, the 2 **Scaffold Site** is directly in front. The building immediately to your left is Waterloo Barracks, where the 3 **Crown Jewels** are housed. These are the absolute highlight of a Tower visit, so keep an eye on the entrance and pick a time to visit when it looks relatively quiet. Once inside, take things at your own pace. Slow-moving travelators shunt you past the dozen or so crowns that are the treasury's centrepieces, but feel free to double-back for a second or even third pass.

Allow plenty of time for the 4 **White Tower**, the core of the whole complex, starting with the exhibition of royal armour. As you continue onto the 1st floor, keep an eye out for 5 **St John's Chapel**.

The famous 6 **ravens** can be seen in the courtyard south of the White Tower. Next, visit the 7 **Bloody Tower** and the torture displays in the dungeon of the Wakefield Tower. Head next through the towers that formed the 8 **Medieval Palace**, then take the 9 **East Wall Walk** to get a feel for the castle's mighty battlements. Spend the rest of your time poking around the many other fascinating nooks and crannies of the Tower complex.

BEAT THE QUEUES

➡ Buy tickets online, avoid weekends and aim to be at the Tower first thing in the morning, when queues are shortest.

➡ The London Pass (www.londonpass.com) allows you to jump the queues and visit the Tower (plus some other 80 attractions) as often as you like.

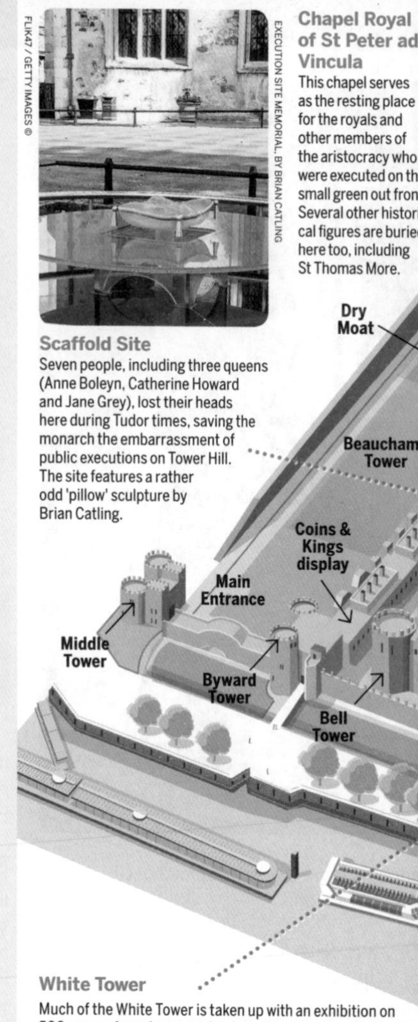

FLIK47 / GETTY IMAGES ©

EXECUTION SITE MEMORIAL, BY BRIAN CATLING

Chapel Royal of St Peter ad Vincula
This chapel serves as the resting place for the royals and other members of the aristocracy who were executed on the small green out front. Several other historical figures are buried here too, including St Thomas More.

Scaffold Site
Seven people, including three queens (Anne Boleyn, Catherine Howard and Jane Grey), lost their heads here during Tudor times, saving the monarch the embarrassment of public executions on Tower Hill. The site features a rather odd 'pillow' sculpture by Brian Catling.

White Tower
Much of the White Tower is taken up with an exhibition on 500 years of royal armour. Look for the virtually cuboid suit made to match Henry VIII's bloated 49-year-old body, complete with an oversized armoured codpiece to protect, ahem, the crown jewels.

CHRISDORNEY / SHUTTERSTOCK ©

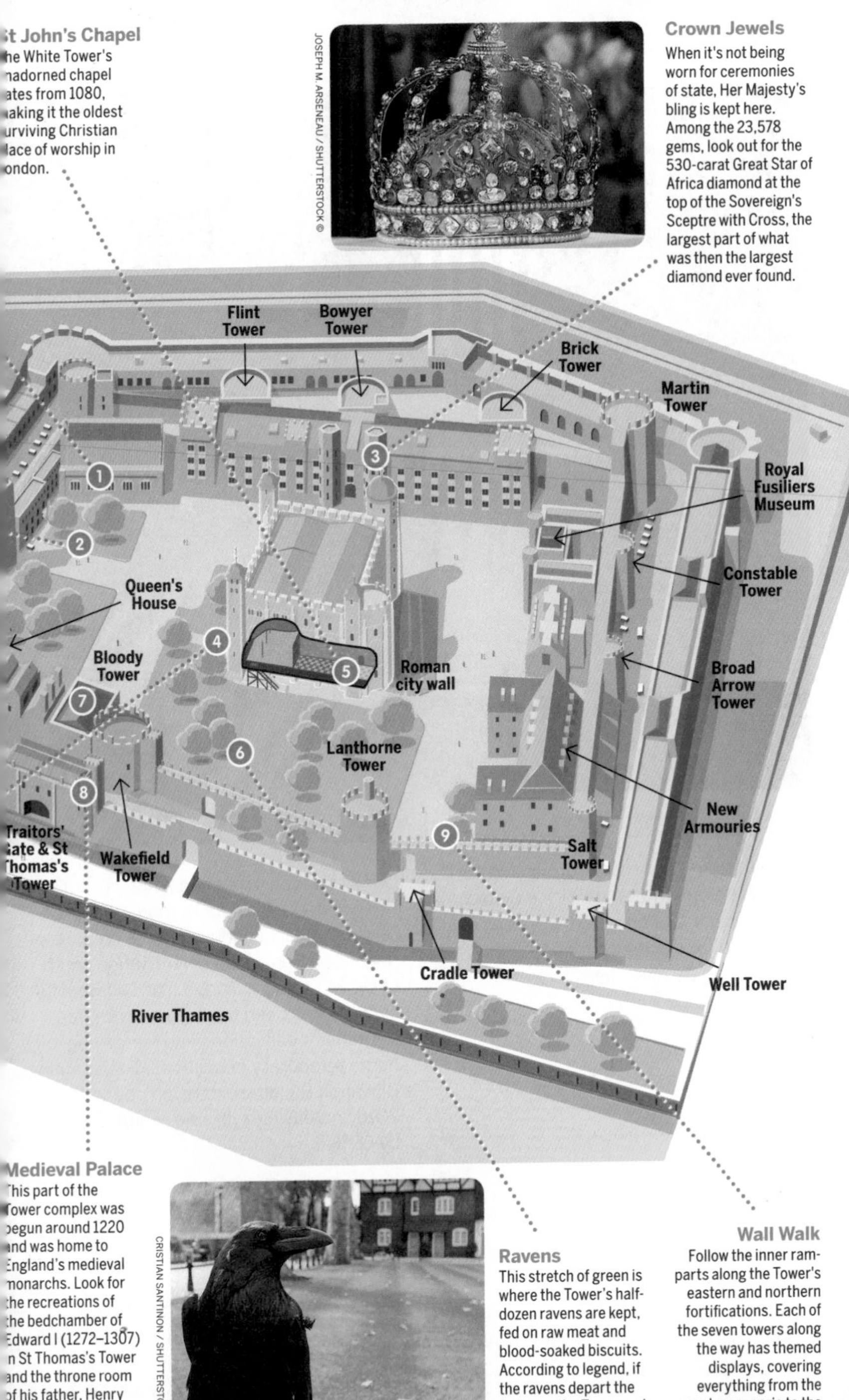

:t John's Chapel

he White Tower's ıadorned chapel ates from 1080, ıaking it the oldest urviving Christian lace of worship in ondon.

Crown Jewels

When it's not being worn for ceremonies of state, Her Majesty's bling is kept here. Among the 23,578 gems, look out for the 530-carat Great Star of Africa diamond at the top of the Sovereign's Sceptre with Cross, the largest part of what was then the largest diamond ever found.

Medieval Palace

'his part of the 'ower complex was ›egun around 1220 ınd was home to :ngland's medieval ıonarchs. Look for :he recreations of :he bedchamber of :dward I (1272–1307) n St Thomas's Tower ınd the throne room of his father, Henry II (1216–72) in the Vakefield Tower.

Ravens

This stretch of green is where the Tower's half-dozen ravens are kept, fed on raw meat and blood-soaked biscuits. According to legend, if the ravens depart the fortress, the Tower and the kingdom will fall.

Wall Walk

Follow the inner ramparts along the Tower's eastern and northern fortifications. Each of the seven towers along the way has themed displays, covering everything from the royal menagerie to the Tower during WWI.

Turbine Hall

TOM EVERSLEY/SHUTTERSTOCK ©

Tate Modern

A spellbinding synthesis of modern art and capacious industrial brick design, Tate Modern has been extraordinarily successful in taking challenging works and making us love them.

Great For...

☑ **Don't Miss**

Works by big-name artists, including Henri Matisse, Nan Goldin and Damien Hirst.

One of London's most amazing attractions, this outstanding modern- and contemporary-art gallery is housed in the creatively revamped Bankside Power Station south of the Millennium Bridge. The secret of its success has been to combine both free permanent collections and fee-paying, big-name temporary exhibitions. The stunning Blavatnik Building extension opened in 2016, increasing available exhibition space by 60%.

The Building

The 4.2 million bricks of the 200m-long Tate Modern is an imposing sight, designed by Swiss architects Herzog and de Meuron, who scooped the prestigious Pritzker Prize for their transformation of the empty power station. Leaving the building's central 99m-high chimney, adding a

MATT MUNRO/LONELY PLANET ©

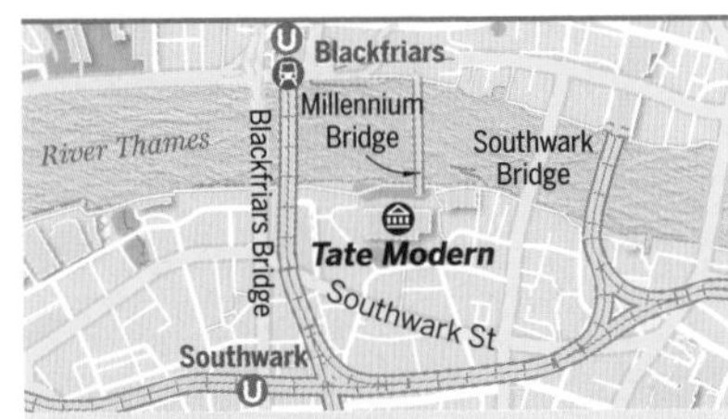

Need to Know

Map p72; ☎020-7887 8888; www.tate.org.uk; Bankside, SE1; ⏰10am-6pm Sun-Thu, to 10pm Fri & Sat; Ⓤ Southwark; FREE

Take a Break

The Tate Modern Cafe dishes up sandwiches, drinks and light meals to hungry art fans.

★ Top Tip

Free guided tours of sections of the permanent collection depart at noon, 1pm and 2pm daily.

two-storey glass box onto the roof and employing the cavernous Turbine Hall as a dramatic entrance space were three huge achievements. Herzog and de Meuron also designed the new 10-storey Tate extension.

The Collections

As a supreme collection of modern art, the contents of the museum are, however, the main draw. At their disposal, the curators have paintings by Georges Braque, Henri Matisse, Piet Mondrian, Andy Warhol, Mark Rothko and Jackson Pollock as well as pieces by Joseph Beuys, Damien Hirst, Louise Bourgeois, Claes Oldenburg and Auguste Rodin.

Tate Modern's permanent collection is arranged by both theme and chronology on levels 2 and 4 of the Natalie Bell Building and levels 0, 2, 3 and 4 of the Blavatnik Building. With more than 60,000 works on constant rotation, if there's a particular piece you want to see, check the website to find out if (and where) it's hanging.

Don't miss sublime city views from the 10th-floor Viewing Level of the Blavatnik Building and the view of the River Thames and St Paul's Cathedral from the 6th-floor cafe in the Natalie Bell Building.

To visit the sister-museum Tate Britain (p67), hop on the **Tate Boat** (www.thamesclippers.com; one way adult/child £8.70/4.35) from Bankside Pier.

What's Nearby

The elegant steel, aluminium and concrete **Millennium Bridge** (Ⓤ Blackfriars) staples the south bank of the Thames, in front of Tate Modern, to the north. The low-slung frame designed by Sir Norman Foster and Anthony Caro looks spectacular, particularly when lit up at night, and the view along it to St Paul's has become an iconic image.

Performers at Shakespeare's Globe (p50)

Entertainment Capital

The West End is synonymous with musicals, and no trip to London would be complete without an evening of Hamilton, Dear Evan Hansen or Six! The Musical. If musicals don't float your boat, there are more alternatives than you'll have evenings to fill: fringe theatre, comedy, dance, opera and classical concerts.

Great For...

Need to Know

For the latest theatre re-openings and show information after the Covid-19 closures go to What's on Stage (www.whatsonstage.com)

★ **Top Tip**

Buy cheap tickets on the day from Leicester Sq ticket booths or with the app Today Tix.

PADMAYOGINI/SHUTTERSTOCK ©

Theatre

A night out at the theatre is as much a must-do London experience as a ride on the top deck of a double-decker bus. London's Theatreland in the dazzling West End – from Aldwych in the east, past Shaftesbury Ave to Regent St in the west – has a concentration of theatres only rivalled by New York's Broadway. It's a thrillingly diverse scene, encompassing Shakespeare's classics performed with old-school precision, edgy new works, raise-the-roof musicals and some of the world's longest-running shows.

There are around 40 theatres in the West End alone, but 'Theatreland' is just the brightest facet of London's sparkling theatre world, where venues range from highbrow institutions to warehouses with new works and tiny fringe stages tucked away above pubs across town.

If you love Shakespeare and the theatre, the **Globe** (Map p72; 020-7401 9919; www.shakespearesglobe.com; 21 New Globe Walk, SE1; box office 10am-6pm; Blackfriars, London Bridge) will knock your theatrical socks off. This authentic Shakespearean theatre is a wooden 'O' without a roof over the central stage area, and although there are covered wooden bench seats in tiers around the stage, many people (there's room for 700) do as 17th-century 'groundlings' did, standing in front of the stage.

The **National Theatre** (Map p72; 020-7452 3000; www.nationaltheatre.org.uk; Upper Ground, SE1; Waterloo), England's flagship theatre (its full name is the Royal National Theatre), showcases a mix of classic and contemporary plays performed by often

National Theatre

well-recognised actors in three theatres (Olivier, Lyttelton and Dorfman).

The cosy **Donmar Warehouse** (Map p64; ☎020-3282 3808; www.donmarwarehouse.com; 41 Earlham St, WC2; Ⓤ Covent Garden) is London's 'thinking person's theatre'. The recently opened **Bridge Theatre** (Map p 72; ☎0333 320 0051; https://bridgetheatre.co.uk; 3 Potters Fields Park, SE1; Ⓤ London Bridge), London's first new major theatre in 80 years, stages some challenging new work.

Opera, Ballet & Classical Music

With multiple world-class orchestras and ensembles, quality venues, reasonable ticket prices and performances covering the whole musical gamut from traditional crowd-pleasers to innovative compositions, London will satisfy even the fussiest classical music, opera or ballet buff.

The **Royal Albert Hall** (Map p78; ☎0845 401 5034; 020-7589 8212; www.royalalberthall.com; Kensington Gore, SW7; Ⓤ South Kensington) hosts classical music, rock and other performances, but is famously the venue for the BBC-sponsored Proms. Booking is possible, but from mid-July to mid-September Proms punters queue for £5 standing (or 'promenading') tickets that go on sale one hour before curtain-up. Otherwise, the box office and prepaid-ticket collection counter are through door 12 (south side of the hall).

A three-year, £50-million revamp gave classic opera a fantastic setting in the **Royal Opera House** (Map p64; ☎020-7304 4000; www.roh.org.uk; Bow St, WC2; ⏰gift shop & cafe from 10am; Ⓤ Covent Garden), and coming here for a night is a sumptuous affair. Although the program has been modernised, the main attractions are still the opera and classical ballet – all are wonderful productions and feature world-class performers.

☑ Don't Miss

Book an informative one-hour front-of-house grand tour, operating most days at the Royal Albert Hall.

RON ELLIS/SHUTTERSTOCK © ARCHITECT: DENYS LASDUN

Tickets

- Book well ahead for live performances and if you can, buy directly from the venue.
- Enquire at the theatre's own box office about cut-price standby tickets or limited late releases for otherwise sold-out shows.
- Shakespeare's Globe offers 700 standing tickets (£5) for each performance.
- Midweek matinees are usually cheaper than evening performances; restricted-view seats can be very cheap.
- Be careful of ticket sales scammers online. Use reputable ticket agencies only.

Camden Market (p54) stall

London's Markets

The capital's famed markets are a treasure trove of foodie treats, small designers, unique jewellery pieces, colourful vintage items and bric-a-brac. They're a joyful antidote to impersonal, carbon-copy shopping centres.

Great For...

Need to Know

BYO cloth bags: as Britain moves to plastic-free shopping you'll be charged for every bag you accept no matter what you're purchasing.

★ Top Tip

Camden Market comprises four distinct market areas. They tend to sell similar kinds of things, but each has its own specialities and quirks.

IVAN/GETTY IMAGES ©

Borough Market

Located here in some form or another since the 13th century (and possibly since 1014), the **'London's Larder'** (Map p72; https://boroughmarket.org.uk; 8 Southwark St, SE1; ⌚full market 10am-5pm Wed & Thu, to 6pm Fri, 8am-5pm Sat, limited market 10am-5pm Mon & Tue; Ⓤ London Bridge) has enjoyed an astonishing renaissance in the past 20 years. Always overflowing with food-loving visitors and Londoners in search of inspiration for their dinner party, this busy central market has become firmly established as a sight in its own right. The market specialises in high-end fresh products; but there are also plenty of street-food vendors and an unreasonable number of cake stalls!

Portobello Road Market

Lovely on a warm summer's day, **Portobello Road Market** (Map p78; www.portobellomarket.org; Portobello Rd, W10; ⌚9am-6pm Mon-Wed, to 7pm Fri & Sat, to 1pm Thu; Ⓤ Notting Hill Gate or Ladbroke Grove) is an iconic London attraction with an eclectic mix of street food, fruit and veg, antiques, curios, collectables, vibrant fashion and trinkets. Although the shops along Portobello Rd open daily and the fruit-and-veg stalls (from Elgin Cres to Talbot Rd) only close on Sunday, the busiest day by far is Saturday, when antique dealers set up shop (from Chepstow Villas to Elgin Cres).

Camden Market

Although – or perhaps because – it stopped being cutting-edge several thousand cheap leather jackets ago, **Camden Market** (Map p78;

Portobello Road Market

www.camdenmarket.com; Camden High St, NW1; 10am-late; Camden Town, Chalk Farm) attracts millions of visitors each year and is one of London's most popular attractions. What started out as a collection of attractive craft stalls by Camden Lock on the Regent's Canal now extends most of the way from Camden Town Tube station to Chalk Farm Tube station.

Old Spitalfields Market

Traders have been hawking their wares here since 1638 and it's still one of London's best markets. Today's covered **market** (Map p72; www.oldspitalfieldsmarket.com; Commercial St, E1; 10am-8pm, to 6pm Sat, to 5pm Sun; Liverpool St, Shoreditch High St, Aldgate East) was built in the late 19th century, with the more modern development added in 2006. Sundays are the biggest and best days, but Thursdays are good for antiques and Fridays for independent designers. There are plenty of food stalls, too.

☑ Don't Miss

The Colombia Road Flower Market in London's East End only pops up on Sunday mornings.

GIORGIOGALANO/GETTY IMAGES ©

Sunday UpMarket

The **Sunday UpMarket** (Map p72; 020-7770 6028; www.sundayupmarket.co.uk; Old Truman Brewery, 91 Brick Lane, E1; 11am-5.30pm Sat, 10am-6pm Sun; Shoreditch High St) within the beautiful red-brick buildings of the Old Truman Brewery is the best of all the Sunday markets, with young designers selling their wares, plus vintage gems and a drool-inducing array of food stalls.

Leadenhall Market

A visit to this covered mall off Gracechurch St is a step back in time. There's been a market on this site since the Roman era, but the architecture that survives is all cobblestones and late-19th-century Victorian ironwork. **Leadenhall Market** (www.leadenhallmarket.co.uk; Gracechurch St, EC3; public areas 24hr; Bank) appears as Diagon Alley in *Harry Potter and the Philosopher's Stone* and an optician's shop was used for the entrance to the Leaky Cauldron wizarding pub in *Harry Potter and the Goblet of Fire*.

Broadway Market

There's been a **market** (www.broadwaymarket.co.uk; Broadway Market, E8; 9am-5pm Sat; 394) down this pretty street since the late 19th century. The focus these days is artisanal food, arty knick-knacks, books, records and vintage clothing. Stock up on edible treats, then head to **London Fields** (Richmond Rd, E8; London Fields) for a picnic.

✕ Take a Break

The **Ten Bells** (www.tenbells.com; 84 Commercial St, E1; noon-midnight, to 1am Thu-Sat; ; Shoreditch High St) pub, perfectly positioned for a pint after a wander around Spitalfields Market.

Upper Ward (Quadrangle)

Windsor Castle

The world's largest and oldest continuously occupied fortress, Windsor Castle is a majestic vision of battlements and towers. It's used for state occasions and is one of the Queen's principal residences; if she's at home, the Royal Standard flies from the Round Tower. Known for its lavish state rooms and beautiful chapels, it's hugely popular.

Great For...

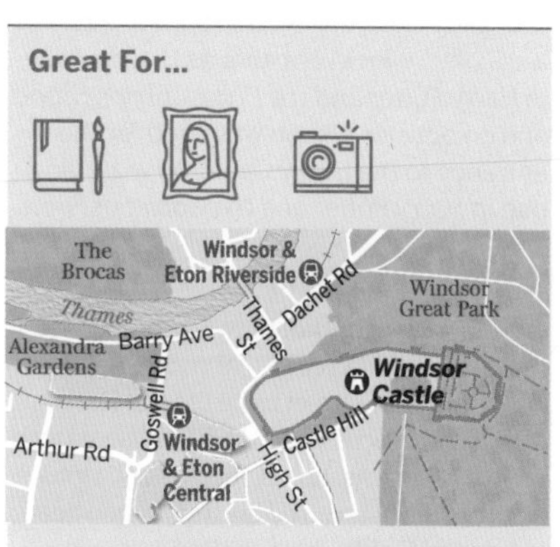

Need to Know

03031-237304; www.royalcollection.org.uk; Castle Hill; adult/child £23.50/13.50; 10am-5.15pm Mar-Oct, to 4.15pm Nov-Feb; ; 702 from London Victoria, London Waterloo-Windsor & Eton Riverside, London Paddington-Windsor & Eton Central via Slough

★ **Top Tip**

Join a free guided tour (frequent) or grab a free audio tour.

KIEV.VICTOR/SHUTTERSTOCK ©

William the Conqueror first established a royal residence in Windsor in 1080. Since then successive monarchs have rebuilt, remodelled and refurbished the castle complex to create the massive, sumptuous palace that stands here today. Henry II replaced the original wooden stockade in 1170 with a stone round tower and built the outer walls to the north, east and south; Edward III turned Windsor into a Gothic palace; Charles II gave the State Apartments a glorious baroque makeover; George IV swept in with his team of artisans; and Queen Victoria refurbished an ornate chapel in memory of her beloved Albert.

Queen Mary's Dolls' House

Your first stop is likely to be the incredible dolls' house designed by Sir Edwin Lutyens for Queen Mary between 1921 and 1924. On a scale of 1:12, the attention to detail is spellbinding: there's running water, electricity and lighting, tiny Crown Jewels, a silver service and wine cellar, and even a fleet of six cars in the garage.

State Apartments

Flanked by armour and weapons, the Grand Staircase sets the tone for the spectacular State Apartments above, dripping in gilt and screaming 'royal' from every painted surface and sparkling chandelier. Presided over by a statue of Queen Victoria, the Grand Vestibule displays artefacts and treasures donated by or captured from the countries of the British Empire, while the Waterloo Chamber celebrates the 1815 victory over Napoleon. St George's Hall beyond still hosts state banquets; its soaring

Changing of the guard

ceiling is covered in the painted shields of the Knights of the Garter.

St George's Chapel

This elegant chapel, commissioned for the Order of the Garter by Edward IV in 1475, is one of England's finest examples of Perpendicular Gothic architecture. The nave and beautiful fan-vaulted roof were completed under Henry VII, but the final nail was driven under Henry VIII in 1528.

Along with Westminster Abbey, it serves as a royal mausoleum. Both Henry VIII and Charles I lie beneath the beautifully carved 15th-century Quire, while the Queen's father (George VI) and mother (Queen Elizabeth) rest in a side chapel. Prince Harry married Meghan Markle here in May 2018.

St George's Chapel closes on Sunday, but you can attend choral evensong at 5.15pm every day except Wednesday.

☑ Don't Miss

As well as the sumptuous decor in the State Apartments, zoom in on the artworks, including pieces by Rubens, Canaletto and Anthony van Dyck.

KIEV.VICTOR/SHUTTERSTOCK ©

Albert Memorial Chapel

Built in 1240 and dedicated to St Edward the Confessor, the small Albert Memorial Chapel was the place of worship for the Order of the Garter until St George's Chapel snatched away that honour. After Prince Albert died at Windsor Castle in 1861, Queen Victoria ordered its elaborate redecoration as a tribute to her husband and consort. A major feature of the restoration is the magnificent vaulted roof, whose gold mosaic pieces were crafted in Venice.

There's a monument to the prince, although he's actually buried with Queen Victoria in the Royal Mausoleum at Frogmore House in Windsor Great Park. Their youngest son, Prince Leopold (Duke of Albany), is, however, buried in the Albert Memorial Chapel.

Changing of the Guard

A fabulous spectacle, with triumphant tunes from a military band and plenty of foot stamping from smartly attired soldiers in red uniforms and bearskin caps, the changing of the guard draws crowds to Windsor Castle each day. Weather permitting, it usually takes place at 11am on Tuesdays, Thursdays and Saturdays.

✕ Take a Break

Duck into the **Two Brewers** (☎01753-855426; www.twobrewerswindsor.co.uk; 34 Park St, Windsor; mains £15-26; ⏰11.30am-10pm Mon-Sat, noon-10pm Sun), an atmospheric inn on the edge of Windsor Great Park. Leave plenty of time to explore this epic park!

London City Walking Tour

The City of London has as much history in its single square mile as the rest of London put together. From churches and finance houses to markets and museums, this walk picks out just a few of its many highlights.

Start Farringdon
Distance 1.5 miles
Duration Three hours

1 Explore the wonderful 12th-century **St Bartholomew-the-Great** (p71), one of London's oldest churches.

2 Head through the Tudor gatehouse toward the colourful Victorian arches of **Smithfield Market**, London's last surviving meat market.

3 Follow the roundabout and nip up the stairs to explore the excellent galleries of the **Museum of London** (p71).

4 Head to Aldermanbury and the impressive 15th-century **Guildhall**. In its courtyard note the black outline of the Roman amphitheatre.

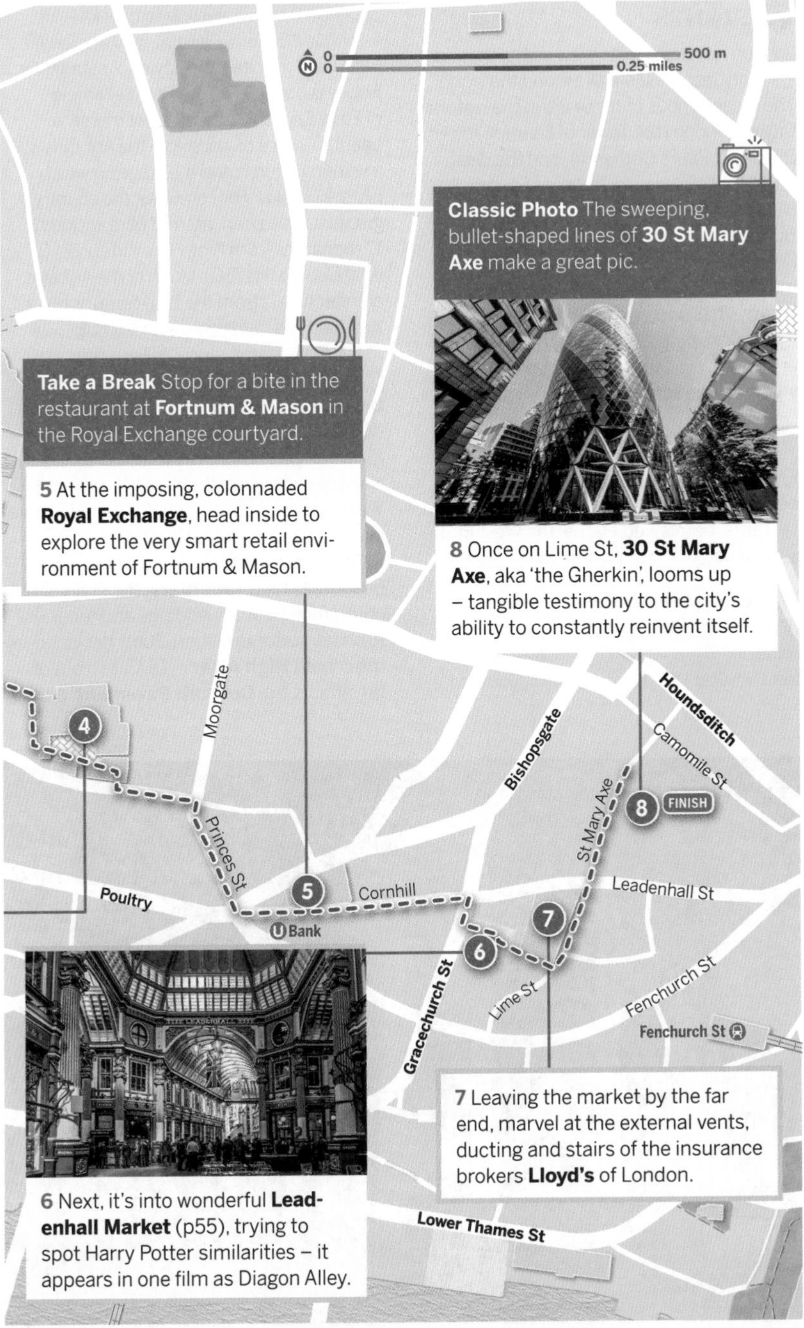

Take a Break Stop for a bite in the restaurant at **Fortnum & Mason** in the Royal Exchange courtyard.

5 At the imposing, colonnaded **Royal Exchange**, head inside to explore the very smart retail environment of Fortnum & Mason.

Classic Photo The sweeping, bullet-shaped lines of **30 St Mary Axe** make a great pic.

8 Once on Lime St, **30 St Mary Axe**, aka 'the Gherkin', looms up – tangible testimony to the city's ability to constantly reinvent itself.

6 Next, it's into wonderful **Leadenhall Market** (p55), trying to spot Harry Potter similarities – it appears in one film as Diagon Alley.

7 Leaving the market by the far end, marvel at the external vents, ducting and stairs of the insurance brokers **Lloyd's** of London.

2 ZOTOV DMITRII/SHUTTERSTOCK © 3 DOUG MCKINLAY/LONELY PLANET © 4 ROMAN BABAKIN/SHUTTERSTOCK © 6 PHILIP BIRD LRPS CPAGB/SHUTTERSTOCK © 8 MAZIARZ/SHUTTERSTOCK ©

SIGHTS

London has more than a few sights that are instantly recognisable all around the world. The most famous of these are in the historic City of London (the Tower of London, Tower Bridge, St Paul's Cathedral) and the West End (British Museum, Trafalgar Square, the Houses of Parliament, Westminster Abbey, Buckingham Palace). Further west, South Kensington is known for its grand Victorian museums, while the South Bank of the Thames has such landmarks as the London Eye, Shakespeare's Globe and the Tate Modern. Other less famous but equally fascinating sights are scattered all around the capital.

The West End

Encompassing many of London's poshest neighbourhoods as well as superlative restaurants, hotels and shops, the West End should be your first port of call.

Westminster Abbey Church

(Map p64; ☎020-7222 5152; www.westminsterabbey.org; 20 Dean's Yard, SW1; adult/child £24/10, half-price Wed 4.30pm; ⏰9.30am-3.30pm Mon, Tue, Thu & Fri, to 6pm Wed, to 3pm Sat May-Aug, to 1pm Sat Sep-Apr; Ⓤ Westminster) A splendid mixture of architectural styles, Westminster Abbey is considered the finest example of Early English Gothic. It's not merely a beautiful place of worship – the Abbey is still a working church and the stage on which history unfolds. For centuries, the country's greatest have been interred here, including 17 monarchs from King Henry III (1272) to King George II (1760). Much of the Abbey's architecture is from the 13th century, but it was founded much earlier, in 960 CE.

Every monarch since William the Conqueror has been crowned here, with the exception of a couple of Eds who were either murdered (Edward V) or abdicated (Edward VIII) before the magic moment. Never a cathedral (the seat of a bishop), Westminster Abbey is what is called a 'royal peculiar', administered by the Crown.

At the heart of the Abbey is the beautifully tiled **sanctuary**, the stage for coronations, royal weddings and funerals. Architect George Gilbert Scott designed the ornate **High Altar** in 1873. In front of the altar is the **Cosmati Pavement**, dating

Westminster Abbey

GRZEGORZ_PAKULA/SHUTTERSTOCK ©

to 1268. It has intricate designs of small pieces of stone and glass inlaid into plain marble, which symbolise the universe at the end of time (an inscription claims the world will end after 19,683 years). At the entrance to the lovely **Chapel of St John the Baptist** is a sublime translucent alabaster *Virgin and Child*, placed here in 1971.

The most sacred spot in the Abbey is the **shrine of St Edward the Confessor**, which lies behind the High Altar; access is restricted to guided tours to protect the fragile 13th-century flooring. King Edward, long considered a saint before he was canonised, was the founder of the Abbey, and the original building was consecrated a few weeks before his death in 1066. Henry III added a new shrine with Cosmati mosaics in the mid-12th century where the sick prayed for healing – and also chipped off a few souvenirs to take home.

The **Quire** (choir), a stunning space of gold, blue and red Victorian Gothic above a black-and-white chequerboard tiled floor, dates to the mid-19th century. It sits where the original choir for the monks' worship would have been but bears little resemblance to the original. Nowadays, the Quire is still used for singing, but its regular occupants are the Choir of Westminster Abbey – about 30 boys and 12 'lay vicars' (men) who sing the daily services and evensong (5pm on weekdays except Wednesday and 3pm on weekends).

Henry III began work on the new Abbey building in 1245 but didn't complete it; the Gothic nave was finished under Richard II in 1388. Henry VII's magnificent Perpendicular Gothic–style **Lady Chapel**, with an impressive fan-vaulted ceiling and tall stained-glass windows, was completed after 13 years of construction in 1516.

Opened in 2018, the **Queen's Diamond Jubilee Galleries** (timed tickets, an additional £5) are a new museum and gallery space located in the medieval triforium, the arched gallery above the nave. Among its exhibits are the death masks and wax effigies of generations of royalty, armour and stained glass. Highlights are the graffiti-

No 10 Downing Street

The official office of British leaders since 1735, when George II presented No 10 to 'First Lord of the Treasury' Robert Walpole, this has also been the prime minister's London residence since refurbishment in 1902. For such a famous address, **No 10** (Map p64; www.number10.gov.uk; 10 Downing St, SW1; ⓤWestminster) is a small-looking Georgian building on a plain-looking street, hardly warranting comparison with the White House, for example. Yet it is actually three houses joined into one and boasts roughly 100 rooms plus a 2000-sq-metre garden.

PCRUCIATTI/SHUTTERSTOCK ©

inscribed chair used for the coronation of Mary II, the beautifully illustrated manuscripts of the *Litlyngton Missal* from 1380 and the 13th-century Westminster Retable, England's oldest surviving altarpiece.

At the western end of the nave near the **Tomb of the Unknown Warrior**, killed in France during WWI and laid to rest here in 1920, is St George's Chapel, which contains the rather ordinary-looking **Coronation Chair**, upon which every monarch since the early 14th century has been crowned (apart from joint monarchs Mary II and William III, who had their own chairs fashioned for the event in 1689).

Apart from the royal graves, you can see many famous commoners interred here, especially in **Poets' Corner**, where you'll find the resting places of Geoffrey Chaucer,

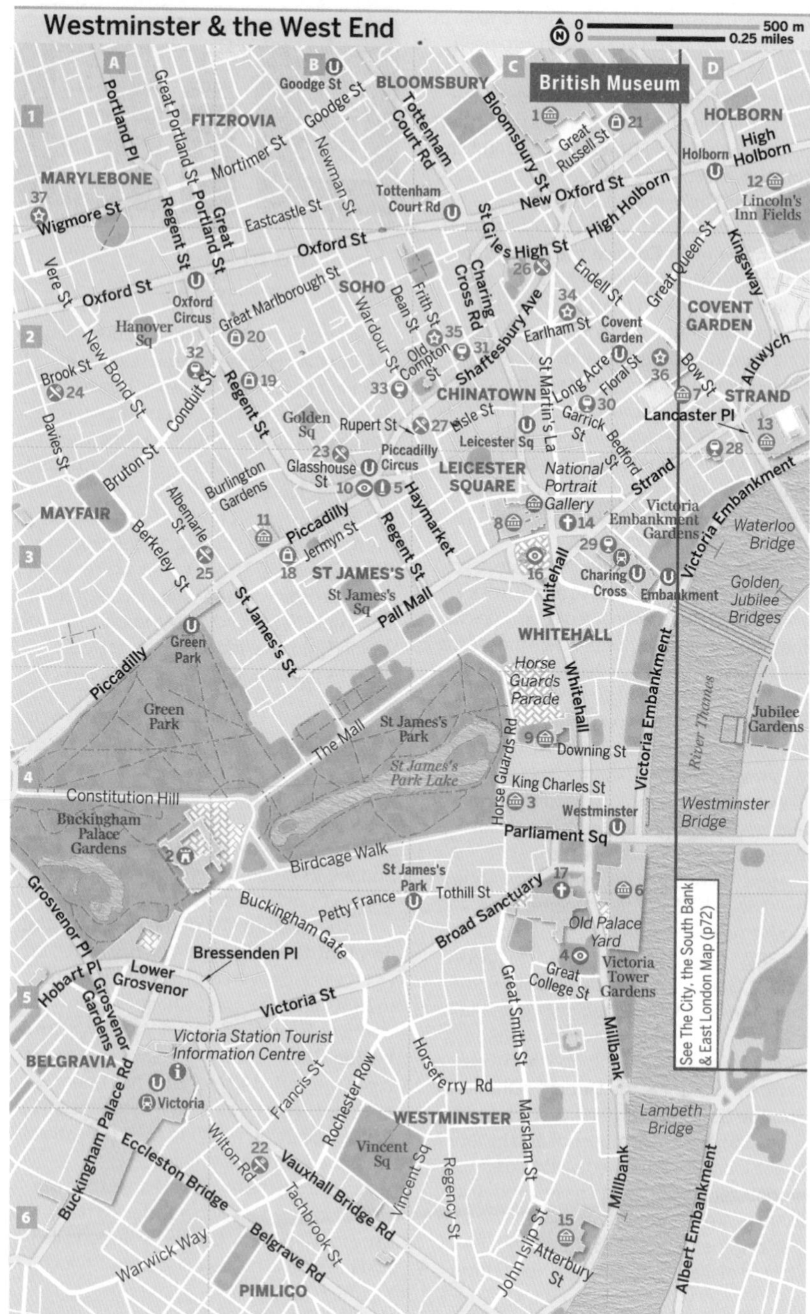
Westminster & the West End
500 m
0.25 miles
British Museum
BLOOMSBURY
FITZROVIA
MARYLEBONE
HOLBORN
SOHO
CHINATOWN
COVENT GARDEN
STRAND
LEICESTER SQUARE
MAYFAIR
ST JAMES'S
WHITEHALL
BELGRAVIA
WESTMINSTER
PIMLICO
Goodge St
Tottenham Court Rd
Oxford Circus
Holborn
Covent Garden
Leicester Sq
Piccadilly Circus
Green Park
Charing Cross
Embankment
Westminster
St James's Park
Victoria
Oxford St
Regent St
Piccadilly
Pall Mall
Whitehall
Strand
Victoria Embankment
Albert Embankment
Millbank
Victoria St
Shaftesbury Ave
Charing Cross Rd
Haymarket
New Oxford St
High Holborn
Kingsway
Aldwych
Lincoln's Inn Fields
Green Park
St James's Park
St James's Park Lake
Buckingham Palace Gardens
Constitution Hill
The Mall
Birdcage Walk
Horse Guards Parade
Downing St
Parliament Sq
Broad Sanctuary
Old Palace Yard
Victoria Tower Gardens
National Portrait Gallery
Victoria Embankment Gardens
Waterloo Bridge
Golden Jubilee Bridges
Jubilee Gardens
River Thames
Westminster Bridge
Lambeth Bridge
Vincent Sq
Victoria Station Tourist Information Centre
Golden Sq
Hanover Sq
St James's Sq
See The City, the South Bank & East London Map (p72)

Westminster & the West End

Sights

1	British Museum	C1
2	Buckingham Palace	A4
3	Churchill War Rooms	C4
4	College Garden	C5
5	Eros Statue	B3
6	Houses of Parliament	D4
7	London Transport Museum	D2
8	National Gallery	C3
9	No 10 Downing Street	C4
10	Piccadilly Circus	B3
11	Royal Academy of Arts	B3
12	Sir John Soane's Museum	D1
13	Somerset House	D2
14	St Martin-in-the-Fields	C3
15	Tate Britain	C6
16	Trafalgar Square	C3
17	Westminster Abbey	C4

Shopping

18	Fortnum & Mason	B3
19	Hamleys	B2
20	Liberty	B2
21	London Review Bookshop	D1

Eating

22	A Wong	B6
23	Brasserie Zédel	B3
24	Foyer & Reading Room at Claridge's	A2
25	Gymkhana	A3
26	Kanada-Ya	C2
27	Palomar	C2
	Spring	(see 13)

Drinking & Nightlife

28	American Bar	D2
29	Heaven	C3
30	Lamb & Flag	C2
31	She Soho	C2
32	Sketch	A2
33	Village	B2

Entertainment

34	Donmar Warehouse	C2
35	Ronnie Scott's	C2
36	Royal Opera House	D2
37	Wigmore Hall	A1

Sleeping

	Claridge's	(see 24)

Charles Dickens, Thomas Hardy, Alfred Tennyson, Samuel Johnson and Rudyard Kipling, as well as memorials to other greats (William Shakespeare, Jane Austen, the Brontë sisters etc). Another set of illustrious stones is in **Scientists' Corner** near the north aisle of the nave, including the final resting places of Sir Isaac Newton, Charles Darwin and the ashes of Stephen Hawking.

Downloadable audio guides are included in the ticket price, but to get more out of your visit, join a 90-minute **verger-led tour** (an additional £7), which includes some 'VIP access', such as Edward's shrine and getting to sit in the Quire stalls.

Parts of the Abbey complex are free to visitors, including the Cloisters, Chapter House and the 900-year-old **College Garden** (Map p64; 10am-4pm Tue-Thu) FREE. The octagonal **Chapter House** dates from the 1250s and was where the monks would meet for daily prayer and their job assignments, before Henry VIII's suppression of the monasteries some three centuries later. To the right of the entrance to Chapter House is what's claimed to be the oldest door in Britain – it's been there since the 1050s. Used as a treasury, the crypt-like **Pyx Chamber** dates from about 1070 and takes its name from boxes that held gold and silver to be tested for purity to make coins.

Photography is not allowed inside the Abbey but is permitted around the Cloisters. Pre-booking tickets required.

National Gallery — Gallery

(Map p64; 020-7747 2885; www.nationalgallery.org.uk; Trafalgar Sq, WC2; 11am-6pm Sat-Thu, to 9pm Fri; U Charing Cross) FREE With more than 2300 European masterpieces in its collection, this is one of the world's great galleries, with seminal works from the 13th to the mid-20th century, including masterpieces by Leonardo da Vinci, Michelangelo, Titian, Vincent van Gogh and Auguste Renoir. Many visitors flock to the eastern rooms on the main floor (1700–1930), where works by British artists such as Thomas Gainsborough, John Constable and JMW Turner, and Impressionist and post-Impressionist masterpieces by Van Gogh, Renoir and Claude Monet await. Pre-booking required.

Changing of the Guard

A London 'must see', this is when the Old Guard (Foot Guards of the Household Regiment) comes off duty to be replaced by the New Guard on the forecourt of Buckingham Palace. Tourists gape – sometimes from behind as many as 10 people – at the bright-red uniforms, bearskin hats and full-on pageantry. The official name for the ceremony is Guard Mounting and it lasts for around 45 minutes.

The ceremony usually takes place daily at 11am in June and July and on Sunday, Monday, Wednesday and Friday, weather permitting, during the rest of the year, but be sure to check the website before setting out.

DAVID STEELE/SHUTTERSTOCK ©

The modern Sainsbury Wing on the gallery's western side houses the oldest paintings, from 1200 to 1500, in rooms 51 to 66. Here you will find largely religious works commissioned for private devotion (such as the *Wilton Diptych* in the alcove of room 51), as well as more unusual masterpieces, such as Sandro Botticelli's *Venus & Mars* (room 58) and Jan van Eyck's *Arnolfini Portrait* (room 63). Leonardo da Vinci's stunning *Virgin of the Rocks* (room 66) is a stroke of genius.

Works from the High Renaissance (1500–1600) embellish rooms 2 to 14, where Michelangelo, Titian, Raphael, Correggio, El Greco and Bronzino hold court; Rubens, Rembrandt and Caravaggio grace rooms 15 to 32 (1600–1700). Notable are two self-portraits of Rembrandt (at age 34 and 63, in room 22) and the beautiful *Rokeby Venus* by Diego Velázquez in room 30.

Before you leave, don't miss the astonishing floor mosaics in the main vestibule.

The comprehensive **audio guides** (adult/family £5/10) are highly recommended, as are the free one-hour tours that leave from the Sainsbury Wing foyer at 2pm Monday to Friday. There are also special trails and activity sheets for children.

Houses of Parliament — Historic Building

(Map p64; ☎tours 020-7219 4114; www.parliament.uk; Parliament Sq, SW1; ⓤWestminster) A visit here is a journey to the heart of UK democracy. The Houses of Parliament are officially called the Palace of Westminster, and its oldest part is 11th-century **Westminster Hall**, one of only a few sections that survived a catastrophic 1834 fire. The rest is mostly a neo-Gothic confection built over 36 years from 1840. Tours inside were suspended at the time of research and online tours were the only option.

Buckingham Palace — Palace

(Map p64; ☎0303 123 7300; www.rct.uk/visit/the-state-rooms-buckingham-palace; Buckingham Palace Rd, SW1; ⏰9am-6pm mid-Jul–end Sep; ⓤGreen Park or St James's Park) Built in 1703 for the Duke of Buckingham, Buckingham Palace replaced St James's Palace as the monarch's official London residence in 1837. Queen Elizabeth II divides her time between here, Windsor Castle and, in summer, Balmoral Castle in Scotland. If she's in residence, the square yellow, red and blue Royal Standard is flown; if not, it's the Union Flag. To protect the wellbeing of visitors and staff, Buckingham Palace was closed to the public in 2020 until further notice.

Trafalgar Square — Square

(Map p64; ⓤCharing Cross or Embankment) Opened to the public in 1844, Trafalgar Sq is the true centre of London, where rallies

Big Ben & the Houses of Parliament

and marches take place, tens of thousands of revellers usher in the New Year and locals congregate for anything from communal open-air cinema and Christmas celebrations to political protests. It is dominated by the 52m-high **Nelson's Column**, guarded by four **bronze lion statues**, and ringed by many splendid buildings, including the National Gallery (p65) and the church of **St Martin-in-the-Fields** (Map p64; ☎020-7766 1100; www.stmartin-in-the-fields.org; Trafalgar Sq, WC2; ⏲8.30am-6pm Mon-Fri, from 9am Sat & Sun; Ⓤ Charing Cross).

Churchill War Rooms Museum

(Map p64; ☎020-7416 5000; www.iwm.org.uk/visits/churchill-war-rooms; Clive Steps, King Charles St, SW1; adult/child £23/11.50; ⏲9.30am-6pm; Ⓤ Westminster) Former Prime Minister Winston Churchill helped coordinate the Allied resistance against Nazi Germany on a Bakelite telephone from this underground complex during WWII. The **Cabinet War Rooms** remain much as they were when the lights were switched off in 1945, capturing the drama and dogged spirit of the time, while the modern multimedia **Churchill Museum** affords intriguing insights into the life and times of the resolute, cigar-smoking wartime leader.

Tate Britain Gallery

(Map p64; ☎020-7887 8888; www.tate.org.uk/visit/tate-britain; Millbank, SW1; ⏲10am-6pm; Ⓤ Pimlico) FREE On the site of the former Millbank Penitentiary, the older and more venerable of the two Tate siblings opened in 1892 and celebrates British art from 1500 to the present, including pieces from William Blake, William Hogarth, Thomas Gainsborough and John Constable, as well as vibrant modern and contemporary pieces from Lucian Freud, Barbara Hepworth, Gillian Ayres, Francis Bacon and Henry Moore. The stars of the show are, undoubtedly, the light-infused visions of JMW Turner in the Clore Gallery.

After Turner died in 1851, his estate was settled by a decree declaring that whatever had been found in his studio – 300 oil

Summer Screen at Somerset House

For a fortnight every summer, Somerset House turns its stunning courtyard into an open-air **cinema** (Map p64; ☎0333 320 2836; www.somersethouse.org.uk; Somerset House, Strand, WC2; tickets from £19; ⌚Aug; Ⓤ Temple) screening an eclectic mix of film premieres, cult classics and popular requests.

KIEV.VICTOR/SHUTTERSTOCKS ©

paintings and about 30,000 watercolours and sketches – would be bequeathed to the nation. The collection here constitutes a grand and sweeping display of his work, including classics such as *The Field of Waterloo* and *Norham Castle, Sunrise*.

Tate Britain is also home to seminal works from Constable, Gainsborough and Joshua Reynolds, as well as the Pre-Raphaelites, including William Holman Hunt's *Strayed Sheep*, John William Waterhouse's sculpture *Hylas Surprised by the Naiades*, *Christ in the House of His Parents* by John Everett Millais and Edward Burne-Jones' *The Golden Stairs*. Look out also for Francis Bacon's *Three Studies for Figures at the Base of a Crucifixion*.

The gallery hosts the prestigious and often controversial **Turner Prize** from October to early January every year (adult/child £13/free), plus a programme of ticketed exhibitions that changes every few months; consult the website for what's on.

Quick 15-minute **Art in Focus talks** on a selected work take place every Tuesday, Thursday and Saturday at 1.15pm; the piece under the microscope changes monthly, so check online or ask at the visitor information desk. Free 45-minute **themed guided tours** are held four times a day, and the 3pm slot is invariably on the work of JMW Turner. Both tours are free; booking is not required.

On the first Friday of each month, **Late at Tate Britain** means the gallery stays open until 9.30pm.

Royal Academy of Arts Gallery

(Map p64; ☎020-7300 8000; www.royalacademy.org.uk; Burlington House, Piccadilly, W1; ⌚10am-6pm; Ⓤ Green Park) FREE Britain's oldest society devoted to fine arts was founded in 1768 and moved here to Burlington House a century later. For its 250th birthday in 2018, the RA gave itself a £56-million makeover. Its collection of drawings, paintings, architectural designs, photographs and sculptures by past and present Royal Academicians, such as Sir Joshua Reynolds, John Constable, Thomas Gainsborough, JMW Turner, David Hockney and Tracey Emin, has historically been male-dominated, but this is slowly changing.

Madame Tussauds Museum

(Map p78; ☎0870 400 3000; www.madame-tussauds.com/london; Marylebone Rd, NW1; adult/child 4-15yr £35/30; ⌚10am-6pm; Ⓤ Baker St) It may be kitschy and pricey, but Madame Tussauds makes for a fun-filled day. There are photo ops with your dream celebrity (be it Daniel Craig, Lady Gaga, Benedict Cumberbatch, or Audrey Hepburn), the Bollywood gathering (sparring studs Hrithik Roshan and Salman Khan) and the Royal Appointment (the Queen, Harry and Meghan, William and Kate). Book online for much cheaper rates and check the website for seasonal opening hours.

Somerset House Historic Building

(Map p64; ☎020-7845 4600; www.somersethouse.org.uk; The Strand, WC2; ⌚10am-7pm;

(Temple) Designed in 1775 for government departments and royal societies – perhaps the world's first office block – Somerset House now contains galleries, restaurants and cafes that encircle a lovely open courtyard and extend to an elevated sun-trap terrace. The **Embankment Galleries** are devoted to temporary exhibitions (usually related to photography, design or fashion). In summer, the grand courtyard hosts open-air live performances, dancing fountains for kids to cool off in and the Film4 Summer Screen (p68), plus an atmospheric ice-skating rink in winter.

Piccadilly Circus Square

(Map p64; Piccadilly Circus) Architect John Nash had originally designed Regent St and Piccadilly in the 1820s to be the two most elegant streets in London but, restrained by city planners, he couldn't fully realise his dream. He may be disappointed, but suitably astonished, by Piccadilly Circus today: a traffic maelstrom, deluged by visitors and flanked by high-tech advertisements.

City of London

London's historic core is a tale of two cities: packed with office workers during the week and eerily quiet at weekends. The current millennium has seen a profusion of daring skyscrapers sprout from the City's fringes, but the essential sights have been standing for hundreds of years: St Paul's Cathedral and the Tower of London.

St Paul's Cathedral Cathedral

(Map p72; 020-7246 8357; www.stpauls.co.uk; St Paul's Churchyard, EC4; adult/child £17/7.20; 8.30am-4.30pm Mon-Sat; St Paul's) Towering over diminutive Ludgate Hill in a superb position that's been a place of Christian worship for more than 1400 years (and pagan before that), St Paul's Cathedral is one of London's most magnificent buildings. For Londoners, the vast dome is a symbol of resilience and pride, standing tall for more than 300 years. Viewing architect Sir Christopher Wren's masterpiece from the inside and climbing to the top for sweeping views of the capital is a celestial experience.

Following the destructive Great Fire of London in 1666, which burned 80% of the city, Wren designed St Paul's to replace the old church, and it was built between 1675 and 1710. The site is ancient hallowed ground, with four other cathedrals preceding Wren's English baroque masterpiece, the first dating from 604 CE.

The cathedral dome, inspired by St Peter's Basilica in the Vatican, is famed for surviving Luftwaffe incendiary bombs in the 'Second Great Fire of London' of December 1940, becoming an icon of London resilience during the Blitz. North of the church is the simple **People of London Memorial**, honouring the 32,000 civilians killed.

Inside, rising more than 85m above the floor, is the dome, supported by eight huge columns. It actually consists of three parts:

The Statue of Anteros, Piccadilly Circus

At the centre of Piccadilly Circus stands the famous aluminium statue mistakenly called **Eros** (Map p64; Piccadilly Circus, W1; Piccadilly Circus) as it actually portrays his twin brother, Anteros. To add to the confusion, the figure is officially the 'Angel of Christian Charity' and dedicated to the philanthropist and social reformer Lord Shaftesbury. The sculpture was at first cast in gold but later replaced by newfangled aluminium, the first outdoor statue in that lightweight metal.

BENJAMIN B/SHUTTERSTOCK ©

Sir John Soane's Museum

This little **museum** (Map p64; ☎020-7405 2107; www.soane.org; 13 Lincoln's Inn Fields, WC2; ⏰10am-5pm Thu-Sat; ⓊHolborn) FREE is one of the most atmospheric and fascinating in London. The building was the bewitching home of architect Sir John Soane (1753–1837), which he left brimming with his vast architectural and archaeological collection, intriguing personal effects and curiosities.

A neoclassical architect and professor of architecture at the Royal Academy, Soane was a country bricklayer's son, most famous for designing the Bank of England. His heritage-listed house is largely as it was when Soane died and is itself a main part of the attraction. The canopy dome brings light right down to the crypt, a colonnade filled with statuary and a picture gallery where paintings are stowed behind each other on folding wooden panes. This is where Soane's choicest artwork is displayed, including paintings by Canaletto and the original *A Rake's Progress*, William Hogarth's satirical cartoons of late-18th-century London lowlife.

Hour-long Highlights Tours (£15), including the private apartment and Model Room, can be booked online. Look out for info on the popular 'Soane Lates' evening candlelit tours on the website.

DANIEL LANGE/SHUTTERSTOCK ©

a plastered brick inner dome, a nonstructural lead outer dome visible on the skyline and a brick cone between them holding it all together. The walkway around its base, accessed via 257 steps from a staircase on the western side of the southern transept, is called the **Whispering Gallery**, which was closed at the time of research but expected to reopen in early 2021. A further 119 steps brings you to the exterior **Stone Gallery**, your first taste of the city vistas, and 152 iron steps more bring you to the **Golden Gallery** at the very top, with unforgettable views of London.

The crypt has memorials to around 300 of Britain's great and the good, including the Duke of Wellington and Vice Admiral Horatio Nelson, whose body lies directly below the dome. But the most poignant is to Wren himself. On a simple tomb slab bearing his name, part of a Latin inscription translates as: 'If you seek his monument, look around you'.

There's no charge to attend a service, but not all areas of the cathedral are accessible. To hear the cathedral choir, attend the 11.30am Sunday Eucharist or Evensong (5pm Monday to Saturday and 3.15pm Sunday), but check the website as a visiting choir may appear for the latter.

Book tickets online in advance for a slight discount and faster entry. Admission includes an audio guide. Free 1½-hour guided tours depart four times a day (10am, 11am, 1pm and 2pm); reserve a place at the tour desk, just past the entrance. About three times a month, one-hour tours (£8) visit the Geometric Staircase, Great Model and astonishing library (closed for renovations until at least autumn 2021), and include impressive views down the nave from above the Great West Doors; check online for timings.

Tower Bridge Bridge

(Map p72; ☎020-7403 3761; www.towerbridge.org.uk; Tower Bridge, SE1; ⓊTower Hill) With its neo-Gothic towers and sky-blue suspension struts, Tower Bridge is one of London's most recognisable sights. London was a thriving port in 1894 when it was built as a much-needed crossing point in the east, equipped with a then-revolutionary steam-driven bascule (counterbalance) mechanism that could raise the roadway to make way for oncoming ships in just three minutes.

The story of building the structure is recounted in the **Tower Bridge Exhibition** (020-7403 3761; www.towerbridge.org.uk; Tower Bridge, SE1; adult/child £10.60/5.30, incl Monument £12/5.50; 9.30am-5pm; Tower Hill). The bridge is still operational, although these days it's electrically powered and raises mainly for pleasure craft. Tower Bridge is in action around 1000 times a year and as often as 10 times a day in summer; check the website for lift times.

Museum of London Museum

(Map p72; 020-7001 9844; www.museumoflondon.org.uk; 150 London Wall, EC2; 10am-6pm; Barbican) FREE Romp through 450,000 years of London history at this entertaining and educational museum, one of the capital's finest. Exhibiting everything from a mammoth's jaw circa 200,000 BCE to Oliver Cromwell's death mask and the desperate scrawls of convicts on a cell from Wellclose Prison, interactive displays and reconstructed scenes transport visitors from Roman Londinium and Saxon Lundenwic right up to the 21st-century metropolis. Free themed tours are offered daily; check at reception for timings and topics.

St Bartholomew the Great Church

(Map p72; 020-7600 0440; www.greatstbarts.com; W Smithfield, EC1; 10am-4pm Mon-Wed, 10am-1pm Thu, 10am-4pm Fri-Sat, 1-6pm Sun; Barbican) FREE Dating from 1123, St Bartholomew the Great is one of London's oldest churches. The Norman arches and profound sense of history lend this holy space an ancient calm, and it's even more atmospheric when entered through the restored 13th-century half-timbered gatehouse. The church was originally part of an Augustinian priory but became the parish church of Smithfield in 1539 when Henry VIII dissolved the monasteries.

St Bartholomew the Great

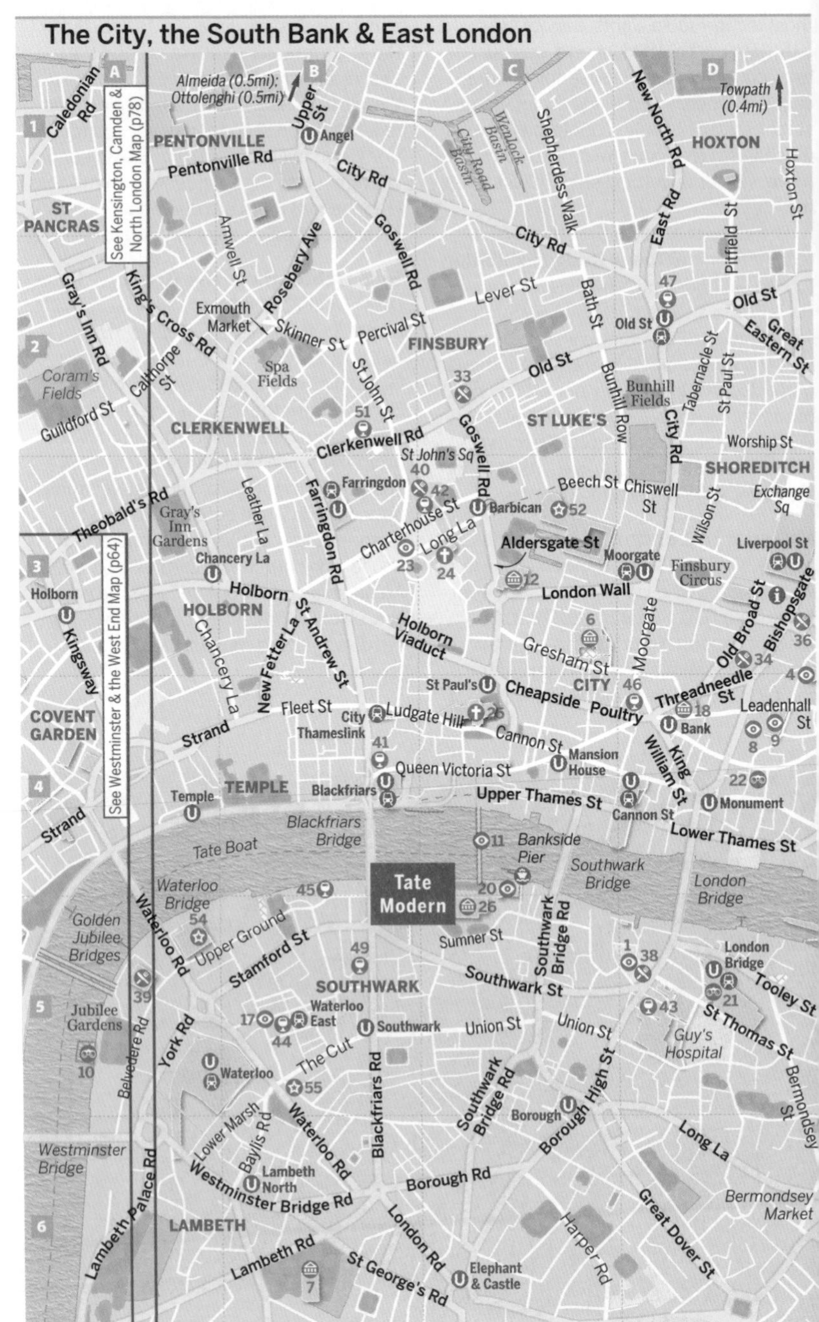
The City, the South Bank & East London
Almeida (0.5mi); Ottolenghi (0.5mi)
Towpath (0.4mi)
See Kensington, Camden & North London Map (p78)
See Westminster & the West End Map (p64)
PENTONVILLE
HOXTON
ST PANCRAS
FINSBURY
CLERKENWELL
ST LUKE'S
SHOREDITCH
HOLBORN
CITY
COVENT GARDEN
TEMPLE
SOUTHWARK
LAMBETH
Caledonian Rd
Upper St
Angel
Pentonville Rd
City Rd
Goswell Rd
Shepherdess Walk
New North Rd
East Rd
Hoxton St
Pitfield St
Wenlock Basin
City Road Basin
Arnwell St
Rosebery Ave
Lever St
Bath St
Old St
Great Eastern St
Gray's Inn Rd
King's Cross Rd
Exmouth Market
Skinner St
Percival St
Coram's Fields
Calthorpe St
Spa Fields
St John St
Bunhill Row
Bunhill Fields
Tabernacle St
St Paul St
Guildford St
Clerkenwell Rd
St John's Sq
Worship St
Farringdon
Beech St
Chiswell St
Wilson St
Exchange Sq
Theobald's Rd
Leather La
Farringdon Rd
Charterhouse St
Barbican
Gray's Inn Gardens
Long La
Aldersgate St
Moorgate
Liverpool St
Chancery La
Finsbury Circus
Holborn
London Wall
Old Broad St
Bishopsgate
Kingsway
St Andrew St
Holborn Viaduct
Gresham St
New Fetter La
St Paul's
Cheapside
Poultry
Threadneedle St
Leadenhall St
Fleet St
City Thameslink
Ludgate Hill
Bank
Strand
Cannon St
Mansion House
King William St
Queen Victoria St
Blackfriars
Upper Thames St
Temple
Monument
Cannon St
Lower Thames St
Blackfriars Bridge
Bankside Pier
Tate Boat
Southwark Bridge
London Bridge
Tate Modern
Waterloo Bridge
Golden Jubilee Bridges
Waterloo Rd
Upper Ground
Sumner St
Southwark Bridge Rd
Stamford St
Southwark St
London Bridge
Tooley St
Jubilee Gardens
Belvedere Rd
Waterloo East
Southwark
Union St
St Thomas St
Guy's Hospital
York Rd
The Cut
Waterloo
Borough High St
Bermondsey St
Blackfriars Rd
Borough
Lower Marsh
Baylis Rd
Long La
Westminster Bridge
Lambeth North
Borough Rd
Westminster Bridge Rd
Bermondsey Market
Lambeth Palace Rd
London Rd
Harper Rd
Great Dover St
Lambeth Rd
St George's Rd
Elephant & Castle
A
B
C
D
1
2
3
4
5
6
1
4
6
7
8
9
10
11
12
17
18
20
21
22
23
24
25
26
33
34
36
38
39
40
41
42
43
44
45
46
47
49
51
52
54
55

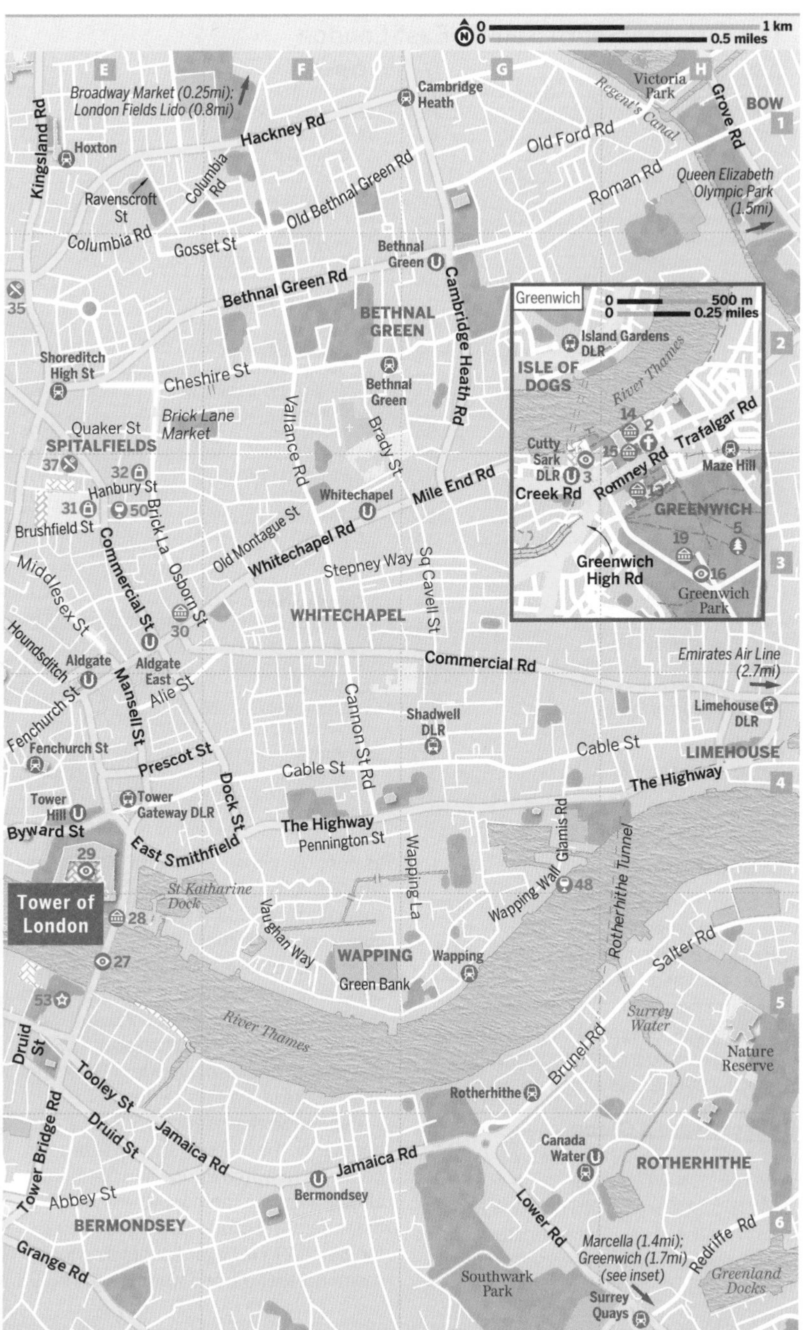

0 1 km
0 0.5 miles
Broadway Market (0.25mi); London Fields Lido (0.8mi)
Kingsland Rd
Hackney Rd
Hoxton
Columbia Rd
Ravenscroft St
Gosset St
Cambridge Heath
Old Bethnal Green Rd
Victoria Park
Regent's Canal
Grove Rd
BOW
Old Ford Rd
Roman Rd
Queen Elizabeth Olympic Park (1.5mi)
Bethnal Green
Bethnal Green Rd
Cambridge Heath Rd
BETHNAL GREEN
Shoreditch High St
Cheshire St
Brick Lane Market
Quaker St
SPITALFIELDS
Hanbury St
Brushfield St
Vallance Rd
Brady St
Whitechapel
Mile End Rd
Old Montague St
Whitechapel Rd
Stepney Way
Cavell St
Middlesex St
Commercial St
Brick La
Osborn St
WHITECHAPEL
Houndsditch
Aldgate
Aldgate East
Mansell St
Alie St
Fenchurch St
Commercial Rd
Cannon St Rd
Shadwell DLR
Emirates Air Line (2.7mi)
Limehouse DLR
LIMEHOUSE
Prescot St
Cable St
Tower Hill
Tower Gateway DLR
Dock St
The Highway
Byward St
East Smithfield
Pennington St
Wapping La
Glamis Rd
Rotherhithe Tunnel
St Katharine Dock
Wapping Wall
Tower of London
Vaughan Way
WAPPING
Wapping
Green Bank
Salter Rd
River Thames
Surrey Water
Nature Reserve
Druid St
Tooley St
Jamaica Rd
Brunel Rd
Rotherhithe
Tower Bridge Rd
Canada Water
ROTHERHITHE
Bermondsey
Abbey St
BERMONDSEY
Lower Rd
Marcella (1.4mi); Greenwich (1.7mi) (see inset)
Redriffe Rd
Grange Rd
Southwark Park
Greenland Docks
Surrey Quays
Greenwich
0 500 m
0 0.25 miles
Island Gardens DLR
ISLE OF DOGS
River Thames
Trafalgar Rd
Cutty Sark DLR
Creek Rd
Romney Rd
Maze Hill
GREENWICH
Greenwich High Rd
Greenwich Park

The City, the South Bank & East London

Sights

1 Borough Market ... D5
2 Chapel of St Peter & St Paul ... H2
3 Cutty Sark ... G3
4 Gherkin ... D4
5 Greenwich Park ... H3
6 Guildhall ... C3
7 Imperial War Museum ... B6
8 Leadenhall Market ... D4
9 Lloyd's Building ... D4
10 London Eye ... A5
11 Millennium Bridge ... C4
12 Museum of London ... C3
13 National Maritime Museum ... H3
14 Old Royal Naval College ... H2
15 Painted Hall ... H2
16 Peter Harrison Planetarium ... H3
17 Roupell St ... B5
18 Royal Exchange ... D4
19 Royal Observatory ... H3
20 Shakespeare's Globe ... C4
21 Shard ... D5
22 Sky Garden ... D4
23 Smithfield Market ... B3
24 St Bartholomew the Great ... C3
25 St Paul's Cathedral ... C4
26 Tate Modern ... C5
27 Tower Bridge ... E5
28 Tower Bridge Exhibition ... E5
29 Tower of London ... E4
30 Whitechapel Gallery ... E3

Shopping

31 Old Spitalfields Market ... E3
32 Sunday Upmarket ... E3

Eating

Arabica Bar & Kitchen ... (see 1)
33 Breddos Tacos ... C2
34 City Social ... D3
35 Clove Club ... E2
36 Duck & Waffle ... D3
37 Hawksmoor Spitalfields ... E3
38 Padella ... D5
39 Skylon ... A5
40 St John ... C3

Drinking & Nightlife

41 Blackfriar ... B4
42 Fox & Anchor ... C3
43 George Inn ... D5
44 Kings Arms ... B5
45 Lyaness ... B4
46 Nickel Bar ... D4
47 Nightjar ... D2
48 Prospect of Whitby ... G4
49 Seabird ... B5
50 Ten Bells ... E3
51 Zetter Townhouse Cocktail Lounge ... B2

Entertainment

52 Barbican Centre ... C3
53 Bridge Theatre ... E5
54 National Theatre ... A5
55 Old Vic ... B5
Shakespeare's Globe ... (see 20)

Sleeping

Hoxton Southwark ... (see 49)
The Ned ... (see 46)

South Bank

The South Bank is a must-visit area for art lovers, theatre-goers and culture hounds, and has been significantly re-energised by the renowned Tate Modern. Come for iconic Thames views, great food markets, first-rate pubs, dollops of history, striking examples of modern architecture, and a sprinkling of fine bars and restaurants.

Shakespeare's Globe Theatre

(Map p72; ☎020-7401 9919; www.shakespearesglobe.com; 21 New Globe Walk, SE1; tour adult/child £17/10; ⊙box office 10am-6pm; Ⓤ Blackfriars or London Bridge) The reconstructed Shakespeare's Globe was designed to resemble the 16th-century original as closely as possible, constructed with 600 oak pegs (there's not a nail or screw in the house), specially fired Tudor-style bricks and a circular thatch roof that leaves the theatre's centre – and the groundlings watching the performance – vulnerable to the elements. Guided tours take in the architecture and give access to the exhibition space, with displays on Shakespeare, life in Bankside and theatre in the 17th century.

Despite Shakespeare's worldwide popularity, the original Globe Theatre, demolished by the Puritans in 1644, was almost a distant memory when American actor Sam Wanamaker came searching for it in 1949. He began fundraising for a memorial theatre, and work started in 1987.

Sadly, Wanamaker died four years before the theatre opened in 1997.

Shakespeare wrote for both outdoor and indoor theatre, and outside the Globe's April to October season, the **Sam Wanamaker Playhouse** – an indoor candlelit Jacobean-style theatre similar to what Shakespeare would have used in winter – puts on year-round performances.

London Eye Viewpoint

(Map p72; www.londoneye.com; near County Hall, SE1; adult/child from £24.50/22; ⌚10am-8.30pm, reduced hours in low season; Ⓤ Waterloo or Westminster) Standing 135m high in a fairly flat city, the London Eye is the world's largest cantilevered observation wheel and affords views 25 miles in every direction (as far as Windsor Castle), weather permitting. Each ride – or 'flight' – takes a gracefully slow 30 minutes. The London Eye is the focal point of the capital's midnight New Year's Eve fireworks display and one of the UK's most popular tourist attractions; book tickets online in advance for a slight discount or fast-track entry to jump the queue.

Kensington & Hyde Park

Splendidly well groomed, Kensington is one of London's most handsome neighbourhoods. You'll find three fine museums here – the V&A, the Natural History Museum and the Science Museum – as well as excellent dining and shopping, graceful parklands and elegant streets of grand period architecture.

Natural History Museum Museum

(Map p78; www.nhm.ac.uk; Cromwell Rd, SW7; ⌚10am-5.50pm; 👪; Ⓤ South Kensington) FREE On a vast 5.7 hectare plot and housing 80 million specimens, this colossal and magnificent building is infused with the irrepressible Victorian spirit of collecting, cataloguing and interpreting the natural world. The **Dinosaurs Gallery** (Blue Zone) is a must for children, who gawp at the animatronic T-rex. Adults will love the intriguing Treasures exhibition in the **Cadogan Gallery** (Green Zone), which displays a host of unrelated objects, each telling its own unique story, from a chunk of moon rock to a dodo skeleton.

Victoria & Albert Museum

The Museum of Manufactures, as the **V&A** (Map p78; V&A; ☎020-7942 2000; www.vam.ac.uk; Cromwell Rd, SW7; ⌚10am-5.45pm Sat-Thu, to 10pm Fri; Ⓤ South Kensington) FREE was known when it opened in 1852, was part of Prince Albert's legacy to the nation in the aftermath of the successful Great Exhibition of 1851. It houses the world's largest collection of decorative arts, from Asian ceramics to Middle Eastern rugs, Chinese paintings, Western furniture, fashion from all ages and modern-day domestic appliances. The (ticketed) temporary exhibitions are another highlight, covering anything from David Bowie retrospectives to designer Alexander McQueen, special materials and trends.

There are more than 100 galleries in the museum, so pick carefully or join a free one-hour guided tour (they meet close to the information desk in the main hall); there are several a day on a variety of themes, including introductory tours, medieval and Renaissance tours, and theatre and performance tours.

PHOTOCRITICAL/SHUTTERSTOCK ©

Science Museum Museum

(Map p78; ☎0333 241 4000, 020-7942 4000; www.sciencemuseum.org.uk; Exhibition Rd, SW7; ⌚10am-6pm, last entry 5.15pm; 👪; Ⓤ South

Science Museum (p75)

Kensington) FREE This scientifically spellbinding museum will mesmerise adults and children alike, with its interactive and educational exhibits covering everything from early technology to space travel. On the ground floor, a perennial favourite is **Exploring Space**, a gallery featuring genuine rockets and satellites and a full-size replica of the *Eagle*, the lander that took Neil Armstrong and Buzz Aldrin to the moon in 1969. The **Making the Modern World Gallery** next door is a visual feast of locomotives, planes, cars and other revolutionary inventions.

Kensington Palace Palace

(Map p78; www.hrp.org.uk/kensingtonpalace; Kensington Gardens, W8; adult/child £21.50/10.70, cheaper weekdays after 2pm; ⌚10am-6pm, to 4pm Nov-Feb; Ⓤ High St Kensington) Built in 1605, Kensington Palace became the favourite royal residence under William and Mary of Orange in 1689, and remained so until George III became king and relocated to Buckingham Palace. Today, it remains a residence for high-ranking royals, including the Duke and Duchess of Cambridge (Prince William and his wife Kate). A large part of the palace is open to the public, however, including the King's and Queen's State Apartments.

North London

North London is framed by Camden's famous eponymous market, its unrivalled music scene and excellent pubs. There's plenty here for quiet enjoyment, too, including gorgeous green spaces as well as canal walks.

British Library Library

(Map p78; ☎0330-333 1144; www.bl.uk; 96 Euston Rd, NW1; ⌚9.30am-8pm Mon-Thu, to 6pm Fri, to 5pm Sat, 11am-5pm Sun; Ⓤ King's Cross St Pancras) FREE Consisting of low-slung red-brick terraces and fronted by a large piazza with an oversized statue of Sir Isaac Newton, Colin St John Wilson's British Library building is an architectural wonder. Completed in 1998, it's home to some of the greatest treasures of the written word, including the *Codex Sinaiticus* (the first complete text of the New Testament), Leonardo da Vinci's notebooks and two copies of the Magna Carta (1215).

The most precious manuscripts are held in the Sir John Ritblat Treasures Gallery, including stunningly illustrated religious texts, Shakespeare's First Folio (1623), a Gutenberg Bible from 1455, a copy of *The Diamond Sutra* in Chinese dating to 868 – the world's oldest block-printed book – as well as handwritten lyrics by the Beatles and the score to Handel's *Messiah*.

Book a one-hour guided library tour (adult/child £10/8) for an eye-opening glimpse into the inner workings of the library and its treasures. Tours can be arranged on the website.

ZSL London Zoo

Zoo

(Map p78; ☎0344-225 1826; www.zsl.org/zsl-london-zoo; Outer Circle, Regent's Park, NW1; depending on date, adult £25-32.50, child £16-20.50; ⏰10am-6pm Apr-Aug, to 5pm mid-Feb–Mar, Sep & Oct, to 4pm Nov–mid-Feb; 👪; 🚌88, 274) Opened in 1828, London Zoo is the oldest in the world. The emphasis nowadays is firmly on conservation, breeding and education, with fewer animals and bigger enclosures. Highlights include **Land of the Lions**, **Gorilla Kingdom**, **Night Life, Penguin Beach** and the walk-through **In with the Lemurs**, . There are regular feeding sessions and talks; various experiences are available, such as Keeper for a Day; and you can even spend the night in one of nine Gir Lion Lodge cabins.

Hampstead Heath

Park

(Map p78; www.cityoflondon.gov.uk/things-to-do/green-spaces/hampstead-heath; Ⓤ Hampstead Heath or Gospel Oak) Sprawling Hampstead Heath, with its rolling woodlands and meadows, feels a million miles away – despite being about 3.5 miles from Trafalgar Sq. It covers 320 hectares and is home to about 180 bird species, 25 species of butterflies, grass snakes, bats and a rich array of flora. It's a wonderful place for a ramble, especially to the top of **Parliament Hill** (Ⓤ Hampstead Heath, Gospel Oak), which offers expansive views across flat-as-a-pancake London.

The Shard

Puncturing the skies above London, the dramatic splinter-like form of the **Shard** (☎0844 499 7111; www.theviewfromtheshard.com; Joiner St, SE1; adult/child from £25/20; ⏰10am-9pm (varies); Ⓤ London Bridge) has rapidly become an icon of London. The viewing platforms on floors 69 and 72 are open to the public and the views are, as you'd expect from a 244m vantage point, sweeping, but they come at a hefty price – book online at least a day in advance to make a big saving.

GANGLIU10/GETTY IMAGES © ARCHITECT: RENZO PIANO

Wellcome Collection

Museum

(Map p78; ☎020-7611 2222; www.wellcomecollection.org; 183 Euston Rd, NW1; ⏰10am-6pm Tue, Wed & Fri-Sun, to 9pm Thu; Ⓤ Euston Sq or Euston) FREE Under a new director Melanie Keen (appointed in 2019), Wellcome Collection committed to addressing the challenges of its less enlightened beginnings. The museum focuses on the interface of art, science and medicine. At its heart is Sir Henry Wellcome's collection of (at times controversial) medical curiosities (saws for amputation, forceps through the ages, sex aids and amulets...). Beyond the permanent galleries, there are absorbing **temporary exhibitions**, plus a great **cafe** and a fantastic **shop**.

Kensington, Camden & North London

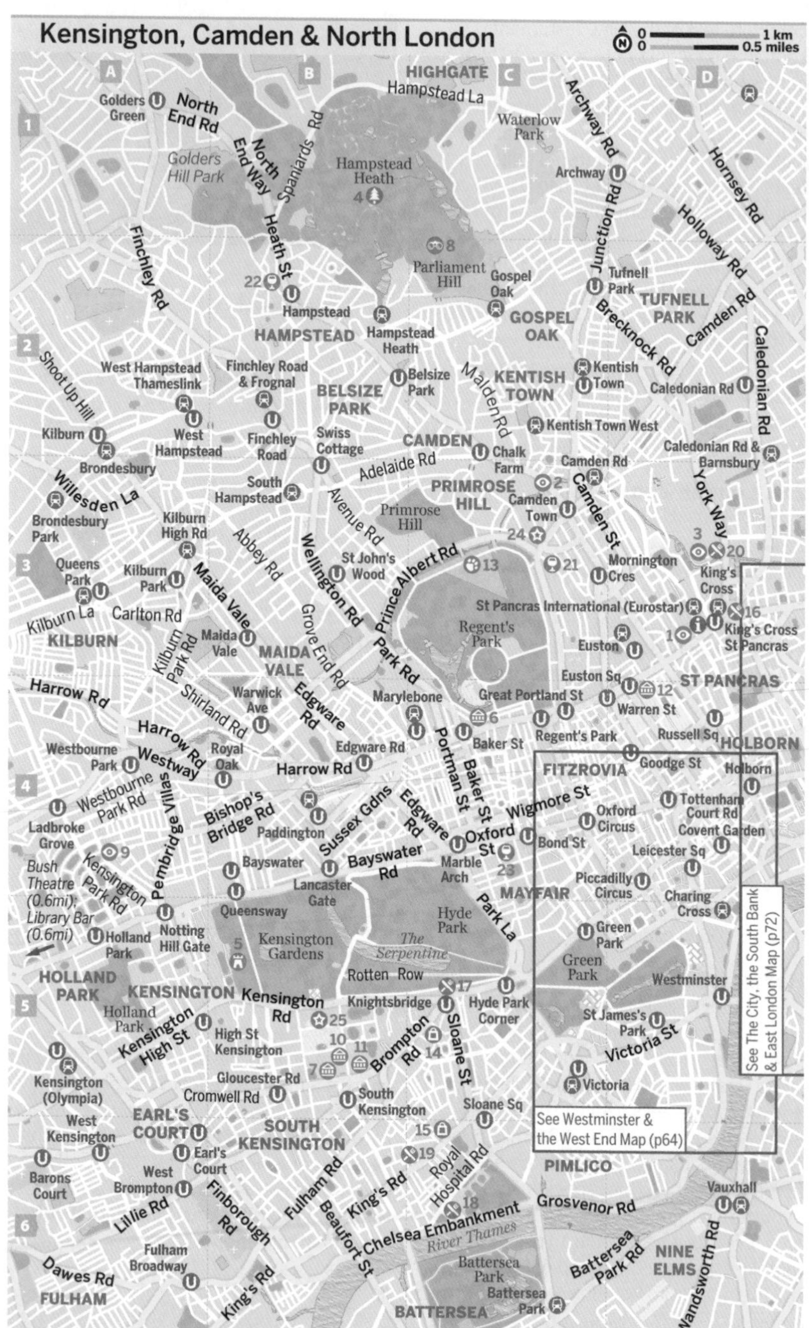

Kensington, Camden & North London

Sights
1 British Library D3
2 Camden Market C3
3 Granary Square D3
4 Hampstead Heath B1
5 Kensington Palace B5
6 Madame Tussauds C4
7 Natural History Museum B5
8 Parliament Hill C2
9 Portobello Road Market A4
10 Science Museum B5
11 Victoria & Albert Museum B5
12 Wellcome Collection D4
13 ZSL London Zoo C3

Shopping
14 Harrods C5
15 John Sandoe Books C6

Eating
16 Bar Pepito D3
17 Dinner by Heston Blumenthal C5
18 Gordon Ramsay C6
19 Rabbit C6
20 Ruby Violet D3

Drinking & Nightlife
21 Edinboro Castle C3
22 Holly Bush B2
23 Magritte Bar C4

Entertainment
24 Green Note C3
25 Royal Albert Hall B5

East London

Anyone with an interest in multicultural London needs to visit the East End. There's standout ethnic cuisine, some interesting museums and galleries, excellent pubs, canal-side eating and drinking, some of London's hippest neighbourhoods, and the vast redeveloped expanse of Queen Elizabeth Olympic Park to explore.

Queen Elizabeth Olympic Park — Park

(www.queenelizabetholympicpark.co.uk; E20; ⓤStratford) The glittering centrepiece of London's 2012 Olympic Games, this vast 227-hectare expanse includes the main Olympic venues as well as playgrounds, walking and cycling trails, gardens and a diverse mix of wetland, woodland, meadow and other wildlife habitats – an environmentally fertile legacy for the future. The main focal point is **London Stadium** (☎020-8522 6157; www.london-stadium.com; tours adult/child £19/11; ⊙tours 10am-4.15pm, to 4.45pm Sat; ⓤPudding Mill Lane), now the home ground for West Ham United FC.

Other signature buildings include the **London Aquatics Centre** (☎020-8536 3150; www.londonaquaticscentre.org; Carpenters Rd, E20; adult/child from £5/3; ⊙6am-10.30pm; ⓤStratford), **Lee Valley VeloPark** (☎0300 003 0613; www.visitleevalley.org.uk/velopark; Abercrombie Rd, E20; 1hr taster £50, pay-and-ride from £5, bike & helmet hire adult/child from £12/8; ⊙9am-10pm Mon-Fri, 8am-9pm Sat & Sun; ⓤStratford International), **ArcelorMittal Orbit** (☎0333 800 8099; www.arcelormittalorbit.com; 3 Thornton St, E20; adult/child £12.50/7.50, with slide £17.50/12.50; ⊙11am-3pm Mon-Fri, 10am-7pm Sat & Sun; ⓤStratford) and the **Copper Box Arena** (☎020-8221 4900; http://copperboxarena.org.uk; Copper St, E20; ⓤHackney Wick), a 7000-seat indoor venue for sports and concerts. There's **Here East**, a vast 'digital campus' covering an area equivalent to 16 football fields. Development of the **East Bank**, a waterfront cultural and educational district, is in the works.

For a different perspective on the park, or if you're feeling lazy, take a tour through its waterways with **Lee & Stort Boats** (☎0845 116 2012; www.leeandstortboats.co.uk; Stratford waterfront pontoon, E20; adult/child £9/5; ⊙daily Apr-Sep, Sat & Sun Mar & Oct; ⓤStratford).

Whitechapel Gallery — Gallery

(Map p72; ☎020-7522 7888; www.whitechapelgallery.org; 77-82 Whitechapel High St, E1; ⊙11am-6pm Tue, Wed & Fri-Sun, to 9pm Thu; ⓤAldgate East) FREE A firm favourite of art students and the avant-garde cognoscenti, this ground-breaking gallery doesn't have a permanent collection but is devoted to hosting edgy exhibitions of contemporary art. It made its name by staging exhibitions by both established and emerging artists, including the first UK shows by Pablo Picasso, Jackson Pollock, Mark Rothko and Frida Kahlo. The gallery's ambitiously themed shows change every couple of months (check online) and there's also often live music, talks and films on Thursday evenings.

Greenwich & South London

Regal riverside Greenwich complements its village feel with some grand architecture, grassy parkland and riverside pubs.

Royal Observatory Museum

(Map p72; 020-8312 6565; www.rmg.co.uk/royal-observa tory; Greenwich Park, Blackheath Ave, SE10; adult/child £16/8; 10am-5pm Sep-Jun, to 6pm Jul & Aug; Greenwich or Cutty Sark) Rising like a beacon of time atop **Greenwich Park** (www.royalparks.org.uk/parks/greenwich-park; SE10; 6am-sunset; Greenwich, Maze Hill or Cutty Sark), the Royal Observatory is home to the **prime meridian** (longitude 0° 0' 0"). Tickets include access to the Christopher Wren–designed **Flamsteed House** (named after the first Royal Astronomer) and the **Meridian Courtyard**, where you can stand with your feet straddling the eastern and western hemispheres. You can also see the Great Equatorial Telescope (1893) inside the onion-domed observatory and explore space and time in the **Weller Astronomy Galleries**.

In a small brick structure next to the Meridian Courtyard, the astonishing **camera obscura** projects a live image of Queen's House – as well as the people moving around it and the boats on the Thames behind – onto a table. Enter through the thick, light-dimming curtains and close them behind you to keep the room as dark as possible.

Night-sky shows are projected daily on the inside of the roof of the **Peter Harrison Planetarium** (020-8858 4422; www.rmg.co.uk/whats-on/planetarium-shows; adult/child £10/5; ; Greenwich or Cutty Sark).

The Royal Observatory was built by order of Charles II in 1675 to help solve the riddle of longitude. In 1884, Greenwich was

Royal Observatory

LUKASZ PAJOR/SHUTTERSTOCK ©

designated as the prime meridian of the world, and Greenwich Mean Time (GMT) became the universal measurement of standard time.

Old Royal Naval College Historic Building

(Map p72; https://ornc.org; SE10; ⏲8am-11pm; Ⓤ Cutty Sark) FREE Home to the University of Greenwich and Trinity Laban Conservatoire of Music and Dance, the Christopher Wren–designed Old Royal Naval College is a masterpiece of baroque architecture. The sprawling grounds are open to the public, as well as the recently restored **Painted Hall** (☎020-8269 4799; www.ornc.org; adult/child £12/free), nicknamed the 'Sistine Chapel of the UK' and covered from floor to ceiling with extraordinary 18th-century art, and the neoclassical **Chapel of St Peter and St Paul** (☎020-8269 4788; https://ornc.org; ⏲10am-5pm) FREE. Tours of the grounds are included in the price of the Painted Hall ticket.

National Maritime Museum Museum

(Map p72; ☎020-8312 6565; www.rmg.co.uk/national- maritime-museum; Romney Rd, SE10; ⏲10am-5pm; 👪; Ⓤ Cutty Sark) FREE Narrating the long, briny and eventful history of seafaring Britain, this excellent museum has three floors of engrossing exhibits. Highlights include JMW Turner's huge oil painting *Battle of Trafalgar* (1824), the 19m-long gilded state barge built in 1732 for the prince of Wales, and the colourful figureheads installed on the ground floor. Families will love the children's galleries, as well as the Great Map splayed out near the upper-floor cafe.

Imperial War Museum Museum

(Map p72; ☎020-7416 5000; www.iwm.org.uk; Lambeth Rd, SE1; ⏲10am-6pm; Ⓤ Lambeth North) FREE Fronted by an intimidating pair of 15in naval guns and a piece of the Berlin Wall, this riveting museum is housed in what was the Bethlem Royal Hospital, a psychiatric facility also known as Bedlam. Although the museum's focus is on military action involving British or Commonwealth troops, largely

Imperial War Museum

DANIEL GALE/SHUTTERSTOCK ©

Hamleys

Claiming to be the world's oldest (and some say, the largest) toy store, **Hamleys** (Map p64; ☎0371 704 1977; www.hamleys.com; 188-196 Regent St, W1; ⏰10am-9pm Mon-Fri, from 9.30am Sat, noon-6pm Sun; 👪; Ⓤ Oxford Circus) moved to its address on Regent St in 1881. From the basement's Star Wars Collection and ground floor where staff blow bubbles and glide foam boomerangs through the air with practised nonchalance, to Lego World and a cafe on the 5th floor, it's a rich layer cake of playthings.

TOM EVERSLEY/SHUTTERSTOCK ©

during the 20th century, it also covers war in the wider sense. Must-see exhibits include the state-of-the-art **First World War** galleries and **Witnesses to War** in the forecourt and atrium.

Cutty Sark Ship

(Map p72; ☎020-8312 6565; www.rmg.co.uk/cuttysark; King William Walk, SE10; adult/child £15/7.50; ⏰10am-5pm; Ⓤ Cutty Sark) The last of the great clipper ships to sail between China and England in the 19th century, the *Cutty Sark* was launched in 1869 and carried almost 4.5 million kg of tea in just seven years of service. Nearly a century later, it was dry-docked in Greenwich and opened to the public. Films, interactive maps, illustrations and props give an idea of what life on board was like. Book online.

TOURS

Guide London Tours

(Association of Professional Tourist Guides; ☎020-7611 2545; www.guidelondon.org.uk; half-/full-day tours £176/288) Hire a prestigious Blue Badge Tourist Guide, knowledgeable guides who have studied for two years and passed a dozen written and practical exams to do their job. They can tell you stories behind the sights that you'd only hear from them or whisk you on a themed tour (eg Royalty, the Beatles, museums, parks). Go by car, public transport, bike or on foot.

Hidden London Tours

(☎020-7565 7298; www.ltmuseum.co.uk/whats-on/hidden-london; tours £35-85) Get under the skin of London on an incredible insider-access tour run by the **London Transport Museum** (☎020-7379 6344; www.ltmuseum.co.uk; Covent Garden Piazza, WC2; adult/child £18.50/free; ⏰10am-6pm; 👪; Ⓤ Covent Garden). Excursions take you to the depths of the city's abandoned Tube stations, which have been film sets for a number of flicks including *Skyfall* and *V for Vendetta*, and to the heights of London's first skyscraper at 55 Broadway, Transport for London's art-deco HQ.

Sign up for email alerts to get notice of when the next tours are going on sale, and book early.

Original Tour Bus

(www.theoriginaltour.com; tours adult/child/family £34/16/84; ⏰8.30am-8.30pm; 👪) Hop-on, hop-off bus service in 11 languages (plus kids' commentary) on six routes, and includes discounts on a host of London attractions. Buses run every five to 15 minutes; you can buy tickets on the bus or online. Also available: 48-hour tickets (adult/child/family £44/21/109) and 72-hour tickets (adult/child/family £54/26/134).

Black History Walks History

(www.blackhistorywalks.co.uk; 2hr tours £10) Learn a little of London's 2000 years of black history in Soho, St Paul's and Notting Hill, to name a few locations where these informative, paradigm-shifting tours are run. Also runs online seminars.

SHOPPING

From charity-shop finds to designer bags, there are thousands of ways to spend your hard-earned cash in London. Many of the big-name shopping attractions, such as Harrods, Hamleys, Camden Market and Old Spitalfields Market, have become must-sees in their own right. Chances are that with so many temptations, you'll give your wallet a full workout.

Fortnum & Mason Department Store

(Map p64; 020-7734 8040; www.fortnumandmason.com; 181 Piccadilly, W1; 10am-9pm Mon-Sat, 11.30am-6pm Sun; Green Park or Piccadilly Circus) With its classic eau-de-Nil (pale green) colour scheme, the 'Queen's grocery store' (established in 1707) refuses to yield to modern times. Its staff – men and women – still wear old-fashioned tailcoats, and its glamorous food hall is supplied with hampers, marmalade and speciality teas. Stop for a spot of afternoon tea at the **Diamond Jubilee Tea Salon**, visited by Queen Elizabeth II in 2012.

Harrods Department Store

(Map p78; 020-7730 1234; www.harrods.com; 87-135 Brompton Rd, SW1; 10am-9pm Mon-Sat, 11.30am-6pm Sun; Knightsbridge) Garish and stylish in equal measure, perennially crowded Harrods is an obligatory stop for visitors, from the cash-strapped to the big spenders. The stock is astonishing, as are many of the price tags. Many visitors don't make it past the ground floor where designer bags, myriad scents from the perfume hall and the mouthwatering counters of the food hall provide plenty of entertainment.

John Sandoe Books Books

(Map p78; 020-7589 9473; www.johnsandoe.com; 10 Blacklands Tce, SW3; 9.30am-6.30pm Mon-Sat, 11am-5pm Sun; Sloane Sq) Steeped in literary charm and a perfect antidote to impersonal book superstores, this three-storey bookshop in an 18th-century premises inhabits its own universe. A treasure trove of literary gems and hidden surprises, it's been in business for over six decades. Loyal customers swear by it, and knowledgeable booksellers spill forth with well-read pointers and helpful advice.

Sky Garden

The City's sixth-tallest building didn't get off to a good start when it opened in 2014. Officially called 20 Fenchurch St, it was quickly dubbed the 'Walkie Talkie' by unimpressed Londoners, and its highly reflective windows melted the bodywork of several cars parked below. However, the opening of this 155m-high, three-storey **public garden** (Map p72; 020-7337 2344; https://skygarden.london; 20 Fenchurch St, EC3; 10am-6pm Mon-Fri, 11am-9pm Sat & Sun; Monument) FREE in the glass dome at the top has helped win naysayers over. Entry is free, but you'll need to book a slot in advance.

DRIMAFILM/SHUTTERSTOCK © ARCHITECT: RAFAEL VIÑOLY

Liberty Department Store

(Map p64; 020-7734 1234; www.libertylondon.com; Regent St, entrance on Great Marlborough St, W1; 10am-8pm Mon-Sat, 11.30am-6pm Sun; ; Oxford Circus) One of London's most recognisable shops, Liberty department store has a white-and-wood-beam Tudor Revival facade that lures shoppers in to browse luxury contemporary fashion, homewares, cosmetics and accessories, all at sky-high prices. Liberty is known for its fabrics and has a full haberdashery department; a classic London gift or souvenir is a Liberty fabric print, especially in the form of a scarf.

Liberty department store (p83)

CHRISPICTURES/SHUTTERSTOCK ©

EATING

Once the butt of many a culinary joke, London has transformed itself over the last few decades and today is a global dining destination. World-famous chefs can be found at the helm of several top-tier restaurants, but it is the sheer diversity on offer that is head-spinning: from Afghan to Zambian, London delivers an A to Z of world cuisine.

The West End

Kanada-Ya Ramen £

(Map p64; ☎020-7240 0232; www.kanada-ya.com; 64 St Giles High St, WC2; mains £11-13; ⏰noon-3pm & 5-10.30pm Mon-Sat, to 8.30pm Sun; Ⓤ Tottenham Court Rd) In the debate over London's best ramen, we're still voting for this one. With no reservations taken, queues can get impressive outside this tiny and enormously popular canteen, where ramen cooked in *tonkotsu* (pork-bone broth) draws in diners from near and far. The noodles arrive at just the right temperature and hardness, steeped in a delectable broth and rich flavours.

Palomar Israeli ££

(Map p64; ☎020-7439 8777; www.thepalomar.co.uk; 34 Rupert St, W1; mains £14-16; ⏰6-10pm Mon-Wed, 12.30-2.30pm & 6-10pm Thu-Sun; 📶; Ⓤ Piccadilly Circus) Packed and praised from the day it opened, Palomar is a wonderful Israeli/Levantine restaurant with the look of a 1930s diner and the constant theatre of expert chefs whipping up magic behind the central zinc bar. Unusual dishes such as date-glazed octopus with harissa will blow you away, as will slow-cooked Tel Aviv seafood and beetroot labneh with parsley vinaigrette.

Brasserie Zédel French ££

(Map p64; ☎020-7734 4888; www.brasseriezedel.com; 20 Sherwood St, W1; mains £15-18; ⏰11.30am-midnight Mon-Sat, to 11pm Sun; 📶; Ⓤ Piccadilly Circus) This restaurant in the renovated art-deco ballroom of a former hotel may be the most French brasserie north of Calais. Favourites include *choucroute alsacienne* (sauerkraut with sausages and charcuterie) and *steak haché* (chopped steak) with pepper sauce and *frites*. Set menus (£11/14 for two/three courses) and *plats du jour* such as rabbit with mustard offer value and variety.

Foyer & Reading Room at Claridge's British £££

(Map p64; ☎020-7107 8886; www.claridges.co.uk; Brook St, W1; afternoon tea £70, with champagne £80-90; ⏰7am-10pm Mon-Sat, from 8am Sun, afternoon tea 2.45-5.30pm; 📶; Ⓤ Bond St) Refreshing the better sort of West End shopper since 1856, the jaw-dropping Foyer and Reading Room at **Claridge's** (☎020-7629 8860; www.claridges.co.uk; Brook St, W1; r/ste from £450/780; ❄@📶🐾; Ⓤ Bond St), refulgent with art-deco mirrors and a Dale Chihuly glass sculpture, really is a memorable dining space. Refined food is served at all mealtimes, but many choose to nibble in best aristocratic fashion on the finger sandwiches and pastries of a classic afternoon tea.

Spring British £££

(Map p64; ☎020-3011 0115; www.springrestaurant.co.uk; New Wing, Somerset House, Lancaster Pl, WC2; mains £29-33, 2-/3-course lunch £29/32; ⏰noon-2.30pm & 5.30-10pm Mon-Sat; Ⓤ Temple) White walls, ball chandeliers and columns are offset by the odd blossom in this restored Victorian drawing room in Somerset House (p68). Award-winning Australian chef Skye Gyngell leads a team dedicated to sustainability – no single-use plastic – and an early-evening scratch menu (£25 for three courses) using food that would otherwise be wasted. Desserts are legendary.

Gymkhana Indian £££

(Map p64; ☎020-3011 5900; www.gymkhanalondon.com; 42 Albemarle St, W1; mains £17-38, 4-course menus £40; ⏰noon-2.30pm & 5.30-10.15pm Mon-Sat; 📶; Ⓤ Green Park) The rather sombre setting at this serious Indian fine-dining establishment is intended to invoke the 'good old days' of the British Raj – lazily whirling fans in oak ceilings, period cricket photos and hunting trophies – but the food is anything but dull. Seven-course tasting meat/vegetarian menus are offered (£85/80), and the bar, reminiscent of a 17th-century East India punch-house, opens until 1am.

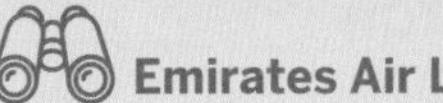

Emirates Air Line

Capable of ferrying 2400 people per hour across the Thames in either direction, this **cable car** (www.emiratesairline.co.uk; 27 Western Gateway, E16; 1-way adult/child £4.50/2.30, with Oyster Card £3.50/1.70; ⏰7am-9pm Mon-Thu, to 11pm Fri, 8am-11pm Sat, 9am-9pm Sun; Royal Victoria DLR, Ⓤ North Greenwich) makes quick work of the journey from the Greenwich Peninsula to the Royal Docks. Although it's mostly patronised by tourists for the views over the river – and the views are ace – it's also listed on the London Underground map as part of the transport network, meaning you can pay with your Oyster Card and nab a discount while you're at it.

PHIL MADDOCKS/SHUTTERSTOCK ©

City of London

Duck & Waffle British ££

(Map p72; ☎020-3640 7310; www.duckandwaffle.com; Heron Tower, 110 Bishopsgate, EC2; mains £14-44; ⏰24hr; 📶; Ⓤ Liverpool St) London tends to have an early bedtime, but Duck and Waffle is the best restaurant that's ready to party all night. Survey the kingdom from the highest restaurant in town (on the 40th floor) over a helping of the namesake dish: a fluffy waffle topped with a crispy leg of duck confit and a fried duck egg, drenched in mustard-seed maple syrup.

LGBTQI+ London

The city of Oscar Wilde, Virginia Woolf and Elton John is a queer life capital, with visible LGBTQI+ communities and laws to protect them. The West End, particularly Soho, is the centre of action, with venues clustered around Old Compton St and its surrounds.

Village (Map p64; ☎020-7478 0530; www.villagesoho.co.uk; 81 Wardour St, W1; ⌚4pm-2am Mon-Thu, to 3am Fri & Sat, to 11.30pm Sun; ⓤPiccadilly Circus) The Village is always up for a party. Take your pick from karaoke nights, 'discolicious' nights, go-go-dancer nights... If you can't wait until the clubs open to strut your stuff, there's a dance floor downstairs.

She Soho (Map p64; ☎020-7437 4303; www.she-soho.com; 23a Old Compton St, W1; ⌚4-11.30pm Mon-Thu, to midnight Fri & Sat, to 10.30pm Sun; ⓤLeicester Sq) This intimate, dimly lit basement bar has DJs, comedy, cabaret, burlesque, live music and party nights. Open till 3am on the last Friday and Saturday of the month. Everybody is welcome at this friendly lesbian spot.

Heaven (Map p64; ☎020-7930 2020; www.heaven nightclub-london.com; Villiers St, WC2; ⌚11pm-5am Mon, to 4am Thu & Fri, 10.30pm-5am Sat; ⓤEmbankment or Charing Cross) This perennially popular mixed/gay club under the arches beneath Charing Cross Station hosts excellent live gigs and club nights. Monday's Popcorn (mixed dance party, with an all-welcome door policy) offers one of the best week-night's clubbing in the capital.

MARIO-GALAS/SHUTTERSTOCK ©

City Social British **£££**

(Map p72; ☎020-7877 7703; www.citysociallondon.com; Tower 42, 25 Old Broad St, EC2; mains £26-37; ⌚noon-2.30pm & 6-10.30pm Mon-Fri, 5-10.30pm Sat; ⓤBank) City Social pairs sublime skyscraper views from its 24th-floor digs with delicate Michelin-starred cuisine. The interior is all art-deco inspired low-lit glamour. If you don't want to splash out on the full menu, opt for the bar, **Social 24**, which has longer hours and a compelling menu of nibbles (don't miss the goats'-cheese churros with locally sourced truffle-infused honey).

South Bank

Padella Italian **£**

(Map p72; www.padella.co; 6 Southwark St, SE1; dishes £4-12.50; ⌚noon-3.45pm & 5-10pm Mon-Sat, noon-3.45pm & 5-9pm Sun; ✎; ⓤLondon Bridge) Come hungry for the best pasta this side of Italy. Padella is a small, energetic bistro specialising in handmade noodles, inspired by the owners' extensive culinary adventures. The portions are small, which means that you can (and should!) have more than one dish. Download the WalkIn app to join the queue virtually to dine here then head to the market or pub.

Arabica Bar & Kitchen Middle Eastern **£**

(Map p72; ☎020-3011 5151; www.arabicabarandkitchen.com; 3 Rochester Walk, Borough Market, SE1; dishes £6-14; ⌚noon-10.30pm Mon-Fri, from 9am Sat, 10am-9.30pm Sun; ✎; ⓤLondon Bridge) Set in a brick-lined railway arch, Arabica specialises in classic Middle Eastern favourites served mezze-style, so round up a group to sample and share as many of the small plates as possible. Stars of the menu include creamy baba ganoush, made with perfectly smoked aubergine and saffron yoghurt, and charcoal-grilled lamb kebab.

Skylon European **£££**

(Map p72; ☎020-7654 7800; www.skylon-restaurant.co.uk; 3rd fl, Royal Festival Hall, Southbank Centre, Belvedere Rd, SE1; mains £16.50-34; ⌚noon-10pm Mon-Fri, 11.30am-3pm & 5-10pm Sat, 11.30am-10pm Sun; 📶👪; ⓤWaterloo)

Named after the original structure in this location for the 1951 Festival of Britain, Skylon brings the 1950s into the modern era, with retro-futuristic decor (cool then, cooler now) and a season-driven menu of contemporary British cuisine. But its biggest selling point might be the floor-to-ceiling windows that bathe you in magnificent views of the Thames and the city.

Kensington & Hyde Park

Rabbit Modern British ££

(Map p78; ☎020-3750 0172; www.rabbit-restaurant.com; 172 King's Rd, SW3; mains £6-20; ⏰noon-9pm Tue-Sat, noon-8pm Sun; 🌿; Ⓤ Sloane Sq) Three brothers grew up on a farm. One became a farmer, another a butcher, while the third worked in hospitality. So they pooled their skills and came up with Rabbit, a breath of fresh air in upmarket Chelsea. The restaurant rocks the agri-chic look, and the creative, seasonal and oft-changing Modern British menu is fabulous.

A Wong Chinese ££

(Map p64; ☎020-7828 8931; www.awong.co.uk; 70 Wilton Rd, SW1; dim sum from £2.50 each, mains £11-35, 'Taste of China' menu £100; ⏰noon-2.30pm & 5.30-10pm Tue-Sat; Ⓤ Victoria) With its relaxed, appealing vibe and busy open kitchen, Michelin-starred A Wong excels at lunchtime dim sum but also casts its net wide to haul in some very tasty sensations from across China: Shanghai *xiaolongbao* dumplings, Shaanxi *roujiamo* (pulled-lamb burger in a bun), Chengdu *doufuhua* (Chengdu 'street tofu'), spicy Sichuan aubergines, Peking duck and more, deliciously reinterpreted.

Dinner by Heston Blumenthal Modern British £££

(Map p78; ☎020-7201 3833; www.dinnerbyheston.com; Mandarin Oriental Hyde Park, 66 Knightsbridge, SW1; 3-course set lunch £48, mains £44-52; ⏰noon-2.15pm & 6-9.30pm Sun-Wed, noon-2.30pm & 6-10pm Thu-Sat; 📶; Ⓤ Knightsbridge) With two Michelin stars, sumptuously presented Dinner is a gastronomic tour de force, taking diners on a journey through British culinary history

Brunch at Duck & Waffle (p85)

Padella (p86)

(with inventive modern inflections). Dishes carry historical dates to convey context, while the restaurant interior is a design triumph, from the glass-walled kitchen and its overhead clock mechanism to the large windows looking onto the park. Book ahead.

Gordon Ramsay French £££

(Map p78; 020-7352 4441; www.gordonramsayrestaurants.com/restaurant-gordon-ramsay; 68 Royal Hospital Rd, SW3; 3-course lunch/dinner £70/130; noon-2.15pm & 6.30-9.45pm Mon-Fri; ; Sloane Sq) One of Britain's finest restaurants and London's longest-running with three Michelin stars (held since 2001), this is hallowed turf for those who worship at the altar of the stove. The blowout Menu Prestige (£160) is seven courses of perfection, also available in vegetarian form (£160); a three-course vegetarian menu (£130) is also at hand. Smart dress code (enquire); reserve early.

Clerkenwell, Shoreditch & Spitalfields

Breddos Tacos Tacos £

(Map p72; 020-3535 8301; www.breddostacos.com; 82 Goswell Rd, EC1; tacos from £5, mains £7.50-17; noon-3pm & 5-11pm Mon-Fri, noon-11.30pm Sat; ; Old St or Farringdon) Started in an East London car park in 2011, Breddos found its first permanent home in Clerkenwell, dishing out some of London's best Mexican grub. Grab some friends and order each of the eight or so tacos, served in pairs, on the menu: fillings vary, but past favourites include confit pork belly, and veggie-friendly mole, queso fresco and egg.

St John British ££

(Map p72; 020-7251 0848; www.stjohnrestaurant.com; 26 St John St, EC1; mains £17-26.50; noon-3pm & 6-11pm Mon-Fri, 6-11pm Sat, 12.30-4pm Sun; Farringdon) Around the corner from London's last remaining meat market, St John is the standard-bearer for nose-to-tail cuisine. With whitewashed brick walls, high ceilings and simple wooden furniture, it's surely one of the most humble Michelin-starred restaurants anywhere. The menu changes daily but is likely to include the signature roast bone marrow and parsley salad.

Clove Club Gastronomy £££
(Map p72; 020-7729 6496; www.thecloveclub.com; Shoreditch Town Hall, 380 Old St, EC1; lunch £65, dinner £95-145; noon-1.45pm Tue-Sat, 6-10.30pm Mon-Sat; ; Old St) From humble origins as a supper club in a London flat, the Clove Club has transformed into this impressive Michelin-starred restaurant, named one of the world's best in 2017. The menu is a mystery until dishes arrive at the table; expect intricately arranged plates with impeccably sourced ingredients from around the British Isles. Your wallet might feel empty, but you sure won't.

Hawksmoor Spitalfields Steak £££
(Map p72; 020-7426 4850; www.thehawksmoor.com; 157a Commercial St, E1; mains £15-60; noon-3pm & 5-10.30pm Mon-Fri, noon-10.30pm Sat, noon-9pm Sun; ; Shoreditch High St) You could easily miss Hawksmoor, discreetly signed and clad in black brick, but dedicated carnivores will find it worth seeking out. The dark wood and velvet curtains make for a handsome setting in which to gorge yourself on the best of British beef. The Sunday roasts (£22) are legendary, but it's *the* place in London to order a steak.

North London

Ruby Violet Ice Cream £
(Map p78; 020-7609 0444; www.rubyviolet.co.uk; Midlands Goods Shed, 3 Wharf Rd, N1; 1 scoop £3; 11am-7pm Mon & Tue, to 10pm Wed-Sun; King's Cross St Pancras) Ruby Violet takes ice cream to the next level: flavours are wonderfully original (masala chai, raspberry and sweet potato) and toppings and hot sauces are shop-made. Plus, there's Pudding Club on Friday and Saturday nights, when you can dive into a mini baked Alaska or hot chocolate fondant. Eat in or sit by the fountain on **Granary Sq** (www.kingscross.co.uk; Stable St, N1; King's Cross St Pancras).

Blackfriar

Built in 1875 on the site of a Dominican monastery (hence the name and the corpulent chap above the door), this prominent **pub** (020-7236 5474; www.nicholsonspubs.co.uk; 174 Queen Victoria St, EC4; 10am-11pm Mon, Thu & Fri, to midnight Tue, noon-10.30pm Wed, 9am-11pm Sat, noon-10.30pm Sun; Blackfriars) was famously saved from demolition in the 1960s by poet Sir John Betjeman. The unusual monastic-themed friezes date from an art-nouveau makeover in 1905. It serves a good selection of ales, along with speciality sausages and chops.

ALPHOTOGRAPHIC/GETTY IMAGES ©

Bar Pepito Tapas £
(Map p78; 020-7841 7331; https://camino.uk.com/res taurant/bar-pepito; 3 Varnishers Yard, The Regent Quarter, N1; tapas £2.50-15; 5pm-midnight Mon-Fri, from 6pm Sat; King's Cross St Pancras) This tiny, intimate Andalusian bodega specialises in sherry and tapas. Novices fear not: the staff are on hand to advise. They're also experts at food pairings (top-notch ham and cheese selections). To go the whole hog, try a tasting flight of selected sherries with snacks to match.

Ottolenghi Mediterranean ££
(020-7288 1454; www.ottolenghi.co.uk; 287 Upper St, N1; breakfast £5.90-12.50, mains lunch/dinner from £16.50/10; 8am-10.30pm Mon-Sat, 9am-7pm Sun; ; Highbury & Islington) Mountains of meringues tempt you through the door of this deli-restaurant, where a sumptuous array of baked goods and

Barge East

fresh salads greets you. Meals are as light and bright as the brilliantly white interior design, with a strong influence from the eastern Mediterranean. Mains at lunch are full platters and include two salads.

East London

Barge East British ££

(020-3026 2807; www.bargeeast.com; River Lee, Sweetwater Mooring, White Post Ln, E9; small plates £7-8.50, mains £14-19; 5-11pm Mon-Thu, noon-11.30pm Fri, 10am-10.30pm Sat, 11am-10.30pm Sun; Hackney Wick) Moored along the River Lee in Hackney Wick is the *De Hoop*, a 100-tonne barge that sailed from Holland to offer seasonal fare and delicious drinks with waterside views. Small plates like nduja scotch eggs with black garlic or large dishes of Szechuan aubergine with cashew cream wash down splendidly with cocktails like the Earl Grey–based East London iced tea.

Silo British £££

(020-7993 8155; https://silolondon.com; Unit 7, Queen's Yard, E9; 6-course tasting menu £50, brunch dishes £7.50-11.50; 6-10pm Tue-Fri, 11am-3pm & 6-10pm Sat, 11am-3pm Sun; Hackney Wick) Brighton's Silo, the world's first zero-waste restaurant, has moved to Hackney Wick. Here, trailblazing chef Doug McMaster fashions lesser-loved ingredients and wonky produce into the likes of beetroot prune with egg yolk fudge or Jerusalem artichoke in brown butter. The canalside space – where everything down to the lampshades is upcycled – is as gorgeous as the dishes on the ever-changing menu.

Greenwich & South London

Marcella Italian ££

(020-3903 6561; https://marcella.london; 165a Deptford High St, SE8; mains £12-16; noon-2.30pm & 6-10pm Wed-Thu, to 10.30pm Fri & Sat, noon-4pm Sun; ; Deptford) If you avoid pasta restaurants because you think you can make it just as easily at home,

Marcella is here to prove you wrong. Perfect house-made pasta comes with seasonally changing sauces in simple but delicious combinations. Starters are equally tasty (the house ricotta is creamy heaven), as are the generously large fish- and meat-based mains, made to share.

DRINKING & NIGHTLIFE

The metropolis offers a huge variety of venues to wet your whistle in – from cosy neighbourhood pubs to glitzy all-night clubs, and everything in between.

The West End

Sketch Cocktail Bar
(Map p64; 020-7659 4500; www.sketch.london; 9 Conduit St, W1; 7am-2am Mon-Fri, 8am-2am Sat, 8am-midnight Sun; Oxford Circus) Merrily undefinable, Sketch has all at once a two-Michelin-starred restaurant, a millennial-pink dining room lined with nonsensical cartoons by British artist David Shrigley, a mystical-forest-themed bar with a self-playing piano, and toilets hidden inside gleaming white egg-shaped pods. We don't know what's happening either, but we're here for it.

Magritte Bar Cocktail Bar
(Map p78; 020-7499 1001; www.thebeaumont.com/dining/american-bar; Beaumont, Brown Hart Gardens, W1; 11.30am-midnight Mon-Sat, to 11pm Sun; ; Bond St) Sip a bourbon or a classic cocktail in the 1920s art-deco ambience of this stylish bar at the hallmark Beaumont hotel. It's central, glam and like a private members' club, but far from stuffy. Only a few years old, the Margritte Bar feels like it's been pouring drinks since the days of the flapper and the jazz age.

American Bar Cocktail Bar
(Map p64; 020-7836 4343; www.fairmont.com/savoy- london/dining/americanbar; The Savoy Hotel, Strand, WC2; 11.30am-midnight Mon-Sat, from noon Sun; ; Temple, Charing Cross or Embankment) Home of the Lonely

Prospect of Whitby

Once known as the Devil's Tavern due to its unsavoury clientele, the **Prospect** (Map p72; 020-7481 1095; www.greeneking-pubs.co.uk; 57 Wapping Wall, E1; noon-11pm Mon-Thu, 11am-midnight Fri & Sat, noon-10.30pm Sun; ; Wapping) first opened its doors in 1520, although the only part of the original pub remaining is the flagstone floor. Famous patrons have included Charles Dickens and Samuel Pepys. There's a smallish terrace overlooking the Thames, a restaurant upstairs, open fires in winter and a pewter-topped bar.

JUSTIN FOULKES/LONELY PLANET ©

Street, Concrete Jungle and other house cocktails named after iconic songs collected in the 'Savoy Songbook', the seriously dishy American Bar is a London icon, with soft blue furniture, gleaming art-deco lines and live piano jazz from 6.30pm nightly. Cocktails start at £20 and peak at a stupefying £5000 (for the Sazerac, containing cognac from 1858).

Lamb & Flag Pub
(Map p64; 020-7497 9504; www.lambandflagcoventgarden.co.uk; 33 Rose St, WC2; 11am-11pm Mon-Sat, noon-10.30pm Sun; Covent Garden) Perpetually busy, the pint-sized Lamb & Flag is full of charm and history: there's been a public house here since at least 1772, when it was known as the Cooper's Arms and infamous for staging bare-knuckle boxing matches. Rain or shine, you'll have

LITTLENYSTOCK/SHUTTERSTOCK ©

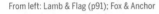

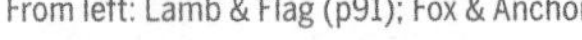
From left: Lamb & Flag (p91); Fox & Anchor

to elbow your way through the merry crowd drinking outside to get to the bar.

City of London

Nickel Bar Cocktail Bar

(Map p72; 020-3828 2000; www.thened.com/restaurants/the-nickel-bar; 27 Poultry, EC2; 8am-2am Mon-Fri, 9am-3am Sat, to midnight Sun; Bank) There's something *Great Gatsby*–ish about **The Ned** (020-3828 2100; www.thened.com; 27 Poultry, London, EC2; r £230-400; Bank) hotel: the elevated jazz pianists, the vast verdite columns, the classy American-inspired cocktails. Of all the public bars inside this magnificent former banking hall, the Nickel Bar soaks up the atmosphere best. Inspired by the glamorous art-deco saloons and the ocean-liner-era elegance, this is timeless nightcap territory.

South Bank

George Inn Pub

(Map p72; 020-7407 2056; www.nationaltrust.org.uk/george-inn; 77 Borough High St, SE1; 11am-11pm Mon-Thu, to midnight Fri & Sat, noon-10.30pm Sun; London Bridge) This magnificent galleried coaching inn is the last of its kind in London. The building, owned by the National Trust, dates from 1677 and is mentioned in Charles Dickens' *Little Dorrit*. In the evenings, the picnic benches in the huge cobbled courtyard fill up (no reservations); otherwise, find a spot in the labyrinth of dark rooms and corridors inside.

Kings Arms Pub

(Map p72; 020-7207 0784; www.thekingsarmslondon.co.uk; 25 Roupell St, SE1; 11am-11pm Mon-Sat, noon-10.30pm Sun; Waterloo) Set on old-school **Roupell St** (Roupell St, SE1; Waterloo), this charming backstreet neighbourhood boozer serves up a rotating selection of traditional ales and bottled beers. The after-work crowd often makes a pit stop here before heading to Waterloo station, spilling out onto the street at peak hours. The farmhouse-style room at the back of the pub serves decent Thai food.

Lyaness Cocktail Bar

(Map p72; 020-3747 1063; https://lyaness.com; Sea Containers, 20 Upper Ground, SE1; 4pm-1am Mon-Wed, noon-2am Thu-Sat, to

The Kings Arms

12.30am Sun; 📶; Ⓤ Southwark) Six months after Dandelyan was named the best bar in the world, renowned mixologist Ryan Chetiyawardana closed it down. Reincarnated in that space with much the same atmosphere and modus operandi is Lyaness. The bar prides itself on unusual ingredients; look out for vegan honey, whey liqueur and onyx, a completely new type of alcohol.

Seabird Rooftop Bar

(Map p72; ☎020-7903 3050; https://seabirdlondon.com; Hoxton Southwark, 40 Blackfriars Rd, SE1; ⏲noon-midnight Mon-Thu, to 1am Fri, 11am-1am Sat, to midnight Sun; Ⓤ Southwark) South Bank's latest rooftop bar might also be its best. Atop the new **Hoxton Southwark** (☎020-7903 3000; https://thehoxton.com/london/southwark; Blackfriars Rd, SE1; r £140-300; ❄@📶🐾; Ⓤ Southwark) hotel, sleek Seabird has palm-filled indoor and outdoor spaces where you can spy St Paul's from the comfort of your wicker seat. If you're hungry, seafood is the speciality, and the restaurant claims London's longest oyster list.

Clerkenwell, Shoreditch & Spitalfields

Fox & Anchor Pub

(Map p72; ☎020-7250 1300; www.foxandanchor.com; 115 Charterhouse St, EC1; ⏲7am-11pm, from 8.30am Sat, from 11am Sun; 📶; Ⓤ Barbican) Behind the Fox & Anchor's wonderful 1898 art-nouveau facade is a stunning traditional Victorian boozer, one of the last remaining market pubs in London that's permitted to serve alcohol before 11am. Fully celebrating its proximity to Smithfield Market, the grub is gloriously meaty. Only the most voracious of carnivores should opt for the City Boy Breakfast (£19.50).

Nightjar Cocktail Bar

(Map p72; ☎020-7253 4101; https://barnightjar.com; 129 City Rd, EC1V; music cover £5-8; ⏲6pm-1am, to 2am Thu, to 3am Fri & Sat; Ⓤ Old St) Behind a nondescript, gold-knobbed door just north of the Old Street roundabout is this bona fide speakeasy, pouring award-winning libations from a four-section menu that delineates the evolution of the cocktail. Leather banquettes, brick-walled booths and art-deco liquor cabinets stocked with vintage spirits set the perfect scene for jazz and blues acts that take the stage nightly at 9.30pm.

Zetter Townhouse Cocktail Lounge Cocktail Bar

(Map p72; ☎020-7324 4545; www.thezettertownhouse.com/clerkenwell/bar; 49-50 St John's Sq, EC1; ⏲7am-midnight, to 1am Thu-Sat; 📶; UFarringdon) Behind an unassuming door on St John's Sq, this ground-floor bar is decorated with plush armchairs, stuffed animal heads and a legion of lamps. The cocktail list takes its theme from the area's distilling history – recipes of yesteryear plus homemade tinctures and cordials are used to create interesting and unusual tipples.

North London

Holly Bush Pub

(Map p78; ☎020-7435 2892; www.hollybushhampstead.co.uk; 22 Holly Mount, NW3; ⏲noon-11pm Mon-Sat, to 10.30pm Sun; 📶👪🐾; UHampstead) This beautiful Grade II–listed Georgian pub boasts a splendid antique interior, with open fires in winter. It has a knack for making you stay longer than you planned. Set above Heath St, in a secluded hilltop location, it's reached via the Holly Bush Steps.

Edinboro Castle Pub

(Map p78; ☎020-7255 9651; www.edinborocastlepub.co.uk; 57 Mornington Tce, NW1; ⏲noon-11pm Mon-Sat, to 10.30pm Sun; 📶; UCamden Town) Large and relaxed, the Edinboro offers a fun atmosphere, a fine bar and a full menu. The highlight, however, is the huge beer garden, complete with warm-weather barbecues and decorated with coloured lights on long summer evenings. Patio heaters appear in winter.

ENTERTAINMENT

Whatever it is that sets your spirits soaring or your booty shaking, you'll find it in London. The city's been a world leader in theatre ever since a young man from Stratford-upon-Avon set up shop here in the 16th century. And if London started swinging in the 1960s, its live rock and pop scene has barely let up since.

Holly Bush

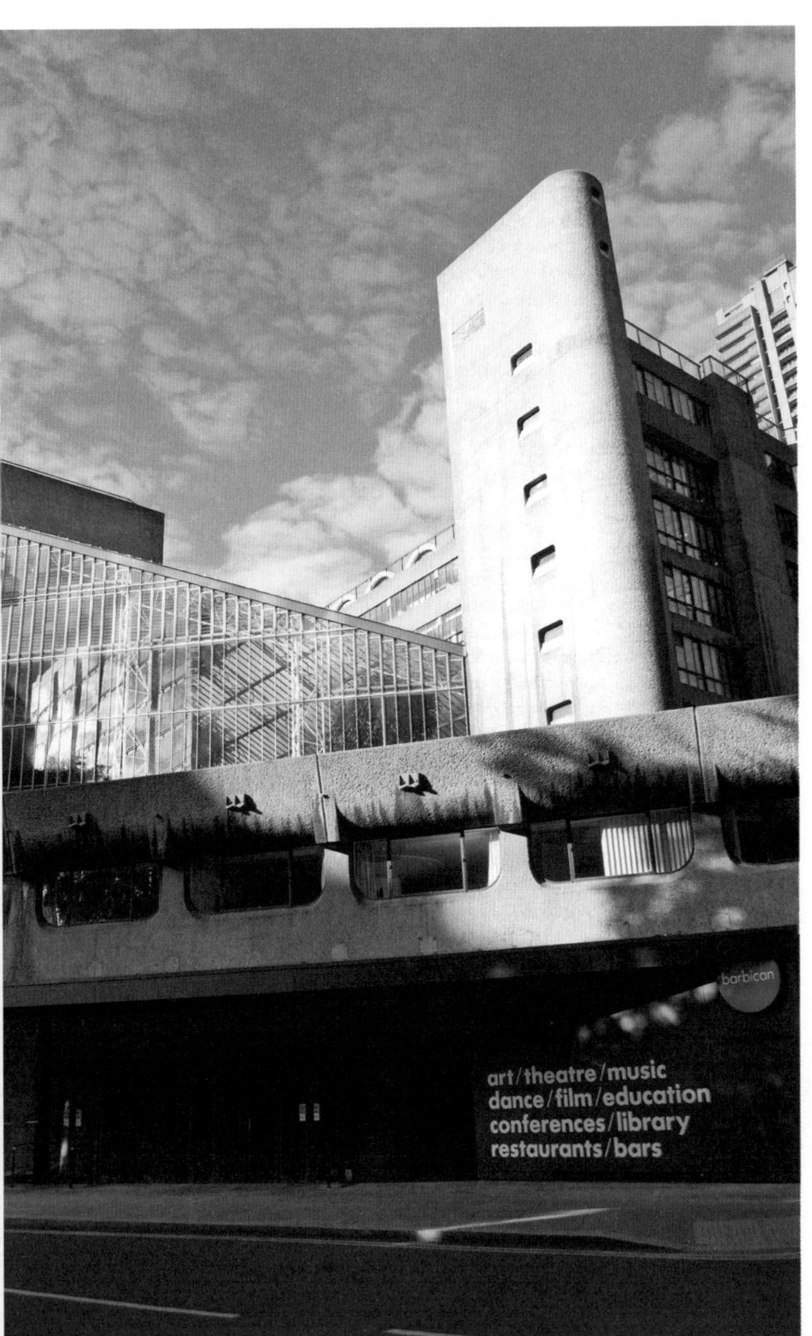
barbican
art/theatre/music
dance/film/education
conferences/library
restaurants/bars

Green Note Live Music
(Map p78; ☎020-7485 9899; www.greennote.co.uk; 106 Parkway, NW1; ⏲7-11pm Sun-Thu, to midnight Fri & Sat; Ⓤ Camden Town) Camden may be the home of punk, but it also has the Green Note: one of the best places in London to see live folk and world music, with gigs every night of the week. The setting is intimate: a tiny bare-brick room with mics set up in a corner, backdropped by red curtains. Most tickets are under £10 (£12 at the door).

Bush Theatre Theatre
(☎020-8743 5050; www.bushtheatre.co.uk; 7 Uxbridge Rd, W12; ⏲10am-11pm Mon-Sat; Ⓤ Shepherd's Bush) Located in the former Passmore Edwards Public Library building, this West London theatre is renowned for encouraging new writing. Its success since 1972 is down to strong plays from the likes of Jonathan Harvey, Conor McPherson, Stephen Poliakoff, Caroline Horton and Tanya Ronder. The Holloway Theatre is the main space; the Studio is the smaller, 70-seat venue. There's an excellent **cafe and bar** (www.bushtheatre.co.uk; 7 Uxbridge Rd; ⏲10am-11pm Mon-Sat; ᯤ; Ⓤ Shepherd's Bush Market).

Wigmore Hall Classical Music
(Map p64; ☎020-7935 2141; www.wigmore-hall.org.uk; 36 Wigmore St, W1; Ⓤ Bond St) Wigmore Hall, built in 1901 as a piano showroom, is one of the best and most active classical-music venues in town, with more than 460 concerts a year. This isn't just because of its fantastic acoustics, beautiful Arts and Crafts–style cupola over the stage and great variety of concerts, but also because of the sheer quality of the performances.

Almeida Theatre
(☎020-7359 4404; www.almeida.co.uk; Almeida St, N1; tickets £10-42.50; Ⓤ Highbury & Islington) Housed in a Grade II–listed Victorian building, this plush 325-seat theatre can be relied on for imaginative programming. Its emphasis is on new, up-and-coming talent. For theatre-goers aged 25 and under, £5 tickets (two per person) are available for select performances.

Ronnie Scott's Jazz
(Map p64; ☎020-7439 0747; www.ronniescotts.co.uk; 47 Frith St, W1; ⏲6pm-3am Mon-Sat, noon-4pm & 6.30pm-midnight Sun; Ⓤ Leicester Sq or Tottenham Court Rd) Ronnie Scott's jazz club opened in 1959 and became widely known as Britain's best, hosting such luminaries as Miles Davis, Charlie Parker, Ella Fitzgerald, Count Basie and Sarah Vaughan. The club continues to build upon its formidable reputation by presenting a range of big names and new talent. Book in advance, or come for a more informal gig at **Upstairs @ Ronnie's**.

Barbican Centre Performing Arts
(Map p72; ☎020-7638 8891; www.barbican.org.uk; Silk St, EC2; ⏲box office 10am-9pm Mon-Sat, noon-8pm Sun; Ⓤ Barbican) You'll get as lost in the astounding programme as you will in the labyrinthine brutalist building. Home to the **London Symphony Orchestra**, the **BBC Symphony Orchestra** and the **Royal Shakespeare Company**, the Barbican Centre is the City's premier cultural venue. It hosts concerts, theatre and dance performances, and screens indie films and Hollywood blockbusters at the cinema on Beech St.

Old Vic Theatre
(Map p72; ☎0344 871 7628; www.oldvictheatre.com; The Cut, SE1; Ⓤ Waterloo) This 1000-seater nonprofit theatre celebrated its 200th season in 2018 and continues to bring eclectic programming occasionally bolstered by big-name actors, such as Daniel Radcliffe.

INFORMATION

DANGERS & ANNOYANCES

London is a fairly safe city for its size, but exercise common sense.

- Several high-profile terrorist attacks have afflicted London in recent years, but the risk to individual visitors is remote. Report

Old Vic

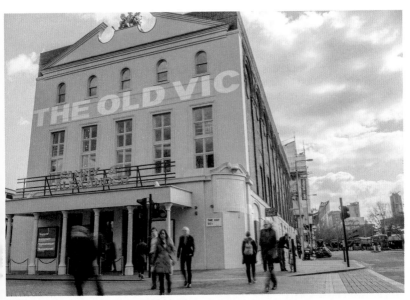

anything suspicious to the police by calling 999 (emergency) or 101 (non-emergency).

- Keep an eye on your handbag and wallet, especially in bars and nightclubs, and in crowded areas.
- Be discreet with your tablet/smartphone – snatching happens.

MONEY

ATMs (cash points) are widespread. Major credit cards are accepted everywhere. Change money at post offices, which don't charge a commission.

TOURIST INFORMATION

Visit London (www.visitlondon.com) can fill you in on everything from attractions and events to tours and accommodation. Kiosks are dotted about the city and can also provide maps and brochures; some branches are able to book theatre tickets.

Key locations:

Heathrow Airport (www.visitlondon.com/tag/tourist-information-centre; Terminal 1, 2 & 3 Underground station concourse; 7.30am-8.30pm)

King's Cross St Pancras Station (www.visitlondon.com/tag/tourist-information-centre; Western Ticket Hall, Euston Rd, N1; 8am-6pm)

Liverpool Street Station (www.visitlondon.com/tag/tourist-information-centre; Liverpool St Underground station, EC2; U Liverpool St)

Victoria Station (www.visitlondon.com/tag/tourist-information-centre; Victoria Station; 9am-5pm; U Victoria)

GETTING THERE & AWAY

AIR

Most people arrive in London by air, but an increasing number of visitors coming from Europe take the train, and buses from across the continent are another option.

The city has six airports: Heathrow, which is the largest, to the west; Gatwick to the south; Stansted to the northeast; Luton to the northwest; London City in the Docklands; and London Southend to the east.

Most trans-Atlantic flights land at Heathrow (average flight time from the US East Coast is between 6½ and 7½ hours, 10 to 11 hours from the West Coast; slightly more on the return). Visitors from Europe are more likely to arrive at Gatwick, Stansted or Luton (the latter two are used exclusively by low-cost airlines such as easyJet and Ryanair). Most flights to continental Europe last from one to three hours.

RAIL

Check **National Rail** (www.nationalrail.co.uk) for timetables and fares. **Eurostar** (www.eurostar.com) is a high-speed passenger rail service linking London St Pancras International with Paris, Brussels, Amsterdam and Marseilles, with up to 19 daily departures. Fares vary greatly, from £29 for a one-way standard-class ticket to around £245 one-way for a fully flexible business premier ticket (prices based on return journeys).

 GETTING AROUND

Both **Transport for London** (TfL; https://tfl.gov.uk/plan-a-journey) and **Citymapper** (https://citymapper.com/london) will give you route options for trip planning with up-to-date information on departures and delays.

The cheapest way to get around London is with an **Oyster Card** (https://oyster.tfl.gov.uk/oyster/entry.do) or a UK contactless card (foreign cardholders should check for extra international transaction charges first) with a daily fare cap.

Tube (London Underground) The fastest and most efficient way of getting around town, but you won't see anything. First/last trains operate from around 5.30am to 12.30am and 24 hours on Friday and Saturday on five lines.

Train The DLR and Overground networks are ideal for connecting between distant parts of the city. The route from Peckham to Shoreditch is fondly called 'the hipster line'.

Bus The London bus network is very extensive and efficient and, best of all, above ground; in heavy traffic it can be quicker to walk.

Taxis Black cabs are ubiquitous and available around the clock. Although not cheap, it's an experience.

Bicycle Santander Cycles are good for shorter journeys around central London, but you need to be fairly road-wise.

Where to Stay

Landing the right accommodation is integral to your London experience, and there's no shortage of choice, from hip hostels to boutique B&Bs and prestigious five-star properties.

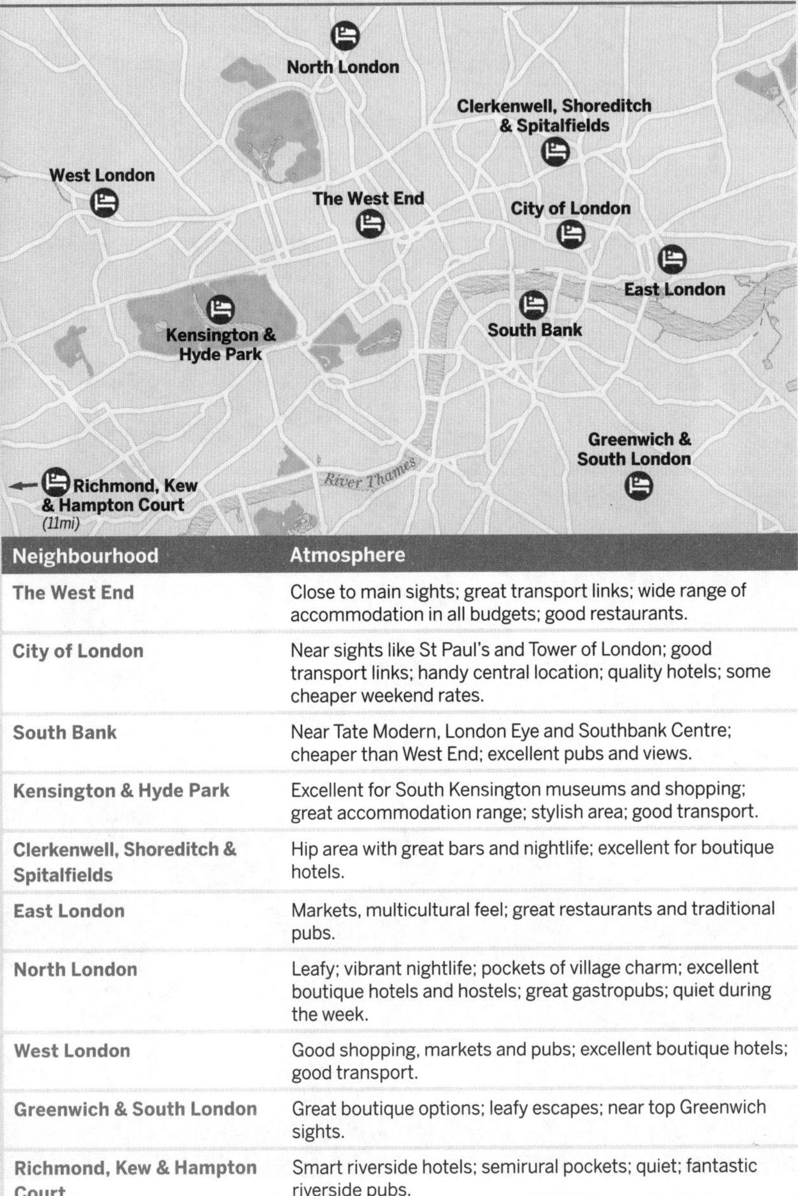

Neighbourhood	Atmosphere
The West End	Close to main sights; great transport links; wide range of accommodation in all budgets; good restaurants.
City of London	Near sights like St Paul's and Tower of London; good transport links; handy central location; quality hotels; some cheaper weekend rates.
South Bank	Near Tate Modern, London Eye and Southbank Centre; cheaper than West End; excellent pubs and views.
Kensington & Hyde Park	Excellent for South Kensington museums and shopping; great accommodation range; stylish area; good transport.
Clerkenwell, Shoreditch & Spitalfields	Hip area with great bars and nightlife; excellent for boutique hotels.
East London	Markets, multicultural feel; great restaurants and traditional pubs.
North London	Leafy; vibrant nightlife; pockets of village charm; excellent boutique hotels and hostels; great gastropubs; quiet during the week.
West London	Good shopping, markets and pubs; excellent boutique hotels; good transport.
Greenwich & South London	Great boutique options; leafy escapes; near top Greenwich sights.
Richmond, Kew & Hampton Court	Smart riverside hotels; semirural pockets; quiet; fantastic riverside pubs.

STONEHENGE

In this Chapter

Stonehenge at a Glance...

The verdant landscape in which Stonehenge sits is rich in the reminders of ritual and packed with not-to-be-missed sights. Dotted with more mysterious stone circles and processional avenues than anywhere else in Britain, it's a place that teases the imagination. Here you'll experience the prehistoric majesty of Stonehenge itself, the historic cathedral city of Salisbury and the supremely stately homes at Stourhead and Longleat. It's an area crammed full of English charm waiting to be explored.

Two Days in Stonehenge

Arrive early on day one to delight in a less busy **Stonehenge** (p104). Next, have a (perhaps picnic) lunch, and explore the fascinating ruined settlement of **Old Sarum** (p109). On your second day, tour **Salisbury Cathedral** (p108), taking in the ornate statuary, glorious stained glass and soaring spire, before exploring the intriguing exhibits at **Salisbury Museum** (p108).

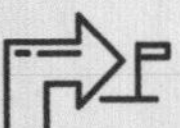

Four Days in Stonehenge

Head to stunning **Stourhead** (p108) to roam around spectacular landscaped grounds; give yourself enough time to explore. Then its back to Salisbury for a drink at the ancient, (purportedly) haunted **Haunch of Venison** (p109). On day four motor to **Longleat** (p109) to drive through the vast safari park. Then nip back to Salisbury for dinner at **Anokaa** (p109) or the **Craft Bar** (p109).

Previous page: Stonehenge
DRONEMYBUSINESS/SHUTTERSTOCK ©

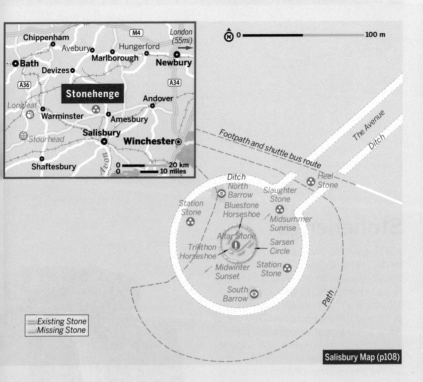

Salisbury Map (p108)

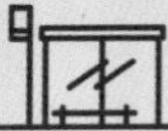

Arriving in Stonehenge

Stonehenge is 10 miles north of Salisbury. The Stonehenge Tour bus (adult/child £16/10) leaves Salisbury's railway station frequently while Stonehenge is open.

Salisbury's transport connections include frequent train and bus services to London and the southwest.

Where to Stay

With a good range of places to sleep, from characterful B&Bs to sleek hotels, Salisbury makes an ideal base for exploring Stonehenge and its outlying sights. The city also offers diverse eating and drinking options, ranging from an acclaimed Indian restaurant to a history-rich pub.

Stone Circle

Stonehenge

You've seen the photos, now prepare to be dazzled by Britain's most recognisable archaeological site. This compelling ring of monolithic stones has been attracting a steady stream of pilgrims, poets and philosophers for 5000 years and it's still a mystical, ethereal place – a haunting echo from Britain's ancient past and a reminder of those who once walked the ceremonial avenues across Salisbury Plain.

Great For...

Need to Know

EH; 0370 333 1181; www.english-heritage.org.uk; near Amesbury; adult/child £21/13; 9.30am-5pm, hours may vary; P

★ **Top Tip**

Book your Stone Circle Experience (p106) at least three months in advance to walk inside the stone circle itself.

MR NAI/SHUTTERSTOCK ©

An ultramodern makeover at Stonehenge has brought an impressive visitor centre and the closure of an intrusive road (now restored to grassland). The result is a far stronger sense of historical context.

Planning

Admission to Stonehenge is through pre-booked timed tickets – secure yours at least two weeks in advance. At the time of writing opening hours were reduced; check whether summer-time early-evening visits have resumed. The **Stone Circle Experience** (☎0370 333 0605; www.english-heritage.org.uk; adult/child £47/28), where you walk within the stone circle itself, sees you wandering around the core of the site, getting up-close views of the iconic bluestones and trilithons.

Access

A pathway frames the ring of massive stones, which are 1.5 miles from the visitor centre. A fleet of trolley buses makes the 10-minute trip, although it's more atmospheric to walk, via a 2.6-mile circular trail through the ancient landscape.

Visitor Centre

Stonehenge's swish **visitor centre** (EH; ☎0370 333 1181; www.english-heritage.org.uk; incl access to Stonehenge adult/child £21/13; ⏰9.30am-5pm, hours may vary) sees you standing in the middle of an atmospheric 360-degree projection of the stone circle through the ages and seasons – complete with midsummer sunrise and swirling star-scape. Engaging audiovisual displays detail the transportation of the stones and the

Stonehenge Visitor Centre

building stages, while 300 finds from the wider site include bone pins and arrowheads. There's also a striking recreation of the face of a Neolithic man whose body was found nearby.

Building Phases

The first phase of building started around 3000 BCE, when the outer circular bank and ditch were erected. Within this were 56 pits – it's thought they may also have held timber posts or stones. Some 500 years later, Stonehenge's main stones were dragged to the site, erected in a circle and crowned by massive lintels to make the trilithons (two vertical stones topped by a horizontal one). The 30 huge slabs of stone were worked carefully to ensure they locked together.

Two curving rows of smaller 'bluestones' were also added. The four Station stones were probably set up at around the same time. Then in around 2300 BCE the central bluestones were rearranged forming inner circles and ovals, which were later rearranged to form a bluestone horseshoe.

Today, three of the five sets of stones in the trilithon horseshoe are intact; the other two have just a single upright. Of the major sarsen circle of 30 massive vertical stones, 17 uprights and six lintels remain.

☑ Don't Miss

The Slaughter Stone, Heel Stone and Avenue, which provide intriguing glimpses into Stonehenge's place in what was a much wider ritual landscape.

PETER TITMUSS/SHUTTERSTOCK ©

A Place of Pilgrimage

Like many stone circles in Britain (including Avebury, 22 miles away), the stones are aligned to coincide with sunrise at the midsummer solstice, which some claim supports the theory that the site was some kind of astronomical calendar.

Prehistoric pilgrims would have entered the site via the Avenue, whose entrance to the circle is marked by the Slaughter Stone and the Heel Stone, located slightly further out on one side.

Prehistoric Engineers

It's thought some of the mammoth 4-tonne bluestone blocks were hauled from the Preseli Mountains in South Wales, some 250 miles away – an extraordinary feat for Stone Age people equipped with only the simplest of tools. Although no one is entirely sure how the builders transported the stones so far, it's thought they probably used a system of ropes, sledges and rollers fashioned from tree trunks – Salisbury Plain was still covered by forest during Stonehenge's construction.

Take a Break

The visitor centre has a large cafe serving sandwiches, soup, drinks and cakes; you can eat inside or in the picnic area.

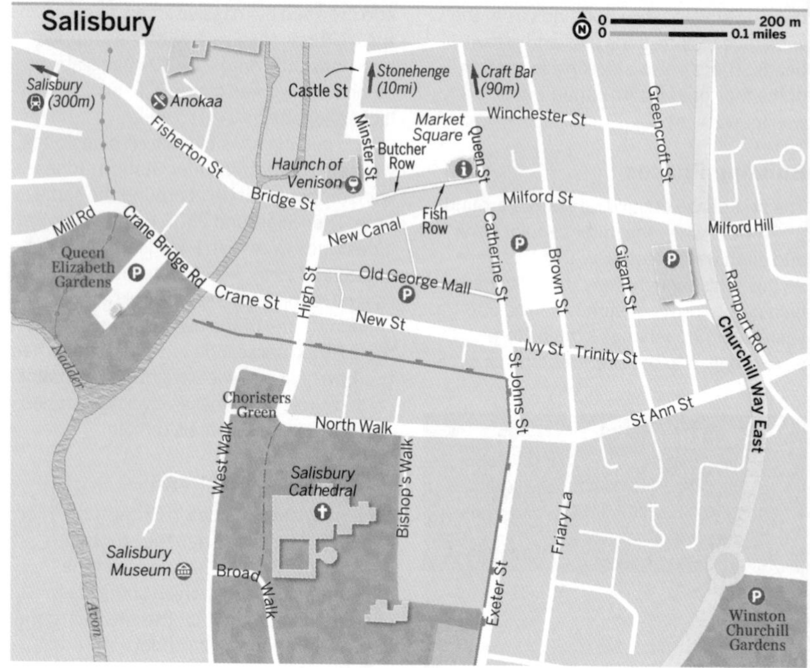

Salisbury

The ancient cathedral city of Salisbury makes an appealing base.

SIGHTS

Salisbury Cathedral Cathedral

(☎01722-555150; www.salisburycathedral.org.uk; The Close; requested donation adult/child £7.50/3; ⏰9am-4pm Mon-Sat) Few of England's stunning churches can hold a candle to the grandeur and sheer spectacle of 13th-century Salisbury Cathedral. This elaborate, early English Gothic–style structure has pointed arches, flying buttresses, a sombre, austere interior and outstanding statuary and tombs. Check the website to see if the daily tower tours have resumed and if the cathedral's 13th-century copy of the **Magna Carta** is on display. If not, look out for the high-resolution facsimile in the North Transept.

Salisbury Museum Museum

(☎01722-332151; www.salisburymuseum.org.uk; 65 The Close; adult/child £8/4; ⏰11am-4pm Thu-Sun) The hugely important archaeological finds in the Wessex Gallery include the Stonehenge Archer, the bones of a man found in the ditch near the stone circle – one of the arrows found alongside probably killed him. With gold coins dating from 100 BCE and a Bronze Age gold necklace, it's a powerful introduction to Wiltshire's prehistory.

Stourhead Historic Building

(NT; ☎01747-841152; www.nationaltrust.org.uk; Mere; gardens adult/child £13/6.50; ⏰gardens 9am-5pm; P) Overflowing with vistas, temples and exotic trees, Stourhead is landscape gardening at its finest. The magnificent 18th-century gardens spread across the valley, with a picturesque 2-mile garden circuit taking you past ornate follies, around a centrepiece lake and to the Georgian Temple of Apollo. A 3.5-mile side trip can be made from near the Pantheon to a 50m-high folly called King Alfred's Tower. Stourhead is off the B3092, 10 miles south of Frome.

Longleat Zoo

(☎01985-844400; www.longleat.co.uk; near Warminster; adult/child £26/19; ⏰10am-5pm, hours may vary; P) Half ancestral mansion, half wildlife park, Longleat was transformed into Britain's first safari park in 1966, turning Capability Brown's landscaped grounds into an amazing drive-through zoo populated by a menagerie of animals more at home in the African wilderness than the fields of Wiltshire. There's a throng of attractions, too: the historic house, animatronic dinosaur exhibits, narrow-gauge railway, mazes, pets' corner, butterfly garden and bat cave.

It's just off the A362, 3 miles from Frome. Check whether you need to pre-book your visit.

Old Sarum Archaeological Site

(EH; ☎01722-335398; www.english-heritage.org.uk; Castle Rd; adult/child £5.90/3.50; ⏰10am-5pm Apr-Oct, to 4pm Nov-Mar; P) The vast ramparts of Old Sarum sit on a turf-covered hill 2 miles north of Salisbury. You can wander the grassy ramparts, see the original cathedral's stone foundations and look across the Wiltshire countryside to the spire of the present Salisbury Cathedral. Buses X4 and R11 regularly run from Salisbury to Old Sarum (£4.40, 10 minutes). It's also a stop on the Stonehenge Tour bus.

EATING

Craft Bar Burgers £

(Salisbury Arms; ☎01722-41170; www.thecraftbar.wordpress.com; 31 Endless St; meals £11; ⏰6-9.30pm Wed-Sat) It's a winning combo: towering burgers, hand-cut fries, creative cocktails and craft beer and cider. All set in a pub with a relaxed vibe.

Anokaa Indian ££

(☎01722-414142; www.anokaa.com; 60 Fisherton St; mains £16-19; ⏰5-9pm Sun-Fri, noon-9pm Sat; 🌶) The neon and ultra-modern decor signals what's in store here: a contemporary, multilayered take on high-class Indian cuisine. The spice and flavour combos make the ingredients sing, the meat-free menu makes vegetarians gleeful, and the early evening deal (two courses with wine for £16) makes everyone smile.

DRINKING & NIGHTLIFE

Haunch of Venison Pub

(☎01722-411313; www.haunchpub.co.uk; 1 Minster St; ⏰11am-11pm Mon-Sat, to 6pm Sun) Featuring wood-panelled snugs, spiral staircases and crooked ceilings, this 14th-century drinking den is packed with atmosphere – and ghosts. One is a cheating whist player whose hand was severed in a game – look out for his mummified bones on display inside.

INFORMATION

Tourist Office (☎01722-342860; www.visitwiltshire.co.uk/salisbury; Fish Row; ⏰9am-5pm Mon-Fri, 10am-4pm Sat; 📶)

GETTING THERE & AWAY

Bus Daily National Express services to Bath (£11, 1½ hours) and London Victoria via Heathrow (£12, three hours).

Train Half-hourly trains run to Bath (£12, one hour) and London Waterloo (£25, 1½ hours).

BATH

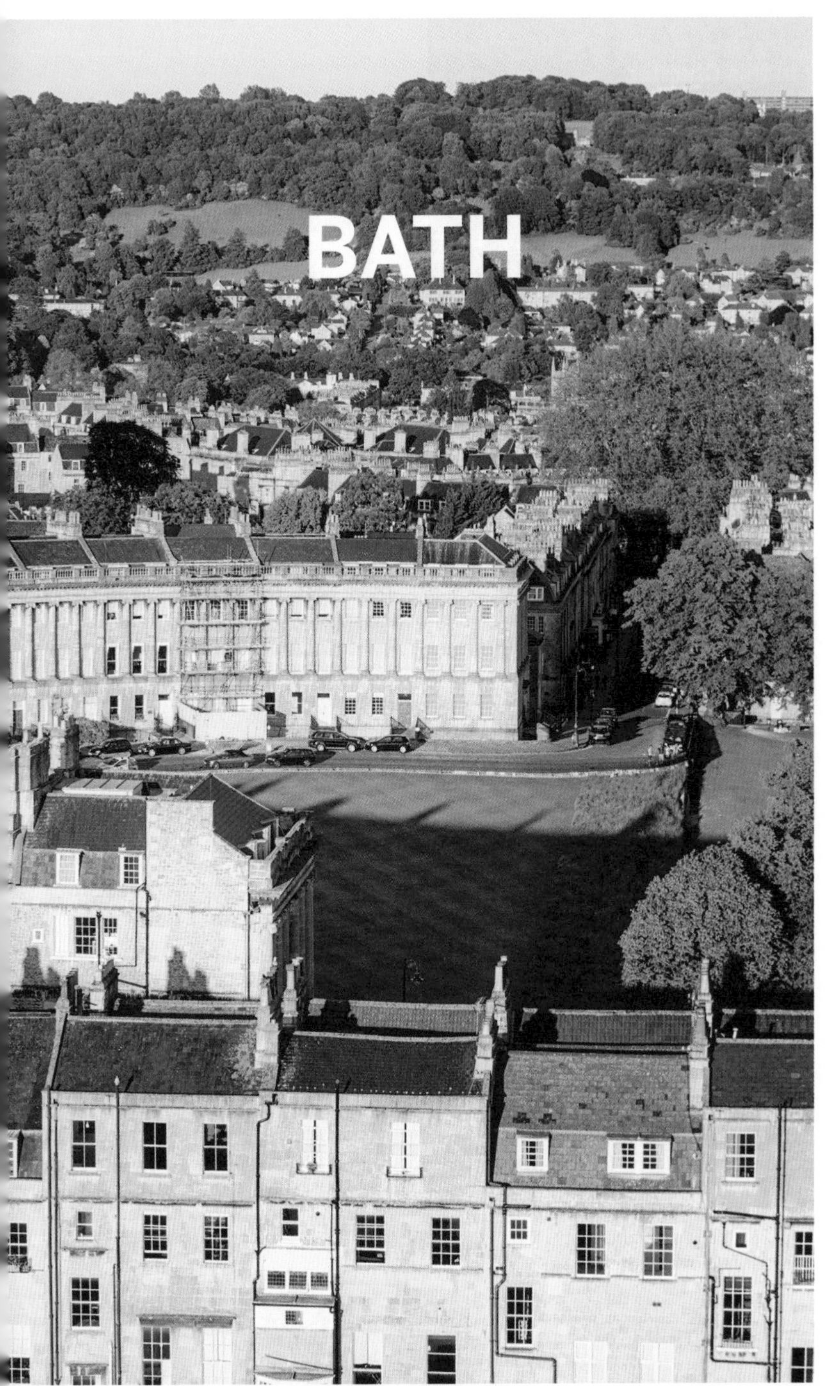

In this Chapter

Bath at a Glance...

Home to some of the nation's grandest Georgian architecture – not to mention one of the world's best-preserved Roman bathhouses – this chic city, founded on top of natural hot springs, has been a tourist draw for nigh on 2000 years. Bath's heyday really began during the 18th century, when local entrepreneur Ralph Allen and his team of father-and-son architects, John Wood the Elder and Younger, turned this sleepy backwater into the toast of Georgian society, and constructed fabulous landmarks such as the Circus and Royal Crescent.

Two Days in Bath

Start by touring the **Roman Baths** (p114), then sip some spring water and sample afternoon tea in the **Pump Room** (p122), before a stylish supper at **Acorn** (p121). On day two, Bath's glorious architecture awaits: first the Royal Crescent – ducking inside **No 1** (p117) – then the **Circus** (p117), stopping at the Circus **restaurant** (p121) for lunch. Next up, browse for books at **Topping & Company** (p121), then have dinner at local favourite **Noya's Kitchen** (p121).

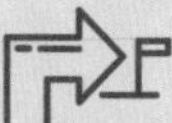

Four Days in Bath

On day three, clamber up Bath Abbey's **tower** (p119), then discover the **Jane Austen Centre** (p118). Take in a barmy comedy **walk** (p119) before dropping by live-music pub, the **Bell Inn** (p122). After starting day four with a lazy cruise down the **Avon** (p119), continue chilling out at **Thermae Bath Spa** (p119); saving the roof-top swim until dusk. End with still more indulgence at **Menu Gordon Jones** (p122).

Previous page: Royal Crescent (p117)
GEORGECLERK/GETTY IMAGES ©

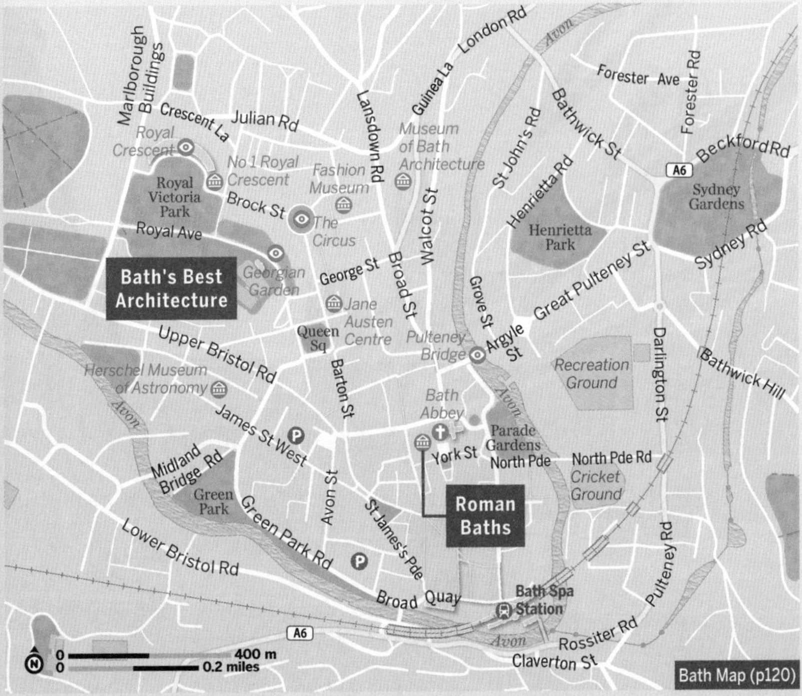

Bath's Best Architecture

Roman Baths

Bath Map (p120)

Arriving in Bath

Bus National Express coaches run to London Victoria (£15, three hours, hourly) and London Heathrow (£27, 2½ hours, two-hourly).

Car Bath is 115 miles (2½ hours) from London and 34 miles (one hour) from Stonehenge.

Train Direct services include London Paddington (£35, 1½ hours, hourly) and Salisbury (for Stonehenge; £12, one hour, half-hourly).

Where to Stay

Bath has a wide range of hotels and B&Bs, and gets extremely busy in the height of summer when prices peak. Be aware, they also rise by anything from £15 to £65 a room at weekends year-round. Few hotels have on-site parking, although some offer discounted rates at municipal car parks.

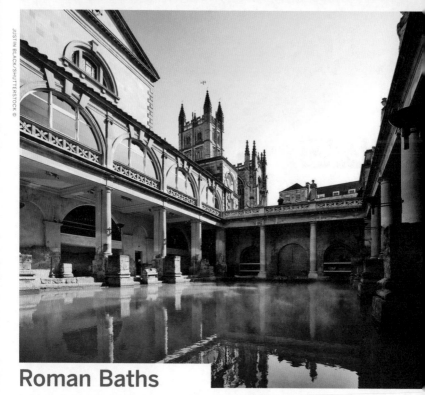

JUSTIN BLACK/SHUTTERSTOCK ©

Roman Baths

In typically ostentatious style, the Romans built a bathhouse complex above Bath's hot springs. Set alongside a temple to a goddess with healing powers, they're now one of the best-preserved Roman-era spas in the world.

You could say Bath the city originated with these Roman baths – legend has it that King Bladud, a Trojan refugee and father of King Lear, founded Bath some 2800 years ago when his pigs were cured of leprosy by a dip in the muddy swamps. The Romans established the town of Aquae Sulis in 44 CE, building the extensive baths complex and a temple to the goddess Sulis-Minerva.

The Great Bath

The heart of the complex is the Great Bath, a lead-lined pool filled with steaming, geothermally heated water to a depth of 1.6m. It emerges at a toasty 46°C (115°F) from the so-called 'Sacred Spring'. Though now open-air, the bath would originally have been covered by a 45m-high, barrel-vaulted roof.

Great For...

☑ Don't Miss

Sampling a glass of Bath's disconcertingly warm spring waters (50p) in the on-site restaurant.

Bust of Minerva at the Roman baths

ALECS ROMANISIN/500PX ©

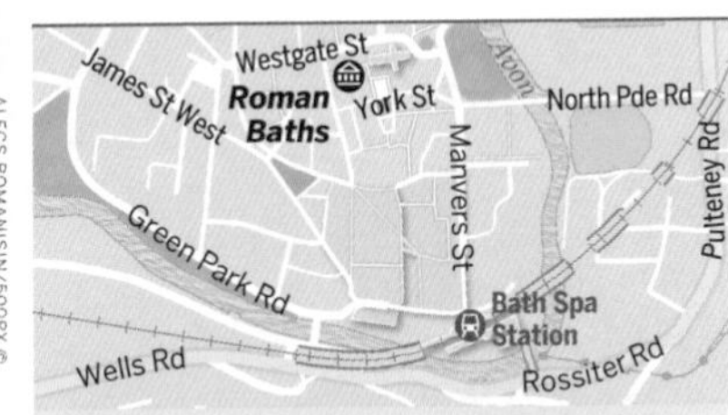

Need to Know

☎01225-477785; www.romanbaths.co.uk; Abbey Church Yard; adult £16-23, child £8.50-15.50; ⌚9.30am-5pm Nov-Feb, 9am-5pm Mar–mid-Jun, Sep & Oct, 9am-9pm mid-Jun–Aug

Take a Break

The bath's Pump Room Restaurant (p122) is an elegant spot for light bites and afternoon tea.

★ Top Tip

Tickets covering the Fashion Museum (p118) and the Roman Baths cost £26/16/70 per adult/child/family. They're 10% cheaper online.

The Pools

More bathing pools and changing rooms are situated to the east and west, with excavated sections revealing the hypocaust system that heated the bathing rooms. After luxuriating in the baths, Romans would have reinvigorated themselves with a dip in the circular cold-water pool, which now has life-size films of bathers projected onto the walls.

The King's Bath

The King's Bath was added sometime during the 12th century around the site of the original Sacred Spring. Every day, 1.5 million litres of hot water still pour into the pool. Beneath the Pump Room are the remains of the Temple of Sulis-Minerva.

The Museum

Look out for the famous gilded bronze head of Minerva and a striking carved Gorgon's Head, as well as some of the 12,000-odd Roman coins thrown into the spring as votive offerings to the goddess.

The Wider Complex

The complex of buildings around the baths were built in stages during the 18th and 19th centuries. The two John Woods designed the buildings around the Sacred Spring, while the famous Pump Room was built by their contemporaries, Thomas Baldwin and John Palmer, in neoclassical style, complete with soaring Ionic and Corinthian columns.

Tours

Admission includes an entertaining audio guide, featuring commentary in 12 languages – there's also one especially for children.

Royal Crescent

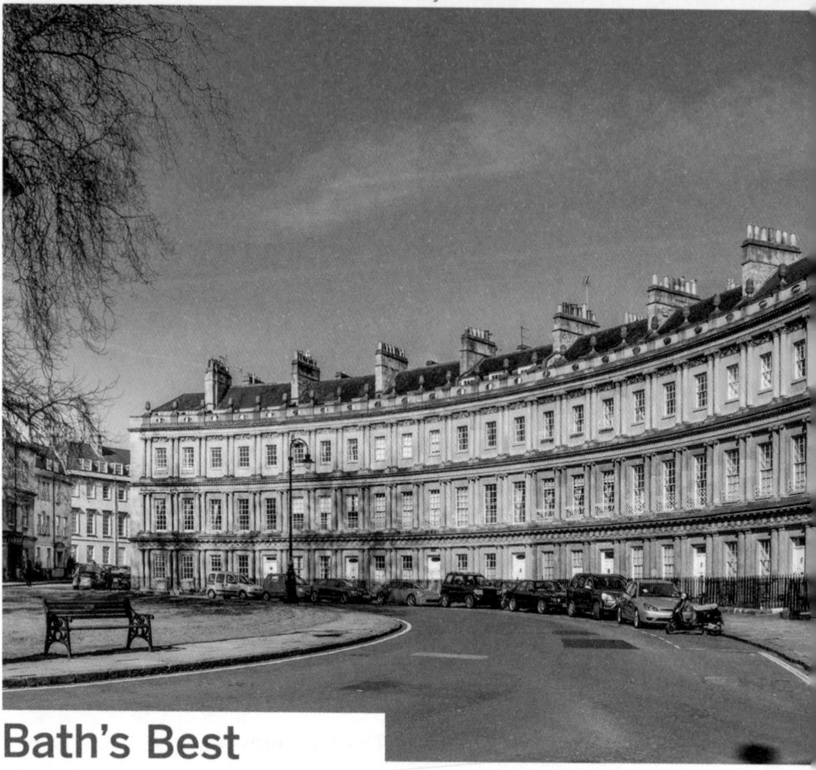

SHUANG LI/SHUTTERSTOCK ©

Bath's Best Architecture

Most cities would count themselves blessed to have a site as special as the Roman Baths, but Bath boasts exquisite 18th-century buildings dotted all around the compact centre.

In the early 18th century Ralph Allen and the celebrated dandy Richard 'Beau' Nash made Bath the centre of fashionable society. Allen developed the quarries at nearby Coombe Down and employed the two John Woods (father and son) to create Bath's signature buildings.

During WWII, Bath was hit by the Luftwaffe during the so-called Baedeker raids, which targeted historic cities. But the grand buildings survived and in 1987 Bath was declared a Unesco World Heritage Site in its entirety.

Great For...

☑ Don't Miss

The view of the other side of the famous Circus terrace from the restored Georgian Garden.

Royal Crescent

Bath's glorious Georgian architecture doesn't get any grander than this semicircular terrace of majestic town houses overlooking the green sweep of Royal Victoria Park. Designed by John Wood the

Pulteney Bridge

AMRA PASIC/SHUTTERSTOCK ©

Younger (1728–82) and built between 1767 and 1775, the houses appear perfectly symmetrical from the outside, but the owners were allowed to tweak the interiors, so no two houses are quite the same.

For a revealing glimpse into the splendour of Georgian life, head inside beautifully restored **No 1 Royal Crescent** (☎01225-428126; www.no1royalcrescent.org.uk; 1 Royal Cres; adult/child/family £11/5.40/27; ⏲10am-5pm). Among the rooms on display are the drawing room, several bedrooms and a huge kitchen. Costumed guides add to the heritage feel.

The Circus

The Circus (The Circus) is a Georgian masterpiece. Built to John Wood the Elder's design and completed in 1768, it's said to have been inspired by the Colosseum. Arranged over three terraces, the 33 mansions form a circle which surrounds a group of plane trees. Famous residents have included Thomas Gainsborough, David Livingstone and American actor Nicholas Cage.

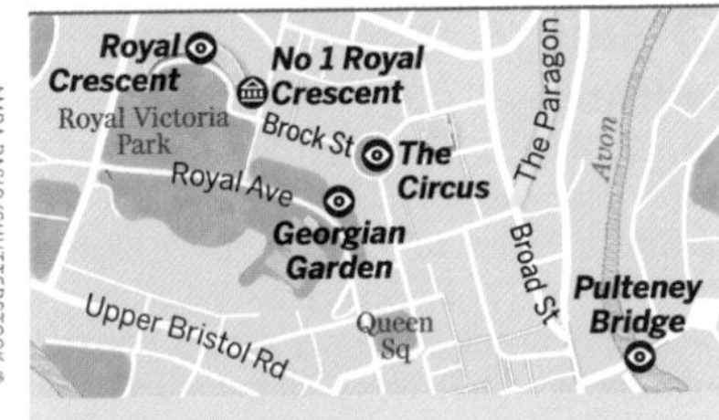

Need to Know

The **Tourist Office** (☎01225-614420; www.visitbath.co.uk; 2 Terrace Walk; ⏲9.30am-5.30pm Mon-Sat, 10am-4pm Sun, closed Sun Nov-Jan) has more info on Bath's architecture.

Take a Break

Book a table at the swish Circus (p121) bistro for stylish British cuisine.

★ Top Tip

Save money on a joint ticket for No 1 Royal Crescent, the Museum of Bath Architecture and the Herschel Museum of Astronomy.

The Georgian Garden

These tiny, walled **gardens** (☎01225-394041; off Royal Ave; ⏲9am-7pm) FREE feature period plants and gravel walkways. They've been carefully restored and provide an intriguing insight into the private spaces behind the Circus' grand facades.

Pulteney Bridge

Elegant, 18th-century Pulteney Bridge is one of only four bridges in the world with shops lining both sides. The best views are from Grand Parade.

SIGHTS

Bath Abbey — Church

(☎01225-422462; www.bathabbey.org; Abbey Church Yard; suggested donation adult/child £5/2.50; ⏰9.30am-5.30pm Mon, 9am-5.30pm Tue-Fri, to 6pm Sat, 12.15-1.45pm & 4-6.30pm Sun) Looming above the city centre, Bath's huge abbey church was built between 1499 and 1616, making it the last great medieval church raised in England. Its most striking feature is the west facade, where angels climb up and down stone ladders, commemorating a dream of the founder, Bishop Oliver King.

Jane Austen Centre — Museum

(☎01225-443000; www.janeausten.co.uk; 40 Gay St; adult/child £12/6.20; ⏰9.45am-5.30pm Apr-Oct, 10am-4pm Sun-Fri, 9.45am-5.30pm Sat Nov-Mar) Bath is known to many as a location in Jane Austen's novels, including *Persuasion* and *Northanger Abbey*. Although Austen lived in Bath for only five years, from 1801 to 1806, she remained a regular visitor and a keen student of the city's social scene. Here, guides in Regency costumes regale you with Austen-esque tales as you tour memorabilia relating to the writer's life in Bath.

Museum of Bath Architecture — Museum

(☎01225-333895; www.museumofbatharchitecture.org.uk; The Countess of Huntingdon's Chapel, off the Paragon; adult/child £7/3.50; ⏰1-5pm Mon-Fri, 10am-5pm Sat & Sun mid-Feb–Nov) The intriguing stories behind the building of Bath's most striking structures are explored here, using maps, drawings, antique tools, displays on Georgian construction methods and a 1:500 scale model of the city. On weekdays in July and August, it opens at 11am.

Fashion Museum — Museum

(☎01225-477789; www.fashionmuseum.co.uk; Assembly Rooms, 19 Bennett St; adult/child £9.50/7.25; ⏰10.30am-5pm Mar-Oct, to 4pm Nov-Feb) The world-class collections on display here include costumes from the 17th to late 20th centuries. Some exhibits change annually; check the website for the latest.

Bath Abbey

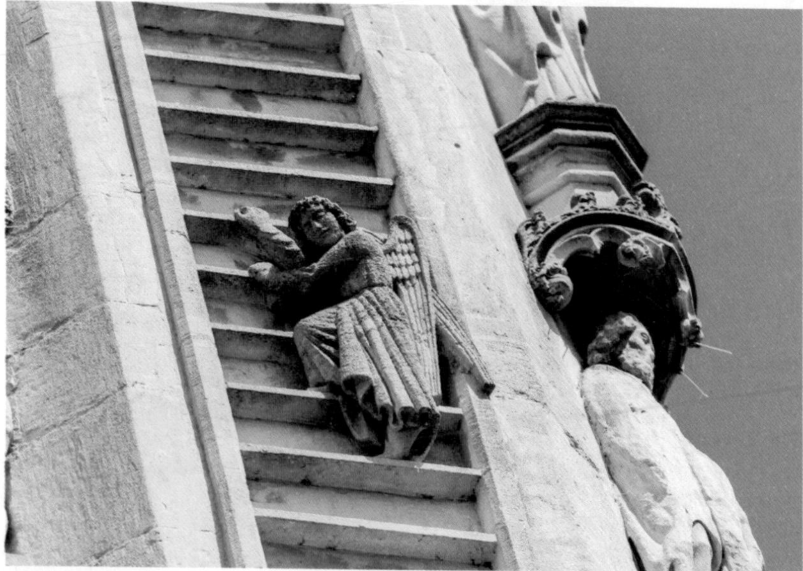

VALDIS SKUDRE/SHUTTERSTOCK ©

The museum sits in the basement of the city's fine, unfurnished Georgian **Assembly Rooms** (free), providing the chance to wander the Great Octagon, tearoom and ballroom.

Herschel Museum of Astronomy Museum

(☎01225-446865; www.herschelmuseum.org.uk; 19 New King St; adult/child £7/3.50; ⏰1-5pm Mon-Fri, 10am-5pm Sat & Sun) In 1781 astronomer William Herschel discovered Uranus from the garden of his home, now converted into a museum. Herschel shared the house with his wife, Caroline, also an important astronomer. Their home is little changed since the 18th century; an astrolabe in the garden marks the position of the couple's telescope.

ACTIVITIES

Thermae Bath Spa Spa

(☎01225-331234; www.thermaebathspa.com; Hot Bath St; spa £37-42; treatments from £72; ⏰9am-9.30pm, last entry 7pm) Taking a dip in the Roman Baths might be off limits, but you can still sample the city's curative waters at this fantastic modern spa complex, housed in a shell of local stone and plate glass. The showpiece is the open-air rooftop pool, where you can bathe in naturally heated, mineral-rich waters with a backdrop of Bath's cityscape – a don't-miss experience, best enjoyed at dusk.

TOURS

Bizarre Bath Comedy Walk Walking

(www.bizarrebath.co.uk; adult/student £10/7; ⏰8pm Apr-Oct) A multi-award-winning stroll that's billed as 'hysterical rather than historical'. That it actually has little to do with Bath doesn't matter a bit. Leaves nightly from outside the Huntsman Inn. There's no need to book.

Bath Abbey Tower Tours

The 50-minute **tours** (☎01225-422462; www.bathabbey.org; adult/child £8/4; ⏰10am-4pm Mon-Sat) of Bath Abbey's tower see you standing above the abbey's fan-vaulted ceiling, sitting behind the clock face and visiting the ringing and bell chamber. The views of the city and surrounding countryside from the roof are superb. Tours can only be booked at the abbey shop, on the day. They leave on the hour Monday to Friday, and on the half-hour on Saturday.

NIGEL JARVIS/SHUTTERSTOCK ©

Bath Boating Station Boating

(☎01225-312900; www.bathboating.co.uk; Forester Rd; adult/child per hour £8/4, per day £20/10; ⏰10am-5.30pm Wed-Sun Easter-Sep) You can pilot your own vessel down the Avon from this Victorian-era boathouse, which rents out traditional rowing boats, punts, kayaks and Canadian canoes. It's in the suburb of Bathwick, a 20-minute walk northeast from the city centre.

Pulteney Cruisers Boating

(☎01225-863600; www.bathboating.com; Pulteney Bridge; adult/child £10/5; ⏰mid-Mar–Oct) Pulteney Cruisers offers frequent, hour-long cruises up and down the River Avon from the Pulteney Bridge area.

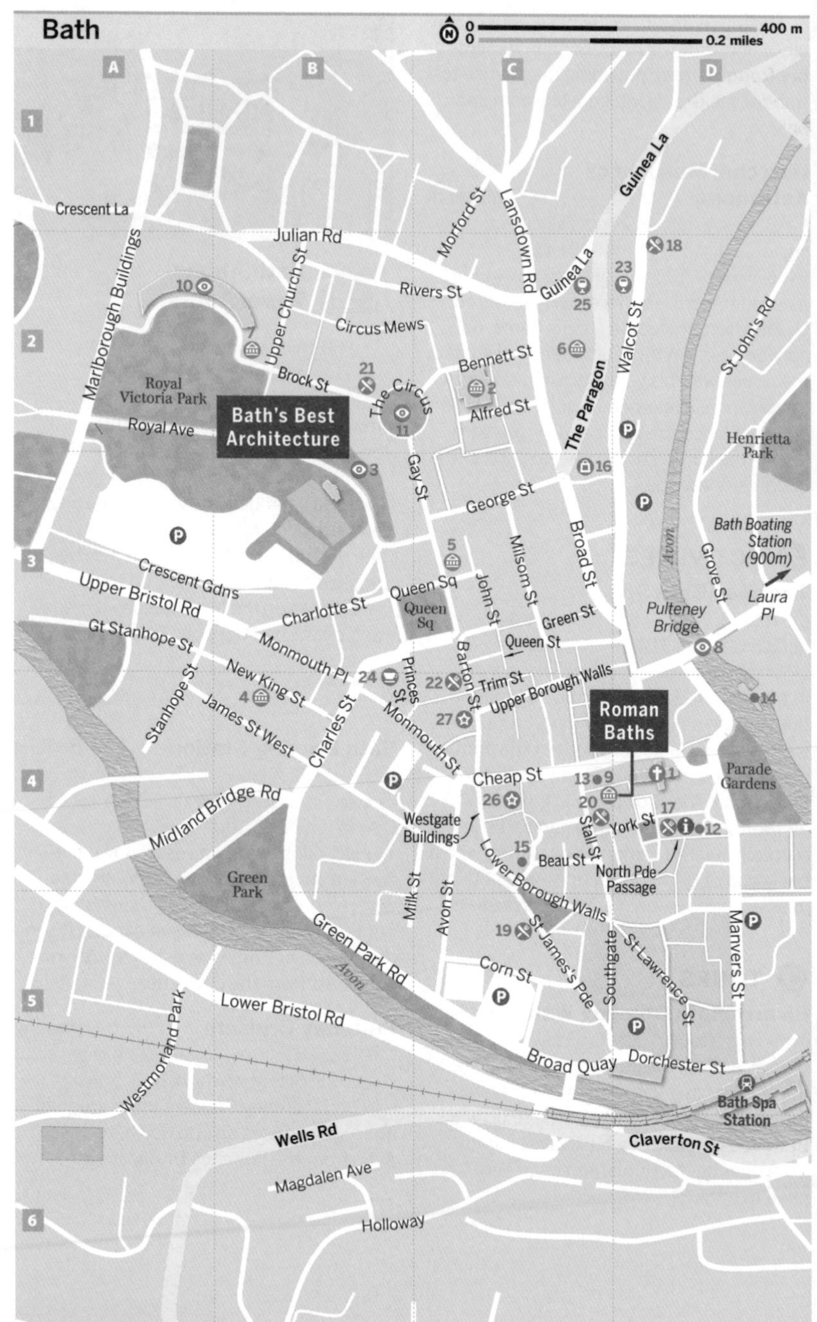
Bath
0 400 m
0 0.2 miles
A
B
C
D
1
2
3
4
5
6
Crescent La
Julian Rd
Marlborough Buildings
Upper Church St
Morford St
Lansdown Rd
Guinea La
Guinea La
Rivers St
Circus Mews
Walcot St
St John's Rd
Royal Victoria Park
Brock St
The Circus
Bennett St
Alfred St
The Paragon
Henrietta Park
Royal Ave
Bath's Best Architecture
Gay St
George St
Milsom St
Broad St
Avon
Bath Boating Station (900m)
Grove St
Laura Pl
Crescent Gdns
Upper Bristol Rd
Queen Sq
Queen Sq
Charlotte St
John St
Green St
Pulteney Bridge
Gt Stanhope St
Monmouth Pl
Queen St
Stanhope St
New King St
Princes St
Barton St
Trim St
Upper Borough Walls
James St West
Charles St
Monmouth St
Roman Baths
Parade Gardens
Cheap St
Midland Bridge Rd
Westgate Buildings
York St
Stall St
Beau St
North Pde Passage
Green Park
Milk St
Avon St
Lower Borough Walls
Manvers St
St James's Pde
Southgate
St Lawrence St
Green Park Rd
Avon
Corn St
Lower Bristol Rd
Broad Quay
Dorchester St
Westmorland Park
Bath Spa Station
Wells Rd
Claverton St
Magdalen Ave
Holloway

Bath

Sights

1 Bath Abbey D4
2 Fashion Museum C2
3 Georgian Garden B3
4 Herschel Museum of Astronomy B4
5 Jane Austen Centre C3
6 Museum of Bath Architecture C2
7 No 1 Royal Crescent B2
8 Pulteney Bridge D3
9 Roman Baths C4
10 Royal Crescent A2
11 The Circus B2

Activities, Courses & Tours

Bath Abbey Tower Tours .... (see 1)
12 Bizarre Bath Comedy Walk D4
13 Mayor's Guide Tours C4
14 Pulteney Cruisers D4
15 Thermae Bath Spa C4

Shopping

16 Topping & Company C3

Eating

17 Acorn D4
18 Corkage D2
19 Noya's Kitchen C5
20 Pump Room Restaurant C4
21 The Circus B2
22 Thoughtful Bread Company C4

Drinking & Nightlife

23 Bell D2
24 Colonna & Smalls B4
25 Star C2

Entertainment

26 Little Theatre Cinema C4
27 Theatre Royal C4

SHOPPING

Chain and independent stores surround Bath's SouthGate Centre. Walcott St features weaving and glassblowing workshops, a vintage clothes store, a superb cheesemonger and, in nearby **Topping & Company** (01225-428111; www.toppingbooks.co.uk; The Paragon; 8.30am-8pm), a bookshop to fall in love with.

EATING

Noya's Kitchen — Vietnamese £

(01225-684439; www.noyaskitchen.co.uk; 7 St James's Pde; mains £7-12; 11.45am-3pm Tue-Sat, plus 6-9pm Wed & Thu, 7-10pm Fri & Sat) Let the fragrances wafting from this intimate Vietnamese restaurant draw you in for fresh, aromatic, delicately flavoured dishes. Lunch menus are admirably short, evenings bring *pho* (noodle soup) on Wednesday, zingy curries on Thursday and the immensely popular, five-course Supper Club (£45) on Friday and Saturday – book well in advance.

Thoughtful Bread Company — Bakery £

(01225-471747; www.thethoughtfulbreadcompany.com; 19 Barton St; 8am-5pm Tue-Sat, 9am-4pm Sun) Come lunchtime they could well be queuing out the door of this snug artisan bakery, where chunky loaves sit alongside delicate macaroons and salted-caramel bombs. Its vegan donuts are fruit-dotted, multi-coloured works of art.

The Circus — Modern British ££

(01225-466020; www.thecircusrestaurant.co.uk; 34 Brock St; mains lunch £14-20, dinner £18-25; 10am-11pm Mon-Sat) Chef Ali Golden has turned this bistro into one of Bath's destination addresses. The menu mixes traditional British fare with global influences – here slow-cooked lamb and caramelised cauliflower meet harissa-infused aubergine, and rabbit in velouté cream sauce.

Acorn — Vegetarian ££

(01225-446059; www.acornvegetariankitchen.co.uk; 2 North Pde Passage; lunch 2/3 courses £20/25, dinner 2/3 courses £30/39; noon-3pm & 5.30-9.30pm) Revelling in an ethical and eco ethos, Bath's premier vegetarian restaurant brings vegetables and grains to a whole new level of deliciousness. Contemporary fine dining using imaginative cookery methods and global flavours result in beautiful plates of food. The six-course taster menu (£50) is worth

Mayor's Guide Tours of Bath

Excellent historical **tours** (www.bathguides.org.uk; ⏱10.30am & 2pm Sun-Fri, 10.30am Sat) FREE are provided free by the Mayor's Corp of Honorary Guides. Tours cover about 2 miles and are wheelchair-accessible. They leave from within the Abbey Churchyard, outside the Pump Room.

Grand Pump Room

CHRISTIAN MUELLER/SHUTTERSTOCK ©

the outlay – it's a true celebration of plant-based food.

Pump Room Restaurant Cafe ££

(☎01225-444477; www.romanbaths.co.uk; Stall St; snacks £5-9, 1/2/3 courses £16/22/28; ⏱9.30am-4pm) Elegance is everywhere in this tall, Georgian room, from the string trio and Corinthian columns to the oil paintings and glinting chandeliers. It sets the scene perfectly for morning coffee, classic lunches and the dainty sandwiches and cakes of its famous afternoon tea (£20 to £36 per person).

Corkage Bistro ££

(☎01225-422577; www.corkagebath.com; 132a Walcot St; ⏱5-11pm Tue, 5-11.30pm Wed & Thu, noon-11.30pm Fri & Sat) At this intimate, friendly neighbourhood bistro the aromas of imaginative dishes fill the air and regiments of bottles fill the shelves. It offers scaled-down versions of main courses (£6 to £13) and an extensive international wine list.

Menu Gordon Jones Modern British £££

(☎01225-480871; www.menugordonjones.co.uk; 2 Wellsway; 7 courses £65, with wines £120; ⏱12.30-2pm & 7-9pm Tue-Sat; ✍) Gordon Jones delights in delivering dining laced with surprise. Menus are dreamt up daily and showcase the chef's taste for experimental ingredients such as wild New Forest mushrooms and Dorset snails. The presentation is eye-catching (perhaps featuring test tubes or paper bags) and Gordon himself often pops out to explain the dishes. Reservations essential.

DRINKING & NIGHTLIFE

Colonna & Smalls Cafe

(☎07766 808067; www.colonnaandsmalls.co.uk; 6 Chapel Row; ⏱8am-5.30pm Mon-Fri, from 8.30am Sat, 10am-4pm Sun; 📶) If you're keen on caffeinated beans, this is a cafe not to miss. A mission to explore coffee means there are three guest espresso varieties and smiley staff happy to share their expertise. They'll even tell you that black filter coffee – yes, filter coffee – is actually the best way to judge high-grade beans.

Bell Pub

(www.thebellinnbath.co.uk; 103 Walcot St; ⏱11.30am-11pm Mon-Thu, to midnight Fri & Sat, noon-10.30pm Sun; 📶) The locals loved the Bell so much they bought it; the pub is a co-operative, owned by more than 500 customers and staff. Get chatting to some of them over table football, bar billiards, backgammon and chess, while sipping one of nine real ales. Or enjoy the DJ sets and live music spanning folk and jazz to the blues.

Star Pub

(☎01225-425072; www.abbeyales.co.uk; 23 The Vineyards, The Paragon; ⏱noon-midnight Sun-Wed, to 12.30am Thu, to 1am Fri & Sat) Few pubs are registered relics, but the Star is just that. First licensed in 1760, historic features include 19th-century bar fittings, wooden

Theatre Royal

benches and four drinking snugs. It's the brewery tap for Bath-based Abbey Ales; some beers are served in traditional jugs, and you can even ask for a pinch of snuff in the 'smaller bar'.

ENTERTAINMENT

Theatre Royal Theatre
(☎01225-448844; www.theatreroyal.org.uk; Sawclose) Bath's historic theatre dates back more than 200 years. Major touring productions appear in the main auditorium and smaller shows take place in the **Ustinov Studio**.

Little Theatre Cinema Cinema
(☎0871 9025735; www.picturehouses.com; St Michael's Pl) An excellent art-house cinema screening fringe films and foreign-language flicks in art-deco surrounds.

INFORMATION

Bath Tourist Office (p117)

GETTING AROUND

Bicycle A 10-minute walk from the centre, **Bath Bike Hire** (☎01225-447276; www.bath-narrowboats.co.uk; Sydney Wharf, Bathwick Hill; adult/child per day £18/15; ⏰9am-5pm) is handy for the canal and railway paths.

Bus Bus U1 Runs from the bus station, via High St and Great Pulteney St, up Bathwick Hill, past the YHA to the university every 20 minutes (£2.50).

Car Bath has serious traffic problems, especially at rush hour, making **Park & Ride** (☎0871 200 22 33; www.firstgroup.com; return Mon-Fri £3.60, Sat & Sun £3.10; ⏰6.15am-8.30pm Mon-Sat, 9.30am-6pm Sun) services appealing. There's a central car park underneath the SouthGate shopping centre (two/eight hours £3.50/11).

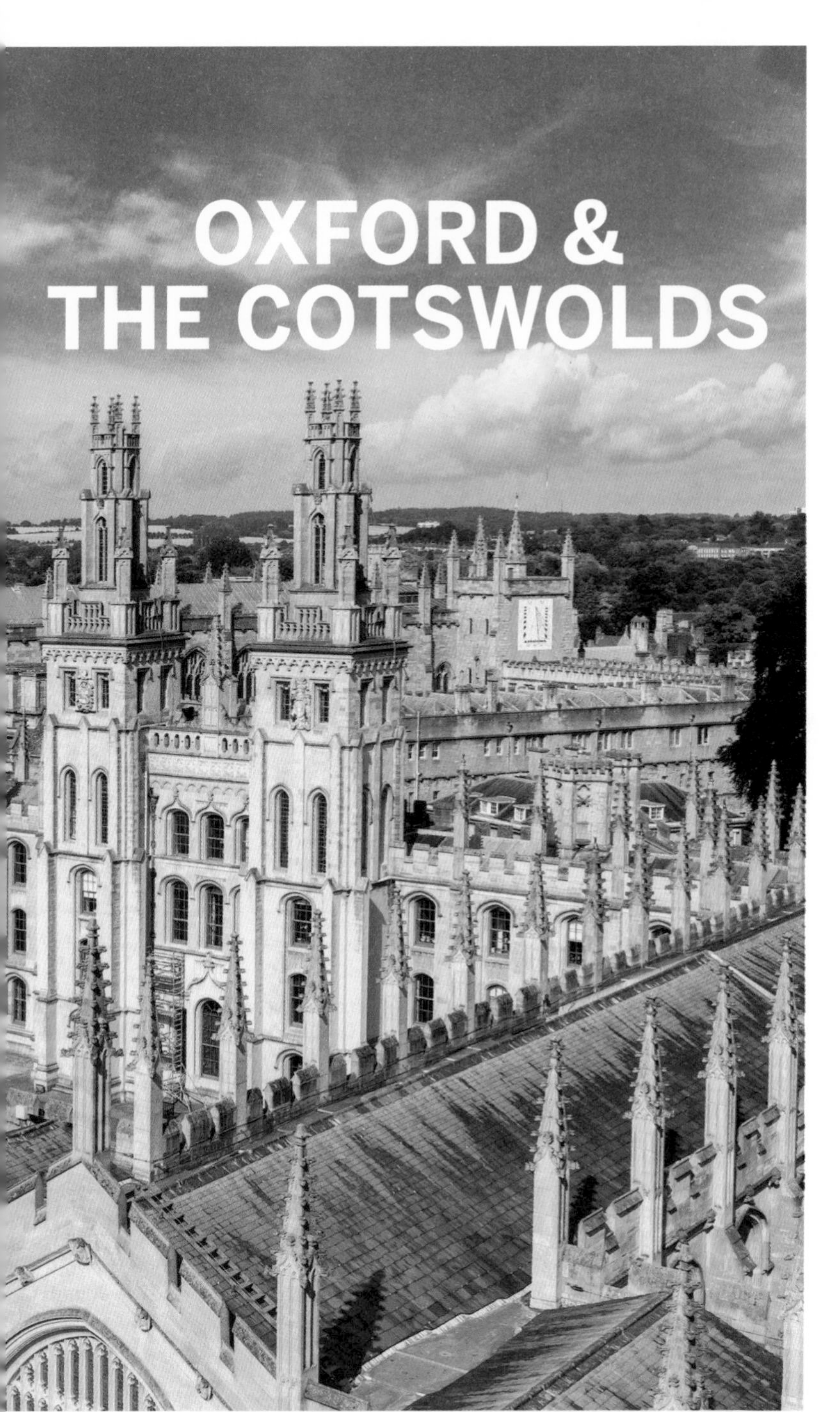
OXFORD &
THE COTSWOLDS

In this Chapter

Oxford & the Cotswolds at a Glance...

One of the world's most famous university cities, Oxford is steeped in history and studded with grandiose buildings, yet maintains a vibrant atmosphere, thanks in part to large student numbers. A few miles west, rolling gracefully across six counties, the Cotswolds are a delightful tangle of charming villages, thatch-roofed cottages and ancient mansions of gold-coloured stone. Like exposed beams, cream teas and cuisine full of local produce? Then the Cotswolds are calling.

Two Days in Oxford & the Cotswolds

Start day one gently – stroll through **college quads** (if they've reopened to visitors), marvel at fine buildings, and stop for a drink at a classic Oxford **pub** (p142). Then head to **Spiced Roots** (p141) for a delicious feed. On day two, take in the city's other sights, targeting the **Bodleian Library** (p138), the **Ashmolean Museum** (p138) and the **Pitt Rivers Museum** (p138). End the day with a feast at **Magdalen Arms** (p142).

Four Days in Oxford & the Cotswolds

On day three, after breakfast at **Vaults & Garden** (p141) immerse yourself in the ornate beauty of **Blenheim Palace** (p136) and its exquisite grounds. For supper, repair to **Two One Five** (p142) back in Oxford followed by a nightcap at roof-top **Varsity Club** (p142).
Next morning, begin your Cotswolds road trip, touring **Stow-on-the-Wold** (p134) and the **Slaughters** (p134) for starters. Foodie treats come courtesy of **Daylesford Organic** (p134) or **Mount Inn** (p144).

Previous page: All Souls College, Oxford University (p131)
S-F/SHUTTERSTOCK ©

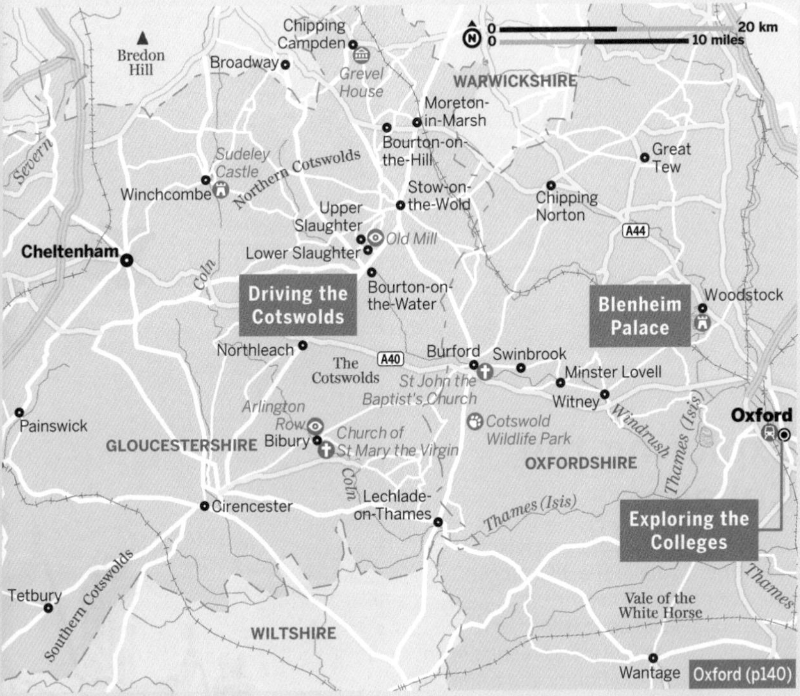

Arriving in Oxford & the Cotswolds

Oxford's excellent transport connections include rail services to London Paddington (£28, 1¼ hours), and National Express bus connections to Bath (£11.30, two hours) and London Victoria (£16, two hours).

Oxford Bus Company (www.oxfordbus.co.uk) services go to Heathrow (£23, 1½ hours) and Gatwick (£28, two hours) airports. Trains and buses run to key Cotswolds towns, but it's easier to explore the villages by car.

Where to Stay

In Oxford, book ahead between May and September and on weekends. If stuck, there are plenty of B&Bs along Iffley, Abingdon, Banbury and Headington Rds. Budget accommodation options are clustered near the train station.

The Cotswolds overflow with exquisite hotels, but have fewer budget options (except in walker-friendly Winchcombe and Chipping Campden). Book ahead, especially during festivals and between May and August.

Brasenose College, Oxford University

Exploring the Colleges

Oxford is a glorious place in which to wander. Some of the 38 colleges date from the 13th century, and each is individual in its appearance and academic specialities. This results in an enchanting air of antiquity and tradition that infuses the city and its quads, halls, chapels and inns.

Great For...

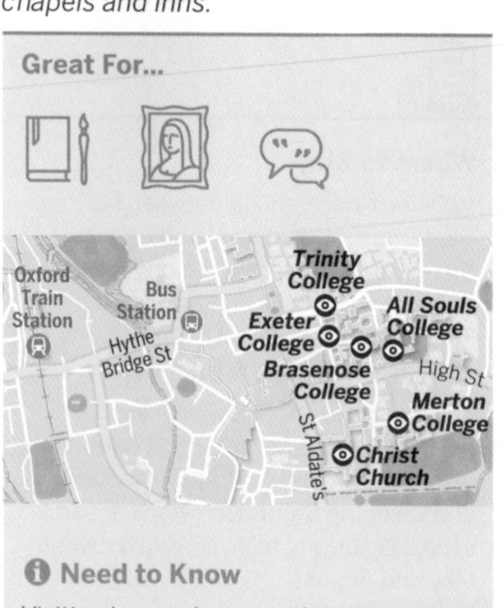

Need to Know

Visiting hours change with terms and exam schedules. Check www.ox.ac.uk for full details.

★ Top Tip

Take your time: atmosphere and details are the appeal here. Lingering and looking bring rewards.

CARONB/GETTY IMAGES ©

Much of Oxford's centre is taken up by elegant university buildings. The gorgeous architecture and compact geography make strolling between them a joy.

Christ Church

The largest of all of Oxford's colleges, and the one with the grandest quad, **Christ Church** (☎01865-276492; www.chch.ox.ac.uk; St Aldate's; adult/child £15/14, pre-booking essential; ⏰10am-5pm Mon-Sat, from 2pm Sun) is also its most popular. It was founded in 1525 by Cardinal Thomas Wolsey. Past students include Albert Einstein, John Locke, WH Auden, Charles Dodgson (Lewis Carroll), and no fewer than 13 British prime ministers.

The main entrance to Christ Church, Tom Gate, stands immediately below the imposing 17th-century Tom Tower. Sir Christopher Wren, who studied at Christ Church, was responsible for its topmost portions. Pass by at 9.05pm, and you'll hear 101 chimes from its 6-tonne bell, Great Tom, to commemorate the curfew inflicted on the college's original students.

The college's imposing Great Hall, with its hammer-beam roof and distinguished portraits of past scholars, was replicated in film studios as the Hogwarts dining hall for the Harry Potter films. The grand fan-vaulted staircase that leads from it is where Professor McGonagall welcomed Harry in *Harry Potter and the Philosopher's Stone*.

Merton College

Founded in 1264, **Merton** (☎01865-276310; www.merton.ox.ac.uk/visitor-information; Merton St) is the oldest of Oxford's colleges. Its celebrated architectural features include large gargoyles, the charming 14th-century Mob Quad, and a 13th-century chapel. The Old

Great hall at Christ Church college

Library is the oldest medieval library in use; it's said that JRR Tolkien, a Merton English professor, spent many hours here writing *The Lord of the Rings* and that the trees in the Fellows' Garden inspired the ents of Middle Earth. Other literary alumni include TS Eliot and Louis MacNeice.

All Souls College

One of the wealthiest and most tranquil Oxford colleges, **All Souls** (☎01865-279379; www.asc.ox.ac.uk; High St; ⏲2-4pm Sun-Fri, closed Aug) FREE was founded in 1438 as a centre of prayer and learning. Much of the college facade dates from the 1440s and the smaller Front Quad is largely unchanged in five centuries. Most eye-catching are the twin mock-Gothic towers on the North Quad, which also contains a 17th-century sundial designed by Christopher Wren.

☑ Don't Miss

Christ Church's Harry Potter film connections; seek out the Great Hall and its sweeping staircase.

EXPOSE/SHUTTERSTOCK ©

Brasenose College

The main draw at **Brasenose** (☎01865-277830; www.bnc.ox.ac.uk; Radcliffe Sq; £2; ⏲10-11.30am & 2-5pm Mon-Fri, 9.30-10.30am & 2-5pm Sat & Sun) is a chapel with a fine painted, fan-vaulted ceiling. This small elegant college was founded in 1509. Famous alumni include *Lord of the Flies* author William Golding, Monty Python's Michael Palin and British prime minister David Cameron.

Exeter College

Founded in 1314, **Exeter** (☎01865-279600; www.exeter.ox.ac.uk; Turl St; ⏲2-5pm) FREE is known for its elaborate 17th-century dining hall, which celebrated its 400th birthday in 2018, and ornate Victorian Gothic chapel which holds a tapestry created by former students William Morris and Edward Burne Jones, *The Adoration of the Magi*. Exeter also inspired former student Philip Pullman to create fictional Jordan College in *His Dark Materials*.

Trinity College

The highlight of this small **college** (☎01865-279900; www.trinity.ox.ac.uk; Broad St; adult/child £3/2; ⏲9.30am-noon & 2pm-dusk), founded in 1555, is a lovely 17th-century garden quad designed by Christopher Wren. Its exquisitely carved chapel is one of the city's most beautiful and a masterpiece of English baroque. Famous students have included Cardinal Newman and British prime minister William Pitt the Elder.

✕ Take a Break

After strolling around Christ Church's Great Hall and Tom Quad, peel off into the nearby streets for a drink or a snack at the ancient and atmospheric **Bear Inn** (☎01865-728164; www.bearoxford.co.uk; 6 Alfred St; ⏲11am-11pm Mon-Thu, 11am-midnight Fri & Sat, 11.30am-10.30pm Sun).

Lower Slaughter

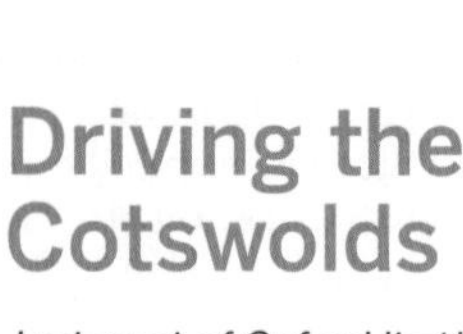

Driving the Cotswolds

Just west of Oxford lie the Cotswolds, a bewitching network of winding country lanes that link ancient market towns, time-warped villages and majestic stately homes. The landscape is England's second-largest protected area after the Lake District and the gentle yet dramatic hills are perfect for touring by car.

Great For...

Need to Know

The most popular villages can be besieged by traffic and visitors, especially in summer. Visit the main centres early in the morning or late in the evening.

★ **Top Tip**

Stretch your trip to two or three days to really soak up the local life.

CHRISATPPS/SHUTTERSTOCK ©

The Slaughters

The picture-postcard villages of Upper and Lower Slaughter have maintained their unhurried medieval charm. The village names have nothing to do with abattoirs; they are derived from the Old English 'sloughtre', meaning slough or muddy place. Today the River Eye is contained within limestone banks and meanders sleepily through the two villages, past classic gold-tinged Cotswolds houses and the **Old Mill** (☎01451-820052; www.oldmill-lowerslaughter.com; Lower Slaughter; ⏰10am-6pm Mar-Oct, to dusk Nov-Feb), now home to a cafe, crafts shop and small museum.

Stow-on-the-Wold & Daylesford Organic

The highest town in the Cotswolds (244m), Stow is anchored by a large market square surrounded by handsome buildings and steep-walled alleyways, originally used to funnel sheep into the fair. The town is famous for its twice-yearly **Stow Horse Fair** (⏰mid-May & late Oct), but it attracts plenty of visitors year-round.

Four miles east of Stow, **Daylesford Organic** (☎01608-731700; www.daylesford.com; Daylesford; ⏰8am-8pm Mon-Sat, 10am-4pm Sun) is a country-chic temple to the Cotswolds' organic movement. The award-winning agricultural operation includes a gleaming food hall crammed

Knot garden, Sudeley Castle

with Daylesford-brand produce and an excellent cafe-restaurant that dishes up a daily-changing menu of organic treats.

Chipping Campden

Pretty Chipping Campden boasts an array of fine terraced houses and ancient inns, most made of beautiful honey-coloured Cotswolds stone. There are particularly striking thatch-roofed cottages along Westington, at the southwestern end of town.

☑ Don't Miss

The extraordinary Tudor-style gardens at Sudeley Castle, where you'll find pathways once strolled by queens, and brightly coloured pheasants strutting their stuff.

STOCKER1970/SHUTTERSTOCK ©

One of the grandest residences is the 14th-century **Grevel House** (High St; ⏲closed to the public) – look out for its splendid Perpendicular Gothic–style gabled window and sundial.

Winchcombe

In Winchcombe, butchers, bakers and independent shops still line the main streets. The capital of the Anglo-Saxon kingdom of Mercia, it was one of the major towns in the Cotswolds until the Middle Ages. Today reminders of this past can be seen in Winchcombe's dramatic stone and half-timbered buildings, and the picturesque cottages on Vineyard St and Dents Tce.

Set on Winchcombe's southeast edge, the magnificent **Sudeley Castle** (☎01242-604244; www.sudeleycastle.co.uk; adult/child £12/5; ⏲10.45am-5pm mid-Mar–Oct; P 👪) has welcomed many a monarch over its thousand-year history, including Richard III, Henry VIII and Charles I. It's most famous as the home and final resting place of Catherine Parr (Henry VIII's widow), who lived here with her fourth husband, Thomas Seymour. You'll find Catherine's tomb in the castle's Perpendicular Gothic St Mary's Church, making this the only private house in England where a queen is buried.

The 10 splendid gardens include spectacular avenues of sculpted yews and an intricate knot garden. The rose-filled Queen's Garden gets its name from having been strolled in by four English queens: Anne Boleyn, Catherine Parr, Lady Jane Grey and Elizabeth I.

✂ Take a Break

Book a table at long-standing Michelin-starred 5 North St (p144) in Winchcombe, which serves creative cuisine in ancient surroundings.

Blenheim Palace

One of Britain's greatest stately homes, Blenheim Palace is a monumental baroque fantasy. With ornate architecture and lush parklands, it's also the birthplace of Sir Winston Churchill.

Great For...

☑ **Don't Miss**

Exploring the impressive grounds – full of features, they were landscaped by 'Capability' Brown.

Blenheim Palace was designed by Sir John Vanbrugh and Nicholas Hawksmoor, and built between 1705 and 1722. The land and funds to build the house were granted to John Churchill, Duke of Marlborough, by a grateful Queen Anne, after his victory over the French at the 1704 Battle of Blenheim. Sir Winston Churchill was born here in 1874. Now a Unesco World Heritage Site, Blenheim is still home to the 12th duke.

The Great Hall

Beyond majestic oak doors, the house is stuffed with statues, tapestries, ostentatious furniture, priceless china, and giant oil paintings in elaborate gilt frames. Visits start in the Great Hall, a soaring space topped by a 20m-high ceiling adorned with images of the first duke. To the right upon entering is the Churchill Exhibition, dedicated to the life,

JUDY DEAN/500PX ©

Need to Know

01993-810530; www.blenheimpalace.com; Woodstock; adult/child £28.50/16.50, park & gardens only £18.50/8.60; palace 10.30am-4.30pm, park & gardens 9.30am-6.30pm or dusk; P

Take a Break

Blenheim's Orangery Restaurant serves everything from three-course lunches to afternoon tea.

★ Top Tip

Free, 45-minute guided tours depart every 30 minutes, except on Sunday, when there are guides in all rooms.

work, paintings and writings of Sir Winston Churchill. The British war-time prime minister was a descendant of the Dukes of Marlborough and is buried nearby in Bladon graveyard.

House Highlights

Must-sees include the famous Blenheim Tapestries, a set of 10 large wall hangings commemorating the first duke's triumphs; the State Dining Room, with its painted walls and trompe l'oeil ceilings; and the magnificent Long Library, overlooked by an elaborate 1738 statue of Queen Anne.

The Untold Story

Upstairs, the Untold Story exhibit sees a ghostly chambermaid leading you through a series of tableaux recreating important scenes from the palace's history.

Tours

As well as free, 45-minute guided tours of the house (Monday to Saturday), from February to September you can also join tours (adult/child £5/4.50) of the Duke's private apartments, the palace bedrooms or the household staff areas.

The Grounds

If the crowds in the house become too oppressive, escape into the vast, lavish gardens and parklands, parts of which were landscaped by the great Lancelot 'Capability' Brown. A mini train (£1) takes visitors to the Pleasure Gardens, which feature a yew maze, adventure playground, lavender garden and butterfly house.

For quieter and longer strolls, there are glorious walks of up to 4.5 miles, leading past lakes to an arboretum, rose garden, cascade and temple, and Vanbrugh's Grand Bridge.

Oxford

SIGHTS

Ashmolean Museum Museum

(☎01865-278000; www.ashmolean.org; Beaumont St; ⏰10am-5pm Tue-Sun, to 8pm last Fri of month; 👪) FREE Britain's oldest public museum, Oxford's wonderful Ashmolean Museum is surpassed only by the British Museum in London. It was established in 1683, when Elias Ashmole presented Oxford University with a collection of 'rarities' amassed by the well-travelled John Tradescant, gardener to Charles I. You could easily spend a day exploring this magnificent neoclassical building, and family-friendly pamphlets draw kids into select exhibits. Pre-booking required.

Pitt Rivers Museum Museum

(☎01865-270927; www.prm.ox.ac.uk; South Parks Rd; ⏰10am-5pm; 👪) FREE If exploring an enormous room full of eccentric and unexpected artefacts sounds like your idea of the perfect afternoon, welcome to the amulets-to-zithers extravaganza that is the Pitt Rivers museum. Tucked behind Oxford's natural history museum, and dimly lit to protect its myriad treasures, it's centred on an anthropological collection amassed by a Victorian general, and revels in exploring how differing cultures have tackled topics like 'Smoking and Stimulants' and 'Treatment of Dead Enemies'.

Bodleian Library Library

(☎01865-287400; www.bodleian.ox.ac.uk/bodley; Catte St; ⏰9am-5pm Mon-Sat, from 11am Sun) At least five kings, dozens of prime ministers and Nobel laureates, and luminaries such as Oscar Wilde, CS Lewis and JRR Tolkien have studied in Oxford's Bodleian Library, a magnificent survivor from the Middle Ages. Wander into its central 17th-century quad, and you can admire its ancient buildings for free. Both Blackwell Hall and the exhibition rooms in the Weston Library can be visited free of charge. Audio and guided tours available.

Radcliffe Camera Library

(☎01865-287400; www.bodleian.ox.ac.uk; Radcliffe Sq; tours £15; ⏰tours 9.15am Wed & Sat,

Ashmolean Museum

11.15am & 1.15pm Sun) Surely Oxford's most photographed landmark, the sandy-gold Radcliffe Camera is a beautiful, light-filled, circular, columned library. Built between 1737 and 1749 in grand Palladian style as 'Radcliffe Library', it's topped by Britain's third-largest dome. It's only been a 'camera', which simply means 'room', since 1860, when it lost its independence and became what it remains: a reading room of the Bodleian Library. The only way for nonmembers to see the interior is on an extended 1½-hour tour of the Bodleian.

Museum of the History of Science Museum

(☎01865-277293; www.mhs.ox.ac.uk; Broad St; ⊙noon-5pm Tue-Sun) FREE Students of science will swoon at this fascinating museum, stuffed to the ceilings with awesome astrolabes, astonishing orreries and early electrical apparatus. Housed in the lovely 17th-century building that held the original Ashmolean Museum, it displays everything from cameras that belonged to Lewis Carroll and Lawrence of Arabia, to a wireless receiver used by Marconi in 1896 and a blackboard that was covered with equations by Einstein in 1931, when he was invited to give three lectures on relativity.

University Church of St Mary the Virgin Church

(☎01865-279111; www.university-church.ox.ac.uk; High St; church free, tower £5; ⊙10am-6pm Mon-Sat, from noon Sun) The ornate 14th-century spire of Oxford's university church is arguably the dreamiest of the city's legendary 'dreaming spires'. The church is famous as the site where three Anglican bishops, including the first Protestant archbishop of Canterbury, Thomas Cranmer, were tried for heresy in 1556, during the reign of Mary I. All three were later burned at the stake on Broad St. Visitors can climb the church's 1280 tower for excellent views of the adjacent Radcliffe Camera.

Bridge of Sighs Bridge

(Hertford Bridge; New College Lane) As you stroll along New College Lane, look up at the steeped Bridge of Sighs linking the two halves of Hertford College. Completed in 1914, it's sometimes erroneously described as a copy of the famous bridge in Venice, but it looks much more like that city's Rialto Bridge.

Worth a Punt

Punting, the quintessential Oxford experience, is all about lounging back in a flat-bottomed boat and sipping Pimms (the classic, cooling English summer drink) as you watch the city's glorious architecture drift by. Right beside Magdalen Bridge, the **boathouse** (☎01865-202643; www.oxfordpunting.co.uk; High St; chauffeured 4-person punts per 30min £30, punt rental per hr £22; ⊙9.30am-dusk Feb-Nov) is the most central location to hire a punt, chauffeured or otherwise. From here you can either head downstream around the Botanic Garden and Christ Church Meadow, or upstream around Magdalen Deer Park.

DAISY DAISY/SHUTTERSTOCK ©

SHOPPING

Ashmolean Shop Gifts & Souvenirs

(☎01865-278000; www.ashmolean.org; Beaumont St; ⊙10am-5pm Tue-Sun, to 8pm last Fri of month) Appropriately enough, the shop at the Ashmolean reflects the scope and variety of Oxford's finest museum. William Morris would certainly approve – everything is either beautiful or useful, and most are both. From postcards of Japanese

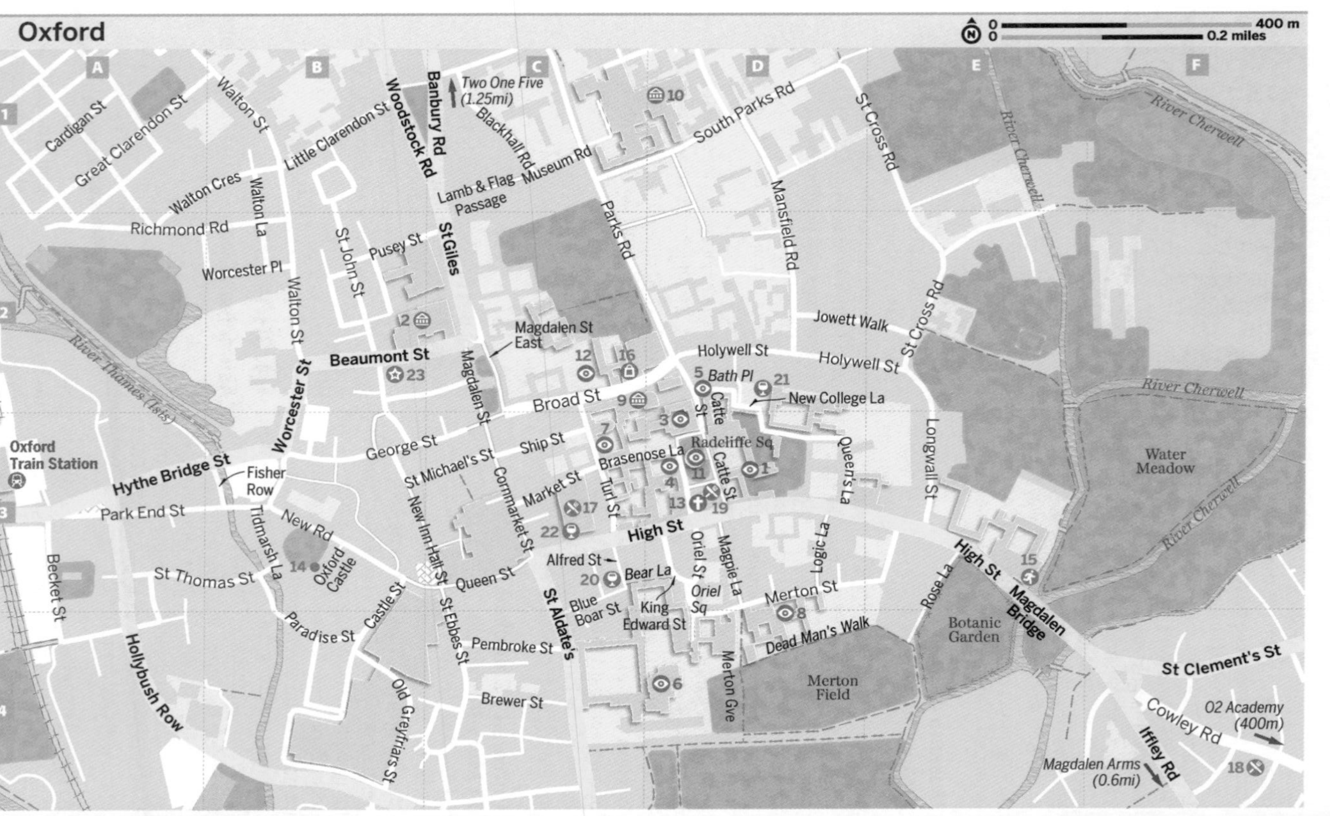
Oxford
400 m
0.2 miles
Cardigan St
Great Clarendon St
Walton St
Little Clarendon St
Woodstock Rd
Banbury Rd
Two One Five (1.25mi)
Blackhall Rd
Museum Rd
South Parks Rd
St Cross Rd
River Cherwell
Walton Cres
Walton La
Lamb & Flag Passage
Richmond Rd
Worcester Pl
St John St
Pusey St
St Giles
Parks Rd
Mansfield Rd
Magdalen St East
Jowett Walk
Beaumont St
Holywell St
Bath Pl
New College La
River Thames (Isis)
Broad St
Catte St
Radcliffe Sq
Magdalen St
Oxford Train Station
Worcester St
George St
Ship St
Brasenose La
Queen's La
Longwall St
Water Meadow
Hythe Bridge St
Fisher Row
St Michael's St
Cornmarket St
Market St
Turl St
Park End St
Tidmarsh La
New Rd
High St
Oriel St
Magpie La
Logic La
Oxford Castle
New Inn Hall St
Queen St
Alfred St
Bear La
Becket St
St Thomas St
St Aldate's
Blue Boar St
King Edward St
Oriel Sq
Merton St
Rose La
Magdalen Bridge
Botanic Garden
Castle St
Paradise St
St Ebbes St
Pembroke St
Dead Man's Walk
St Clement's St
Hollybush Row
Old Greyfriars St
Brewer St
Merton Gve
Merton Field
Cowley Rd
O2 Academy (400m)
Iffley Rd
Magdalen Arms (0.6mi)

Oxford

Sights

1 All Souls College.......D3
2 Ashmolean Museum.......B2
3 Bodleian Library.......D3
4 Brasenose College.......D3
5 Bridge of Sighs.......D2
6 Christ Church.......D4
7 Exeter College.......C3
8 Merton College.......D4
9 Museum of the History of Science.......C2
10 Pitt Rivers Museum.......D1
11 Radcliffe Camera.......D3
12 Trinity College.......C2
13 University Church of St Mary the Virgin.......D3

Activities, Courses & Tours

14 Bill Spectre's Oxford Ghost Trail.......B3
15 Magdalen Bridge Boathouse.......E3

Shopping

Ashmolean Shop.......(see 2)
16 Blackwell's.......C2

Eating

17 Covered Market.......C3
18 Spiced Roots.......F4
19 Vaults & Garden.......D3

Drinking & Nightlife

20 Bear Inn.......C3
21 Turf Tavern.......D2
22 Varsity Club.......C3

Entertainment

23 Oxford Playhouse.......B2

woodblock prints to Juan Gris mirrors and Cressida Bell–designed notepaper, it's the perfect place to pick up classy gifts and souvenirs.

Blackwell's Books

(☎01865-792792; www.blackwells.co.uk; 48-51 Broad St; 9am-6.30pm Mon & Wed-Sat, 9.30am-6.30pm Tue, 11am-5pm Sun) The most famous bookshop in the most studenty of cities, Blackwell's is, with its vast range of literature, treatises and guilty pleasures, a book-lover's dream. Be sure to visit the basement Norrington Room, an immense inverted step pyramid, lined with 3 miles of shelves and hailed in the Guinness Book of Records as the largest book-selling room in the world.

EATING

Covered Market Market £

(www.oxford-coveredmarket.co.uk; Market St; prices vary; 8am- 5.30pm Mon-Sat, 10am-5pm Sun;) A haven for impecunious students, this indoor marketplace holds 20 restaurants, cafes and takeaways. Let anyone loose here, and something's sure to catch their fancy. Brown's no-frills cafe, famous for its apple pies, is the longest-standing veteran. Look out too for Georgina's upstairs; two excellent pie shops; and good Thai and Chinese options. Traders keep their own varied hours.

Vaults & Garden Cafe £

(☎01865-279112; www.thevaultsandgarden.com; University Church of St Mary the Virgin, Radcliffe Sq; mains £9-10.50; 9am-5pm;) This beautiful lunch venue spreads from the vaulted 14th-century Old Congregation House of the University Church into a garden facing the Radcliffe Camera. Come early and queue at the counter to choose from wholesome organic specials such as carrot and nutmeg soup, chicken panang curry, or slow-roasted lamb shoulder with red currant. Breakfast and afternoon tea (those scones!) are equally good.

Spiced Roots Caribbean ££

(☎01865-249888; www.spicedroots.com; 64 Cowley Rd; mains from £12; 6-10pm Tue & Wed, noon-3pm & 6-10pm Thu-Sat, noon-8pm Sun;) From black rice with pomegranates to oxtail with mac cheese and plantains – and, of course, spicy jerk chicken – everything is just perfection at this flawless Caribbean restaurant. There are plenty of vegetarian options, as well as curried fish or goat. And adding a cocktail or two from the thatched rum bar is pretty much irresistible. Look out for tasting classes.

Oxford Ghost Trail

For a theatrical and entertaining voyage through Oxford's uncanny underbelly, plus the occasional magic trick, take a 1¾-hour **tour** (07941-041811; www.ghosttrail.org; Oxford Castle; adult/child £10/7; 6.30pm Fri & Sat;) with Victorian undertaker Bill Spectre. No bookings needed, audience participation more than likely.

ACOBA/SHUTTERSTOCK ©

Magdalen Arms British ££
(01865-243159; www.magdalenarms.co.uk; 243 Iffley Rd; mains £14-42; 11am-10pm Tue-Sat, to 9pm Sun;) A mile beyond Magdalen Bridge, this extra-special neighbourhood gastropub has won plaudits from the national press. A friendly, informal spot, it offers indoor and outdoor space for drinkers, and dining tables further back. From vegetarian specials such as broad-bean tagliatelle to the fabulous sharing-size steak-and-ale pie (well, it's a stew with a suet-crust lid, really) everything is delicious, with gutsy flavours.

Two One Five Modern British £££
(01865-511149; www.twoonefive.co.uk; 215 Banbury Rd; 2-/3-course menus £35/40; noon-2.30pm & 6-9.30pm Tue-Sat) Oxford's not renowned for high-end, cutting-edge cuisine, so if you're crying out for something special, make haste to Summertown's relaxed-yet-contemporary successor to its Michelin-starred Oxford Kitchen. Expect flavoursome dishes like gin-cured Loch Duart salmon with cucumber, lemon, tonic and dill or 48-hour hay-smoked pork fillet with carrot and pineapple.

DRINKING & NIGHTLIFE

Turf Tavern Pub
(01865-243235; www.turftavern-oxford.co.uk; 4-5 Bath Pl; noon-10pm;) Squeezed down an alleyway and subdivided into endless nooks and crannies, this medieval rabbit warren dates from around 1381. The definitive Oxford pub, it's where Bill Clinton famously 'did not inhale'. Other patrons have included Oscar Wilde, Stephen Hawking and Margaret Thatcher. Home to a fabulous array of real ales and ciders, it's always pretty crowded, but there's outdoor seating, too.

Varsity Club Cocktail Bar
(01865-248777; www.tvcoxford.co.uk; 9 High St; noon-midnight;) At this sleekly minimalist rooftop cocktail bar, spectacularly located in the town centre, cocktails and small dishes are served with sensational views across Oxford's dreaming spires. Heaters, blankets and canopies keep things cosy in colder weather, while lounges and dance spaces sprawl across three floors below.

ENTERTAINMENT

Creation Theatre Theatre
(01865-766266; www.creationtheatre.co.uk) This ambitious theatre company produces highly original shows – often Shakespeare, but also anything from *Dracula* to *The Wind in the Willows* – that are bursting with magic, quirk and special effects. It then performs them in all sorts of non-traditional venues, including city parks, the Westgate Shopping Centre, various colleges and Oxford Castle. During the Covid-19 pandemic shows continued via Zoom.

Oxford Playhouse Theatre
(01865-305305; www.oxfordplayhouse.com; Beaumont St) Oxford's main stage for quality drama also hosts an impressive selection of touring music, dance and theatre

performances. The Burton Taylor Studio often features quirky student productions and other innovative pieces.

O2 Academy Live Music

(☎01865-813500; www.academymusicgroup.com/o2academyoxford; 190 Cowley Rd) Oxford's busiest club and live-music venue (previously known as the Venue and the Zodiac, way back when) hosts everything from big-name DJs and international touring artists to indie bands and hard rock.

INFORMATION

The Oxford tourist office website (www.experienceoxfordshire.org) covers the whole of Oxfordshire, makes reservations for local accommodation and walking tours, and sells tickets for events and attractions.

GETTING THERE & AROUND

All major attractions lie within half a mile of the city centre, so most visitors walk pretty much everywhere. Cycling is the perfect way to get around. A car can be useful to explore the surrounding countryside, or reach rural pubs and restaurants, but it's a liability in the city centre.

Bus The main bus companies are **Oxford Bus Company** (☎01865-785400; www.oxfordbus.co.uk), **Stagecoach** (☎01865-772250; www.stagecoachbus.com) and **Swanbrook** (☎01452-712386; www.swanbrook.co.uk).

Car If driving, head to one of the Park & Ride spots on the edge of town.

Train Oxford's main train station is conveniently located just west of the city centre.

Burford

Gliding down a steep hillside to an ancient (and still single-lane) crossing point on the River Windrush, 20 miles west of Oxford, Burford has hardly changed since its medieval glory days. Locals insist it's a town not a village, having received its charter in 1090, but it's a very small town, and a very picturesque one too, home to an appealing mix of stone cottages, gold-tinged Cotswold town houses, and the odd Elizabethan or Georgian treasure.

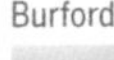

Burford

BEN MOLYNEUX/SHUTTERSTOCK ©

The Cotswolds' Best Eateries

Wheatsheaf (☎01451-860244; www.cotswoldswheatsheaf.com; West End; mains £14.50-24; ⊙8-10am, noon-3pm & 6-9pm Mon-Thu & Sun, to 10pm Fri & Sat; P 📶 👪) Lively, stylish and laid-back, this beautifully revamped coaching inn in Northleach serves excellent seasonal British dishes with a contemporary kick.

5 North St (☎01242-604566; www.5northstreetrestaurant.co.uk; 5 North St; 2-/3-course lunch £26/32, 3-/7-course dinner £54/74; ⊙12.30-1.30pm Tue-Sun, plus 7-9pm Wed-Sat; 🌱) This veteran gourmet restaurant in Winchcombe is a treat from start to finish, from its splendid 400-year-old timbered exterior to the inventive creations you find on your plate.

Badgers Hall (☎01386-840839; www.badgershall.com; High St; afternoon tea per person £7.50-24.50; ⊙8am-5.30pm Thu-Sat; 🌱) Set in a glorious old mansion facing the market hall in Chipping Campden, this definitive Cotswold tearoom is renowned for its no-holds-barred afternoon teas, served from 2.30pm onward.

Mount Inn (☎01386-584316; www.themount-inn.co.uk; Stanton; mains £13-22; ⊙noon-2pm & 6-9pm Mon-Sat, to 8pm Sun; P) Revelling in glorious hilltop views above pretty honey-washed Stanton, just off the Cotswolds Way 3.5 miles southwest of Broadway, this pub (pictured) is idyllically located and serves hearty country favourites, prepared with contemporary flair.

STEPHEN DOREY/GETTY IMAGES ©

SIGHTS

St John the Baptist's Church — Church

(www.burfordchurch.org; Church Lane) Burford's splendid church, near the river, took over three centuries to build, from 1175 onwards. Its fan-vaulted ceiling, Norman west doorway and 15th-century spire remain intact. The star attraction is the macabre 1625 Tanfield tomb, depicting local nobleman Sir Lawrence Tanfield and his wife lying in finery above a pair of carved skeletons, one leg bone of which is said to be real.

Cotswold Wildlife Park — Zoo

(☎01993-823006; www.cotswoldwildlifepark.co.uk; Bradwell Grove; adult/child £14.50/9.90; ⊙10am-6pm Apr-Oct, to 5pm or dusk Nov-Mar, last admission 2hr before closing; P 👪) 🍃 Younger visitors in particular will enjoy this hugely popular wildlife centre, 3 miles south of Burford. Its vast 250-species menagerie includes penguins, zebras, lions, reindeer, anacondas, endangered white rhinos and a giant tortoise. A miniature train takes the excitement up a notch.

EATING & DRINKING

Several of Burford's lively pubs have pretty back gardens to enjoy in sunny weather.

Huffkins — Cafe £

(☎01993-824694; www.huffkins.com; 98 High St; mains £6-15; ⊙9am-4.30pm Mon-Fri, 9am-5pm Sat, 10am-5pm Sun; 👪) The original outlet of a Cotswolds chain that's been baking and serving delicious scones, cakes and pies since 1890, this lively, friendly cafe is usually busy with locals enjoying quiches, soups, macaroni cheese or burgers. It also offers all-day cooked breakfasts and full-blown afternoon teas. For a quick snack, pick up baked goods in its adjoining deli.

Swan Inn — Modern British ££

(☎01993-823339; www.theswanswinbrook.co.uk; Swinbrook; mains £16-26; ⊙noon-2pm & 7-9pm; P) With a maze of lively rooms, roaring winter fires and bench tables overlooking a gorgeous orchard, this popular riverside gastropub, 3 miles east of Burford, oozes appeal. Its seasonal British menu mixes a pinch of creativity with quality, mostly local ingredients, offering original starters (like Stilton soufflé) and sharing platters alongside succulent meaty mains. Bookings recommended.

INFORMATION

Tourist Office (☎01993-823558; www.oxfordshirecotswolds.org; 33a High St; ⊙9.30am-5pm Mon-Sat, 10am-4pm Sun) Information on local walks.

GETTING THERE & AWAY

Bus Stagecoach and Swanbrook buses run to/from Burford, including to Oxford (route 853; £6.30, 45 minutes to 1¼ hours).

Car Standing conveniently just north of the A40, Burford is one of the easiest Cotswold towns to reach by road. It's often the first port of call for drivers coming from Oxford (20 miles east) or London (75 miles southeast).

Bibury

Memorably described as 'England's most beautiful village' by no less an authority than William Morris, Bibury, 8 miles northeast of Cirencester, epitomises the Cotswolds at its most picturesque. With a cluster of perfect cottages beside the River Coln, and a tangle of narrow streets flanked by attractive stone buildings, small wonder that it's a major halt on large-group Cotswold tours.

SIGHTS

Arlington Row Street

Bibury's most famous attraction, this ravishing row of rustic cottages – as seen in movies like *Stardust* – was originally a 14th-century wool store, before being converted into workers' lodgings. They overlook Rack Isle, a low-lying, marshy area once used to dry cloth and graze cattle, and now a wildlife refuge. Visitors are reminded to admire the cottages but respect the residents' privacy as you stroll the flower-lined lane alongside.

Church of St Mary the Virgin Church

(Church Rd; ⊙10am-dusk) Bibury's Saxon-built church has been much altered since its original construction, but many 8th-century features are still visible among the 12th-, 13th- and 15th-century additions. It's just off the B4425 in the village centre.

EATING & DRINKING

A handful of pubs in Bibury itself serve meals, but the best restaurants in the vicinity can be found in nearby Barnsley and Coln St Aldwyns, or slightly further afield in Cirencester.

Bibury holds a couple of mellow pubs, and so too do the nearby villages of Coln St Aldwyns and Barnsley.

GETTING THERE & AWAY

Most drivers approach Bibury along the B4425, which passes through the village centre halfway between Burford (9 miles northeast) and Cirencester (8 miles southwest).

Pulhams Coaches bus 855 heads to/from Cirencester (15 minutes) and Northleach (20 minutes); there's no Sunday service.

See www.traveline.info for fares and timetables.

Great Coffees
Breakfasts
Light Lunches
Salads
Paninis
Afternoon Teas
Pastries & Cakes
Daily Specials
Famously Independent since 1989

STRATFORD-UPON-AVON

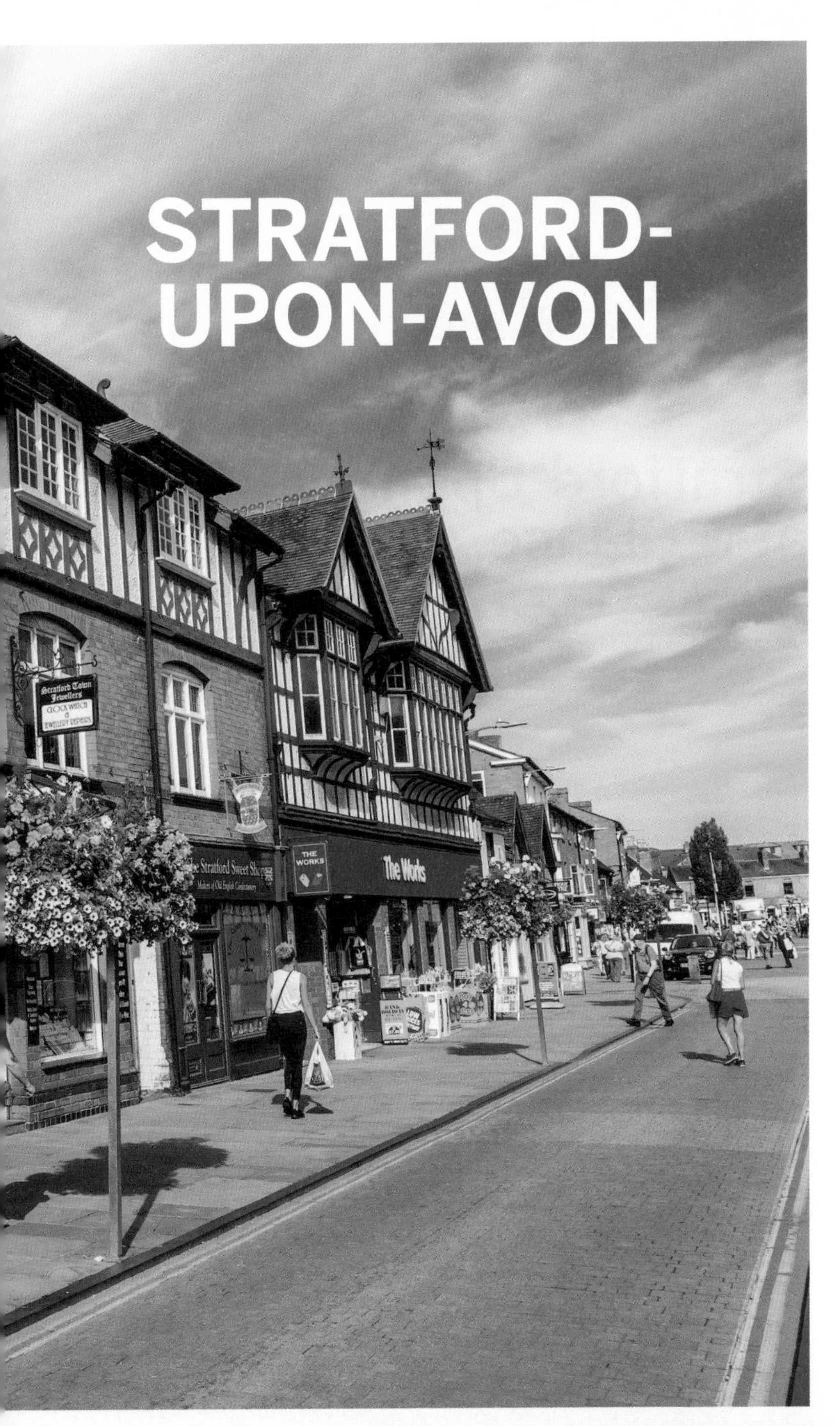

In this Chapter

Stratford-Upon-Avon at a Glance...

The author of some of the most quoted lines ever written in the English language, William Shakespeare, was born in Stratford in 1564 and died here in 1616. Experiences linked to his life in this unmistakably Tudor town are rich and varied, ranging from the intriguing (his schoolroom) via the humbling (his grave) to the sublime (a performance at the Royal Shakespeare Company).

Two Days in Stratford-Upon-Avon

Discover the Bard's home town on a two-hour guided **walk** (p154). Continue explorations at his **birthplace** (p152) and **classroom** (p152), before repairing to **Salt** (p156) for a lovely evening meal. On day two, take in the outlying Bard-related sights: **Anne Hathaway's Cottage** (p152) and **Mary Arden's Farm** (p153). For supper, it's back to town for more treats at **Townhouse** (p156).

Four Days in Stratford-Upon-Avon

Start day three in grand style at the extravagantly Elizabethan **Charlecote Park** (p154), before a cruise down the **Avon** (p157) and dinner at **Edward Moon's** (p156). On your fourth day, shop for that perfect Shakespeare souvenir; have a pint at the oldest pub in town, **Old Thatch Tavern** (p156); then delight in an outstanding performance at the **Royal Shakespeare Company** (p157).

Previous page: Half-timbered buildings in Stratford-Upon-Avon
S-F/SHUTTERSTOCK ©

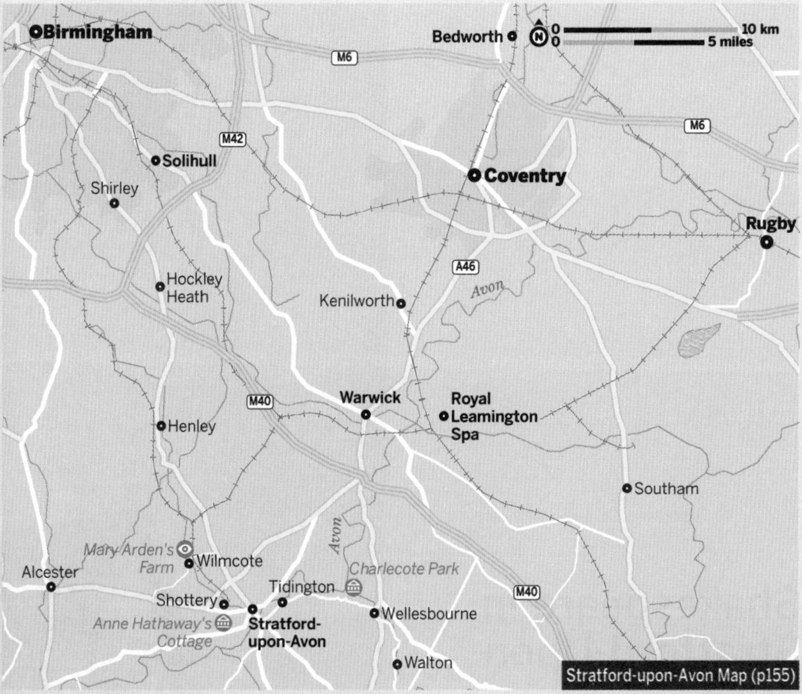

Stratford-upon-Avon Map (p155)

Arriving in Stratford-Upon-Avon

Bus National Express coach services include those to London Victoria (£10.50, three hours, four daily) and Oxford (£10.10, one hour, one daily).

Car Stratford is 100 miles (two hours) northwest of London and 85 miles (two hours) north of Bath. Town car parks charge high fees.

Train Services include those to London Marylebone (£38.20, 2¾ hours, up to two per hour).

Where to Stay

B&Bs are plentiful, particularly along Grove Rd and Evesham Pl, but vacancies can be hard to find during the high season – check listings on www.shakespeare-country.co.uk. The tourist office can help with bookings.

Shakespeare's birthplace

Shakespeare in Stratford-Upon-Avon

Stratford (the 'upon Avon' is dropped locally) is a delightful Tudor town that's fascinating to wander – even a short stroll here leads around a living, breathing map of Shakespeare's life. As well as being home to both his birth and burial place, the town also stages world-class performances of the Bard's plays.

Great For...

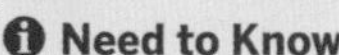

Need to Know

The Shakespeare Birthplace Trust (www.shakespeare.org.uk) offers combined tickets (adult/child £22/14.50) to five key sights.

★ Top Tip

Visit the arboretum at Anne Hathaway's Cottage (p152) for examples of the trees mentioned in Shakespeare's plays.

GARY718/SHUTTERSTOCK ©

Shakespeare's Birthplace

Start your Shakespeare quest at the **house** (☎01789-204016; www.shakespeare.org.uk; Henley St; adult/child £15/11; ⏰10am-4pm Mon-Fri, to 5pm Sat & Sun) where the renowned playwright was born in 1564 and spent his childhood days. John Shakespeare owned the house for a period of 50 years. William, as the eldest surviving son, inherited it upon his father's death in 1601 and spent his first five years of marriage here. Behind a modern facade, the house has restored Tudor rooms, live presentations from famous Shakespearean characters and an engaging exhibition on Stratford's favourite son.

Shakespeare's Childhood

Shakespeare's alma mater, King Edward VI School (still a prestigious grammar school today), incorporates a vast black-and-white timbered building, dating from 1420, that was once the town's guildhall. Upstairs, in the Bard's former **classroom** (☎01789-203170; www.shakespearesschoolroom.org; King Edward VI School, Church St; adult/child £8.50/5.50, combination ticket with MAD Museum £13.10/8.60; ⏰11am-5pm), you can sit in on mock-Tudor lessons, watch a short film and test yourself on Tudor-style homework.

Shakespeare's Family

Before tying the knot with Shakespeare, Anne Hathaway lived in Shottery, 1 mile west of the centre of Stratford, in a delightful thatched **cottage** (☎01789-338532; www.shakespeare.org.uk; Cottage Lane, Shottery; adult/child £12.50/8; ⏰9am-5pm Apr-Aug, to 4.30pm Sep & Oct, 10am-3.30pm Nov-Mar). As well as period furniture, the farmhouse has

Anne Hathaway's Cottage

gorgeous gardens and an orchard and fine arboretum. A footpath (no bikes allowed) leads to Shottery from Evesham Pl.

The childhood home of Mary Arden, Shakespeare's mother, can be found at Wilmcote, 3 miles west of Stratford. Aimed squarely at families, the working **farm** (01789-338535; www.shakespeare.org.uk; Station Rd, Wilmcote; adult/child £15/10; 10am-5pm Apr-Aug, to 4.30pm Sep & Oct;) traces country life over the centuries, with nature trails, falconry displays and a collection of rare-breed farm animals. You can get here on the City Sightseeing bus (p154) or cycle via Anne Hathaway's Cottage, following the Stratford-upon-Avon Canal towpath.

Hall's Croft (01789-338533; www.shakespeare.org.uk; Old Town; adult/child £8.50/5.50; 10am-5pm Apr-Aug, to 4.30pm Sep & Oct, 11am-3.30pm Nov-Feb), the handsome Jacobean town house belonging to Shakespeare's daughter Susanna and her husband, respected doctor John Hall, stands south of the centre. The exhibition offers fascinating insights into medicine in the 16th and 17th centuries, and the lovely walled garden sprouts with aromatic herbs employed in medicinal preparations.

☑ Don't Miss

Adjacent to the guildhall housing Shakespeare's classroom, the 1269-founded Guild Chapel contains 15th- and early 16th-century frescoes.

DAVID STEELE/SHUTTERSTOCK ©

Later Years

When Shakespeare retired, he swapped the bright lights of London for a comfortable town house at **New Place** (01789-338536; www.shakespeare.org.uk; cnr Chapel St & Chapel Lane; adult/child £12.50/8; 10am-5pm Apr-Aug, to 4.30pm Sep & Oct, to 3.30pm Nov-Feb). The house has long been demolished, but an attractive Elizabethan knot garden occupies part of the grounds. A major restoration project has uncovered Shakespeare's kitchen and incorporated new exhibits in a re-imagining of the house as it would have been. You can also explore the adjacent Nash's House, where Shakespeare's granddaughter Elizabeth lived.

Shakespeare's Grave

Set inside a **church** (01789-266316; www.stratford-upon-avon.org; Old Town; Shakespeare's grave adult/child £3/2; noon-2pm Mon-Thu, to 4pm Fri, 11am-4pm Sat) featuring handsome 16th-century tombs and carved choir stalls, the grave of William Shakespeare bears the ominous epitaph: 'cvrst be he yt moves my bones'.

Take a Break

The Townhouse (p156) is a delightful spot in which to pause the Shakespearean sightseeing for a while to feast in a 400-year-old building.

SIGHTS

Charlecote Park Historic Building

(NT; ☎01789-470277; www.nationaltrust.org.uk; Loxley Lane, Charlecote CV35 9ER; house & garden adult/child £11.45/5.70, garden only £8/4; ⏲house 11am-4.30pm Thu-Tue mid-Mar–Oct, noon-3.30pm Thu-Tue mid-Feb–mid-Mar, noon-3.30pm Sat & Sun Nov & Dec, garden 9am-5pm Mar-Oct, to 4.30pm Nov-Feb) A youthful Shakespeare allegedly poached deer in the grounds of this lavish Elizabethan pile on the River Avon, 5 miles east of Stratford-upon-Avon. Fallow deer still roam the grounds today. The interiors were restored from Georgian chintz to Tudor splendour in 1823. Highlights include Victorian kitchens, filled with culinary moulds, and an original 1551 Tudor gatehouse.

Bus X17 runs to Charlecote hourly from Stratford (£5.50, 30 minutes, two per hour Monday to Friday, hourly Saturday and Sunday).

MAD Museum Museum

(☎01789-269356; www.themadmuseum.co.uk; 4-5 Henley St; adult/child £7.80/5.20, combination ticket with Shakespeare's School Room £13.10/8.60; ⏲10am-5.30pm) Fun, hands-on exhibits at Stratford's Mechanical Art & Design Museum (aka MAD) make physics accessible for kids, who can build their own gravity-propelled marble run, use their energy to light up electric panels, and pull levers and turn cranks to animate displays. Tickets are valid all day, so you can come and go as you please.

Gower Memorial Monument

(Bancroft Gardens, Bridge Foot) Aristocratic sculptor Lord Ronald Gower is the master behind this multi-sculpture homage to Shakespeare, which features the characters of Hamlet (representing philosophy), Prince Hal (history), Lady Macbeth (tragedy) and Falstaff (comedy) as well the Bard himself. The figures and decorative bronze work were cast in France in 1881; the final statues were installed across from the Holy Trinity Church in 1888 (Oscar Wilde officiated at the unveiling). The memorial shifted to its current location in Bancroft Gardens in 1933.

American Fountain Monument

(Market Sq, Rother St) Gifted by American publisher George W Childs in 1887 to mark Queen Victoria's Golden Jubilee, and designed by Birmingham architect Jethro Cossins, this ornate Victorian Gothic clock tower was unveiled by Shakespearean actor Henry Irving. Lions, eagles, owls and Tudor roses adorn the tower; a fairy sits atop each clock face representing *A Midsummer Night's Dream*. Although the fountain no longer runs, the clocks and bell still work. The horse troughs, once filled with water, now bloom with flowers.

TOURS

Stratford Town Walk Walking

(☎07855 760377; www.stratfordtownwalk.co.uk; town walk adult/child £7/3, ghost walk £8/5; ⏲town walk 11am Sun-Fri, 11am & 2pm Sat, ghost walk by reservation 7.30pm Sat) Popular two-hour guided town walks depart from Waterside, opposite Sheep St (prebooking not necessary). Chilling ghost walks lasting 90 minutes leave from the same location but must be booked ahead.

City Sightseeing Bus

(☎01789-299123; www.city-sightseeing.com; adult/child 24hr £15/7.50, 48hr £23/11.50; ⏲9.30am-5pm Apr-Oct) Open-top, hop-on/hop-off bus tours leave from the tourist office on Bridge Foot, rolling to each of the Shakespeare properties, and making 11 stops in all. Buy tickets online, at the tourist office or from the driver.

Shopping

Chaucer Head Books

(www.chaucerhead.com; 21 Chapel St; ⏲11am-5.30pm Mon-Fri, 10am-5pm Sat) Bargain-priced paperbacks through to rare antiquarian books worth thousands of pounds are stocked at the Chaucer Head, which was originally founded in Birmingham in 1830 and relocated to literary-famed Stratford in 1960.

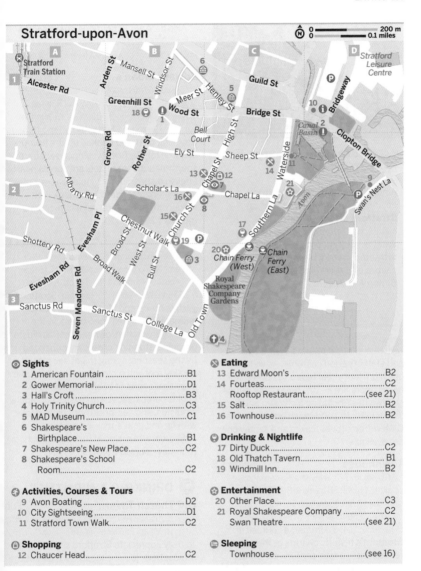

Stratford-upon-Avon

Sights

1 American Fountain B1
2 Gower Memorial D1
3 Hall's Croft B3
4 Holy Trinity Church C3
5 MAD Museum C1
6 Shakespeare's Birthplace B1
7 Shakespeare's New Place C2
8 Shakespeare's School Room C2

Activities, Courses & Tours

9 Avon Boating D2
10 City Sightseeing D1
11 Stratford Town Walk C2

Shopping

12 Chaucer Head C2

Eating

13 Edward Moon's B2
14 Fourteas C2
Rooftop Restaurant .... (see 21)
15 Salt B2
16 Townhouse B2

Drinking & Nightlife

17 Dirty Duck C2
18 Old Thatch Tavern B1
19 Windmill Inn B2

Entertainment

20 Other Place C3
21 Royal Shakespeare Company C2
Swan Theatre .... (see 21)

Sleeping

Townhouse .... (see 16)

EATING

Sheep St is rammed with upmarket eating options, mostly aimed at theatre goers (look out for good-value pre-theatre menus).

Fourteas — Cafe £

(☎01789-293908; www.thefourteas.co.uk; 24 Sheep St; dishes £4.50-9.50, afternoon tea with/without Prosecco £20/15; ⏰9.30am-5.30pm Mon-Sat, from 10.30am Sun) Breaking with Stratford's Shakespearean theme, this tearoom takes the 1940s as its inspiration

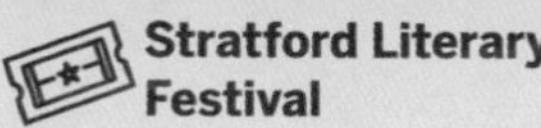

Stratford Literary Festival

A highlight of Stratford's cultural calendar is the week-long annual **Stratford Literary Festival** (☎01789-470185; www.stratfordliteraryfestival.co.uk; ⊙late Apr/early May), which has attracted literary big-hitters of the calibre of Robert Harris, PD James and Simon Armitage.

CLAUDIO DIVIZIA/SHUTTERSTOCK ©

with beautiful old teapots, framed posters and staff in period costume. As well as premium loose-leaf teas and homemade cakes, there are all-day breakfasts, soups, sandwiches (including a chicken and bacon 'Churchill club') and lavish afternoon teas. Gluten-free scones, cakes and sandwiches are available.

Townhouse Bistro **££**

(☎01789-262222; www.stratfordtownhouse.co.uk; 16 Church St; mains £13-21; ⊙kitchen noon-3pm & 5-9.30pm Mon-Fri, noon-9.30pm Sat, to 8pm Sun, bar 8am-midnight Mon-Sat, to 10.30pm Sun;) Immerse yourself in Stratford's historic charms at this lovely restaurant in a four-century-old timber building. Rare-breed steaks and seafood dishes such as dressed crab with truffled mayo are specialities. Music students from Shakespeare's old grammar school across the way tinkle the piano ivories at 5.30pm Monday to Saturday, though it can be hard to hear over the bar noise.

Also here are 12 boutique **guest rooms** (☎01789-262222; www.stratfordtownhouse.co.uk; 16 Church St; d incl breakfast from £140;).

Edward Moon's British **££**

(☎01789-267069; www.edwardmoon.com; 9 Chapel St; mains £12-20; ⊙noon-2.30pm & 5-9pm Tue-Thu, noon-2.30pm & 5-9.30pm Fri & Sat, noon-3pm Sun;) Named after a famous travelling chef who cooked up the flavours of home for the British colonial service, this snug independent restaurant serves hearty English dishes, such as steak-and-ale pie and meltingly tender lamb shank with redcurrant gravy. Kids get a two-course menu for £7.95.

Salt British **£££**

(☎01789-263566; www.salt-restaurant.co.uk; 8 Church St; 4-/6-course lunch menu £45/55, 8-course dinner menu £78; ⊙noon-2pm & 6.30-10pm Wed-Sat, noon-2pm Sun) Stratford's gastronomic (and Michelin) star is this intimate, beam-ceilinged bistro. In the semi-open kitchen, owner-chef Paul Foster produces stunning creations influenced by the seasons: spring might see glazed parsley root with chicory and black-truffle shavings, onglet of beef with malted artichoke, cured halibut with oyster and apple emulsion, and sea-buckthorn mille-feuille with fig and goat's-milk ice cream.

Recreate its magic at its cookery school (half-day courses from £95).

DRINKING & NIGHTLIFE

Old Thatch Tavern Pub

(www.oldthatchtavernstratford.co.uk; Greenhill St; ⊙11.30am-11pm Mon-Sat, from noon Sun;) To truly appreciate Stratford's olde-worlde atmosphere, join the locals for a pint at the town's oldest pub. Built in 1470, this thatch-roofed treasure has great real ales and a gorgeous summertime courtyard.

Dirty Duck Pub

(Black Swan; www.greeneking-pubs.co.uk; Waterside; ⊙noon-11.30pm Mon-Thu, to midnight Fri & Sat, to 11pm Sun;) Also called the 'Black Swan', this enchanting riverside alehouse is the only pub in England to be licensed under two names. It's a favourite thespian watering hole, with a roll call of former regulars (Olivier, Attenborough et al) that reads like a who's who of actors.

Windmill Inn Pub
(www.greeneking-pubs.co.uk; Church St; ⏲11am-11pm Sun-Thu, to midnight Fri & Sat;) Ale was already flowing at this low-ceilinged pub when rhyming couplets gushed from Shakespeare's quill. Flowers frame the whitewashed facade; there's a shaded rear beer garden.

ENTERTAINMENT

Royal Shakespeare Company Theatre
(RSC; ☎box office 01789-331111; www.rsc.org.uk; Waterside) Stratford has two grand stages run by the world-renowned Royal Shakespeare Company – the **Royal Shakespeare Theatre** and the **Swan Theatre** (☎01789-331111; www.rsc.org.uk; Waterside) on Waterside – as well as the smaller **Other Place** (☎box office 01789-331111; www.rsc.org.uk; 22 Southern Lane). The theatres have witnessed performances by such legends as Lawrence Olivier, Richard Burton, Judi Dench, Helen Mirren, Ian McKellan and Patrick Stewart. One-hour guided tours (on hold at the time of research) take you behind the scenes.

Zipping up the lift/elevator of the Royal Shakespeare Theatre's **tower** rewards with panoramic views over the town and River Avon. Spectacular views also unfold from its 3rd-floor **Rooftop Restaurant** (☎01789-403449; www.rsc.org.uk; 3rd fl, Royal Shakespeare Theatre, Waterside; mains £14-26; ⏲10.30am-9.30pm Mon-Thu, to 9.45pm Fri & Sat, to 3.30pm Sun;), which opens to a terrace.

Contact the RSC for performance times, and book well ahead as capacity is limited (though there are plans to stream performances as well).

There are often special deals for under-25-year-olds, students and seniors. A few tickets are held back for sale on the day of performances but get snapped up fast.

Boating on the Avon

Avon Boating (☎01789-267073; www.avon-boating.co.uk; The Boathouse, Swan's Nest Lane; river cruises adult/child £7/5; ⏲9am-dusk Easter-Oct) runs 40-minute river cruises that depart every 20 minutes from either side of the main bridge. It also hires rowboats, canoes and punts (per hour £7, minimum charge £12) and motorboats (per hour £50).

CARON BADKIN/SHUTTERSTOCK ©

INFORMATION

Tourist Office (☎01789-264293; www.shakespeares-england.co.uk; Bridge Foot; ⏲9am-5.30pm Mon-Sat, 10am-4pm Sun) Just west of Clopton Bridge.

GETTING AROUND

From 10am to 6pm April to October, a 1937-built, hand-wound chain ferry yo-yos across the Avon between the **west bank** (one-way 20p; ⏲10am-6pm Apr-Oct) and the **east bank** (one-way 20p; ⏲10am-6pm Apr-Oct).

A bicycle is handy for getting out to the outlying Shakespeare properties. **Stratford Bike Hire** (☎07711-776340; www.stratfordbikehire.com; The Stratford Greenway, Seven Meadows Rd; bike hire per half/full day from £10/15; ⏲9.30am-5pm) will deliver to your accommodation for free within a 6-mile radius of Stratford.

CAMBRIDGE

In this Chapter

Cambridge at a Glance...

Bursting with extravagant architecture, dripping with history, and as English as high tea on a checked picnic blanket, the university city of Cambridge is the story of learning written large. Cyclists negotiate cobbled passageways, students picnic on manicured lawns and great minds debate the issues of the day in historic pubs after dark. Add in first-rate museums, great eating and punting on the River Cam (the Granta) and it's easy to see the appeal.

Two Days in Cambridge

Prime yourself at the **Fitzwilliam Museum** (p166), then hit the historic colleges, starting with **King's College Chapel** (p164) and **St John's** (p165). For supper, try the agreeably hip **Pint Shop** (p169). On day two explore more colleges – don't miss **Trinity** (p164) and its famous **Wren Library** – and climb the tower of **Great St Mary's Church** (p163) for epic views. Dine at **Chop House** (p169) in the heart of the action.

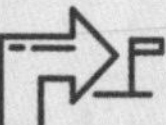

Four Days in Cambridge

Day three is for fresh air – glide along the college Backs in a chauffeur-driven **punt** (p167) (or pilot your own), then head over to Grantchester's gorgeous **tea garden** (p167). You'll have earned a slap-up dinner at **Smokeworks** (p169). On day four, see art at **Kettle's Yard** (p167) and nature's beauty at the **Botanic Garden** (p166). End your Cambridge visit with a gourmet treat at **Midsummer House** (p169).

Previous page: Great Court, Trinity College (p164)
PREMIER PHOTO/SHUTTERSTOCK ©

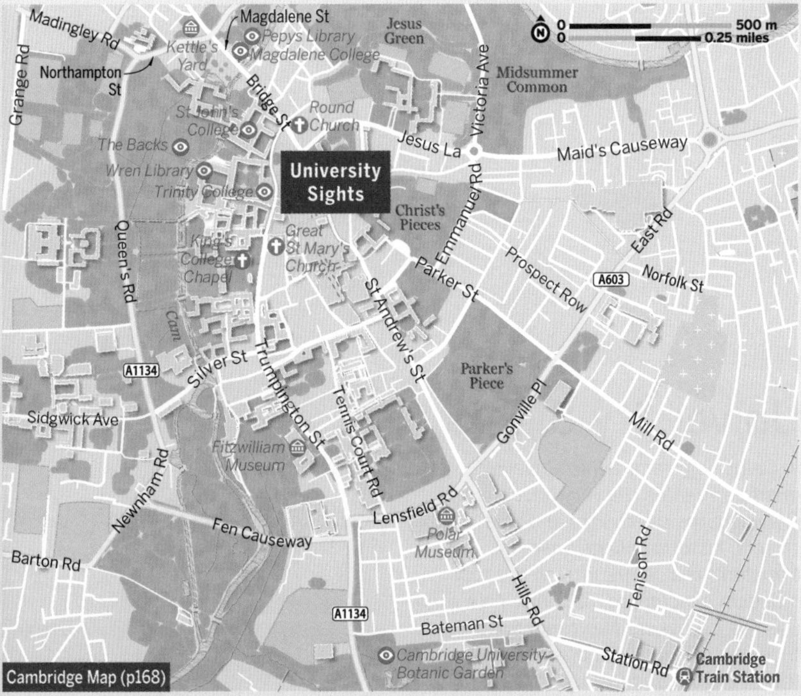

Cambridge Map (p168)

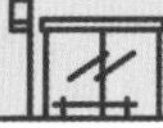

Arriving in Cambridge

Bus There are up to 12 National Express buses daily from London Victoria (from £19, 2½ hours), dropping you at Parkside just east of Cambridge's city centre.

Train Trains zip very regularly to London (from £19.90, one hour), Ely (£4.70, 15 minutes, half-hourly), Stansted Airport (£11.40, 30 minutes to one hour, every 20 minutes) and other local hubs.

Where to Stay

Cambridge has lots of appealling accommodation, but booking ahead is advised. Options range from hostels, college halls and B&Bs to elegant boutique hotels, but prices reflect the popularity of this historic city.

Market Square and Great St Mary's Church

University Sights

In Cambridge, academic achievement permeates the very pavements. Crowding the riverbanks and side streets, historic college buildings transform the centre into an outdoor museum of sculpted masonry. This was the city where Newton refined his theory of gravity, Whipple invented the jet engine and Crick and Watson discovered DNA; you can almost feel the creativity in the air.

Great For...

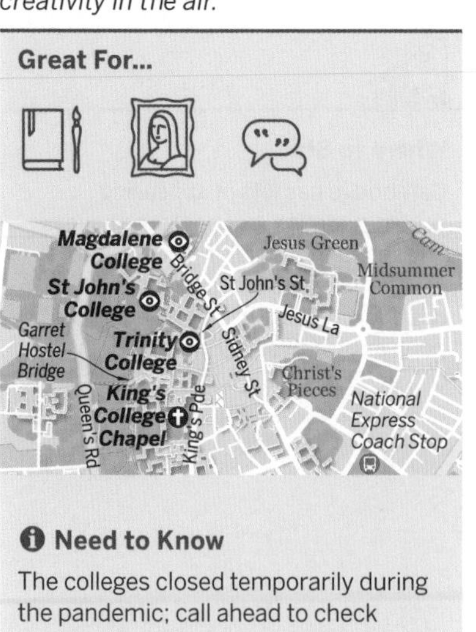

Need to Know

The colleges closed temporarily during the pandemic; call ahead to check they're open. All close at Christmas and from early April to mid-June for exams.

★ Top Tip

Before you start your explorations, climb the tower of **Great St Mary's Church** (☎01223-747273; www.gsm.cam.ac.uk; Senate House Hill; tower per person/family £6/16; ⏰11am-5pm Tue-Sun) FREE or have a drink on the Roof Terrace (p170) at the Varsity Hotel, so you can see the layout of the city from above.

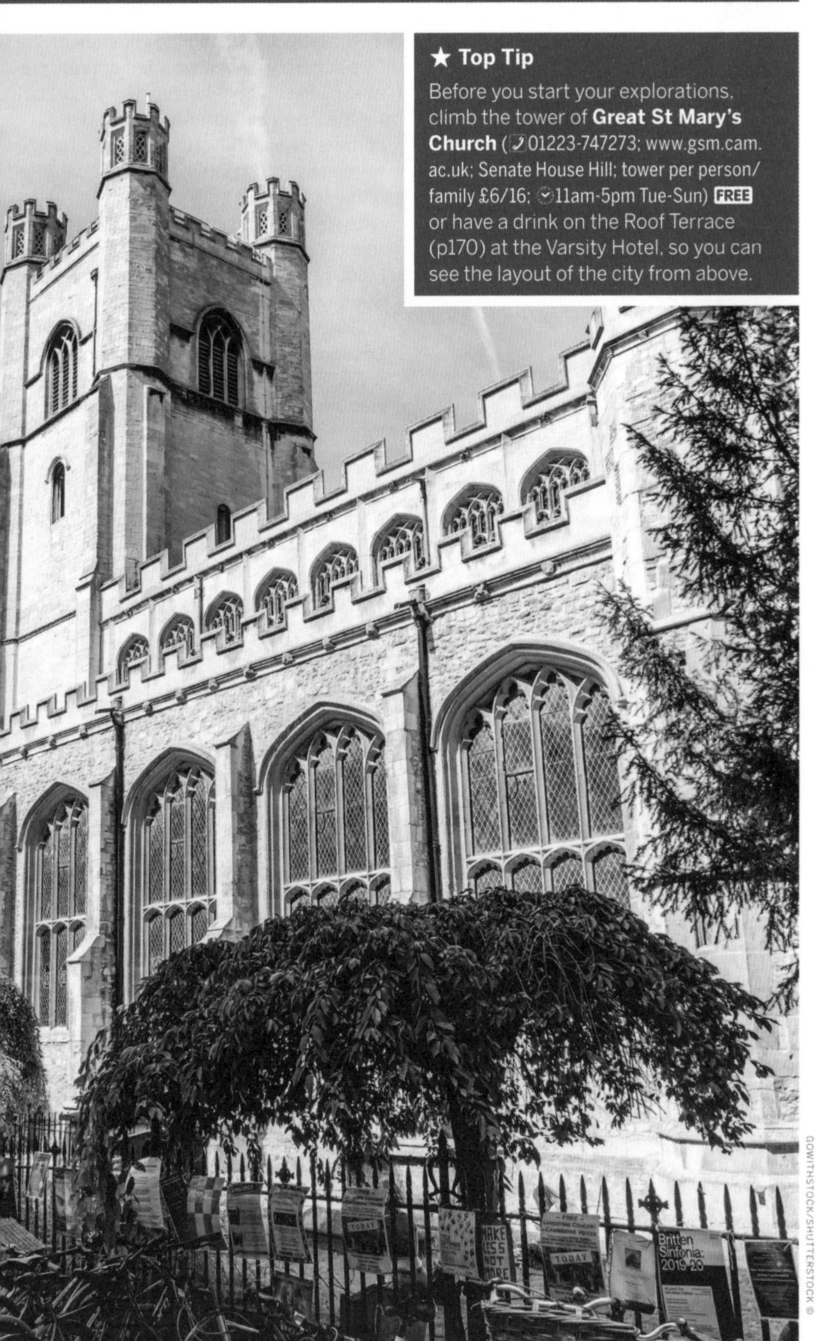

GOWITHSTOCK/SHUTTERSTOCK ©

King's College Chapel

This grandiose, limestone-faced 16th-century **chapel** (01223-331100; www.kings.cam.ac.uk; King's Pde; adult/child £10/8; 9.30am-3.15pm Mon-Sat, 1.15-2.30pm Sun term time, 9.30am-4.30pm rest of year) is one of England's most extraordinary Gothic monuments. During services, the sound of the chapel's famous choir rises to an almost impossibly intricate fan-vaulted ceiling – the world's largest. Think of it as a firework display, expressed as architecture.

Founded in 1446 as an act of piety by Henry VI, the chapel was only finished by Henry VIII around 1516. The glass in the lofty windows that flank the chapel's sides is original, spared from the excesses of England's 17th-century Civil War on the orders of Oliver Cromwell.

The antechapel and the choir are divided by a superbly carved **wooden screen**, created by Peter Stockton for Henry VIII. Look for the king's initials entwined with those of Anne Boleyn. Beyond, the high altar is framed by Rubens' masterpiece *Adoration of the Magi* (1634).

Under normal circumstances, visitors congregate for **Evensong** (5.30pm Monday to Saturday, 10.30am and 3.30pm Sunday). Each Christmas Eve, King's College Chapel stages the **Festival of Nine Lessons & Carols**, broadcast globally by the BBC. At the time of writing, the chapel was only open at set times – check ahead for the latest.

Trinity College

The largest of Cambridge's colleges, **Trinity** (01223-338400; www.trin.cam.ac.uk; Trinity

King's College Chapel

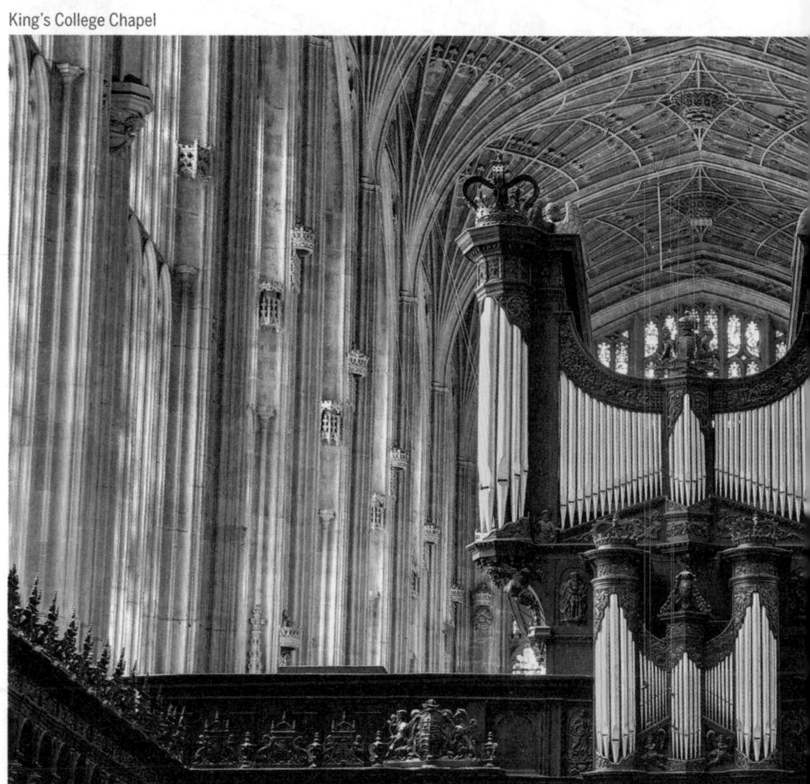

St) grabs attention with an extraordinary Tudor gateway, capped by a stern-looking statue of the college founder, Henry VIII. Beyond lies the vast **Great Court** flanked by cloisters and Gothic halls and spires. The famous, musty **Wren Library** (☎01223-338400; www.trin.cam.ac.uk; Trinity St) FREE contains more than 55,000 books published before 1820, including works by Shakespeare, St Jerome, Newton and Swift – and an original *Winnie the Pooh* (AA Milne and his son, Christopher Robin, were graduates). Other famous alumni include Sir Isaac Newton, Francis Bacon, Lord Byron, Tennyson and HRH Prince Charles. Contact the college for current hours and entry fees.

☑ Don't Miss

The statue of Henry VIII at Trinity College's gates – his left hand holds a table leg, left in place of the original sceptre by student pranksters.

RADEK STURGOLEWSKI/SHUTTERSTOCK ©

St John's College

Alma mater of six prime ministers (including India's Manmohan Singh), poet William Wordsworth, anti-slavery campaigner William Wilberforce and Douglas Adams (author of *The Hitchhiker's Guide to the Galaxy*), **St John's** (☎01223-33860; www.joh.cam.ac.uk; St John's St) is highly photogenic. Founded in 1511 by Henry VII's mother, Margaret Beaufort, it sprawls along both riverbanks, connected by the ecclesiastical-looking **Bridge of Sighs**, a common focus for student pranks. Contact the college for current hours and entry fees.

Magdalene College

A former Benedictine hostel, riverside **Magdalene** (☎01223-332100; www.magd.cam.ac.uk; Magdalene St) – properly pronounced 'Maud-lyn' – is home to the famous **Pepys Library** (☎01223-332115; www.magd.cam.ac.uk; Magdalene St) FREE, housing 3000 books bequeathed by the mid-17th-century diarist to his old college. This idiosyncratic library covers everything from illuminated medieval manuscripts to the *Anthony Roll*, a 1540s depiction of the Royal Navy's ships. Contact the college for current hours and entry fees.

The Backs

Behind the Cambridge colleges' grandiose facades and stately courts, a series of gardens and parks line up beside the river, linked by a number of historic bridges. Collectively known as the **Backs**, these tranquil green spaces offer timelessly evocative snapshots of student life.

Take a Break

Rest feet and boost sugar levels at Fitzbillies (p169), less a bakery, more an institution, famed for its plump Chelsea buns.

SIGHTS

Fitzwilliam Museum Museum

(www.fitzmuseum.cam.ac.uk; Trumpington St; by donation; 10am-5pm Tue-Sat, from noon Sun) Fondly dubbed 'the Fitz' by locals, this colossal neoclassical treasure house was one of the first public art museums in Britain, built to house the fabulous collection that the seventh Viscount Fitzwilliam bequeathed to his old university. There are obvious parallels to the British Museum, and highlights include Roman, Egyptian and Cypriot grave goods, artworks by great masters and one of the country's finest collections of ancient, medieval and modern pottery. Check ahead for the latest hours.

Polar Museum Museum

(01223-336540; www.spri.cam.ac.uk/museum; Lensfield Rd) FREE In this compelling university museum, the trials, victories and tragic mistakes of such great Polar explorers as Roald Amundsen, Ernest Shackleton and Captain Scott are powerfully evoked, using paintings, photographs, equipment, maps, journals and even last messages left for loved ones. The museum was temporarily closed in 2020 – check ahead for the latest opening times.

Round Church Church

(01223-311602; www.roundchurchcambridge.org; Bridge St; £3.50; 10am-4.30pm Fri & Sat, from 12.30pm Sun) Looking like a prime setting for a Dan Brown novel, Cambridge's atmospheric Round Church is one of only four round medieval churches in England. It was built by the mysterious Knights Templar in 1130, making it older than the university, and the unusual circular knave is ringed by chunky Norman pillars. Guided walks explore the church and local area, leaving on Saturday and Sunday at 2.15pm.

Cambridge University Botanic Garden Gardens

(01223-336265; www.botanic.cam.ac.uk; 1 Brookside; adult/child £6.60/free; 10am-6pm Apr-Sep, to 5pm Feb, Mar & Oct, to 4pm Nov-Jan;) Founded by Charles Darwin's mentor, Professor John Henslow, the beautiful Botanic Garden is a gorgeous green expanse, full of hidden corners, tiny paths and secret

Round Church

spaces. There are more than 8000 plant species here, from mature trees in the arboretum to an army of carnivorous pitcher plants in Victorian-era greenhouses. Under normal circumstances, hour-long guided tours (free) run from May through to September; check to see if they've resumed.

Kettle's Yard Gallery
(☎01223-748100; www.kettlesyard.co.uk; Castle St; ⏲11am-5pm Wed-Sun) FREE If you've ever wondered what art gallery curators do at home, pop into Kettle's Yard, a living art gallery created by HS 'Jim' Ede, a former curator at the Tate Gallery in London. A lifetime's collection of artworks and found objects is displayed inside a line of elegantly converted cottages, including works by Miró, Henry Moore and lesser-known artists such as WWI-era sculptor Henri Gaudier-Brzeska and primitive nautical artist Alfred Wallis.

ACTIVITIES

Scudamore's Punting Boating
(☎01223-359750; www.scudamores.com; Mill Lane; chauffeured punt trips per bench/boat from £70/120, 6-person punt hire from £51; ⏲10am-7pm Mon-Fri, to 8pm Sat & Sun) At this long-established operator, you can hire punts to pole yourself along the Granta, or take chauffeured trips to Granchester and the Backs. Prices are flexible and staff cruise the jetty offering discounts. Note that you can hire just a row of seats to reduce rates.

It has a second hire station north of the centre at **Quayside** (☎01223-359750; www.scudamores.com; Quayside; chauffeured punt trips per bench/boat from £70/120, 6-person punt hire from £51; ⏲9am-dusk).

Cambridge Chauffeur Punts Boating
(☎01223-354164; www.punting-in-cambridge.co.uk; Silver St Bridge; chauffeured punts from adult/child £20/12 per hour, 6-person self-punt per hour £30; ⏲9am-8pm Jun & Aug, 10am-dusk Apr, May, Sep & Oct) Runs regular chauffeured punting tours of the Backs and to Granchester; also offers self-hire.

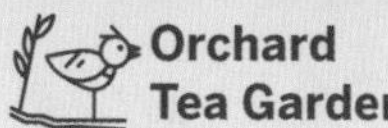

Orchard Tea Garden

After an idyllic punt, walk or cycle beside the River Cam (the Granta) from Cambridge to Granchester, flop into a deckchair under a leafy apple tree and wolf down calorific cakes or light lunches at the **Orchard Tea Garden** (☎01223-840230; www.theorchardteagarden.co.uk; 47 Mill Way; lunch mains £6-10; ⏲9am-6pm Apr-Oct, to 4pm Wed-Sun Nov-Mar), a quintessentially English spot. This was a favourite haunt of the Bloomsbury Group who came to camp, picnic, swim and push back social boundaries.

PREMIER PHOTO/SHUTTERSTOCK ©

TOURS

With the (hopefully temporary) closure of the tourist office, **walking tours** run by official Blue Badge and Green Badge guides run from beside the Guildhall on Peas Hill at 11am and 1.30pm (one-hour tour £10/5 per adult/child), taking in the main sights.

SHOPPING

Cambridge University Press Books
(www.cambridge.org; 1-2 Trinity St; ⏲10am-5.30pm Mon Sat, 11am-5pm Sun) The world's oldest university press has been publishing the results of university research and thinking since 1534. It's always worth popping into the bookstore by King's College to see the latest offerings from the country's leading thinkers.

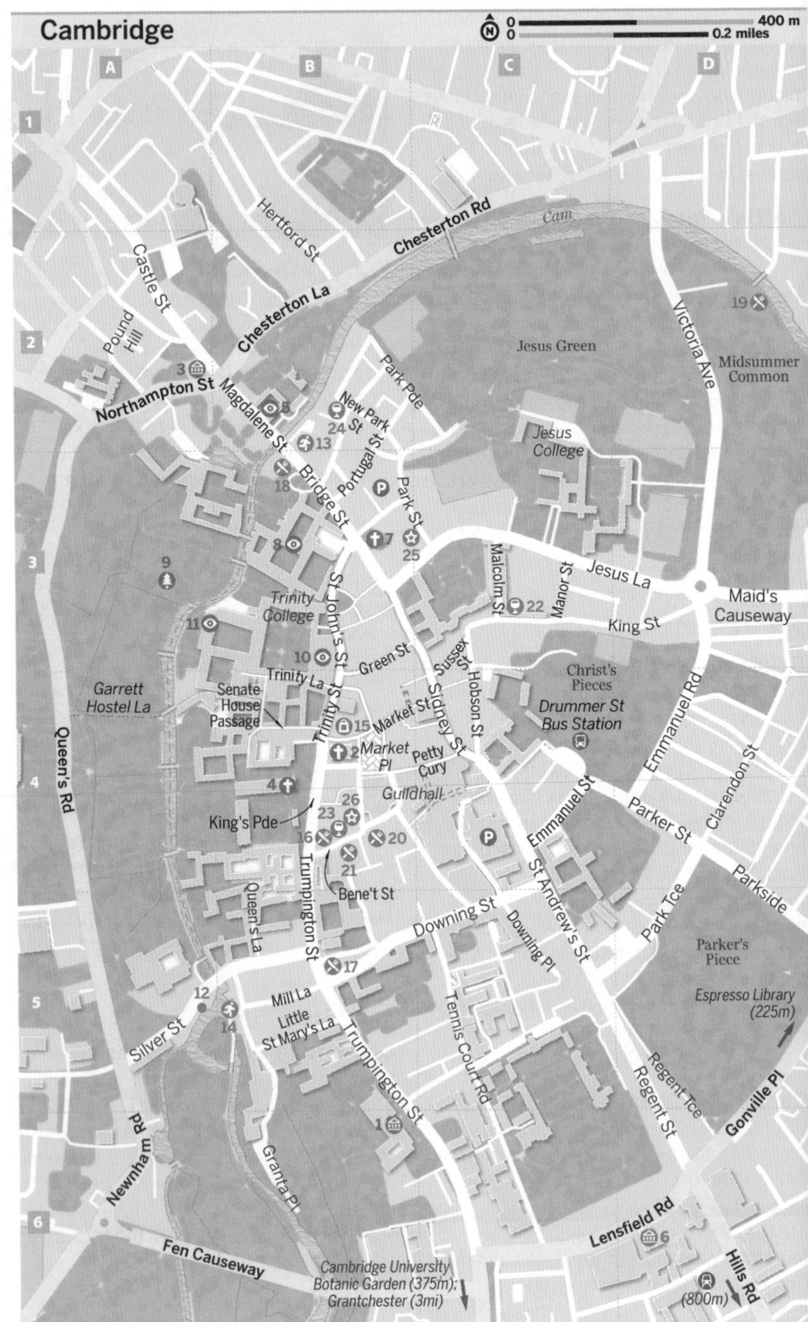
Cambridge
0
400 m
0
0.2 miles
A
B
C
D
1
2
3
4
5
6
Hertford St
Chesterton Rd
Cam
Castle St
Chesterton La
Pound Hill
Northampton St
Magdalene St
New Park St
Park Pde
Portugal St
Bridge St
Park St
Jesus Green
Victoria Ave
Midsummer Common
Jesus College
Malcolm St
Manor St
Jesus La
Maid's Causeway
King St
Trinity College
St John's St
Green St
Sussex St
Hobson St
Christ's Pieces
Drummer St Bus Station
Garrett Hostel La
Senate House Passage
Trinity La
Trinity St
Market St
Sidney St
Market Pl
Petty Cury
Guildhall
Emmanuel Rd
Emmanuel St
Parker St
Clarendon St
Queen's Rd
King's Pde
Bene't St
Trumpington St
Queen's La
Downing St
Downing Pl
St Andrew's St
Parkside
Park Tce
Parker's Piece
Mill La
Little St Mary's La
Silver St
Tennis Court Rd
Regent Tce
Regent St
Espresso Library (225m)
Gonville Pl
Newnham Rd
Granta Pl
Fen Causeway
Lensfield Rd
Hills Rd
(800m)
Cambridge University Botanic Garden (375m); Grantchester (3mi)
1
2
3
4
5
6
7
8
9
10
11
12
13
14
15
16
17
18
19
20
21
22
23
24
25
26

Cambridge

Sights
1 Fitzwilliam Museum B6
2 Great St Mary's Church B4
3 Kettle's Yard A2
4 King's College Chapel B4
5 Magdalene College B2
Pepys Library .... (see 5)
6 Polar Museum D6
7 Round Church B3
8 St John's College B3
9 The Backs A3
10 Trinity College B3
11 Wren Library A3

Activities, Courses & Tours
12 Cambridge Chauffeur Punts A5
13 Scudamore's Punting B2
14 Scudamore's Punting B5

Shopping
15 Cambridge University Press B4

Eating
16 Cambridge Chop House B4
17 Fitzbillies B5
18 Fitzbillies B3
19 Midsummer House D2
20 Pint Shop B4
21 Smokeworks B4

Drinking & Nightlife
22 Cambridge Brew House C3
23 Eagle B4
24 Roof Terrace B2

Entertainment
25 ADC B3
26 Cambridge Arts Theatre B4

Sleeping
Varsity Hotel .... (see 24)

EATING

Fitzbillies — Cafe £

(www.fitzbillies.com; 52 Trumpington St; mains £5-15; 8.30am-5pm Mon-Fri, 9am-5.30pm Sat & Sun) Cambridge's oldest bakery has a soft, doughy place in the hearts of generations of students. Its stock-in-trade is sticky Chelsea buns and cream teas (available to eat in or beautifully boxed to take away), but it also serves upmarket sandwiches, bacon rolls, English breakfasts and salads.

There's a smaller **branch** (www.fitzbillies.com; 36 Bridge St; light mains £5-15; 8.30am-5pm Mon-Fri, 9am-6pm Sat & Sun) on Bridge St.

Espresso Library — Cafe £

(01223-367333; www.espressolibrary.com; 210 East Rd; mains £6-15; 8am-4pm;) Customers with laptops at almost every table send a signal that this industrial-chic cafe is a student favourite. Thank the coffee, the cyclist-friendly attitude, and the wholesome food – sourdough sandwiches, soups, frittata and shaksuka.

Pint Shop — Modern British ££

(01223-981070; www.pintshop.co.uk; 10 Peas Hill; 2/3 courses £22/26; noon-9pm Mon-Wed, to 10pm Thu-Sat, to 6pm Sun) Popular Pint Shop is part craft-beer sampling house, part hearty kitchen. Wash down tasty pub grub (charred salmon, burgers, flatbread kebabs) with artisan ciders, ales and fruit beers (including coconut, passionfruit and mango).

Cambridge Chop House — British ££

(01223-359506; www.cambscuisine.com/cambridge-chop-house; 1 King's Pde; mains £17-27; 11.30am-8.30pm Mon-Fri, to 9pm Fri & Sat, to 5pm Sun) The window seats here look right onto King's College and the food is pure English establishment: hearty steaks, grilled chops, breaded coley, roast meats and grilled lobster. Schedule a long walk afterwards to burn off the calories.

Smokeworks — Barbecue ££

(01223-365385; www.smokeworks.co.uk; 2 Free School Lane; mains £7.50-19.50; noon-8pm Mon & Tue, to 9pm Wed-Sat, to 5pm Sun;) This dark, industrial-looking dining room draws a young, hip crowd of carnivores with melt-in-your-mouth rib racks, wings and wonderfully smoky pulled pork. For drinks, try the house beers or salted-caramel milkshakes in glasses the size of your head.

Midsummer House — Modern British £££

(01223-369299; www.midsummerhouse.co.uk; Midsummer Common; set lunch/tasting menu

Eagle pub

£115/230; ⏲10am-5pm Wed-Sat) A lone house in parkland beside the Granta, the region's top table shows off the culinary creativity of chef Daniel Clifford, recipient of two Michelin stars. Set menus, which include champagne and hot infusions or coffee, might include such delights as salted beetroot with venison tartare and buttermilk poached Cornish cod with champagne beurre blanc.

DRINKING & NIGHTLIFE

Roof Terrace Bar

(☎01223-306030; www.thevarsityhotel.co.uk; Varsity Hotel, Thompson's Lane; ⏲2pm-10pm Mon-Thu, from noon Fri & Sat) The rooftop terrace at the **Varsity Hotel** (☎01223-306030; www.thevarsityhotel.co.uk; Thompson's Lane; d £190-325; ❄@📶) is an achingly cool eyrie perched high above the old town, and people flood here every afternoon for sundowners looking out over the rooftops. Smart dress recommended.

Cambridge Brew House Microbrewery

(☎01223-855185; www.thecambridgebrewhouse.com; 1 King St; ⏲4-10pm Mon-Fri, noon-11pm Sat, noon-10pm Sun) Order a pint here and there's a good chance it'll have been brewed in the gleaming vats beside the bar. Add a buzzy vibe, eclectic upcycled decor, dirty burgers and British tapas (mains from £10) and you have the kind of pub you wish was just down your road.

Eagle Pub

(☎01223-505020; www.eagle-cambridge.co.uk; Bene't St; ⏲11am-11pm Mon-Thu, to midnight Fri & Sat, to 10.30pm Sun; 📶👪) Cambridge's most famous pub has loosened the tongues of many an illustrious academic, among them Nobel Prize–winning scientists Crick and Watson, who discussed their research into DNA here. The interior is 15th-century, wood-panelled and rambling; note the WWII airmen's signatures on the ceiling.

ENTERTAINMENT

Live entertainment ground to a halt during the pandemic, but the following venues were expected to reopen in 2021.

ADC Theatre

(01223-300085; www.adctheatre.com; Park St) This famous student-run theatre is home to the university's Footlights comedy troupe, whose past members include Emma Thompson, Rowan Atkinson and Stephen Fry.

Cambridge Arts Theatre Theatre

(01223-503333; www.cambridgeartstheatre.com; 6 St Edward's Passage) Cambridge's biggest bona-fide theatre hosts everything from highbrow drama and dance, to panto and shows fresh from London's West End.

INFORMATION

Visit Cambridge (www.visitcambridge.org) Closed during the pandemic, along with the tourist office in the guildhall on Peas Hill. it's likely to reopen, but in the meantime, brochures on local attractions can be picked up at cafes, tourist sights and the train station.

GETTING AROUND

Bicycle Cambridge is incredibly bike-friendly. **S&G Cycles** (01223-311134; 15 Laundress Lane; per hour/day from £7/18; 9am-4pm Mon-Sat, from 11am Sun) is handily central, near the Silver St bridge, but there's a bigger selection of bikes at **Rutland Cycling** (0330-555 0080; www.rutlandcycling.com; Corn Exchange St; per half-day/day from £12/18; 8am-5pm Mon-Fri, 9am-5pm Sat, 10am-4pm Sun) under the Grand Arcade shopping centre, with another **branch** (01223-352728; www.rutlandcycling.com; 156 Great Northern Rd; per half-day/day from £12/18; 8am-5pm Mon-Fri, 9am-5pm Sat, 10am-4pm Sun) just off Station Rd at the train station.

Bus The main bus hub is the **Drummer St bus station** (Drummer St). Routes C1, C3 and C7 stop at the train station. A city Dayrider ticket (£4.50) provides 24 hours of unlimited bus travel around Cambridge.

Ely

A £4.70, 20-minute train ride from Cambridge, historic Ely is dominated by the Gothic towers of **Ely Cathedral** (01353-667735; www.elycathedral.org; The Gallery; adult/child £8/free; 10am-4pm Mon-Sat, 1-3.30pm Sun), whose medieval Lady Chapel still bears the scars left by Puritan iconoclasts during the English Civil War. Nearby is the home of Oliver Cromwell, who led the revolution against the monarchy and ordered the execution of Charles I; it's now an interesting **museum** (01353-662062; www.olivercromwellshouse.co.uk; 29 St Mary's St; adult/child £5.20/3.50; 10am-5pm Apr-Oct, 11am-4pm Nov-Mar). Pause for a snack lunch with an ecclesiastical view at **The Almonry** (01353-666360; off High St; cream tea £6, light meals from £7; 9am-4pm Mon-Sat, from 11am Sun) behind the cathedral.

PHOTOGRAPHY BY PAULGMCCABE/GETTY IMAGES ©

PEDESTRIAN
ZONE

YORKSHIRE

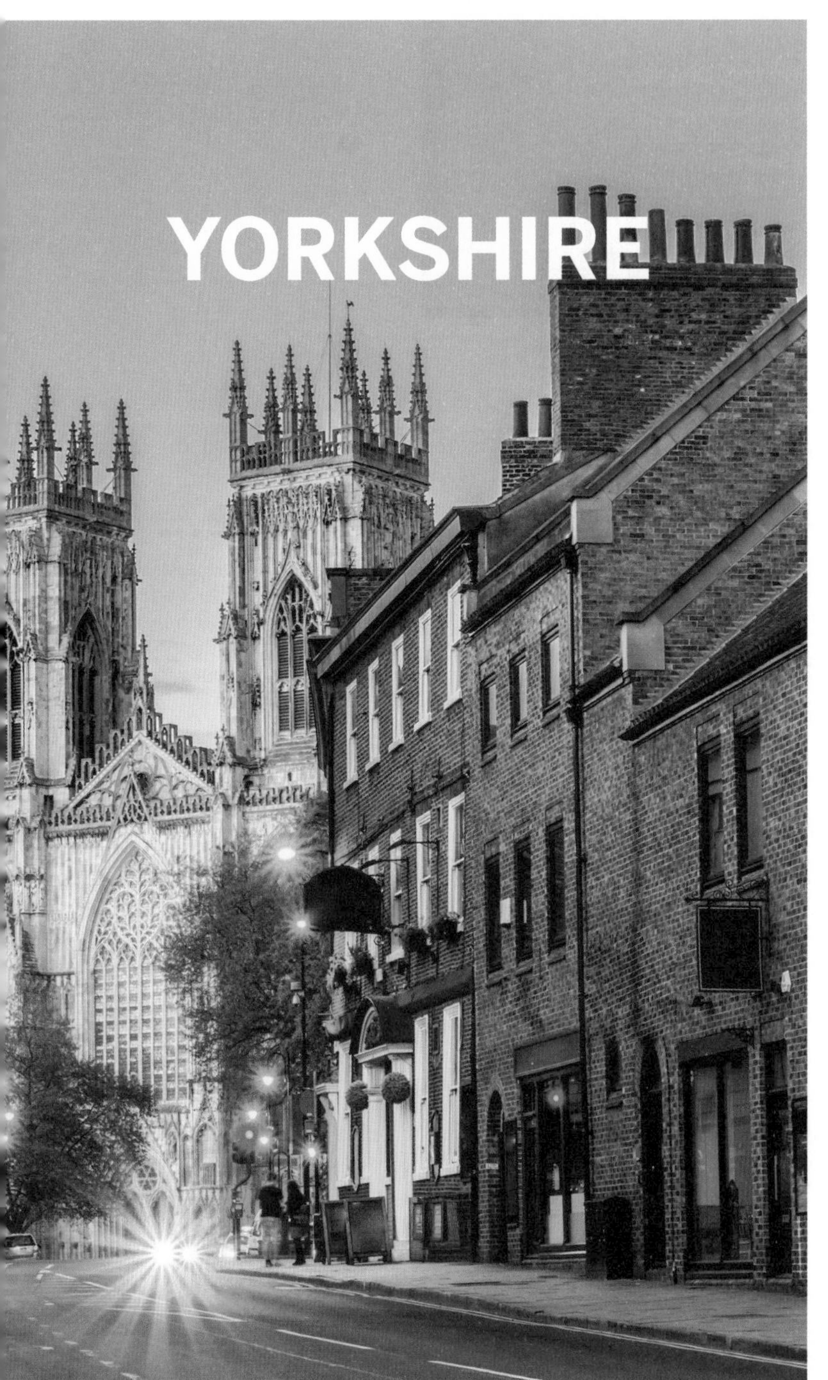

In this Chapter

Yorkshire at a Glance...

No other city in northern England says 'medieval' quite like York, where a magnificent circuit of 13th-century walls encloses an enchanting spider's web of narrow streets. At its heart lies the immense, awe-inspiring York Minster, one of the most beautiful Gothic cathedrals in the world. On York's outskirts is Castle Howard, one of England's most impressive stately homes, and further out you can find the region's wild heart: the brooding Yorkshire dales and moors.

Two Days in Yorkshire

Be awed by **York Minster** (p178) on day one, then tour the **city walls**. Make for **Hairy Fig** (p188) for foodie treats. On day two, head to marvellous **Castle Howard** (p176) and join the peacocks in the grounds. After a detour to **Kirkham Priory** (p177), dine in fine style at **Cochon Aveugle** (p189).

Four Days in Yorkshire

On day three visit **Jorvik** (p182), the **National Railway Museum** (p182), and ancient alleyways galore. Go **ghost hunting** (p185) in the evening, then recover at the **Blue Bell** (p189). Day four, experience Yorkshire's wild, wind-whipped beauty by hiking the moors or **dales** – you'll have earned that supper at **Chopping Block** (p188).

Previous page: York street and York Minster (p178)

DAVID IONUT/SHUTTERSTOCK ©

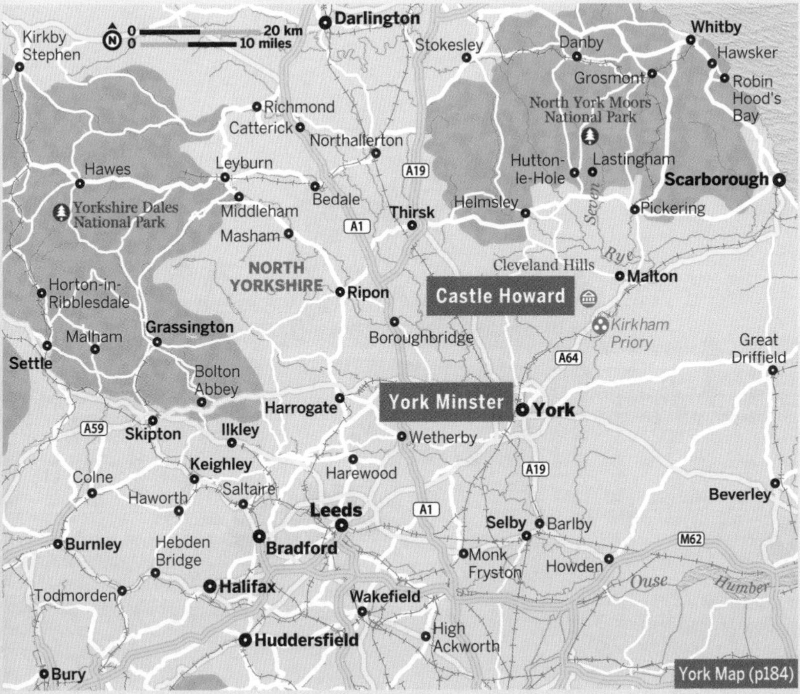

York Map (p184)

Arriving in Yorkshire

Bus Buses are slower than trains, but cheaper – three services shuttle between York and London daily (from £30, 5½ hours).

Car Unless your hotel has parking, a car can be a pain in the city.

Train York has frequent, fast and direct services to many British cities – London King's Cross is two hours away (£57.50, every half-hour).

Where to Stay

Beds can be hard to find in York in midsummer. The tourist office's booking service charges £4, which can be money well spent. City-centre prices are higher, but there are plenty of decent B&Bs on the streets north and south of Bootham. Southwest of the centre, B&Bs are around Scarcroft, Southlands and Bishopthorpe Rds.

Castle Howard

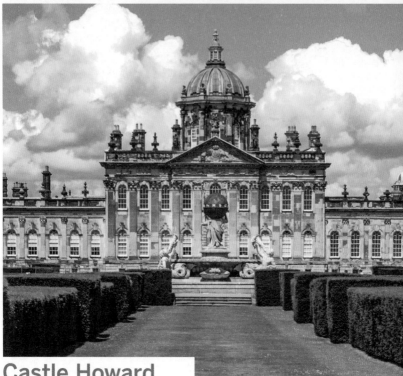

EDWARD HAYLAN/SHUTTERSTOCK ©

Castle Howard

You'll have to try pretty damn hard to find a home as breathtakingly stately as Castle Howard, a work of theatrical grandeur and audacity set in the rolling Howardian Hills.

Great For...

☑ Don't Miss

The Pre-Raphaelite stained glass in Castle Howard's ornate chapel.

Welcome to one of the world's most beautiful buildings, instantly recognisable from its starring role as Sebastian Flyte's home in both screen versions of Evelyn Waugh's 1945 paean to the English aristocracy, *Brideshead Revisited*. Admission is by pre-booked ticket only.

Construction

When the Earl of Carlisle hired his pal Sir John Vanbrugh to design his new home in 1699, he was hiring a man without formal training and best known as a playwright. Luckily, Vanbrugh hired Nicholas Hawksmoor, who had worked as Christopher Wren's clerk of works. Hawksmoor played a big part in the house's design, and he and Vanbrugh later worked wonders with Blenheim Palace. The house is still home to the Hon Nicholas Howard, who can often be seen around the place.

Temple of the Four Winds

MELISSAMATSU/BUDGET TRAVEL ©

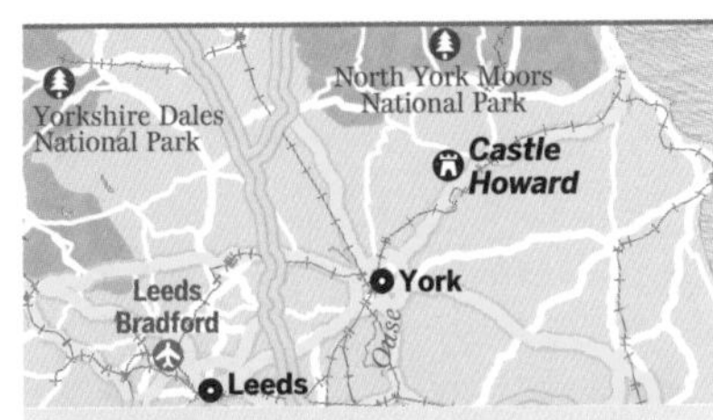

Need to Know

01653-648333; www.castlehoward.co.uk; YO60 7DA; adult/child house & grounds £22/12, grounds only £12.95/8.50; house 10am-2pm Wed, Fri & Sat, grounds to 5.30pm daily, pre-booked tickets only; P

Take a Break

Castle Howard has its own cafe, or head to the nearby Stone Trough Inn.

★ Top Tip

Try to visit on a weekday, when a quieter Castle Howard has even more atmosphere.

The House & Grounds

Vanbrugh and Hawksmoor created a hedonistic mix of art, architecture, landscaping and natural beauty. The great baroque house with its magnificent central cupola – the first on a domestic building in England – is full of treasures, including the breathtaking Great Hall with its soaring Corinthian pilasters.

The entrance courtyard has a good cafe, a gift shop and a lovely farm shop. As you wander around grounds patrolled by peacocks, views open up over Vanbrugh's playful Temple of the Four Winds, Hawksmoor's stately mausoleum and the distant hills.

Getting There & Away

Castle Howard is 15 miles northeast of York, off the A64. Ask at the tourist office (p191) about organised tours from York, or take bus 181 (£10 return, one hour, four daily Monday to Saturday year-round).

What's Nearby

Kirkham Priory Ruins

(EH; www.english-heritage.org.uk; Kirkham; adult/child £5/3; 10am-5pm Wed-Sun; P) The picturesque ruins of Kirkham Priory rise gracefully above the banks of the River Derwent, sporting medieval floor tiles and an impressive 13th-century gatehouse (through which you'll enter) encrusted with heraldic symbols.

Stone Trough Inn Pub Food ££

(01653-618713; www.thestonetroughinn.com; Kirkham; mains £13-21; food served noon-9pm; P) This lovely country inn is full of cosy nooks, with exposed stone walls, timber beams and open fires, and serves gourmet-style pub classics (eg fish and chips, steak pie with peas and gravy) with Yorkshire beers on tap. The outdoor terrace has views over the Derwent valley above Kirkham Priory. Three-course Sunday carvery lunch is £19.

York Minster

Vast, medieval York Minster is one of the world's most beautiful Gothic buildings. Seat of the archbishop of York, it is second in importance only to Canterbury, and York's long history and rich heritage is woven into virtually every brick and beam. If you visit only one English cathedral, York Minster will not disappoint.

Great For...

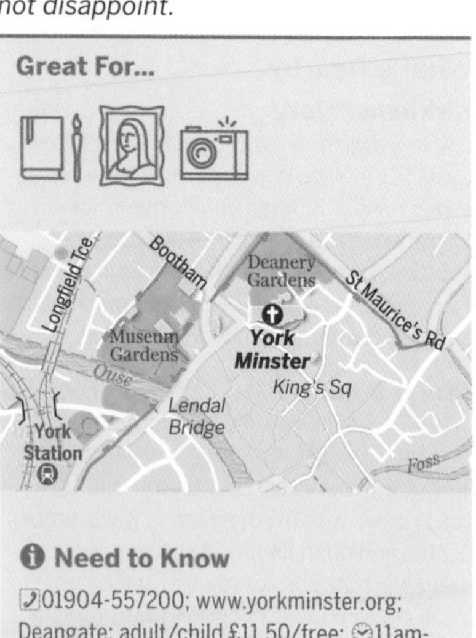

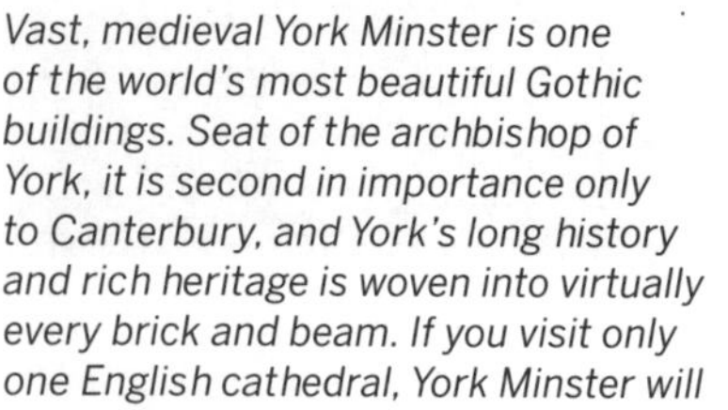

Need to Know

01904-557200; www.yorkminster.org; Deangate; adult/child £11.50/free; 11am-4.30pm Mon-Thu, from 10am Fri & Sat, 12.30-2.30pm Sun

★ **Top Tip**

The YorkPass (one/three days £48/80) provides entry into 30 sights, including York Minster, Jorvik and Castle Howard.

CHRISHEPBURN/GETTY IMAGES ©

Early History

The first church on this site was a wooden chapel built for the baptism of King Edwin of Northumbria on Easter Day 627. It was replaced with a stone church built on the site of a Roman basilica, parts of which can be seen in the foundations – as can fragments of the first 11th-century Norman minster.

Later History

The current minster, built mainly between 1220 and 1480, manages to encompass all the major stages of Gothic architectural development. The transepts (1220–55) were built in Early English style; the octagonal chapter house (1260–90) and nave (1291–1340) in the Decorated style; and the west towers, west front and central (or lantern) tower (1470–72) in Perpendicular style.

Nave

Entrance to the minster is via the west door, which leads into a tall, wide nave lined with painted stone shields of nobles. Also note the dragon's head projecting from the gallery – it's a crane believed to have been used to lift a font cover. There are several fine windows dating from the early 14th century, but the most impressive is the Great West Window (1338) above the entrance, with its beautiful heart-shaped stone tracery.

Transepts & Chapter House

The south transept is dominated by the exquisite Rose Window commemorating the union of the royal houses of Lancaster and York, through the marriage of Henry VII and Elizabeth of York, which ended the Wars of the Roses and began the Tudor dynasty.

Chapter House ceiling in York Minster

Opposite, in the north transept, is the magnificent Five Sisters Window, with five lancets over 15m high. This is the minster's oldest complete window; most of its tangle of coloured glass dates from around 1250. Just beyond it to the right is the 13th-century chapter house, a fine example of the Decorated style. Sinuous and intricately carved stonework – there are more than 200 expressive carved heads and figures – surrounds an airy, uninterrupted space.

☑ Don't Miss

Climbing York Minster's massive tower (£5). It can get busy on the stairs, but the 275 steps lead to unparalleled city views.

PHIL MACD PHOTOGRAPHY/SHUTTERSTOCK ©

Choir Screen & East Window

Separating the choir from the nave is a superb 15th-century choir screen with 15 statues depicting the kings of England from William I to Henry VI. Behind the high altar is the huge Great East Window (1405). At 23.7m by 9.4m – roughly the size of a tennis court – it's the world's largest medieval stained-glass window and the cathedral's single most important treasure. Needless to say, its epic size matches the epic theme depicted within: the beginning and end of the world as described in Genesis and the Book of Revelations.

Undercroft

A set of stairs in the south transept leads down to the undercroft (open 10am to 4.15pm Monday to Saturday, 1pm to 3pm Sunday), the very bowels of the building. In 1967 the minster foundations were shored up when the central tower threatened to collapse; archaeologists uncovered Roman and Norman remains including a Roman culvert, still carrying water to the Ouse. An interactive exhibition here, *York Minster Revealed,* leads you through 2000 years of history on the site of the cathedral. The nearby treasury houses 11th-century artefacts including relics from the graves of medieval archbishops.

Crypt

The crypt, entered from the choir close to the altar, contains fragments from the Norman cathedral, including the font showing King Edwin's baptism, which also marks the site of the original wooden chapel. Look out for the Doomstone, a 12th-century carved stone showing a scene from the Last Judgement with demons casting doomed souls into Hell.

✕ Take a Break

The laid-back, music-themed **Café Concerto** (☎01904-610478; www.cafeconcerto.biz; 21 High Petergate; lunch £6-9, dinner £12-15; ⏰9am-9pm) is just a few paces away from York Minster, ready to feed you from breakfast through to dinner.

York

SIGHTS

National Railway Museum Museum

(www.railwaymuseum.org.uk; Leeman Rd; ⏲10am-5pm Wed-Sun; P 👪) FREE York's National Railway Museum – the biggest in the world, with more than 100 locomotives – is well presented and crammed with fascinating stuff. It is laid out on a vast scale and housed in a series of giant railway sheds – allow at least two hours to do it justice. The museum also now includes a high-tech simulator experience of riding on the **Mallard** (£3), which set the world speed record for a steam locomotive in 1938 (126mph). Pre-booking only.

Jorvik Viking Centre Museum

(☎ticket reservations 01904-615505; www.jorvikvikingcentre.co.uk; Coppergate; adult/child £12.50/8.50, with Barley Hall £15/10, with Dig £15.50/12, 3-site ticket £18/12.50; ⏲10am-5pm Apr-Oct, to 4pm Nov-Mar) Interactive multimedia exhibits aimed at bringing history to life often achieve exactly the opposite, but the much-hyped Jorvik manages to pull it off with aplomb. It's a smells-and-all reconstruction of the Viking settlement unearthed here during excavations in the late 1970s, experienced via a 'time-car' monorail that transports you through 9th-century Jorvik (the Viking name for York). Book your timed-entry tickets online.

Barley Hall Historic Building

(☎01904-615505; www.barleyhall.co.uk; 2 Coffee Yard; adult/child £6.50/3.50, with Jorvik £15/10, with Dig £10/7.75, 3-site ticket £18/12.50; ⏲10am-5pm Apr-Oct, to 4pm Nov-Mar) This restored medieval townhouse, tucked down an alleyway, includes a permanent exhibition of life in the times of Henry VIII. It was once the home of York's Lord Mayor. The centrepiece is a double-height banquet hall decorated with the Yorkshire rose – peek at it through a window in the alleyway if you don't want to pay to enter.

Yorkshire Museum Museum

(www.yorkshiremuseum.org.uk; Museum St; adult/child £8/free; ⏲10am-5pm) Most of York's Roman archaeology is hidden

York Castle Museum

beneath the medieval city, so the superb displays in the Yorkshire Museum are invaluable if you want to get an idea of what Eboracum Roman York was like. There are maps and models, funerary monuments, mosaic floors and wall paintings, and a 4th-century bust of Emperor Constantine. Kids will enjoy the dinosaur exhibit, centred on giant ichthyosaur fossils from Yorkshire's Jurassic Coast.

The Shambles Street

The Shambles takes its name from the Saxon word *shamel,* meaning 'slaughterhouse' – in 1862 there were 26 butcher shops on this street. Today the butchers are long gone, but this narrow cobbled lane, lined with 15th-century Tudor buildings that overhang so much they seem to meet above your head, is the most picturesque in Britain, and one of the most visited in Europe, often filled with visitors wielding cameras.

York Castle Museum Museum

(www.yorkcastlemuseum.org.uk; Tower St; adult/child £10/free; ⏲guided tour only, 10am-4pm Thu-Sun) This excellent museum has displays of everyday life through the centuries, with reconstructed domestic interiors, a Victorian street and a prison cell where you can try out a condemned man's bed – and it could be that of highwayman Dick Turpin (imprisoned here before being hanged in 1739). For the time being all visits are by pre-booked guided tour only.

There's a bewildering array of evocative objects from the past 400 years, gathered together by a certain Dr Kirk from the 1920s onwards for fear the items would become obsolete and disappear completely.

Merchant Adventurers' Hall Historic Building

(☎01904-654818; www.merchantshallyork.org; Fossgate; adult/child £6.50/free; ⏲10am-4.30pm Sun-Fri, to 1.30pm Sat) York's most impressive semi-timbered building is still owned by the fraternity that built it almost 650 years ago and it is the oldest surviving guildhall of its kind in Britain. The owner was originally a religious fraternity and one of the hall's chambers is still a chapel, but the building's name refers to the pioneering business exploits that made the fraternity's fortunes while 'adventuring' their money in overseas markets at a time when York was an important international port.

York's City Walls

Don't miss the chance to walk York's City Walls (www.yorkwalls.org.uk), which follow the line of the original Roman walls and give a whole new perspective on the city. Allow 1½ to two hours for the full circuit of 4.5 miles.

Start and finish in the Museum Gardens or at **Bootham Bar** (on the site of a Roman gate), where an exhibit provides some historical context, and travel clockwise. Highlights include **Monk Bar**, which is the best-preserved medieval gate and still has a working portcullis, and **Walmgate Bar**, England's only city gate with an intact barbican.

LEONID ANDRONOV/SHUTTERSTOCK ©

TOURS

Brewtown Brewery

(☎01904-636666; www.brewtowntours.co.uk; £70; ⏲11.30am-5pm) These craft-brewery minivan tours are a fuss-free way to get behind the scenes at Yorkshire's smaller breweries, some of which only open to the public for these tours. Owner Mark runs different routes (around York, Malton or Leeds) depending on the day of the week;

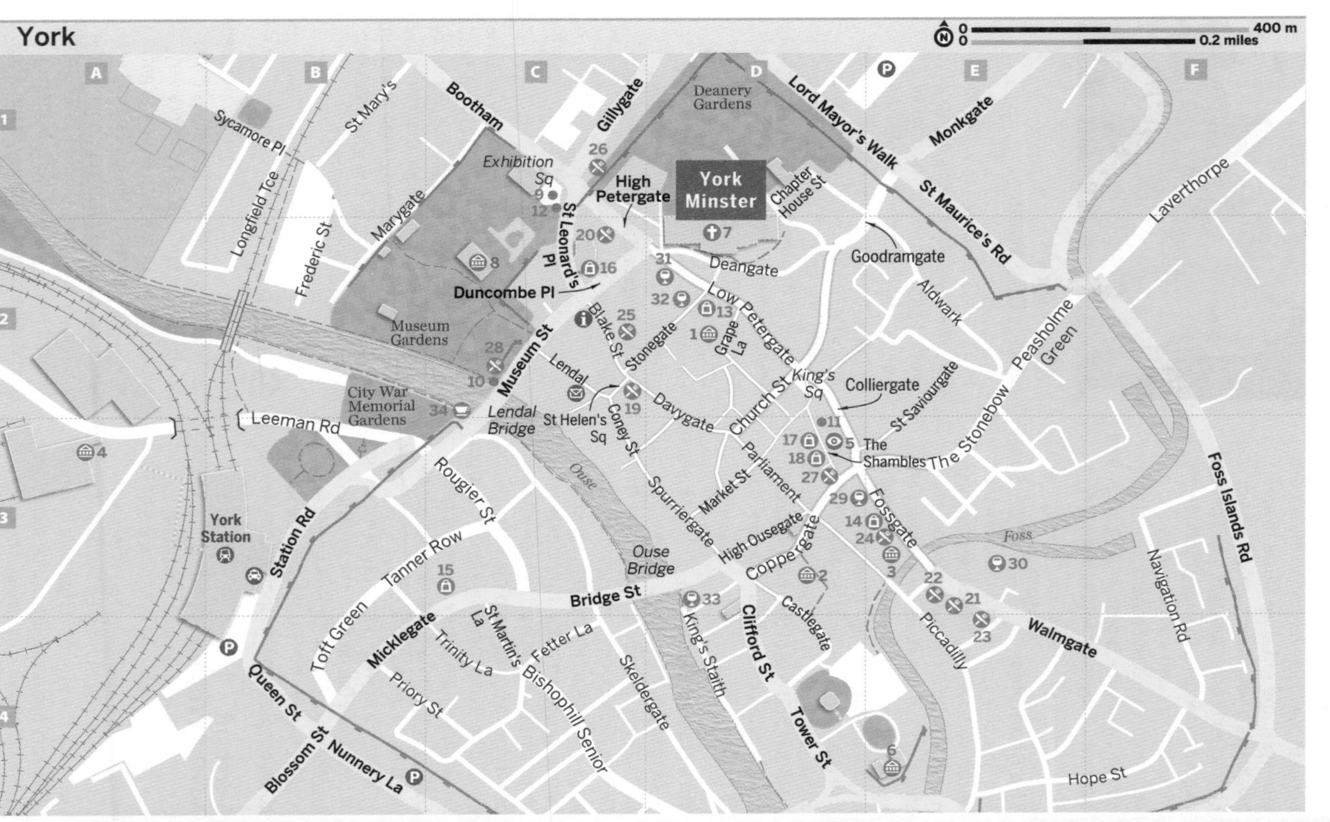
York
0
0
400 m
0.2 miles
A
B
C
D
E
F
1
2
3
4
Sycamore Pl
St Mary's
Bootham
Gillygate
Deanery Gardens
Lord Mayor's Walk
Monkgate
St Maurice's Rd
Lawrence St
Longfield Tce
Frederic St
Marygate
Exhibition Sq
High Petergate
York Minster
Chapter House St
Goodramgate
St Leonard's Pl
Duncombe Pl
Deangate
Low Petergate
Aldwark
Peasholme Green
Museum Gardens
Museum St
Blake St
Stonegate
Grape La
King's Sq
Colliergate
St Saviourgate
The Stonebow
Lendal
City War Memorial Gardens
Lendal Bridge
Leeman Rd
St Helen's Sq
Coney St
Davygate
Church St
The Shambles
Parliament St
Market St
Spurriergate
Fossgate
Foss
Foss Islands Rd
Navigation Rd
Ouse
Rougier St
York Station
Station Rd
Tanner Row
Ouse Bridge
High Ousegate
Coppergate
Bridge St
Toft Green
Micklegate
St Martin's La
Trinity La
Fetter La
Bishophill Senior
Priory St
Skeldergate
King's Staith
Clifford St
Castlegate
Piccadilly
Walmgate
Tower St
Queen St
Blossom St
Nunnery La
Hope St
1
2
3
4
5
6
7
8
9
10
11
12
13
14
15
16
17
18
19
20
21
22
23
24
25
26
27
28
29
30
31
32
33
34

York

Sights

1 Barley Hall ... D2
2 Jorvik Viking Centre ... D3
3 Merchant Adventurers' Hall ... E3
4 National Railway Museum ... A3
5 The Shambles ... D3
6 York Castle Museum ... E4
7 York Minster ... D2
8 Yorkshire Museum ... C2

Activities, Courses & Tours

9 Association of Voluntary Guides ... C1
10 City Cruises York ... C2
11 Ghost Hunt of York ... D3
12 York Citysightseeing ... C1

Shopping

13 Antiques Centre ... D2
14 Fossgate Books ... E3
15 Ken Spelman Booksellers ... C3
16 Red House ... C2
17 Shambles Market ... D3
18 The Shop That Must Not Be Named ... D3

Eating

19 Bettys ... C2
20 Café Concerto ... C2
21 Cave du Cochon ... E3
22 Chopping Block at Walmgate Ale House ... E3
23 Cochon Aveugle ... E4
24 Hairy Fig ... E3
25 Mannion & Co ... C2
26 No 8 Bistro ... C1
27 Shambles Kitchen ... D3
28 Star Inn the City ... C2

Drinking & Nightlife

29 Blue Bell ... D3
30 Brew York ... E3
31 Guy Fawkes Inn ... D2
32 House of Trembling Madness ... D2
33 King's Arms ... D3
34 Perky Peacock ... C2

each tour visits three breweries with tastings along the way, and sometimes even beer-pairing nibbles.

City Cruises York Boating

(www.citycruisesyork.com; Lendal Bridge; adult/child from £10.50/6; tours 10.30am, noon, 1.30pm & 3pm;) These hour-long cruises on the River Ouse depart from King's Staith and, 10 minutes later, Lendal Bridge. Special lunch, afternoon-tea and evening cruises are also offered. You can buy tickets on board or book at the office by Lendal Bridge.

York Citysightseeing Bus

(www.city-sightseeing.com; day ticket adult/child £16/9; 9am-4.30pm Easter-Nov, reduced service rest of yr) Hop-on, hop-off route with 20 stops, calling at all the main sights. Buses leave every 12 to 30 minutes from Exhibition Sq near York Minster.

Ghost Hunt of York Walking

(01904-608700; www.ghosthunt.co.uk; adult/child £10/6.66; tours 6pm & 7.30pm) The kids will just love this award-winning and highly entertaining 75-minute tour laced with authentic ghost stories. It begins on the Shambles, whatever the weather (it's never cancelled), and there's no need to book – just turn up and wait till you hear the handbell ringing...

Association of Voluntary Guides Walking

(www.avgyork.co.uk; tours 10.15am & 1.15pm year-round, 6.15pm Jun-Aug) FREE Free two-hour walking tours of the city, setting out from Exhibition Sq in front of York Art Gallery.

SHOPPING

Coney St, Davygate and the adjoining streets are the hub of York's city-centre shopping scene, but the real treats are the secondhand bookshops, and antique, bric-a-brac and independent shops to be found along Gillygate, Colliergate, Fossgate and Micklegate.

Antiques Centre Antiques

(www.theantiquescentreyork.co.uk; 41 Stonegate; 9.30am-5.30pm Mon-Sat, to 4pm Sun) A Georgian town house with a veritable maze of rooms and corridors, showcasing the wares of about 120 dealers selling everything from lapel pins and snuffboxes

Yorkshire Afternoon Tea

For old-school afternoon tea, with white-aproned waiters, linen tablecloths and a teapot collection ranged along the walls, come to **Bettys** (01904-659142; www.bettys.co.uk; 6-8 St Helen's Sq; mains £6-14, afternoon tea £18.50; 9am-7pm;). The house speciality is the Yorkshire Fat Rascal, a huge fruit scone smothered in melted butter, while breakfast and lunch dishes, like bacon and raclette rösti, and Yorkshire rarebit, show off Betty's Swiss-Yorkshire heritage. No bookings, but be prepared to queue.

JASON BATTERHAM/GETTY IMAGES ©

to oil paintings and longcase clocks. And the house is haunted as well...

Shambles Market Food

(www.shamblesmarket.com; The Shambles; 9am-5pm) Yorkshire cheeses, Whitby fish and local meat make good fodder for self-caterers at this anything-goes market behind the Shambles, which also touts arts, crafts and Yorkshire flat caps. The food-court section near where the Shambles joins Pavement is a good spot for cheap eats, coffee and ice-cream at picnic tables.

Red House Antiques

(www.redhouseyork.co.uk; Duncombe Pl; 9.30am-5.30pm Mon-Fri, to 6pm Sat, 10.30am-5pm Sun) The goods of about 60 antiques dealers are displayed in 10 showrooms spread over two floors, with items ranging from jewellery and porcelain to clocks and furniture.

Ken Spelman Booksellers Books

(www.kenspelman.com; 70 Micklegate; 9am-5.30pm Mon-Sat) This fascinating shop has been selling rare, antiquarian and secondhand books since 1947. With an open fire crackling in the grate in winter, it's a browser's paradise.

The Shop That Must Not Be Named Gifts & Souvenirs

(30 The Shambles; 10am-6pm) This shop on the Shambles – the street said to be the inspiration for Diagon Alley – has everything to cast a spell over Harry Potter fans. Wands? Tick. Quidditch fan gear? Tick. Potions? Tick. Pure magic for muggles. There's now no less than three Potter shops on the Shambles, but this is the original and still the most convincing.

Fossgate Books Books

(01904-641389; fossgatebooks@hotmail.co.uk; 36 Fossgate; 10am-5.30pm Mon-Sat) A classic, old-school secondhand bookshop, with towers of books on the floor and a maze of floor-to-ceiling shelves crammed with titles covering every subject under the sun, from crime fiction and popular paperbacks to arcane academic tomes and first editions.

EATING

Eating well in York is not a problem – there are plenty of fine options throughout the city centre, from high-quality takeaway food to some of the most inventive cuisine in the country; most pubs also serve food.

Mannion & Co Cafe, Bistro £

(01904-631030; www.mannionandco.co.uk; 1 Blake St; mains £7-14; 10am-4pm Sun-Mon & Wed-Thu, 9am-4pm Fri-Sat) Expect to queue for a table at this busy bistro (no reservations), with its convivial atmosphere and selection of delicious daily specials. Regulars on the menu include eggs Benedict for breakfast, a chunky Yorkshire rarebit (cheese on toast) made with home-baked bread, and lunch platters of cheese and charcuterie. Oh, and pavlova for pudding.

The Shambles

York Festivals

Jorvik Viking Festival (www.jorvik-viking-festival.co.uk; mid-Feb) For a week in mid-February, York is invaded by Vikings as part of this festival, which features battle re-enactments, themed walks, markets and other bits of Viking-related fun.

York Christmas (www.visityork.org/whats-on/christmas; Dec) Kicking off with St Nicholas Fayre market in late November, the run-up to Christmas is an extravaganza of street decorations, market stalls, ice-skating, carol singers and mulled wine.

York Food Festival (www.yorkfoodfestival.com; late Sep) A 10-day celebration of all that's good to eat and drink in Yorkshire, with food stalls, tastings, a beer tent, cookery demonstrations and more. The main event is in late September, but there's a small taster festival in June and a chocolate festival on Easter weekend.

MAXINEA/SHUTTERSTOCK ©

Hairy Fig Cafe £

(01904-677074; www.thehairyfig.co.uk; 39 Fossgate; mains £6-12; 9am-4.30pm Mon-Sat) This cafe-deli is a standout in York. On the one side you have the best of Yorkshire tripping over the best of Europe, with Italian white anchovies and truffle-infused olive oil stacked alongside York honey mead and baked pies; on the other you have a Dickensian-style sweet shop and backroom cafe serving dishes crafted from the deli.

Cave du Cochon Pizza £

(01904-633669; www.caveducochon.uk; 19 Walmgate; mains £7-10; 5-10pm Wed-Fri, noon-10pm Sat-Sun) New York–style sourdough pizza is the mainstay at this elegant wine bar – the sister business to the Cochon Aveugle (p189). It also serves some locally sourced charcuterie (£22) and cheese (£15) from one of the UK's very best producers, the Courtyard Dairy near Settle.

Shambles Kitchen Fast Food £

(01904-674684; www.shambleskitchen.co.uk; 28 The Shambles; mains £6.50-8; 11am-3.30pm Sun-Fri, to 4.30pm Sat;) Fast food doesn't mean unhealthy at this hugely popular little takeaway (there are only three tables inside). The place is best known for its pulled-pork sandwiches on sourdough bread, but there are also yummy wraps, daily specials such as Goan curry and Korean chicken, and a choice of freshly made veg juices and smoothies.

Chopping Block at Walmgate Ale House British ££

(www.thechoppingblock.co.uk; 25 Walmgate; mains £14-18; 5-10pm Tue-Fri, noon-10pm Sat, to 9pm Sun;) This restaurant above a pub wears its Yorkshire credentials with pride. Local produce underpins the menu, which turns out mainly meat dishes (lamb shoulder, confit of duck leg, pork belly), given a French-flavoured gourmet twist, that are fine examples of contemporary British cuisine. Vegetarian options include tasty dishes like pea pancakes with spiced cauliflower.

Star Inn the City British ££

(01904-619208; www.starinnthecity.co.uk; Lendal Engine House, Museum St; mains £16-25; 9.30-11.30am, noon-9.30pm Mon-Sat, to 7.30pm Sun;) Its riverside setting in a Grade II–listed engine house and quirky British menu make Andrew Pern's York outpost of the **Star Inn** (01439-770397; www.thestaratharome.co.uk; Harome, YO62 5JE; mains £18-34; noon-2pm Tue-Sat, 4.30-8.30pm Mon-Sat, noon-6.30pm Sun; P) an exceedingly pleasant place to while away the hours. Expect country-themed cosiness in winter, and dining out on the broad terrace in summer.

No 8 Bistro Bistro **££**
(01904-653074; www.cafeno8.co.uk; 8 Gillygate; dinner mains £17; noon-10pm Mon-Fri, 9am-10pm Sat & Sun;) A cool little place with modern artwork mimicking the Edwardian stained glass at the front, No 8 offers a day-long menu of top-notch bistro dishes using fresh local produce, such as Jerusalem artichoke risotto with fresh herbs, and Yorkshire lamb slow-cooked in hay and lavender. Booking recommended.

Cochon Aveugle French **£££**
(01904-640222; www.lecochonaveugle.uk; 37 Walmgate; 4-course lunch £75, 8-course tasting menu £95; 6-9pm Wed-Sat, noon-1.30pm Sat) Black-pudding macaroon? Salt-baked gurnard with lardo? Warm hen's yolk with smoked taramasalata? Fussy eaters beware – this small restaurant with huge ambition serves an ever-changing tasting menu (no à la carte) of infinite imagination and invention. You never know what will come next, except that it will be delicious. Bookings are essential. Its wine bar, Cave du Cochon (p188), is a few doors away.

DRINKING & NIGHTLIFE

The area around Ousegate and Micklegate can get a bit rowdy, especially at weekends. There are cocktail bars with outdoor seating on Swinegate Court (off Grape Lane).

Blue Bell Pub
(01904-654904; 53 Fossgate; 11am-11pm Mon-Thu, to midnight Fri & Sat, noon-10.30pm Sun;) This is what a proper English pub looks like – a tiny, 200-year-old wood-panelled room with a smouldering fireplace, decor untouched since 1903, a

Guy Fawkes Inn (p190)

Yorkshire's Moors & Dales

Yorkshire's varied landscape of wild hills, tranquil valleys, high moors and spectacular coastline offers plenty of opportunities for outdoor activities.

For shorter walks and rambles, the best area is the **Yorkshire Dales**, with a great selection of walks through scenic valleys or over wild hilltops, with a few higher summits thrown in for good measure. The East Riding's **Yorkshire Wolds** hold hidden delights, while the quiet valleys and dramatic, blustery coast of the **North York Moors** also offer sublime rambling opportunities.

DANIEL J. RAO/SHUTTERSTOCK ©

pile of ancient board games in the corner, friendly and efficient bar staff, and weekly cask-ale specials chalked on a board. Bliss, with froth on top – if you can get in (it's often full).

Guy Fawkes Inn Pub

(☎01904-466674; www.guyfawkesinnyork.com; 25 High Petergate; ⏰11am-11pm Mon-Thu & Sun, to midnight Fri & Sat) The man who famously plotted to blow up the Houses of Parliament and inspired Bonfire Night in the UK was born on this site in 1570. Walk through the lovely Georgian wood-panelled pub to find Guy Fawkes' grandmother's cottage at the far end of the back patio, watched over by a giant wall mural.

The inn also has live music on Sunday nights (from 8.30pm) and 13 hotel rooms.

Brew York Microbrewery

(☎01904-848448; www.brewyork.co.uk; Enterprise Complex, Walmgate; ⏰noon-11pm Tue-Sat, to 9pm Sun) Housed in a cavernous old warehouse, half the floor space in this craft brewery is occupied by giant brewing tanks while the rest is given over to simple wooden drinking benches and a bar with rotating keg and cask beers. At the far end of the brewery there's a small riverside terrace overlooking Rowntree Wharf.

House of Trembling Madness Bar

(☎01904-640009; www.tremblingmadness.co.uk; 48 Stonegate; ⏰10am-midnight Mon-Sat, from 11am Sun) When a place describes itself as a 'medieval drinking hall', it clearly deserves investigation. The ground floor and basement host an impressive shop stacked with craft beers, gins, vodkas and even absinthes; but head upstairs to the 1st floor and you'll find the secret drinking den – an ancient timber-framed room with high ceilings, a bar and happy drinkers.

Perky Peacock Cafe

(Lendal Bridge; ⏰7am-5pm Mon-Fri, 9am-5pm Sat, to 4pm Sun) One of York's charms is finding teeny places like this cafe, shoe-horned into historic buildings. In this case the host is a 14th-century, rotund watchtower crouched by the riverbank. Sup an excellent coffee under the ancient wood beams, or grab a street-side table for a tasty pastry.

King's Arms Pub

(☎01904-659435; King's Staith; ⏰noon-11pm Mon-Sat, to 10.30pm Sun) York's best-known pub enjoys a fabulous riverside location, with tables spilling out onto the quayside.

It's the perfect spot on a summer evening, but be prepared to share it with a few hundred other people.

INFORMATION

Post Office (22 Lendal, York; 9am-5.30pm Mon-Fri, to 4pm Sat)

York Tourist Office (01904-550099; www.visityork.org; 1 Museum St, YO1 7DT; 9am-5pm Mon-Sat, 10am-4pm Sun) Visitor and transport info for all of Yorkshire, plus accommodation bookings (for a small fee) and ticket sales.

GETTING AROUND

Central York is easy to get around on foot – you're never more than 20 minutes' walk from any of the major sights.

Bicycle You can rent bikes from **Cycle Heaven** (01904-622701; www.cycle-heaven.co.uk; York Railway Station, Station Rd; rental per 2/24hr £15/25; 8.30am-5.30pm Mon-Fri, 9am-5pm Sat year-round, 11am-4pm Sun May-Sep) at the train station for £25 per 24 hours. The tourist office has a useful free map showing York's cycle routes, or visit iTravel-York (www.itravelyork.info/cycling). Castle Howard (15 miles northeast of York via Haxby and Strensall) is an interesting destination, and there's also a section of the **Trans-Pennine Trail cycle path** (www.transpenninetrail.org.uk) from Bishopthorpe in York to Selby (15 miles) along the old railway line.

Taxi Station Taxis (01904-623332; www.yorkstationtaxis.co.uk; Train Station, Station Rd, York) has a kiosk outside the train station.

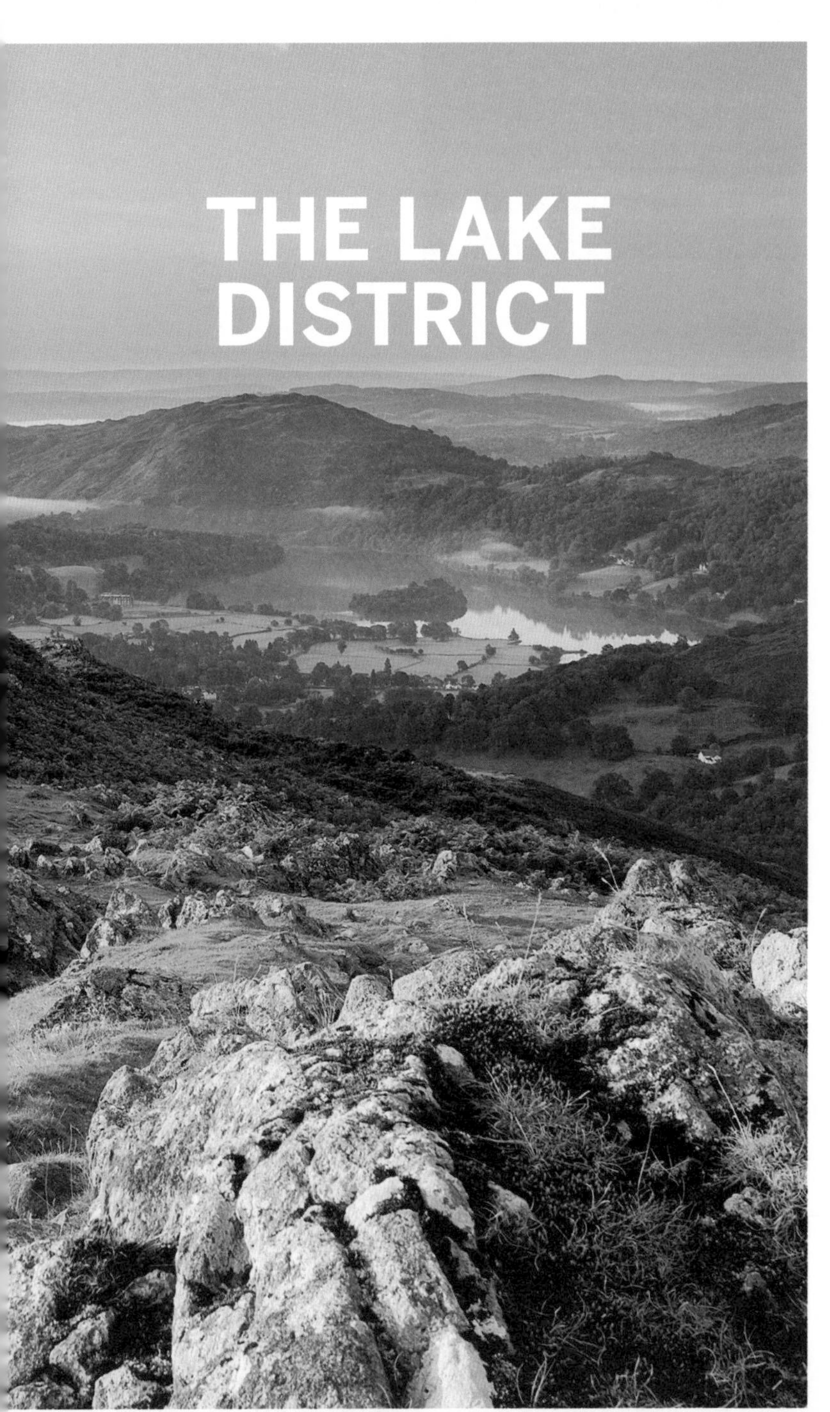

THE LAKE DISTRICT

In this Chapter

The Lake District at a Glance...

The Lake District (or Lakeland, as it's commonly known around these parts) is the UK's most popular national park, with 15 million people pitching up annually. Indeed, ever since the Romantic poets arrived in the 19th century, this postcard panorama of craggy hills and glittering lakes has been stirring the imagination. The region is awash with historic hikes, including the astounding Hadrian's Wall, and literary links to William Wordsworth, Arthur Ransome, Beatrix Potter and other writers.

Two Days in the Lake District

Begin your literary Lakes odyssey with Wordsworth: his **birthplace** (p198) and **cottage** (p198) (and the next-door Jerwood Museum) will do for starters, followed by a visit to his grave in the village churchyard. Day two and onto the poet's family **home** (p198) for more intriguing insights, then hike Lakeland scenery at **Helm Crag** (p205) before dropping by to **The Yan** (p205) for a slap-up supper.

Four Days in the Lake District

On day three it's time to switch writers. Beatrix Potter's **house** (p199) is bound to delight, then play at pirates by cruising (or sailing) **Coniston Water** (p199) – 'home' to Arthur Ransome's *Swallows and Amazons*. Day four sees you travelling back thousands of years as you head to **Housesteads** (p200) and **Vindolanda** (p201) to begin exploring the extraordinary Roman past at Hadrian's Wall.

Previous page: View from Helm Crag overlooking Grasmere (p205)
TRANQUILLIANI/GETTY IMAGES ©

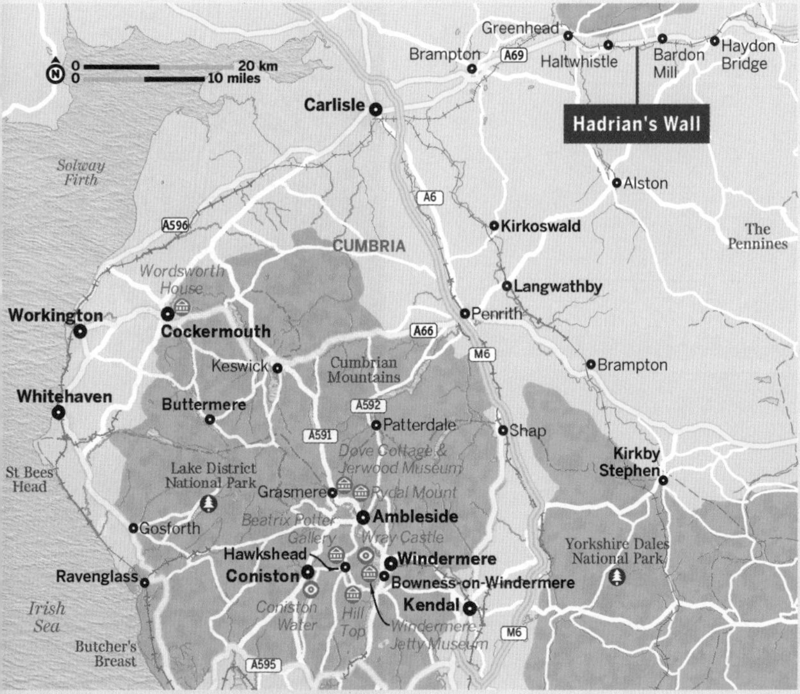

Arriving in the Lake District

Bus National Express coaches run direct from London Victoria and Glasgow to the key towns of Windermere and Kendal.

Car Windermere is 115 miles (2½ hours) northwest of York and 150 miles (three hours) south of Edinburgh.

Train To get to the Lake District via the main West Coast train line, change at Oxenholme for Windermere and Kendal.

Where to Stay

There's a huge range of places to stay in the Lake District: grand country hotels, country inns and boutique B&Bs – there's also a superb collection of hostels (both YHA and independent) and campsites.

Prices tend to be higher inside the national park's boundaries, however, and there are premiums in peak seasons such as Easter and over the summer school holidays.

Dove Cottage

The Lakes & Literature

In terms of natural splendour, few English places can compare to the Lake District. Its beauty has inspired poets and painters for centuries. The legacy is a landscape rich in links to writers who created world-famous Romantic poetry and some of the nation's best-loved children's tales. What's more, the key sites are all within a curving, scenic 45-mile drive.

Great For...

Need to Know

Brockhole National Park Visitor Centre (p204) is the Lake District's flagship visitor centre

★ Top Tip

Several key sights operate by timed ticket; book early and aim for late afternoons or weekdays.

D K GROVE/SHUTTERSTOCK ©

William Wordsworth

Wordsworth House

The Romantic poet was born in 1770 at this handsome Georgian **house** (NT; ☎01900-824805; www.nationaltrust.org.uk/wordsworth-house; Main St; adult/child £8.80/4.40; ⏲11am-5pm Sat-Thu Mar-Oct) in Cockermouth. Built around 1745, the house has been meticulously restored based on accounts from the Wordsworth archive: the kitchen, drawing room, study and bedrooms all look much as they would have to a young William. Costumed guides help bring things to life.

Dove Cottage

On the edge of Grasmere, around 30 miles southeast of Cockermouth, this tiny, creeper-clad **cottage** (☎01539-435544; www.wordsworth.org.uk; adult/child £9.50/4.50; ⏲9.30am-5.30pm Mar-Oct, 10am-4.30pm Nov, Dec & Feb) was famously inhabited by Wordsworth between 1799 and 1808. Its cramped rooms are full of artefacts: try to spot the poet's passport, a pair of his spectacles and a portrait (a gift from Sir Walter Scott) of his favourite dog, Pepper. An informative guided tour is included.

Entry includes the next-door **Jerwood Museum**, which has a significant Romantic-movement collection, including original manuscripts, letters and rare editions by leading Romantic figures.

Rydal Mount

Wordsworth's most famous Lake District residence is Dove Cottage, but he spent a great deal more time at **Rydal Mount** (☎01539-433002; www.rydalmount.co.uk; adult/child £7.50/4, grounds only £5; ⏲9.30am-5pm Apr-Oct, 11am-4pm Wed-Sun Nov, Dec, Feb & Mar). This was the Wordsworth family's home from 1813 until the

Hill Top

poet's death in 1850. You can wander freely around the library, dining room and drawing room; upstairs are the family bedrooms and Wordsworth's attic study, containing his encyclopaedia and a sword belonging to his brother John, who was lost at sea. Recently unveiled exhibits include the Wordsworth's family Bible and William's beloved walking sticks (complete with his silver crest).

Beatrix Potter

Hill Top

Just 9 miles south of Rydal Mount in the tiny village of Near Sawrey, the idyllic **farmhouse** (NT; ☎01539-436269; www.nationaltrust.org.uk/hill-top; garden adult/child £5/2.50; ⏰10am-5.30pm Jun-Aug, to 4.30pm Sat-Thu Apr, May, Sep & Oct, weekends only Nov-Mar) purchased in 1905 by Beatrix Potter was the inspiration for many of her tales: the house features in *Samuel Whiskers, Tom Kitten, Pigling Bland* and *Jemima Puddleduck*, and you might recognise the kitchen garden from *Peter Rabbit*. At the time of research, the house was closed due to Covid-19, but the garden was open for prebooked visits.

☑ Don't Miss

Rowing your own boat, and playing at pirates, on the bewitching lake that inspired the *Swallows and Amazons* children's tales.

PXL.STORE/SHUTTERSTOCK ©

Beatrix Potter Gallery

Potter was also a talented botanical painter and amateur naturalist. This small **gallery** (NT; www.nationaltrust.org.uk/beatrix-potter-gallery; Red Lion Sq; ⏰closed at time of research) in Hawkshead, in what were once the offices of Potter's husband, solicitor William Heelis, has a collection of her watercolours of local flora and fauna (she was particularly fascinated by mushrooms). The gallery celebrated Beatrix Potter's 150th birthday in 2016 with a special exhibition featuring extracts from the author's coded journal.

Arthur Ransome

Coniston's gleaming 5-mile lake, **Coniston Water**, around 6 miles west of Hill Top and the third largest in the Lake District, inspired Ransome's classic children's tale *Swallows and Amazons*. Peel Island, toward the southern end of the lake, supposedly provided the model for Wild Cat Island.

Cruise boats ply the waters; hire dinghies, rowing boats, kayaks and motorboats from the **Coniston Boating Centre** (☎01539-441366; www.conistonboatingcentre.co.uk; Coniston Jetty).

Take a Break

The cheery **Heidi's Cafe** (☎01539-435248; www.heidisgrasmerelodge.co.uk; Red Lion Sq; mains £4-8; ⏰9am-5.30pm) in the heart of Grasmere is a cute place for homemade soup or an indulgent slice of cake.

Ruins at Vindolanda Roman Fort

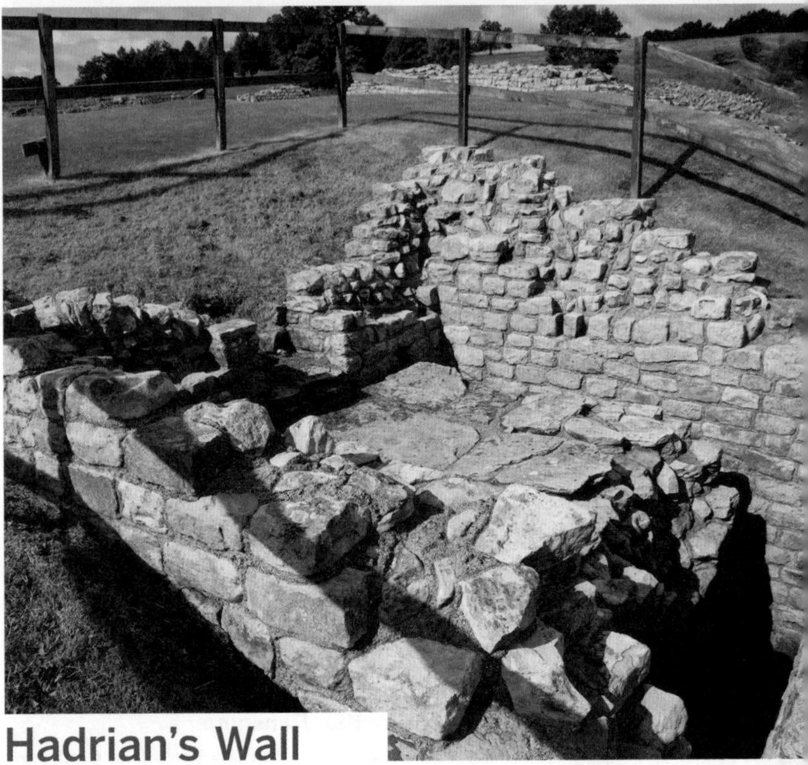

JAIME PHARR/SHUTTERSTOCK ©

Hadrian's Wall

Named in honour of the emperor who ordered its construction, the 73-mile-long Hadrian's Wall was one of Rome's greatest engineering projects, built right across Britain's narrow neck between 122 and 128 CE.

Great For...

☑ **Don't Miss**

The evocative Roman writing tablets on display at Vindolanda Fort.

Designed to separate Romans and Scottish Picts, the remaining sections of enormous Hadrian's Wall are testament to Roman ambition and tenacity.

Housesteads Roman Fort & Museum

The most dramatic site of Hadrian's Wall, and the best-preserved **Roman fort** (EH; 01434-344363; www.english-heritage.org.uk; Haydon Bridge; adult/child £9/5.40; 10am-6pm Apr-Sep, to 5pm Oct, to 4pm Nov-Mar) in the whole country, is at Housesteads, 6.5 miles northeast of Haltwhistle. From here, high on a ridge and covering 2 hectares, you can survey the snaking wall, with a sense of awe at the landscape and the Roman lookouts.

Remains here include an impressive hospital, granaries and spectacularly situated communal flushable latrines.

Hadrian's Wall

JUSTIN FOULKES/LONELY PLANET ©

Need to Know

Hadrian's Wall Country (http://hadrianswallcountry.co.uk) is the official portal for the entire area.

Take a Break

All of the sites featured have cafes for mid-sightseeing stops.

★ Top Tip

Make savings with a joint ticket for Vindolanda Fort and the Roman Army Museum.

Vindolanda Roman Fort & Museum

Handily near Housesteads Roman Fort & Museum, the sweeping site of **Vindolanda** (☎01434-344277; www.vindolanda.com; Bardon Mill; adult/child/family £8/4.75/22.80; ⏰10am-5pm) offers a fascinating glimpse into the daily life of a Roman garrison town. It's a large, extensively excavated site, which includes impressive parts of the fort and town and reconstructed turrets and temple.

Vindolanda is 5.8 miles northeast of Haltwhistle.

Roman Army Museum

On the site of the Carvoran Roman Fort, a mile northeast of Greenhead, this revamped **museum** (☎01697-747485; www.vindolanda.com/roman-army-museum; Greenhead; adult/child/family £6.89/3.80/19; ⏰10am-5pm) has three new galleries covering the Roman army and the empire; the wall (with a 3D film illustrating what the wall was like nearly 2000 years ago and today); and colourful background detail to Hadrian's Wall life.

Birdoswald Roman Fort

Technically in Cumbria, the remains of this once-formidable **fort** (EH; ☎01697-747602; www.english-heritage.org.uk; Gilsland, Greenhead; adult/child £9/5.50; ⏰10am-6pm daily Apr-Sep, 10am-5pm daily Oct, 10am-4pm Sat & Sun Nov–mid-Feb, 10am-4pm Wed-Sun mid-Feb–Mar) on an escarpment overlooking the beautiful Irthing Gorge are on a minor road off the B6318, about 4 miles west of Greenhead. The longest intact stretch of wall extends from here to Harrow's Scar Milecastle. A 4m-high gatehouse leads to interactive, kid-friendly exhibits, which were revamped in 2018.

Hadrian's Wall

ROME'S FINAL FRONTIER

Of all Britain's Roman ruins, Emperor Hadrian's 2nd-century wall, cutting across northern England from the Irish Sea to the North Sea, is by far the most spectacular; Unesco awarded it World Heritage status in 1987.

We've picked out the highlights, one of which is the prime remaining Roman fort on the wall, Housesteads, which we've reconstructed here.

GANNET77 / GETTY IMAGES ©

Housesteads' Granaries

Nothing like the clever underground ventilation system, which kept vital supplies of grain dry in Northumberland's damp and drizzly climate, would be seen again in these parts for 1500 years

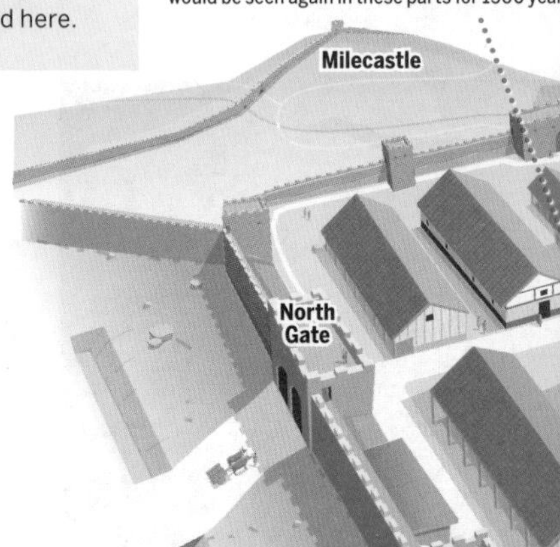

STEPHEN DOREY / GETTY IMAGES ©

Birdoswald Roman Fort

Explore the longest intact stretch of the wall, scramble over the remains of a large fort then head indoors to wonder at a full-scale model of the wall at its zenith. Great fun for the kids.

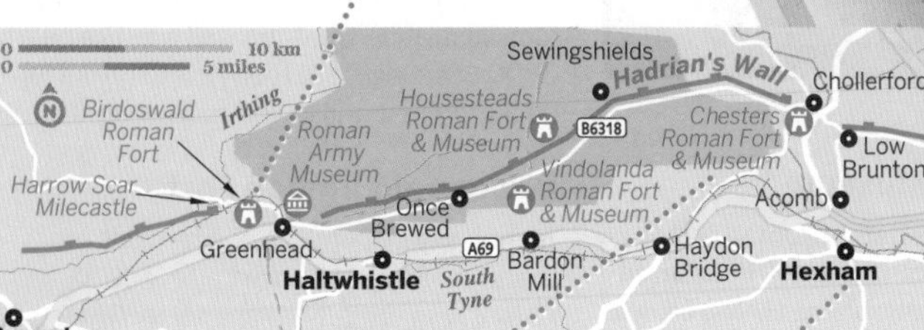

Chesters Roman Fort

Built to keep watch over a bridge spanning the River North Tyne, Britain's best-preserved Roman cavalry fort has a terrific bathhouse, essential if you have months of nippy northern winter ahead.

Hexham Abbey

This may be the finest non-Roman sight near Hadrian's Wall, but the 7th-century parts of this magnificent church were built with stone quarried by the Romans for use in their forts.

STEPHAN GOERLICH / GETTY IMAGES ©

VERITYJOHNSON / SHUTTERSTOCK ©

Housesteads' Hospital

Operations performe at the hospital would have been surprising effective, even without anaesthetics religious rituals and prayers to Aesculapius, the Roman god of healing were possibly less helpful for a hernia or appendicitis

ALISON ROSCOE / GETTY IMAGES ©

Housesteads' Latrines
Communal toilets were the norm in Roman times and Housesteads' are remarkably well preserved – fortunately no traces remain of the vinegar-soaked sponges that were used instead of toilet paper.

QUICK WALL FACTS & FIGURES

Latin name Vallum Aelium

Length 73.5 miles (80 Roman miles)

Construction date 122–128 CE

Manpower for construction
Three legions (around 16,000 men)

Features At least 16 forts, 80 milecastles, 160 turrets

Did you know Hadrian's wasn't the only Roman wall in Britain – the Antonine Wall was built across what is now central Scotland in c140 CE, but it was abandoned soon after.

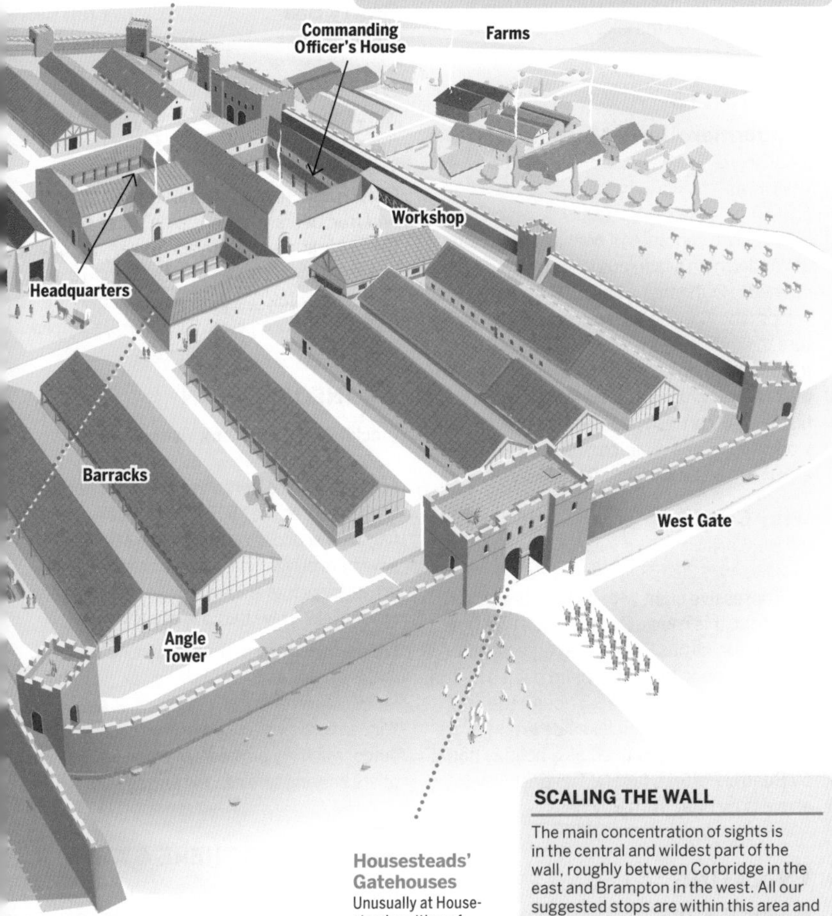

Commanding Officer's House

Farms

Workshop

Headquarters

Barracks

West Gate

Angle Tower

SCALING THE WALL

The main concentration of sights is in the central and wildest part of the wall, roughly between Corbridge in the east and Brampton in the west. All our suggested stops are within this area and follow an east–west route. The easiest way to travel is by car, scooting along the B6318, but special bus AD122 will also get you there. Hiking along the designated Hadrian's Wall Path (84 miles) allows you to appreciate the achievement up close.

Housesteads' Gatehouses
Unusually at Housesteads neither of the gates faces the enemy, as was the norm at Roman forts; builders aligned them east–west. Ruts worn by cart wheels are still

FREE GUIDES

At some sites, knowledgeable volunteer heritage guides are on hand to answer questions and add context and interesting details to what you're seeing.

Windermere

Stretching for 10.5 miles between Ambleside and Newby Bridge, Windermere isn't just the queen of Lake District lakes – it's also the largest body of water anywhere in England, closer in stature to a Scottish loch.

Confusingly, the town of Windermere is split in two: Windermere Town is actually 1.5 miles from the lake, at the top of a steep hill, while touristy, overdeveloped Bowness-on-Windermere (usually shortened just to Bowness) sits on the lake's eastern shore.

SIGHTS

Windermere Jetty Museum Museum

(☎01539-637940; www.lakelandarts.org.uk/windermere-jetty-museum; Rayrigg Rd; adult/child £9/4.50; ⊙10am-5pm Mar-Oct, 10.30am-4.30pm Nov-Feb) Two centuries of boating are explored at Windermere's fabulous lakeside museum, opened in 2019 after a long £20 million redevelopment. Housed in a striking wooden structure that resembles a *Grand Designs* take on a traditional boat shed, it contains a collection of gorgeous vintage vessels from the lake's history. You can also peek into the restoration workshop, pilot a radio-controlled boat or take a cruise in an Edwardian steam launch.

Wray Castle Historic Site

(NT; www.nationaltrust.org.uk/wray-castle; adult/child £10.40/5.20; ⊙10am-6pm, cafe 10am-4pm) An impressive sight with its turrets and battlements, this mock-Gothic castle was built in 1840 for James Dawson, a retired doctor from Liverpool, but it has been owned by the National Trust since 1929. Though the interior is largely empty, the lakeside grounds are glorious. It was once used as a holiday home by Beatrix Potter's family. The best way to arrive is by boat from Bowness.

EATING

Mason's Arms Pub Food **££**

(☎01539-568486; www.masonsarmsstrawberrybank.co.uk; Bowland Bridge; mains £12.95-19.95; ⊙noon-10pm) Three miles east of the lake, near Bowlands Bridge, the marvellous Mason's Arms is a local secret. The rafters, flagstones and cast-iron range haven't changed in centuries, and the patio has to-die-for views across fields and fells. The food is hearty – Cumbrian stewpot, slow-roasted Cartmel lamb – and there are lovely rooms and cottages for rent (£175 to £350). In short, a cracker.

DRINKING & NIGHTLIFE

Crafty Baa Craft Beer

(☎01539-488002; https://thecraftybaa.business.site; 21 Victoria St, Windermere Town; ⊙11am-11pm) Brilliant and slightly bonkers, festooned with a mishmash of upcycled materials, this much-loved Windermere craft bar has scooped numerous awards: choose from Czech pilsners, weissbiers, smoked lagers and fruit beers, chalked up on slates behind the bar and served with accompanying snack platters. It's so successful, it's opened a sister pub in **Keswick** (☎01768-785405; https://thecraftybaa.business.site; 13 Bank St; ⊙11am-11pm).

INFORMATION

Brockhole National Park Visitor Centre (☎01539-446601; www.brockhole.co.uk; ⊙10am-5pm) In a 19th-century mansion 3 miles north of Windermere on the A591, this is the Lake District's flagship visitor centre. It also has a cafe, an adventure playground, gardens and kid-friendly activities such as archery, minigolf, treetop nets and the new 'Brave the Cave' attraction.

Windermere Information Centre (☎01539-446499; www.windermereinfo.co.uk; Victoria St, Windermere Town; ⊙8.30am-5.30pm) Windermere's visitor centre is now run by the outdoor-activity provider Mountain Goat. It also offers booking services and luggage storage.

GETTING THERE & AWAY

Boat To cross Windermere by car, bike or on foot, head south of Bowness to the **Windermere Ferry** (www.cumbria.gov.uk/roads-transport/highways-pavements/windermereferry.asp; car/bicycle/pedestrian £5/2/1; ⊙6.50am-9.50pm Mon-Sat, 8.50am-10pm Sun Apr-Oct, to 8.50pm

Oct-Mar), which shuttles between Ferry Nab on the east bank to Ferry House on the west bank.

Train Windermere is the only town inside the national park accessible by train. It's on the branch line to Kendal and Oxenholme, with onward connections to Edinburgh, Manchester and London Piccadilly.

Grasmere

Huddled at the edge of an island-studded lake surrounded by woods, pastures and slate-coloured hills, Grasmere is most famous as the former home of the grand old daddy of the Romantics himself, poet William Wordsworth, who set up home at nearby Dove Cottage in 1799, and spent much of the rest of his life here.

ACTIVITIES

Helm Crag Hiking

If you only do one fell walk in Grasmere, make it Helm Crag. Sometimes referred to as 'the Lion and the Lamb', after the twin crags atop its summit, it's a rewarding two-hour climb, but it's dauntingly steep in places, with around 335m of elevation gain. The trail starts on Easedale Rd and is fairly well signposted.

SHOPPING

Sarah Nelson's Gingerbread Shop Food

(☎01539-435428; www.grasmeregingerbread.co.uk; Church Cottage; ⊙9.15am-5.30pm Mon-Sat, 12.30-5pm Sun) In business since 1854, this famous sweet shop next to the village church makes Grasmere's essential souvenir: traditional gingerbread with a half-biscuity, half-cakey texture (six/12 pieces for £3.95/7.50), cooked using the original top-secret recipe.

EATING

The Yan Bistro ££

(☎01539-435055; www.theyan.co.uk; Broadrayne Farm; mains £13.95-15.95; ⊙5-10pm Mon-Fri, 3-10pm Sat & Sun) Rustic-meets-refined at the Yan (from an old Cumbrian word for 'one'). Lodged in an ancient farmhouse a mile north of Grasmere, the design marries minimalism with chunky wooden tables, a futuristic fireplace and hefty wood beams, and the food offers a fun, modern spin on traditional classic like fish pie, chicken Kiev and bacon chop. Lovely bedrooms, too.

Windermere Lake Cruises

Since the launch of the first passenger ferry in 1845, taking a **cruise** (☎01539-443360; www.windermere-lakecruises.co.uk; cruises from £9.50) has been an essential part of every Windermere itinerary. The most popular route is the Islands Cruise (adult/child £9.50/4.75), a 45-minute circular cruise around Windermere's shoreline and islands. The north-lake Red Cruise (adult/child £12.40/6.20) goes from Bowness to Ambleside, while the south-lake Yellow Cruise (adult/child/family £13/6.50) heads down to the lake's southern side.

JUSTIN FOULKES/LONELY PLANET ©

GETTING THERE & AWAY

The regular 555 bus (at least hourly, including Sundays) runs from Windermere to Grasmere (15 minutes) via Ambleside, Rydal Church and Dove Cottage, then travels onwards to Keswick.

The open-top 599 (two or three per hour in summer) runs to Grasmere from Windermere and Bowness via Troutbeck Bridge and Ambleside.

Both buses charge the same fares: Grasmere to Ambleside is £4.90; to Bowness and Windermere is £7.40.

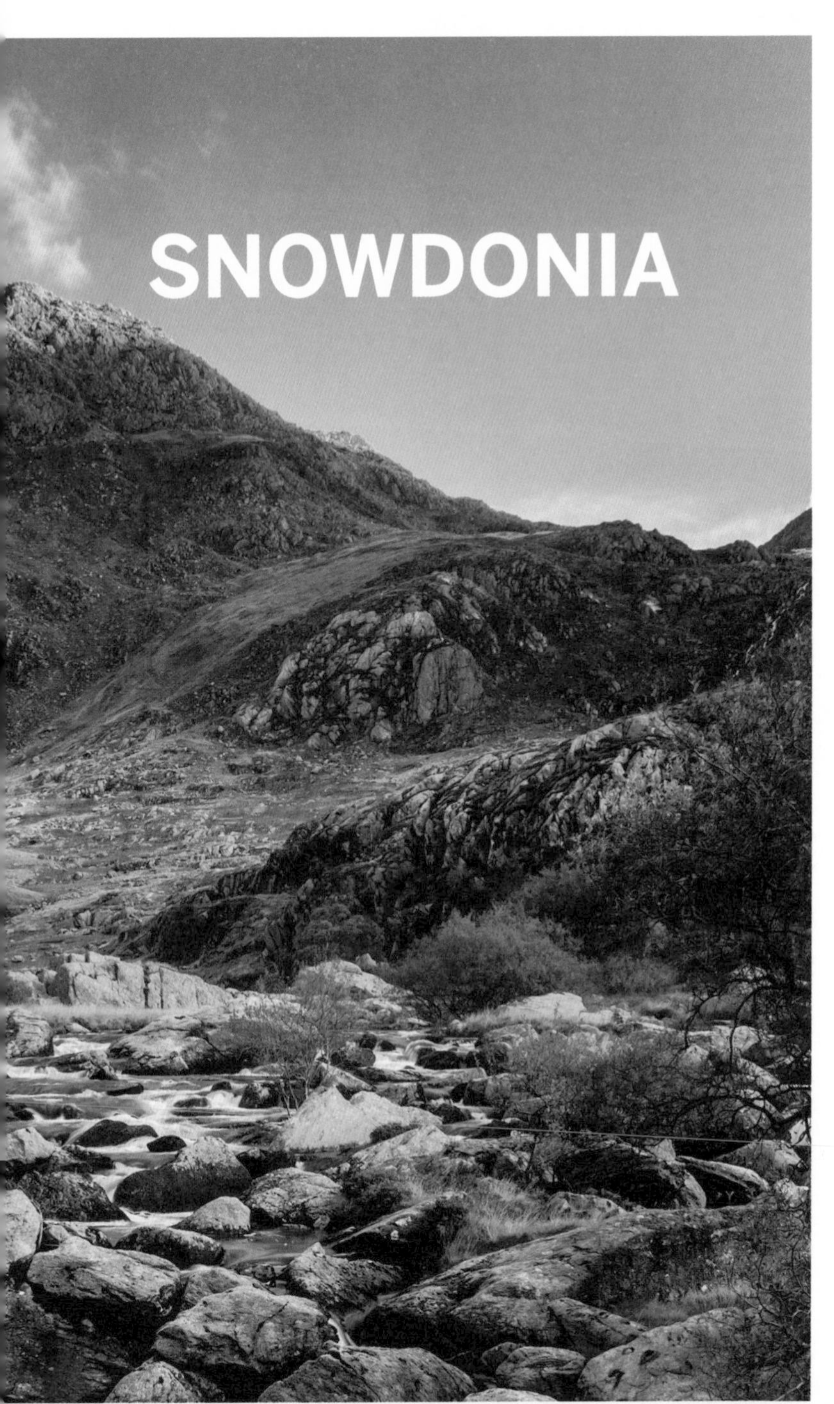
SNOWDONIA

In this Chapter

Snowdonia at a Glance...

Wales is crowned with Snowdonia – a range of rocky peaks, glacier-hewn valleys and bird-filled estuaries stretching across the north of the country. This is Wales' best-known and most visited national park, and every year more than 400,000 people walk, climb or take the train to the 1085m summit of Snowdon. Alongside Wales' biggest natural lake, Snowdonia National Park's 823 sq miles are also home to a breathtaking array of adrenaline pursuits that will sate any fresh-air fiend.

Two Days in Snowdonia

Check the weather, then go for the big one on your first day: climbing **Snowdon** (p212) – or riding the train to the top. Celebrate with hearty dinner at the **Tŷ Gwyn Hotel** (p215). The following day, head underground to explore Snowdonia's slate-mining heritage by scrambling across a **subterranean via ferrata** (p210) and zip-lining through caverns.

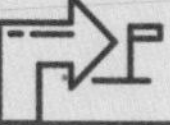

Four Days in Snowdonia

Take it (relatively) easy on day three – white-water rafting at the **National White Water Centre** (p211), or perhaps descending into Blaenau Ffestiniog's **Llechwedd Slate Caverns** (p211) with a knowledgeable guide. For dinner, enjoy fusion tapas and wine at **Olif** (p215). Start day four by hiking up Snowdonia's most challenging mountain, **Tryfan** (p214), before relaxing in front of Wales' highest **waterfalls** (p215). End your Snowdonia adventures with music at **Y Stablau** (p215).

Previous page: Tryfan (p214)
JOE DANIEL PRICE/GETTY IMAGES ©

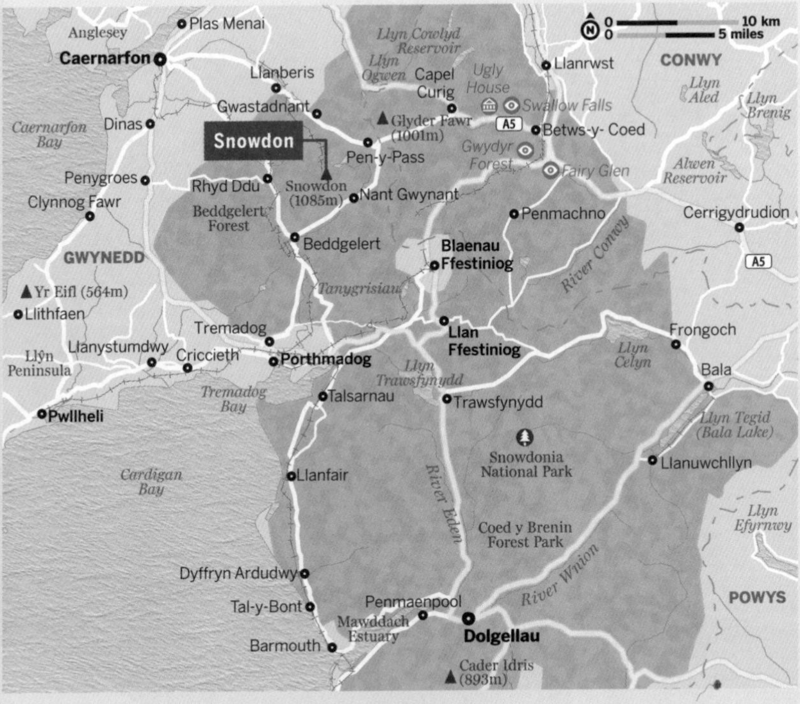

Arriving in Snowdonia

Bus Bus services are extensive, reaching towns such as Betws-y-Coed, Llanberis, Dolgellau and Bala.

Car The A5, A494, A470 and A487 are the principal roads into the park.

Train There are three major rail routes into and around the park: the Cambrian, North Wales Coast and Conwy Valley lines.

Where to Stay

Accommodation is not a problem in well-peopled Snowdonia. Hotels and B&Bs cluster around the towns, especially Betws, and there are numerous hostels, self-catering cottages and campgrounds. Some can close seasonally or be overrun in school holidays.

Bounce Below

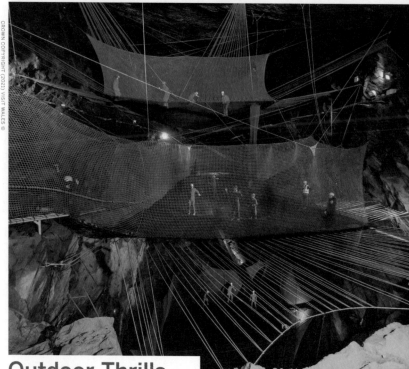

CROWN COPYRIGHT (2021) VISIT WALES ©

Outdoor Thrills

Apart from superb hiking, Snowdonia offers subterranean adventures galore, as well as man-made zip-lining thrills, mountain biking and more.

Great For...

☑ **Don't Miss**

White-knuckle, white-water rafting or kayaking on the foaming waters of the River Tryweryn.

Climbing & Mountaineering

At the western edge of the village of Capel Curig, the **Plas y Brenin National Mountain Sports Centre** (☎01690-720214; www.pyb.co.uk; A4086; 👪) has excellent facilities and a huge array of year-round courses, from basic rock climbing and mountaineering, to kayaking, canoeing and abseiling. **Paul Poole Mountaineering** (☎07786-360347; www.paulpoolemountaineering.co.uk; courses from £130) in Llanberis can teach you everything from rock climbing to winter ascents.

Adrenaline Activities

Head down an old slate mine and try your hand zip-lining across lakes, scrambling along a subterranean via ferrata, and abseiling down shafts with **Go Below Underground Adventures** (☎01690-710108; www.go-below.co.uk; adventures £59-99; ⏲9am-5pm).

Antur Stiniog

CROWN COPYRIGHT (2021) VISIT WALES ©

For trampolining in a mine, head to Bounce Below at **Zip World Slate Caverns** (☎01248-601444; www.zipworld.co.uk; off A470, Llechwedd Slate Caverns; ⏲booking office 8am-6.30pm; 👪), a 'cathedral-sized' cavern with bouncy nets, walkways, tunnels and slides (one hour adult/child £25/20). It also offers Titan, zip wires over deep open pits (£50 per two hours), and zip wires through the caverns (£65). **Zip World Fforest** (☎01248-601444; www.zipworld.co.uk; A470, LL24 0HX; 3 coaster rides £20, 2hr safari £40; ⏲9am-5pm; 👪) offers more buttock-clenching fun with 'Plummet', a free-fall experience through a tower trap door.

Mountain Biking

If you don't know the meaning of fear, check out **Antur Stiniog** (☎01766-238007; www.anturstiniog.com; A470, Llechwedd Slate Caverns; 1 uplift £5, day pass from £31; ⏲8am-5pm Thu-Mon Apr-Aug & Thu-Sun Sep-Mar), which boasts 14 blue, red and black downhill and free-ride runs down the mountainside near Blaenau Ffestiniog's slate caverns. There's also challenging mountain biking in the northern section of Gwydyr Forest (p214).

ℹ Need to Know

Snowdonia National Park Tourist Office (p215) is an invaluable source of information about walking trails, mountain conditions and more.

✕ Take a Break

Pete's Eats (☎01286-870117; www.petes-eats.co.uk; 40 High St; mains £4-7; ⏲8am-8pm; 📶) in Llanberis is a legendary adventurists' cafe.

★ Top Tip

Book activities well in advance and allow some flexibility in case conditions force a reschedule.

White-Water Activities

On the River Tryweryn's reliable white water, rafting, kayaking and canoeing is possible around 200 days per year. Trips with the **National White Water Centre** (Canolfan Dŵr Gwyn Genedlaethol; ☎01678-521083; www.ukrafting.co.uk; Frongoch, off A4212; rafting taster/full session £37/67; ⏲9am-4.30pm Mon-Fri) traverse a 1.5-mile stretch through abundant class-III white water and class IV sections.

Surfing

Lying just outside the national park's eastern border, in the lush Conwy Valley, **Surf Snowdonia** (☎01492-353123; www.adventureparcsnowdonia.com; Conway Rd, Dolgarrog LL32 8QE; ⏲8am-11pm; 👪) is an unexpected slice of Maui: an adventure park centred on a vast artificial wave pool. Choose between surfing (adult/child from £40/35) waves of different intensity, based on your ability, lagoon 'crash and splash' sessions (£25 per hour), kayaking, SUP, walking and more.

Snowdon Mountain Railway

DILCHASPIYAAN/SHUTTERSTOCK ©

Snowdon

No Snowdonia experience is complete without coming face-to-face with Snowdon (1085m), one of Britain's most awe-inspiring mountains. You can climb it on foot or let the train take the strain.

Great For...

☑ Don't Miss

The views over jagged ridges and deep post-glacial lakes. Even on gloomy days you could be above the clouds.

Welcome to Wales' highest mountain. 'Yr Wyddfa' in Welsh (pronounced 'uhr-*with*-vuh', meaning 'The Tomb'), it's the mythical resting place of the giant Rhita Gawr, who demanded King Arthur's beard for his cloak, and was killed for his temerity. On a clear day the views stretch to Ireland and the Isle of Man.

Climbing Snowdon

The most straightforward route to the summit is the **Llanberis Path** (9 miles return) running beside the train line. The two paths starting from Pen-y-Pass require the least amount of ascent, but are nevertheless tougher walks: the **Miner's Track** (8 miles return) starts off wide and gentle but gets steep beyond Llyn Llydaw; and the more interesting **Pyg Track** (7 miles return) is more rugged still.

Hikers on Llanberis Path

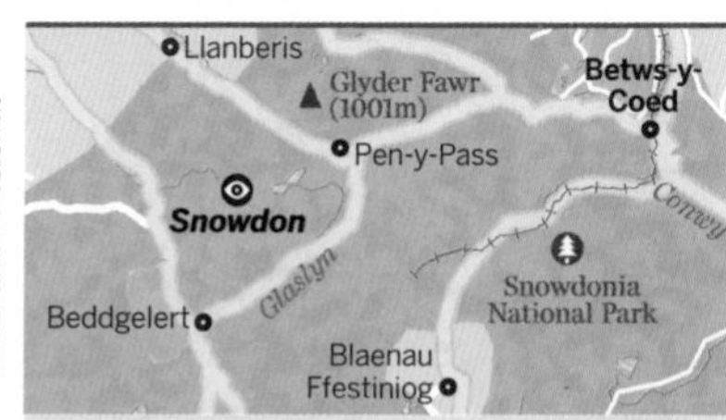

Need to Know

Hafod Eryri (www.snowdonrailway.co.uk; 10.30am-4.30pm May-Oct;) is Snowdon's information centre.

Take a Break

The Hafod Eryri centre on Snowdon's summit has a decent cafe.

★ Top Tip

Arrive early or use public transport – the Pen-y-Pas car park can fill up by 8am.

Two tracks start from the Caernarfon–Beddgelert road (A4085): the **Snowdon Ranger Path** (8 miles return) is the safest route in winter, while the **Rhyd Ddu Path** (8 miles return) is the least-used route and boasts spectacular views. The most challenging route is the **Watkin Path** (8 miles return), involving an ascent of more than 1000m on its southerly approach from Nant Gwynant, and finishing with a scramble across a steep-sided scree-covered slope.

The classic **Snowdon Horseshoe** (7.5 miles return) branches off from the Pyg Track to follow the precipitous ridge of **Crib Goch** (one of the most dangerous routes on the mountains and only recommended for the very experienced) with a descent over the peak of Y Lliwedd and a final section down the Miner's Track.

Snowdon Mountain Railway

If you can't, or would rather not, climb Snowdon, there is another way up. Opened in 1896, the **Snowdon Mountain Railway** (01286-870223; www.snowdonrailway.co.uk; A4086; adult/child return diesel £29/20, steam £37/27; 9am-5pm mid-Mar–Oct) is the UK's highest rack-and-pinion railway. Vintage steam and modern diesel locomotives haul carriages from Llanberis up to Snowdon's summit in an hour. Book tickets well in advance.

Getting to Snowdon

All the trailheads are accessible by Snowdon Sherpa bus services S1, S2, S4 or S97 (single/day ticket £2/5).

The **Welsh Highland Railway** (01766-516000; www.festrail.co.uk; £40 return; Easter-Oct, limited service winter) stops at the trailhead of the Rhyd Ddu Path, and there is a request stop (Snowdon Ranger Halt) where you can alight for the Snowdon Ranger Path.

Mountains Less Trodden

The Ogwen Valley, just 10 miles west of Betws-y-Coed, is home to hiking even more spectacular than Snowdon, and with a fraction of the crowds. Trails depart either from Idwal Cottage or from the vicinity of the Llyn Ogwen lake.

On the south side of the valley, the spiky Glyderau beckon. One of the best day hikes you can do is the ascent of the **Glyder Fach** (994m) and **Glyder Fawr** (1001m), with a ridge walk in between, plus otherworldly rock formations en route, such as the **Castell y Gwynt** (Castle of the Winds), and a scambling detour up the triple-peaked **Tryfan** (918m). Jump between the Adam and Eve rocks if you dare!

Alternatively, look to the rounded, gentler amphitheatre of the Carneddau range on the north side of the valley. Another fantastic day hike takes in four of the Carnedd peaks, including **Carnedd Llewelyn** (1064m), Wales' third-highest, a gentle ridge walk, two glacial lakes and a couple of tough scrambles.

There's parking near Idwal Cottage and along the A5, along Llyn Ogwen.

Glyder Fach

SEBASTIEN COELL/SHUTTERSTOCK ©

Betws-y-Coed

Betws-y-Coed (*bet*-us-ee-*coyd*) sits at the junction of three river valleys (the Llugwy, the Conwy and the Lledr) and on the verge of the Gwydyr Forest. With outdoor-gear shops appearing to outnumber pubs, walking trails leaving right from the centre and guesthouses occupying a fair proportion of its slate Victorian buildings, it's the perfect base for exploring Snowdonia.

SIGHTS

Fairy Glen Waterfall

(A470, LL24 0SH; 50p) Reachable via a walking trail signposted off the A470, 2 miles south of Betws-y-Coed, this is a beautiful gorge, hemmed in by mossy rocks and a small waterfall. It's named after the Welsh sprites, the Tylwyth Teg, who allegedly live in these parts, and the pool at the confluence of Afon Lledr and River Cowny is a great swimming spot.

Gwydyr Forest Forest

The 28-sq-mile Gwydyr Forest, planted since the 1920s with oak, beech and larch, encircles Betws-y-Coed and is scattered with the remnants of lead and zinc mine workings. Named for a more ancient forest in the same location, it's ideal for a day's walking, though it gets very muddy in wet weather. *Walks Around Betws-y-Coed* (£5), available from the National Park Tourist Office (p215), details several circular forest walks.

The northern section of the park is home to the Gwydyr Bach and Gwydyr Mawr Mountain Bike Trail, a challenging 16-mile circuit starting immediately southwest of Llanrwst, 3.5 miles north of Betws. A map and pamphlet detailing the route can be downloaded for free at www.mbwales.com.

Ugly House Historic Building

(Tŷ Hyll; www.theuglyhouse.co.uk; A5; ⌚10.30am-4.30pm daily Easter-Oct, Mon-Fri Nov & Feb-Mar) The Ugly House is a misnomer. This unusual cottage is constructed from huge boulders and is home to a characterful tearoom and, upstairs, the Honeybee Room, with displays devoted to the beleaguered insect, protected by the Snowdonia Society, an environmentalist group that sells locally produced honey in the garden. It's half a mile west of Swallow Falls on the A5.

EATING

Hangin' Pizzeria Pizza £

(☎01690-710393; www.hanginpizzeria.co.uk; Station Rd, The Old Railway Station; pizza £9-12; ⏲noon-8.30pm;) All industrial decor and cheerful, bustling staff, this pizzeria churns out crowd-pleasing, wood-fired pizza, with simple topping combos, some locally inspired (check out the Welsh rarebit pizza). Catering to a captive audience, since pretty much every visitor to Betws rocks up at the train station, but no worse for it.

Olif Tapas ££

(☎01690-733942; www.olifbetws.wales; Holyhead Rd; tapas £5-7; ⏲6-8.30pm Tue-Sun, noon-3pm Sat & Sun May-Oct, closed Mon-Wed Nov-Apr) Breakfast first up, burgers for lunch, and tapas and wine in the evening – Olif morphs to please throughout the day. The tapas has a distinctly Welsh flavour, without straying too far into fusion territory (the croquettes are made with Perl Wen cheese and the ham's from Camarthen) and fun finger foods, like popcorn cockles and cider-cooked mussels, abound.

Tŷ Gwyn Hotel European ££

(☎01690-710383; www.tygwynhotel.co.uk; A5; mains £13-18; ⏲noon-2pm & 6-9pm;) This 400-year-old coaching inn with bare stone walls and exposed beams is hand-down the town's most characterful restaurant. The menu is creative without trying too hard, and the chef does wonderful things with local ingredients to conjure up the likes of slow-braised lamb shoulder and seafood gratin, and the quirky historic building only adds to the appeal.

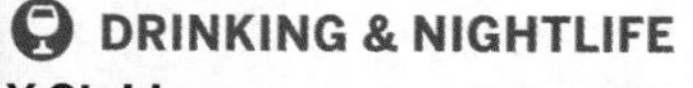

DRINKING & NIGHTLIFE

Y Stablau Pub

(☎01690-710011; www.ystablau.com; A5; ⏲11.30am-11pm;) Doing a roaring trade in ho-hum pub grub and ice-cold pints for weary walkers, motorbikers and daytrippers, the Stables (Y Stablau) is the only pub per se in Betws. The big draw inside this long, low-ceilinged, tile-floored barn of a place is the welcoming atmosphere and chilled craft ales. There's also music, including Dixieland, blues and Welsh male choirs.

Swallow Falls

Betws-y-Coed's main natural tourist draw are these **falls** (Rhaeadr Ewynnol; A5, LL24 0DW; adult/child £1.50/50p), located 2 miles west of town, alongside the A5 on the River Llugwy. It's a beautiful spot, with the 42m torrent, Wales' highest, weaving through the rocks into a green pool below. Outside seasonal opening hours, bring coins for the turnstile (no change is available).

INFORMATION

Snowdonia National Park Tourist Office

(☎01690-710426; www.eryri-npa.gov.uk; Royal Oak Stables; ⏲9.30am-12.30pm & 1.30-4.30pm) More than just a repository of books, maps and local craft, this office is an invaluable source of information about walking trails, mountain conditions and more.

GETTING THERE & AROUND

Bus Snowdon Sherpa bus service S2 heads to Swallow Falls (seven minutes), Capel Curig (15 minutes), Pen-y-Pass (25 minutes), Llanberis (35 minutes) and Bangor (route S6, weekends only April to October, one hour); all trips are £2.

Train Betws-y-Coed is on the Conwy Valley Line (www.conwyvalleyrailway.co.uk), with up to five trains every day to Llandudno (£6.30, 50 minutes) and Blaenau Ffestiniog (£5.10, 35 minutes).

EDINBURGH

In this Chapter

Edinburgh at a Glance...

Draped across a series of rocky hills overlooking the sea, Edinburgh is one of Europe's most beguiling cities. It is here that each summer the world's biggest arts festival rises, phoenix-like, from the ashes of last year's rave reviews and broken box-office records to produce yet another string of superlatives. Deeply cultured but also intrinsically down-to-earth, Edinburgh is a city of loud, crowded pubs, decadent restaurants, beer-fuelled poets and foul-mouthed comedians.

Two Days in Edinburgh

First up, **Edinburgh Castle** (p220) then a stroll down the **Royal Mile** (p230), via **Real Mary King's Close** (p233). Scare yourself silly on a churchyard **ghost tour,** (p241) then recover at cosily romantic **Ondine** (p242). On day two, soak up the culture at the **National Museum of Scotland** (p238) before cracking the code at the **Rosslyn Chapel** (p226) Head to **Outlook** (p242) for dinner.

Four Days in Edinburgh

Get active on day three with a hike up to **Arthur's Seat** (p238), then slow it down at the **Scotch Whisky Experience** (p239). Weave your way to **Grain Store** (p243) for dinner, followed by a **bar crawl** (p245) of the city's whisky bars. On day four, after swanning around the **Royal Yacht Britannia** (p239), explore the Old Town's **alleyways** (p236). Hungry? Stop by excellent **Timberyard** (p242).

Previous page: Edinburgh cityscape

VICHIE81/SHUTTERSTOCK ©

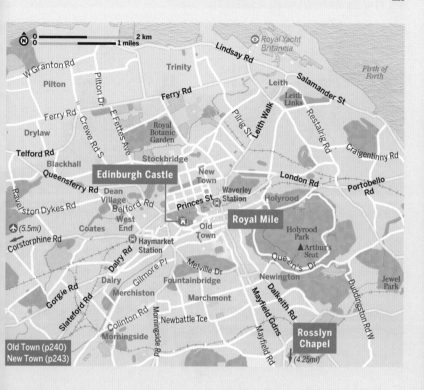

Old Town (p240)
New Town (p243)

Arriving in Edinburgh

Edinburgh Airport Bus 100 shuttles to South St David St (£4.50, 30 minutes, every 10 minutes), outside the main train station, via Haymarket and the West End from 4am to midnight. Trams to the city centre (£6.50, 33 minutes, every six to eight minutes) run from 6am to midnight. Taxis to the city centre cost around £20.

Edinburgh Waverley Train Station The main, central train station. Trains for the west also stop at Edinburgh Haymarket.

Where to Stay

Edinburgh offers a wide range of accommodation options, from moderately priced guesthouses set in lovely Victorian villas and Georgian town houses to expensive and stylish boutique hotels. There are also plenty of international chain hotels, and a few truly exceptional hotels housed in magnificent historic buildings. At the budget end, the youth hostels and independent backpacker hostels often have twins and doubles. For more information on the best neighbourhood to stay in, see p247.

Edinburgh Castle front gate

WINDS/SHUTTERSTOCK ©

Edinburgh Castle

Edinburgh Castle has played a pivotal role in Scottish history, both as a royal residence and as a military stronghold. King Malcolm Canmore (r 1058–93) and Queen Margaret first made their home in Edinburgh Castle in the 11th century. The castle last saw military action in 1745. Today it's one of Scotland's most atmospheric tourist attractions.

Great For...

☑ Don't Miss

The graffiti of American and French prisoners carved into the doors of the Castle Vaults.

Entrance Gateway

The Entrance Gateway, flanked by statues of Robert the Bruce and William Wallace, opens to a cobbled lane that leads up beneath the 16th-century Portcullis Gate to the cannons ranged along the Argyle and Mills Mount Batteries. The battlements here have great views over the New Town to the Firth of Forth.

One O'Clock Gun

At the far end of Mills Mount Battery is the famous One O'Clock Gun, where crowds gather to watch a gleaming WWII 25-pounder fire an ear-splitting time signal at exactly 1pm (every day except Sundays, Good Friday and Christmas Day).

Edinburgh Castle from Princes Street Gardens

GODRICK/SHUTTERSTOCK ©

Need to Know

Map p240; 0131-225 9846; www.edinburghcastle.scot; Castle Esplanade, EH1 2NG; adult/child £17.50/10.50, audio guide £3.50/1.50; 9.30am-6pm Apr-Sep, to 5pm Oct-Mar, last entry 1hr before closing; 23, 27, 41, 42

Take a Break

The **Redcoat Café** (www.edinburghcastle.scot/see-and-do/eat; Crown Sq; mains £5-10; 9.30am-5pm Apr-Oct, 10am-4pm Nov-Mar; ; 23, 27, 41, 42) serves good lunches.

★ Top Tip

Visit at lunchtime for the deafening One O'Clock Gun.

St Margaret's Chapel

South of Mills Mount, the road curls up leftwards to the highest part of Castle Rock, crowned by tiny, Romanesque St Margaret's Chapel, the oldest building in Edinburgh. It was probably built by David I or Alexander I in memory of their mother, Queen Margaret, around 1130. Beside the chapel stands Mons Meg, a giant 15th-century siege gun.

Crown Square

The main group of buildings on the summit of Castle Rock sits around Crown Sq, dominated by the shrine of the Scottish National War Memorial. Opposite is the Great Hall, built for James IV (r 1488–1513) and the meeting place for the Scottish parliament until 1639. Its most remarkable feature is the original 16th-century hammer-beam roof.

Castle Vaults

The Castle Vaults beneath the Great Hall were used variously as storerooms, bakeries and a prison. They've been renovated to resemble 18th-century prisons, where graffiti carved by French and American inmates can be seen on the ancient wooden doors.

The Royal Palace

On the eastern side of the square is the Royal Palace, built during the 15th and 16th centuries. It contains the castle's highlight – the Honours of Scotland (the Scottish crown jewels), comprising a crown made in 1540 from the gold of Robert the Bruce's 14th-century coronet, sword and sceptre. Also here is the Stone of Destiny, on which the ancient kings of Scotland were traditionally crowned.

Edinburgh Festival Fringe

Edinburgh's Festivals

Get set for culture galore – Edinburgh hosts an amazing number of festivals throughout the year. August in particular sees a frenzy of events, with several world-class festivals running at the same time, notably the Edinburgh International Festival, the Festival Fringe and the Military Tattoo. Hogmanay, Scotland's New Year's celebrations, is also peak party time.

Great For...

Need to Know

Find listings for all of Edinburgh's festivals on the umbrella website www.edinburghfestivalcity.com.

★ **Top Tip**

Book as early as possible; the Fringe Office (p224) for the Fringe, the Hub (p225) for the International Festival.

THOMAS ORTEGA/SHUTTERSTOCK ©

The program for the Edinburgh International Festival is usually published at the beginning of April; the Fringe program comes out in early June.

Edinburgh Festival Fringe

When the first Edinburgh International Festival was held in 1947, there were eight theatre companies that didn't make it onto the main program. Undeterred, they grouped together and held their own mini-festival – on the fringe – and an Edinburgh institution was born. Today the **Edinburgh Festival Fringe** (☎0131-226 0026; www.edfringe.com; ⏰Aug) is the biggest festival of the performing arts in the world.

Since 1990 the Fringe has been dominated by stand-up comedy, but the sheer variety of shows on offer is staggering – everything from chainsaw juggling to performance poetry to Tibetan yak-milk gargling. So how do you decide what to see? There are daily reviews in the *Scotsman* – one good review and a show sells out in hours – but the best recommendation is word of mouth.

The big names play at mega venues organised by big agencies such as Assembly (www.assemblyfestival.com) and the Gilded Balloon (www.gildedballoon.co.uk), and charge mega prices (some up to and over £30), but there are plenty of good shows in the £5-to-£20 range and, best of all, lots of free stuff.

The Fringe takes place over three-and-a-half weeks, the last two weeks overlapping with the first two of the Edinburgh International Festival.

For bookings and information, head to the **Edinburgh Festival Fringe Office** (☎0131-226 0026; www.edfringe.com; 180 High St, EH1 1QS; ⏰noon-3pm Mon-Sat mid-Jun–mid-

Edinburgh Military Tattoo

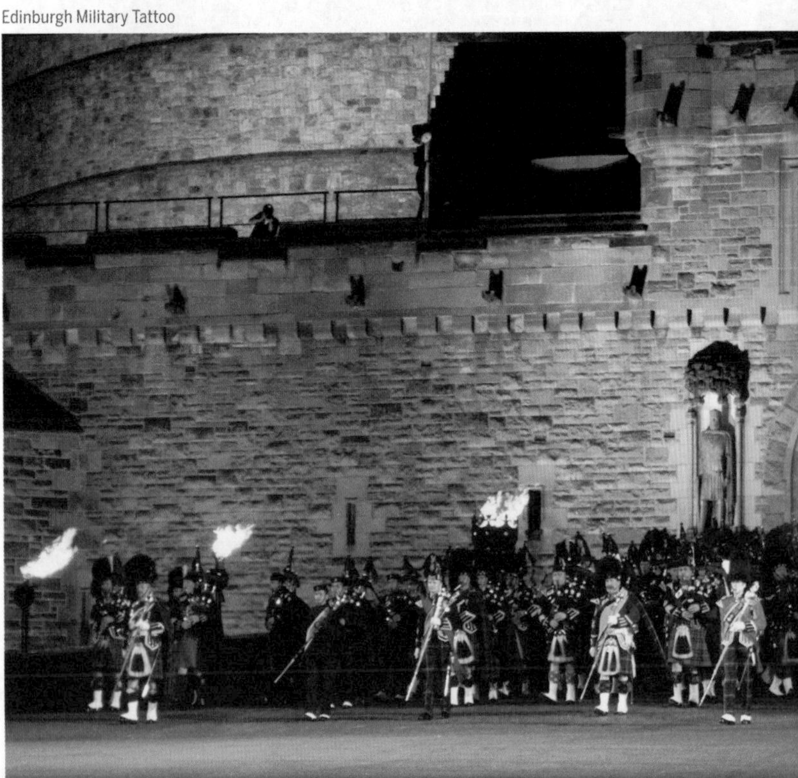

Jul, 10am-6pm daily mid-Jul–1 Aug, 9am-9pm daily Aug; all South Bridge buses).

Edinburgh International Festival

First held in 1947 to mark a return to peace after the ordeal of WWII, the **Edinburgh International Festival** (0131-473 2000; www.eif.co.uk; Aug-Sep) is festooned with superlatives – the oldest, the biggest, the most famous, the best in the world. The original was a modest affair, but today hundreds of the world's top musicians and performers congregate in Edinburgh for three weeks of diverse and inspirational music, opera, theatre and dance.

☑ Don't Miss

Edinburgh Festival Fringe's 'Fringe Sunday'. Usually the second Sunday, it's a smorgasbord of free performances, staged in the Meadows park.

DOMHNALL DODS/SHUTTERSTOCK ©

The festival takes place over the three weeks ending on the first Saturday in September. Tickets for popular events, especially music and opera, sell out quickly, so it's best to book as far in advance as possible. You can buy tickets in person at the **Hub** (0131-473 2015; www.thehub-edinburgh.com; Castlehill, EH1 2NE; ticket centre 10am-5pm Mon-Fri; ; 23, 27, 41, 42), or by phone or internet.

Edinburgh Military Tattoo

August in Edinburgh kicks off with the **Edinburgh Military Tattoo** (0131-225 1188; www.edintattoo.co.uk; Aug), a spectacular display of military marching bands, massed pipes and drums, acrobats, cheerleaders and motorcycle display teams, all played out in front of the magnificent backdrop of the floodlit castle. Each show traditionally finishes with a lone piper, dramatically lit, playing a lament on the battlements. The Tattoo takes place over the first three weeks of August (from a Friday to a Saturday); there's one show at 9pm Monday to Friday and two (at 7.30pm and 10.30pm) on Saturday, but no performance on Sunday.

Edinburgh International Book Festival

Held in a little village of marquees in the middle of Charlotte Sq, the **Edinburgh International Book Festival** (0845 373 5888; www.edbookfest.co.uk; Charlotte Sq Gardens, EH2 4DR; Aug) is a fun fortnight of talks, readings, debates, lectures, book signings and meet-the-author events, with a cafe-bar and tented bookshop thrown in. The festival lasts for two weeks (usually the first two weeks of the Edinburgh International Festival).

Take a Break

Just steps away from the Edinburgh Festival Fringe Office are tasty Italian dishes at cheery **Gordon's Trattoria** (0131-225 7992; www.gordonstrattoria.com; 231 High St, EH1 1PE; mains £12-20; noon-11pm Sun-Thu, to midnight Fri & Sat; ; all South Bridge buses).

ANTON IVANOV/SHUTTERSTOCK ©

Rosslyn Chapel

Many years may have passed since Dan Brown's novel The Da Vinci Code came out, but floods of visitors still descend on the beautiful and enigmatic church made famous by the book – Rosslyn Chapel.

Rosslyn Chapel was built in the mid-15th century for William St Clair, third prince of Orkney, and the ornately carved interior – at odds with the architectural fashion of its time – is a monument to the mason's art, rich in symbolic imagery and shrouded in mystery.

Famous highlights include the Apprentice Pillar; Lucifer, the Fallen Angel; and the Green Man. Alongside these notables, there's plenty more symbolism to explore.

The chapel is owned by the Episcopal Church of Scotland and services are still held here on Sunday mornings.

Great For...

☑ Don't Miss

The Apprentice Pillar with its intricate curved stonework and accompanying murderous back story.

Rosslyn's Symbolism

As well as flowers, vines, angels and biblical figures, the carved stones include many examples of the pagan 'Green

MARK PITT IMAGES/SHUTTERSTOCK ©

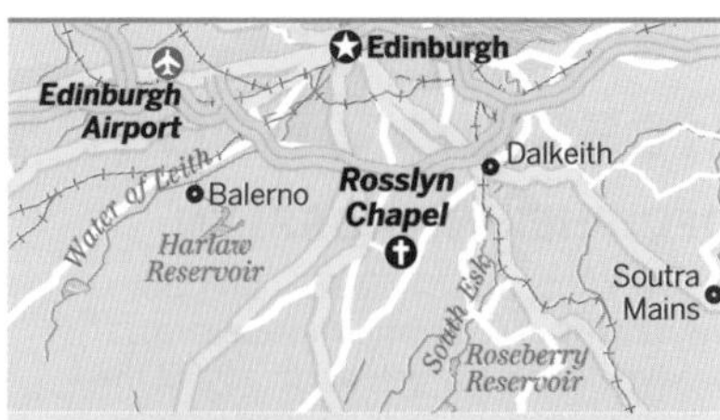

Need to Know

Collegiate Church of St Matthew; 0131-440 2159; www.rosslynchapel.com; Chapel Loan, Roslin, EH25 9PU; adult/child £9/free; 9.30am-6pm Mon-Sat Jun-Aug, to 5pm Sep-May, noon-4.45pm Sun year-round; P; 37;

Take a Break

Rosslyn's visitors-centre **coffee shop** (Chapel Loan, Roslin, EH25 9PU; mains £5-10; 9.30am-6pm Mon-Sat Jun-Aug, to 5pm Sep-May, noon-4.45pm Sun year-round; 37) has views over Roslin Glen.

★ Top Tip

Hourly talks by qualified guides are included in admission.

Man'; other figures are associated with Freemasonry and the Knights Templar. Intriguingly, there are also carvings of plants from the Americas that predate Columbus' voyage of discovery. The symbolism of these images has led some researchers to conclude that Rosslyn is some kind of secret Templar repository, and it has been claimed that hidden vaults beneath the chapel could conceal anything from the Holy Grail or the head of John the Baptist to the body of Christ himself.

The Ceiling

The spectacular ceiling vault is decorated with engraved roses, lilies and stars: look for the sun and the moon.

The Sacristy

Entered to the right of the Apprentice Pillar, the Sacristy (sometimes called the Crypt) was used as a workshop during construction and contains architectural drawings scratched on the walls by medieval masons.

Explore Some More

After visiting the chapel, head downhill to see the spectacularly sited ruins of Roslin Castle, then take a walk along leafy Roslin Glen.

How to Get There

Rosslyn Chapel is on the eastern edge of the village of Roslin, 7 miles south of Edinburgh's centre. Lothian Bus 37 to Penicuik Deanburn links Edinburgh to the village of Roslin. (Bus 37 to Bush does not go via Roslin.)

Rosslyn Chapel

DECIPHERING ROSSLYN

Rosslyn Chapel is a small building, but the density of decoration inside can be overwhelming. It's well worth buying the official guidebook by the Earl of Rosslyn first; find a bench in the gardens and have a skim through before going into the chapel – the background information will make your visit all the more interesting. The book also offers a useful self-guided tour of the chapel, and explains the legend of the Master Mason and the Apprentice.

Entrance is through the 1 **north door**. Take a pew and sit for a while to allow your eyes to adjust to the dim interior; then look up at the ceiling vault, decorated with engraved roses, lilies and stars, (Can you spot the sun and the moon?). Walk left along the north aisle to reach the Lady Chapel, separated from the rest of the church by the 2 **Mason's Pillar** and the 3 **Apprentice Pillar**. Here you'll find carvings of 4 **Lucifer**, the Fallen Angel, and the 5 **Green Man**. Nearby are 6 **carvings** that appear to resemble Indian corn (maize). Finally, go to the western end and look up at the wall – in the left corner is the head of the 7 **Apprentice**; to the right is the (rather worn) head of the 8 **Master Mason**.

VERONICA OLIVOTTO © LUCIFER: CC BY-NC-ND 2.0: HTTPS://FLIC.KR/P/ZWQRB

Lucifer, the Fallen Angel
At head height, to the left of the second window from the left, is an upside-down angel bound with rope, a symbol often associated with Freemasonry. The arch above is decorated with the Dance of Death.

The Apprentice
High in the corner, beneath an empty statue niche, is the head of the murdered Apprentice, with a deep wound in his forehead above the right eye. Legend says the Apprentice was murdered in a jealous rage by the Master Mason. The worn head on the side wall to the left of the Apprentice is that of his mother.

The Master Mason
8

Baptistry

EXPLORE SOME MORE

After visiting the chapel, head downhill to see the spectacularly sited ruins of Roslin Castle, then take a walk along leafy Roslin Glen.

ROSSLYN CHAPEL & THE DA VINCI CODE

Dan Brown was referencing Rosslyn Chapel's alleged links to the Knights Templar and the Freemasons – unusual symbols found among the carvings, and the fact that a descendant of its founder, William St Clair, was a Grand Master Mason – when he chose it as the setting for his novel's denouement. Rosslyn is indeed a coded work, written in stone, but its meaning depends on your point of view. See *The Rosslyn Hoax?* by Robert LD Cooper for an alternative interpretation of the chapel's symbolism.

PRACTICAL TIPS

Local guides give hourly talks throughout the day, which are included in the admission price. No photography is allowed inside the chapel.

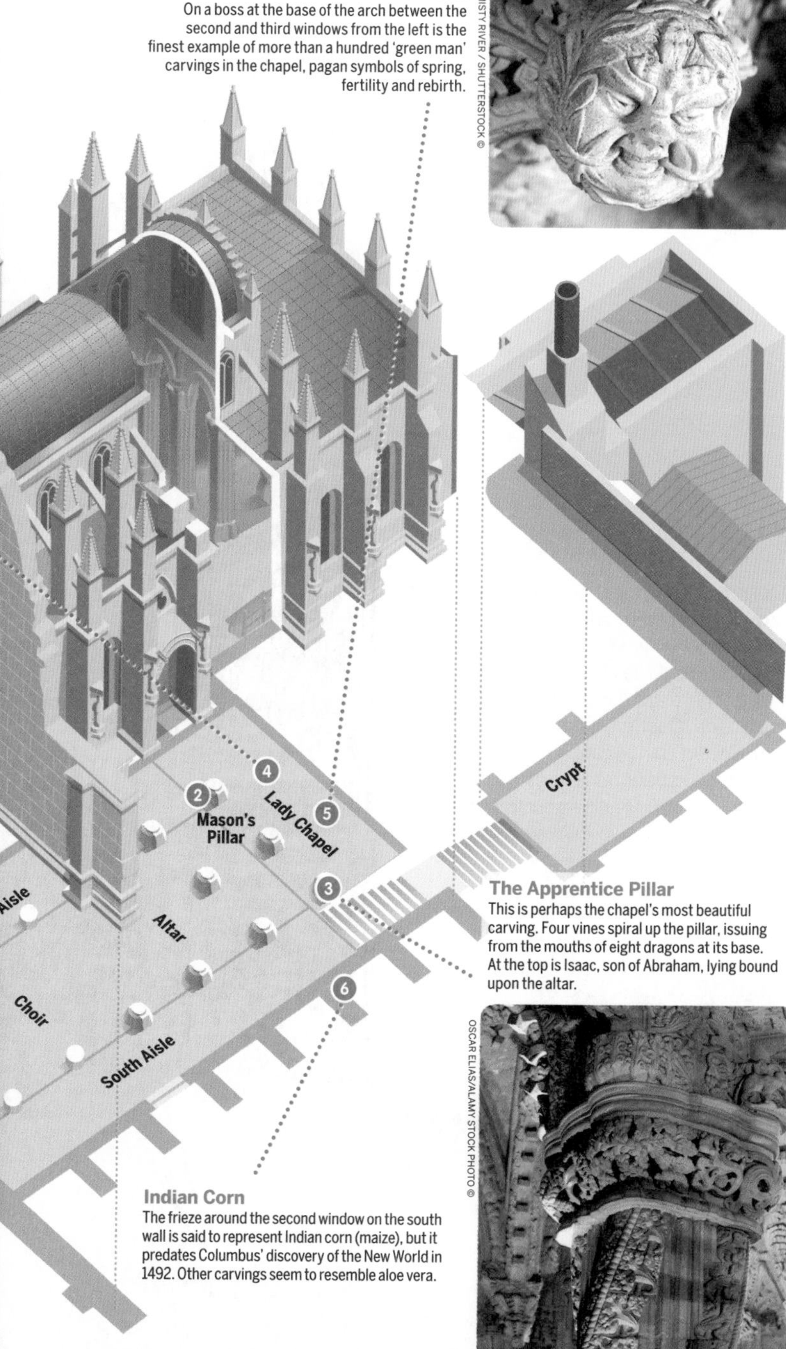
Green Man
On a boss at the base of the arch between the second and third windows from the left is the finest example of more than a hundred 'green man' carvings in the chapel, pagan symbols of spring, fertility and rebirth.
MISTY RIVER / SHUTTERSTOCK ©
Crypt
4
2
Mason's Pillar
Lady Chapel
5
3
Altar
Aisle
Choir
South Aisle
6
The Apprentice Pillar
This is perhaps the chapel's most beautiful carving. Four vines spiral up the pillar, issuing from the mouths of eight dragons at its base. At the top is Isaac, son of Abraham, lying bound upon the altar.
OSCAR ELIAS/ALAMY STOCK PHOTO ©
Indian Corn
The frieze around the second window on the south wall is said to represent Indian corn (maize), but it predates Columbus' discovery of the New World in 1492. Other carvings seem to resemble aloe vera.

The Royal Mile

This infinitely appealing mile-long street earned its nickname in the 16th century when the king used it to travel between the castle and the Palace of Holyroodhouse. There are five sections: Castle Esplanade, Castlehill, Lawnmarket, High St and Canongate. Twisting wynds (alleyways) shoot off alongside.

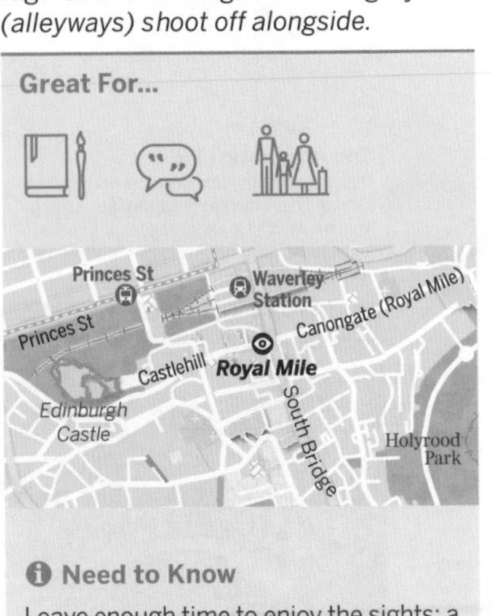

Need to Know

Leave enough time to enjoy the sights; a full day ensures you're not rushed.

★ Top Tip

Head to the Outlook Tower in the Camera Obscura for knockout city views.

MATTHI/SHUTTERSTOCK ©

From big-name attractions along the main streets to tempting detours into the maze of hidden alleyways, the Royal Mile is an irresistible place to explore.

Camera Obscura

This curious 19th-century **device** (Map p240; www.camera-obscura.co.uk; Castlehill, EH1 2ND; adult/child £16.50/12.50; ⌚9am-10pm Jul & Aug, 9.30am-8pm Apr-Jun, Sep & Oct, 9.30am-7pm Nov-Mar; 🚌23, 27, 41, 42) uses lenses and mirrors to throw a live image of the city onto a large horizontal screen.

Gladstone's Land

One of Edinburgh's most prominent 17th-century merchants was Thomas Gledstanes, who in 1617 purchased the tenement later known as **Gladstone's Land** (Map p240; NTS; ☎0131-226 5856; www.nts.org.uk; 477 Lawnmarket, EH1 2NT; 🚌23, 27, 41, 42). It contains fine painted ceilings, walls and beams, and some splendid furniture from the 17th and 18th centuries.

St Giles Cathedral

The great grey bulk of **St Giles Cathedral** (Map p240; www.stgilescathedral.org.uk; High St, EH1 1RE; ⌚9am-7pm Mon-Fri, to 5pm Sat, 1-5pm Sun Apr-Oct, 9am-5pm Mon-Sat, 1-5pm Sun Nov-Mar; 🚌23, 27, 41, 42) FREE dates largely from the 15th century, but much of it was restored in the 19th century. One of the most interesting corners of the kirk is the Thistle Chapel, built in 1911 for the Knights of the Most Ancient and Most Noble Order of the Thistle. The elaborately carved Gothic-style stalls have canopies topped with the helms and arms of the 16 knights – look out for the bagpipe-playing angel amid the vaulting.

Scottish Parliament Building

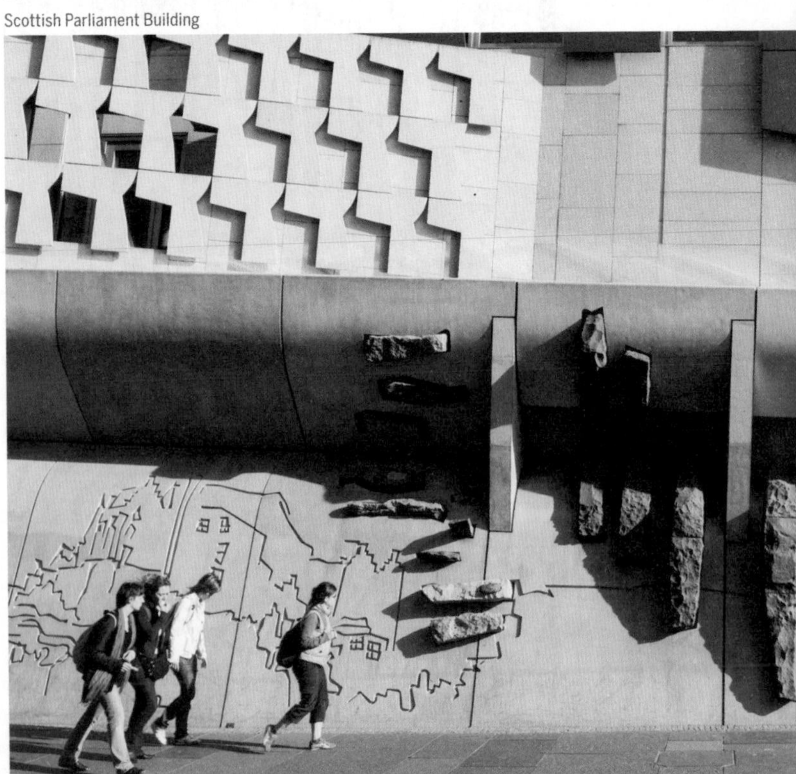

Monuments include the tombs of James Graham, Marquis of Montrose, who led Charles I's forces in Scotland and was hanged in 1650 at the Mercat Cross; and his Covenanter opponent Archibald Campbell, Marquis of Argyll, who was decapitated in 1661 after the Restoration of Charles II.

Real Mary King's Close

Edinburgh's 18th-century City Chambers were built over the sealed-off remains of Mary King's Close, and the lower levels of this medieval Old Town **alley** (Map p240; 0131-225 0672; www.realmarykingsclose.com; 2 Warriston's Close, EH1 1PG; adult/child £17.95/11.25; hours vary, approx 9.30am-9pm Apr-Oct, 10am-5.30pm Nov-Mar; 23, 27, 41, 42) have survived almost unchanged amid the foundations for 250 years. Now open to the public, this spooky, subterranean labyrinth gives a fascinating insight into the everyday life of 17th-century Edinburgh. Costumed characters lead tours through a 16th-century town house and the plague-stricken home of a 17th-century gravedigger; there's something about the crumbling 17th-century tenement room that makes the hairs rise on the back of your neck, with the ghost of a pattern on the walls, and the ancient smell of stone and dust thick in your nostrils.

In one of the former bedrooms off the close, a psychic once claimed to have been approached by the ghost of a little girl called Annie. It's hard to tell what's more frightening – the story of the ghostly child, or the bizarre heap of tiny dolls and teddies left in a corner by sympathetic visitors.

Advance booking is recommended.

☑ Don't Miss

The free one-hour guided tours of the Scottish Parliament, taking in the Debating Chamber, the Garden Lobby and a politician's office. Book ahead.

WILL SALTER/LONELY PLANET ©

Scottish Parliament Building

The **Scottish Parliament Building** (Map p240; 0131-348 5200; www.parliament.scot; Horse Wynd, EH99 1SP; 9am-6.30pm Tue-Thu, 10am-5pm Mon, Fri & Sat in session, 10am-5pm Tue-Thu in recess; ; 35) FREE, on the site of a former brewery, was officially opened by the Queen in October 2004. Designed by Catalan architect Enric Miralles (1955–2000), the ground plan of the parliament complex represents a 'flower of democracy rooted in Scottish soil' (best seen looking down from Salisbury Crags).

Take a Break

Dive off the main drag into the **Jolly Judge** (Map p 240; www.jollyjudge.co.uk; 7a James Ct, EH1 2PB; noon-11pm Mon-Thu, to midnight Fri & Sat, 12.30-11pm Sun; ; 23, 27, 41, 42) for 17th-century atmosphere (low, timber-beamed painted ceilings) and, in cold weather, an open fire.

Royal Mile

A GRAND DAY OUT

Planning your own procession along the Royal Mile involves some tough decisions – it would be impossible to see everything in a single day, so it's wise to decide in advance what you don't want to miss and shape your visit around that. Remember to leave time for lunch, for exploring some of the Mile's countless side alleys and, during festival time, for enjoying the street theatre that is bound to be happening in High St.

The most pleasant way to reach the Castle Esplanade at the start of the Royal Mile is to hike up the zigzag path from the footbridge behind the Ross Bandstand in Princes St Gardens (in springtime you'll be knee-deep in daffodils). Starting at ❶ **Edinburgh Castle** means that the rest of your walk is downhill. Fo a superb view up and down the length of the Mile, climb the ❷ **Camera Obscura's Outlool Tower** before visiting ❸ **Gladstone's Land** and ❹ **St Giles Cathedral**.

CLAUDIO DIVIZIA / SHUTTERSTOCK ©

Edinburgh Castle

If you're pushed for time, visit the Great Hall, the Honours of Scotland and the Prisons of War exhibit. Head for the Half Moon Battery for a photo looking down the length of the Royal Mile.

ROYAL VISITS TO THE ROYAL MILE

1561: Mary, Queen of Scots arrives from France and holds an audience with John Knox.
1745: Bonnie Prince Charlie fails to capture Edinburgh Castle, and instead sets up court in Holyroodhouse.
2004: Queen Elizabeth II officially opens the Scottish Parliament building.

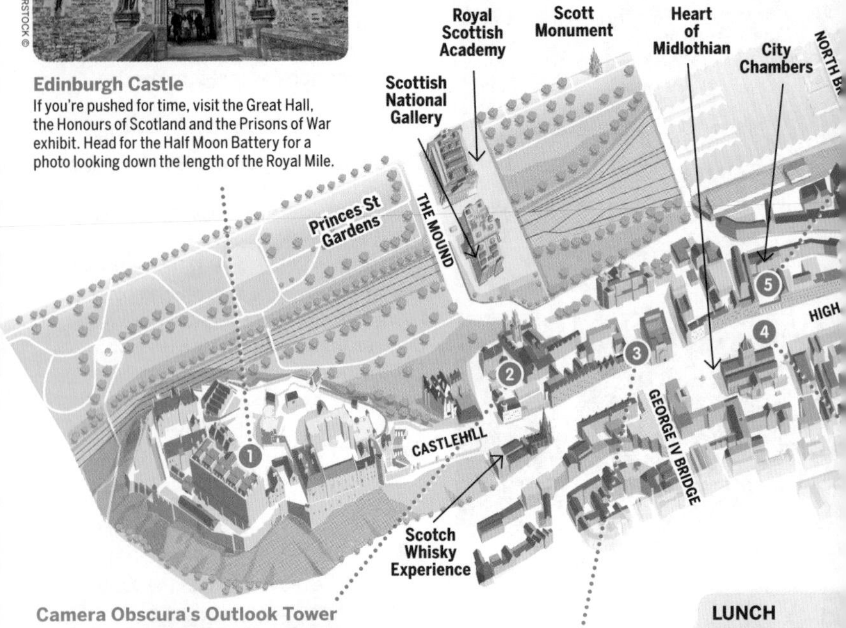

Royal Scottish Academy
Scott Monument
Heart of Midlothian
City Chambers
NORTH B
Scottish National Gallery
Princes St Gardens
THE MOUND
HIGH
5
4
3
2
1
CASTLEHILL
GEORGE IV BRIDGE
Scotch Whisky Experience

Camera Obscura's Outlook Tower

MINGKWAN DOILOM/ SHUTTERSTOCK ©

Gladstone's Land

The 1st floor houses a faithful recreation of how a wealthy Edinburgh merchant lived in the 17th century. Check out the beautiful Painted Bedchamber, with its ornately decorated walls and wooden ceilings.

LUNCH BREAK

Eggs Benedict at **Edinburgh Larder** steak and chips at **Maxie's Bistro**; slap-up seafood at **Ondine**.

f history's your thing, you'll want to add 5 **Real Mary King's Close**, 6 **John Knox House** and the 7 **Museum of Edinburgh** to your must-see list.

At the foot of the mile, choose between modern and ancient seats of power – the 8 **Scottish Parliament** or the 9 **Palace of Holyroodhouse**. Round off the day with an evening ascent of Arthur's Seat or, slightly less strenuously, Calton Hill. Both make great sunset viewpoints.

TAKING YOUR TIME

Minimum time needed for each attraction:

Edinburgh Castle two hours

Gladstone's Land 45 minutes

St Giles Cathedral 30 minutes

Real Mary King's Close one hour (tour)

Scottish Parliament one hour (tour)

Palace of Holyroodhouse one hour

Real Mary King's Close

The guided tour is heavy on ghost stories, but a highlight is standing in an original 17th-century room with tufts of horsehair poking from the crumbling plaster, and breathing in the ancient scent of stone, dust and history.

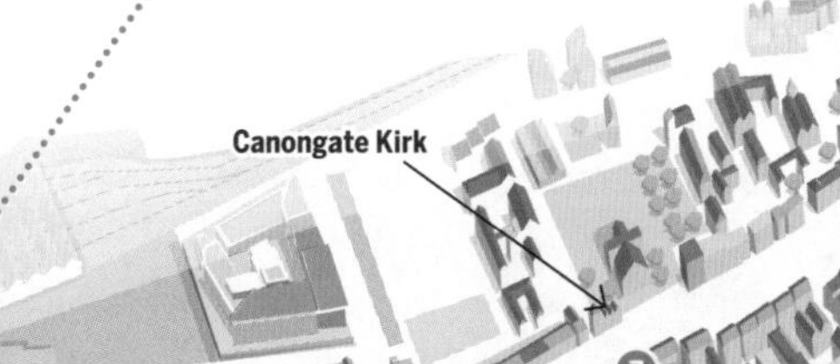

Scottish Parliament

Don't have time for the guided tour? Pick up a 'Discover the Scottish Parliament Building' leaflet from reception and take a self-guided tour of the exterior, then hike up to Salisbury Crags for a great view of the complex.

Palace of Holyroodhouse

Find the secret staircase joining Mary, Queen of Scots' bedchamber with that of her husband, Lord Darnley, who restrained the queen while his henchmen stabbed to death her secretary (and possible lover), David Rizzio.

St Giles Cathedral

Look out for the Burne-Jones stained-glass window (1873) at the west end, showing the crossing of the River Jordan, and the bronze memorial to Robert Louis Stevenson in the Moray Aisle.

HEARTLAND ARTS / SHUTTERSTOCK ©

DAVID IONUT / SHUTTERSTOCK ©

Edinburgh Walking Tour

Edinburgh's winding, ancient alleyways (or wynds) are a big part of the city's appeal. This walk leads you up steep steps and along cobbled streets awash with history and atmosphere. And into a pub, too.

Start Castle Esplanade
Distance 1 mile
Duration Two hours

Classic Photo The **statue of John Knox** framed by the towers of New College.

4 At **New College** visit a courtyard containing a statue of John Knox, a firebrand preacher who led the Protestant Reformation in Scotland.

3 **Ramsay Garden** is one of Edinburgh's most desirable addresses – where late 19th-century apartments were built around the octagonal Ramsay Lodge.

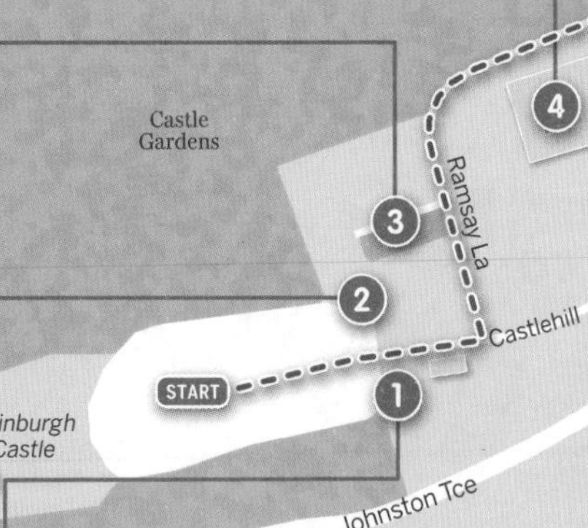

2 On a west-facing wall of this low building, spot the **Witches Well** fountain, commemorating the 4000 people (mostly women), executed on suspicion of sorcery.

King's Stables Rd

1 At Castle Esplanade head to the 17th-century **Cannonball House** to spot the iron ball lodged in the wall between the two largest windows facing the castle.

W Port

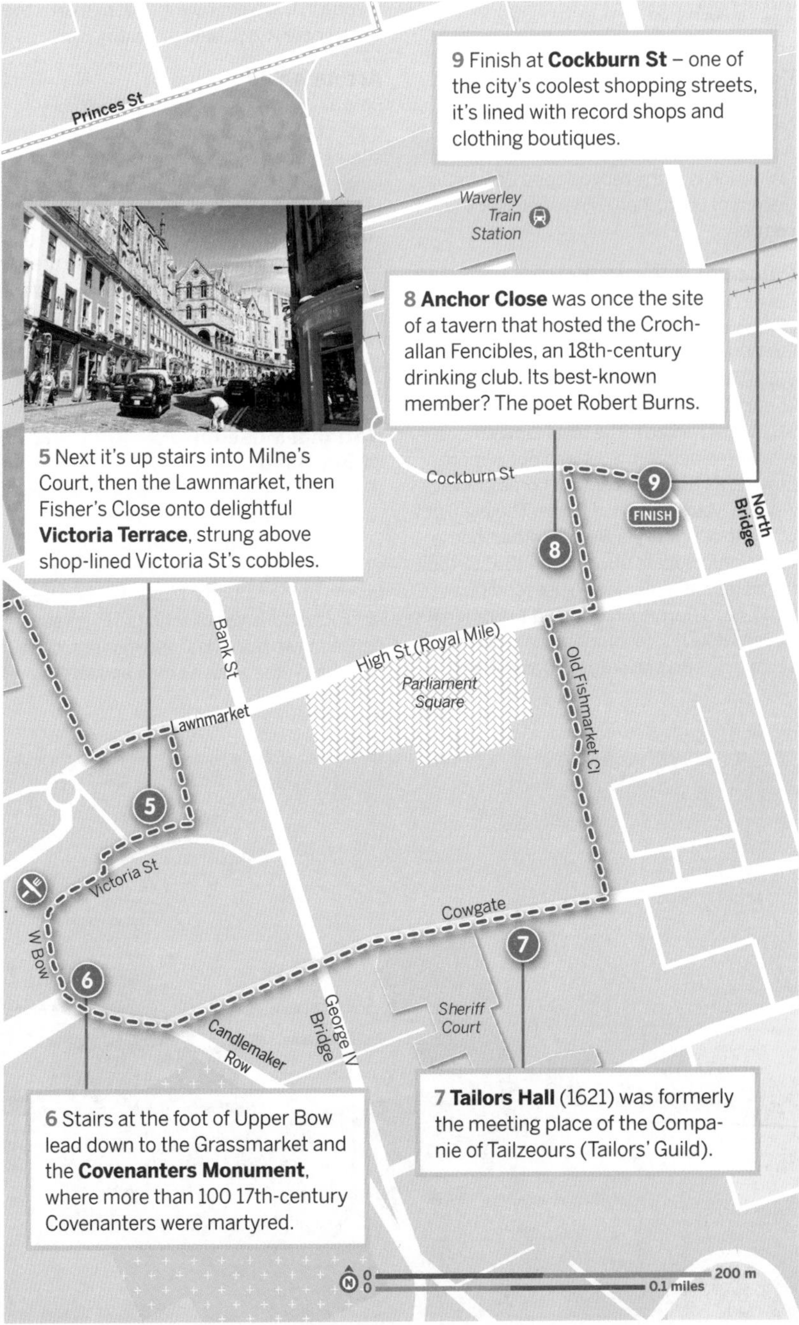

Princes St
Waverley Train Station
Cockburn St
North Bridge
FINISH
Bank St
High St (Royal Mile)
Parliament Square
Old Fishmarket Cl
Lawnmarket
Victoria St
W Bow
Cowgate
Sheriff Court
Candlemaker Row
George IV Bridge
0
200 m
0
0.1 miles

5 Next it's up stairs into Milne's Court, then the Lawnmarket, then Fisher's Close onto delightful **Victoria Terrace**, strung above shop-lined Victoria St's cobbles.

6 Stairs at the foot of Upper Bow lead down to the Grassmarket and the **Covenanters Monument**, where more than 100 17th-century Covenanters were martyred.

7 **Tailors Hall** (1621) was formerly the meeting place of the Companie of Tailzeours (Tailors' Guild).

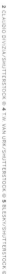

8 **Anchor Close** was once the site of a tavern that hosted the Crochallan Fencibles, an 18th-century drinking club. Its best-known member? The poet Robert Burns.

9 Finish at **Cockburn St** – one of the city's coolest shopping streets, it's lined with record shops and clothing boutiques.

2 CLAUDIO DIVIZIA/SHUTTERSTOCK © 4 T.W. VAN URK/SHUTTERSTOCK © 5 BLESKY/SHUTTERSTOCK ©

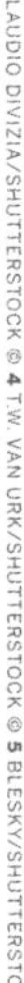

SIGHTS

Edinburgh's main attractions are concentrated in the city centre – on and around the Old Town's Royal Mile between the castle and Holyrood, and in the New Town. A major exception is the Royal Yacht *Britannia,* which is in the redeveloped docklands district of Leith, 2 miles northeast of the centre.

Palace of Holyroodhouse — Palace

(Map p240; 0303 123 7306; www.rct.uk/visit/palace-of-holyroodhouse; Canongate, Royal Mile, EH8 8DX; adult/child incl audio guide £16.50/9.50; 9.30am-6pm, last entry 4.30pm Apr-Oct, to 4.30pm, last entry 3.15pm Nov-Mar; 35) This palace is the royal family's official residence in Scotland but is more famous as the 16th-century home of the ill-fated Mary, Queen of Scots. The highlight of the tour is **Mary's Bedchamber**, home to the unfortunate queen from 1561 to 1567. It was here that her jealous second husband, Lord Darnley, restrained the pregnant queen while his henchmen murdered her secretary – and favourite – David Rizzio. A plaque in the neighbouring room marks the spot where Rizzio bled to death.

Arthur's Seat — Viewpoint

(Map p240; Holyrood Park; 35) The rocky peak of Arthur's Seat (251m), carved by ice sheets from the deeply eroded stump of a long-extinct volcano, is a distinctive feature of Edinburgh's skyline. The view from the summit is well worth the walk, extending from the Forth bridges in the west to the distant conical hill of North Berwick Law in the east, with the Ochil Hills and the Highlands on the northwestern horizon. You can hike from Holyrood to the summit in around 45 minutes.

National Museum of Scotland — Museum

(Map p240; 0300 123 6789; www.nms.ac.uk/national-mu seum-of-scotland; Chambers St, EH1 1JF; 10am-5pm; ; 35, 45) FREE Elegant Chambers St is dominated by the long facade of the National Museum of Scotland. Its extensive collections are spread between two buildings: one modern, one Victorian – the golden stone and striking

Royal Yacht Brittania

JOHN SELWAY/SHUTTERSTOCK ©

architecture of the new building (1998) make it one of the city's most distinctive landmarks. The museum's five floors trace the history of Scotland from geological beginnings to the present, with many imaginative and stimulating exhibits. Audio guides are available in several languages. Fees apply for special exhibitions.

Royal Yacht Britannia Ship

(Map p219; www.royalyachtbritannia.co.uk; Ocean Terminal, EH6 6JJ; adult/child incl audio guide £17/8.75; 9.30am-6pm Apr-Sep, to 5.30pm Oct, 10am-5pm Nov-Mar, last entry 1½hr before closing; P; 11, 22, 34, 36, 200) The former Royal Yacht *Britannia* was the British royal family's floating holiday home from the time of her launch in 1953 until her decommissioning in 1997, and is now permanently moored in front of **Ocean Terminal** (0131-555 8888; www.oceanterminal.com; Ocean Dr, EH6 6JJ; 10am-8pm Mon-Fri, to 7pm Sat, 11am-6pm Sun; ; 11, 22, 34, 36, 200). The tour, which you take at your own pace with an audio guide (available in 30 languages), lifts the curtain on the everyday lives of the royals, and gives an intriguing insight into the Queen's private tastes. It's best to book online in advance.

Scottish National Portrait Gallery Gallery

(Map p243; 0131-624 6200; www.nationalgalleries.org; 1 Queen St, EH2 1JD; 10am-5pm; ; all York Pl buses, St Andrew Sq) FREE The Venetian Gothic palace of the Scottish National Portrait Gallery is one of the city's top attractions. Its galleries illustrate Scottish history through paintings, photographs and sculptures, putting faces to famous names from Scotland's past and present, from Robert Burns, Mary, Queen of Scots, and Bonnie Prince Charlie to the late Sir Sean Connery, comedian Billy Connolly and poet Jackie Kay. There's an admission fee for special exhibitions.

Scotch Whisky Experience Museum

(Map p240; www.scotchwhiskyexperience.co.uk; 354 Castlehill, EH1 2NE; adult/child from £17/8; 10am-6pm Apr-Jul, to 5pm Aug-Mar; 23, 27, 41, 42) A former school houses this

Edinburgh Shopping

Edinburgh's shopping experience extends far beyond the big-name department stores of Princes St. Classic buys include cashmere, Harris tweed, tartan goods, Celtic jewellery, smoked salmon and Scotch whisky.

Kilberry Bagpipes (Map p240; 0131-556 9607; www.kilberrybagpipes.com; 27 St Mary's St, EH1 1TA; 8.30am-4.30pm Mon-Fri, 10am-2pm Sat; 35) This maker and retailer of traditional Highland bagpipes also sells piping accessories, snare drums, books, CDs and learning materials.

Valvona & Crolla (Map p243; 0131-556 6066; www.valvonacrolla.co.uk; 19 Elm Row, EH7 4AA; 9am-6.30pm Mon-Sat; all Leith Walk buses) The queen of Edinburgh delicatessens, established during the 1930s, is packed with Mediterranean goodies and fine wines and has a good cafe.

Jenners (Map p243; 0131-225 2442; www.houseoffraser.co.uk; 48 Princes St, EH2 2YJ; 9.30am-6.30pm Mon-Wed, to 8pm Thu, to 7pm Fri, 9am-7pm Sat, 11am-6pm Sun; Princes St) Founded in 1838, the grande dame of Scottish department stores stocks a wide range of quality goods, both classic and contemporary.

Royal Mile Whiskies (Map p240; 0131-225 3383; www.royalmilewhiskies.com; 379 High St, EH1 1PW; 10am-6pm; 23, 27, 41, 42) This place has a selection of single malts in miniature and full-size bottles. There's also a range of blended whiskies, Irish whiskey and bourbon; you can buy online too.

Dishes at Valvona & Crolla

JONATHAN SMITH/LONELY PLANET ©

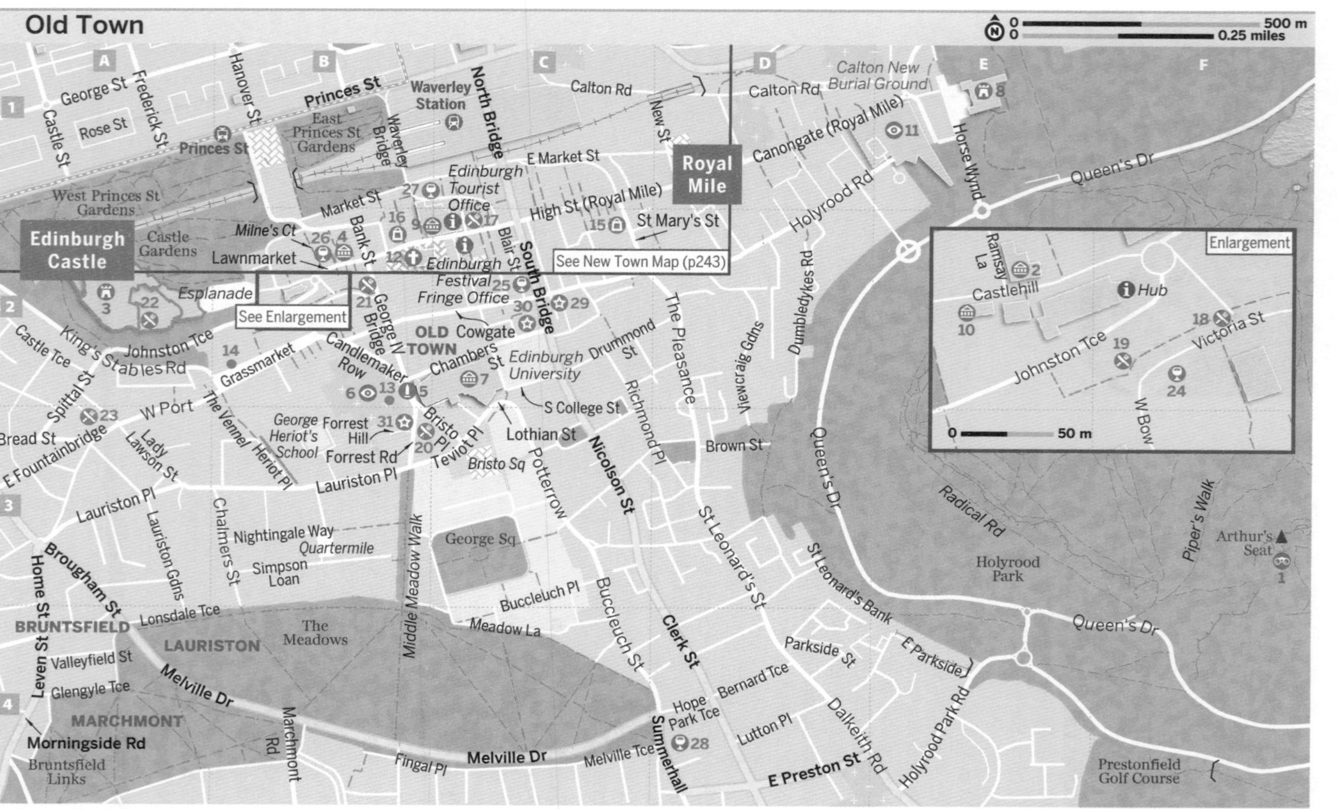
Old Town
500 m
0.25 miles
Princes St
George St
Rose St
Castle St
Frederick St
Hanover St
West Princes St Gardens
East Princes St Gardens
Waverley Station
Waverley Bridge
North Bridge
Calton Rd
New St
E Market St
Royal Mile
Canongate (Royal Mile)
Calton New Burial Ground
Horse Wynd
Queen's Dr
Holyrood Rd
Edinburgh Tourist Office
Market St
High St (Royal Mile)
St Mary's St
Milne's Ct
Bank St
Blair St
Edinburgh Castle
Castle Gardens
Lawnmarket
Edinburgh Festival Fringe Office
South Bridge
See New Town Map (p243)
Esplanade
See Enlargement
George IV Bridge
OLD TOWN
Cowgate
Castle Tce
King's Stables Rd
Johnston Tce
Grassmarket
Candlemaker Row
Chambers St
Edinburgh University
Drummond St
The Pleasance
Viewcraig Gdns
Dumbiedykes Rd
Spittal St
W Port
The Vennel
George Heriot's School
Forrest Hill
Bristo Pl
S College St
Richmond Pl
Bread St
E Fountainbridge
Lady Lawson St
Heriot Pl
Forrest Rd
Teviot Pl
Lothian St
Nicolson St
Brown St
Bristo Sq
Lauriston Pl
Potterrow
Lauriston Gdns
Chalmers St
Nightingale Way
Quartermile
Simpson Loan
Middle Meadow Walk
George Sq
St Leonard's St
Home St
Brougham St
BRUNTSFIELD
Lonsdale Tce
Buccleuch Pl
Buccleuch St
St Leonard's Bank
The Meadows
LAURISTON
Meadow La
Clerk St
Leven St
Valleyfield St
Glengyle Tce
Melville Dr
Marchmont Rd
MARCHMONT
Morningside Rd
Bruntsfield Links
Fingal Pl
Melville Tce
Summerhall
Hope Park Tce
Bernard Tce
Parkside St
Lutton Pl
E Parkside
Dalkeith Rd
E Preston St
Holyrood Park Rd
Radical Rd
Holyrood Park
Piper's Walk
Arthur's Seat
Prestonfield Golf Course
Enlargement
Ramsay La
Castlehill
Hub
Victoria St
Johnston Tce
W Bow
50 m

Old Town

Sights

1	Arthur's Seat	F3
2	Camera Obscura & World of Illusions	E2
3	Edinburgh Castle	A2
4	Gladstone's Land	B2
5	Greyfriars Bobby Statue	B2
6	Greyfriars Kirkyard	B2
7	National Museum of Scotland	C2
8	Palace of Holyroodhouse	E1
9	Real Mary King's Close	B2
10	Scotch Whisky Experience	E2
11	Scottish Parliament Building	E1
12	St Giles Cathedral	B2

Activities, Courses & Tours

13	City of the Dead Tours	B2
14	Edinburgh Literary Pub Tour	B2

Shopping

15	Kilberry Bagpipes	C2
16	Royal Mile Whiskies	B2

Eating

	Amber	(see 10)
17	Gordon's Trattoria	C2
18	Grain Store	F2
19	Maxie's Bistro	F2
20	Mums	B3
21	Ondine	B2
22	Redcoat Café	A2
23	Timberyard	A3

Drinking & Nightlife

24	Bow Bar	F2
25	Cabaret Voltaire	C2
26	Jolly Judge	B2
27	Malt Shovel	B1
28	Royal Dick	D4

Entertainment

29	Caves	C2
30	Jazz Bar	C2
31	Sandy Bell's	B3
	Summerhall	(see 28)

multimedia centre that takes you through the making of whisky, from barley to bottle, in a series of exhibits, demonstrations and talks that combine sight, sound and smell, including the world's largest collection of malt whiskies (3384 bottles!). The pricier tours include extensive whisky tastings and samples of Scottish cuisine. There's also a **restaurant** (0131-477 8477; www.scotchwhiskyexperience.co.uk/restaurant; 354 Castlehill, EH1 2NE; mains £15-20; 11am-8pm; 23, 27, 41, 42) that serves traditional Scottish dishes with, where possible, a dash of whisky thrown in.

Greyfriars Bobby Statue Monument

(Map p240; cnr George IV Bridge & Candlemaker Row, EH1 2QQ; 2, 23, 27, 35, 41, 42, 45) Probably the most popular photo opportunity in Edinburgh, the life-size statue of Greyfriars Bobby, a Skye terrier who captured the hearts of the British public in the late 19th century, stands outside **Greyfriars Kirkyard** (www.greyfriarskirk.com; Candlemaker Row, EH1 2QQ; 24hr; 2, 23, 27, 35, 41, 42, 45). From 1858 to 1872 the wee dog maintained a vigil over the grave of his master, an Edinburgh police officer. The story was immortalised in a novel by Eleanor Atkinson in 1912, and in 1961 was made into a movie by – who else? – Walt Disney.

TOURS

Edinburgh Literary Pub Tour Walking

(www.edinburghliterarypubtour.co.uk; Beehive Inn, Grassmarket, EH1 2JU; adult/student £16/14; 7.30pm daily May-Sep, limited days Oct-Apr) An enlightening two-hour trawl through Edinburgh's literary history – and its associated howffs (pubs) – in the entertaining company of Messrs Clart and McBrain. One of the city's best walking tours (departing from Beehive Inn).

City of the Dead Tours Walking

(0131-225 9044; www.cityofthedeadtours.com; 26a Candlemaker Row, EH1 2QE; adult/concession £14/10; 9pm Easter-Oct, 8.30pm Tue & Thu-Sat Nov-Easter) This nightly tour of Greyfriars Kirkyard is probably the scariest of Edinburgh's 'ghost' tours. Many people have reported encounters with the Mackenzie Poltergeist, the ghost of a 17th-century judge who persecuted the Covenanters and who now haunts their former prison in a corner of the kirkyard. Not suitable for children under 12.

Majestic Tour Bus
(www.edinburghtour.com/majestic-tour; St Andrew Sq, EH2 1BB; adult/child £16/free; ⏲daily year-round except 25 Dec) Hop-on, hop-off tour departing every 15 to 20 minutes from the north side of St Andrew Sq to the Royal Yacht *Britannia* at Ocean Terminal via the New Town, the Royal Botanic Garden and Newhaven, returning via Leith Walk, Holyrood and the Royal Mile.

EATING

Today, Edinburgh has more restaurants per head of population than any other UK city, including a handful of places with Michelin stars.

Mums Cafe £
(Map p240; ☎0131-260 9806; www.monstermashcafe.co.uk; 4a Forrest Rd, EH1 2QN; mains £9-13; ⏲9am-10pm Mon-Sat, 10am-10pm Sun; 📶👪; 🚌2, 23, 27, 35, 41, 42, 45) This nostalgia-fuelled cafe serves up classic British comfort food that wouldn't look out of place on a 1950s menu – bacon and eggs, bangers and mash, shepherd's pie, fish and chips. But there's a twist – the food is all top-quality nosh freshly prepared from local produce. There's also a good selection of bottled craft beers and Scottish-brewed cider.

Gardener's Cottage Scottish ££
(Map p243; ☎0131-558 1221; www.thegardenerscottage.co; 1 Royal Tce Gdns, London Rd, EH7 5DX; 2-/3-course lunch £15/19, 6-course dinner £60; ⏲noon-2pm & 5-10pm Mon-Fri, 10am-2pm & 5-10pm Sat & Sun; 🚌all London Rd buses) This country cottage in the heart of the city, bedecked with flowers and fairy lights, offers one of Edinburgh's most interesting dining experiences – two tiny rooms with communal tables made of salvaged timber, and a set menu based on fresh local produce (most of the vegetables and fruit are from its own organic garden). Bookings essential; brunch served at weekends.

Aizle Scottish ££
(Map p243; ☎0131-527 4747; www.aizle.co.uk; Kimpton Charlotte Square Hotel, 38 Charlotte Sq, EH2 4HQ; 6-course dinner £70; ⏲5-9pm Wed-Sun; 📶; 🚌all Princes St buses) If you tend to have trouble deciding what to eat, Aizle (the name is an old Scots word for 'spark' or 'ember') will do the job for you. There's no menu here, just a six-course dinner conjured from a monthly 'harvest' of the finest and freshest local produce (listed on a blackboard), and presented beautifully – art on a plate.

Timberyard Scottish ££
(Map p240; ☎0131-221 1222; www.timberyard.co; 10 Lady Lawson St, EH3 9DS; mains £16-22, 5-course set menu £50; ⏲noon-2pm & 5.30-9.30pm Tue-Sat; 📶🌱👪; 🚌2, 300) Ancient, worn floorboards, cast-iron pillars, exposed joists, and tables made from slabs of old mahogany create a rustic, retro atmosphere in this slow-food restaurant where the accent is on locally sourced produce from artisan growers and foragers. Typical dishes include honey-glazed monkfish with saffron, samphire and leek, and pigeon with radicchio, chanterelles and sherry.

Outlook Scottish £££
(Map p243; ☎0131-322 1246; www.thelookoutedinburgh.co; Calton Hill, EH7 5AA; lunch/dinner from £28/34; ⏲noon-9.30pm Tue-Thu, 10am-9.30pm Fri-Sun; 🌱) This glass-walled restaurant perched on top of Calton Hill enjoys some of the finest views in the city, and some of the finest food. Run by the same folk as Gardener's Cottage, it has a menu consisting of a tray of seven small dishes (including a vegetarian option) prepared using whatever fresh local produce is in season, plus a choice of sides and wines.

Ondine Seafood £££
(Map p240; ☎0131-226 1888; www.ondinerestaurant.co.uk; 2 George IV Bridge, EH1 1AD; mains £22-38; ⏲noon-9pm Wed-Sat, noon-4pm Sun; 📶; 🚌23, 27, 41, 42) Ondine is one of Edinburgh's finest seafood restaurants, with a menu based on sustainably sourced fish. Take a seat at the curved Oyster Bar

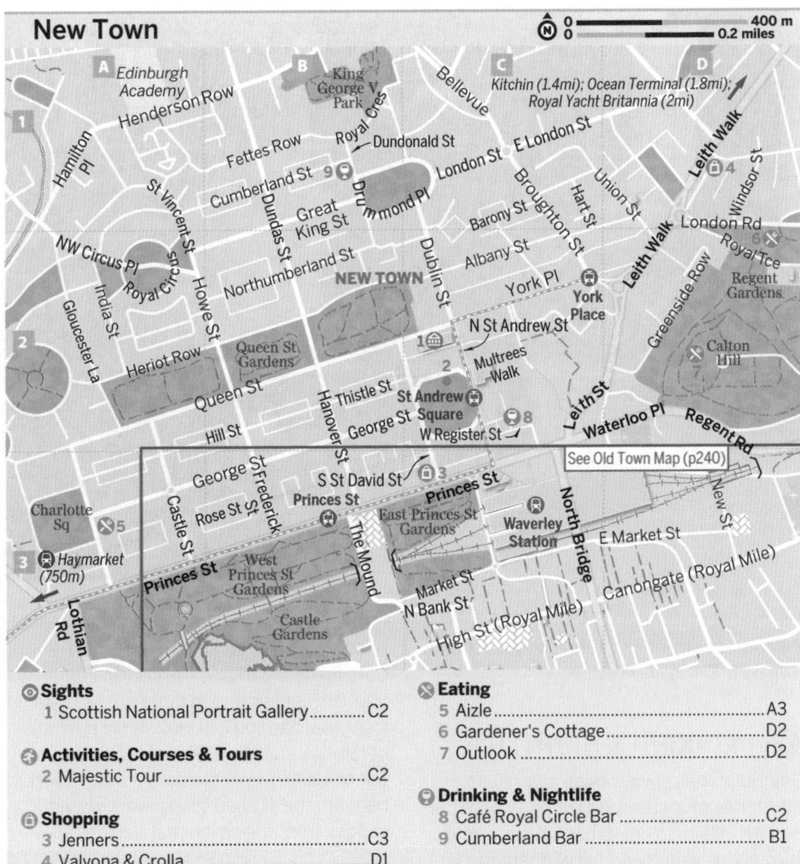

Sights
1 Scottish National Portrait Gallery C2

Activities, Courses & Tours
2 Majestic Tour C2

Shopping
3 Jenners C3
4 Valvona & Crolla D1

Eating
5 Aizle A3
6 Gardener's Cottage D2
7 Outlook D2

Drinking & Nightlife
8 Café Royal Circle Bar C2
9 Cumberland Bar B1

and tuck into oysters with shallot dressing, shellfish bisque, lobster thermidor, a *fruits de mer* platter or just good old haddock and chips (with minted pea puree, just to keep things posh).

Kitchin Scottish £££

(☎0131-555 1755; www.thekitchin.com; 78 Commercial Quay, EH6 6LX; 3-course lunch/dinner £39/90; ⏲noon-2.30pm & 6-10pm Tue-Sat; ✎; 🚌16, 22, 35, 36) Fresh, seasonal, locally sourced Scottish produce is the philosophy that's won a Michelin star for this elegant but unpretentious restaurant. The menu moves with the seasons, of course, so expect fresh salads in summer and game in winter, and shellfish dishes such as Orkney scallops baked in the shell with white wine, vermouth and herbs when there's an 'r' in the month.

Grain Store Scottish £££

(Map p240; ☎0131-225 7635; www.grainstore-restaurant.co.uk; 30 Victoria St, EH1 2JW; mains £24-32; ⏲noon-2.30pm & 6-9.45pm Mon-Sat, noon-2.30pm & 6-9.30pm Sun; 🚌2, 23, 27, 41, 42) An atmospheric upstairs dining room on picturesque Victoria St, the Grain Store has a well-earned reputation for serving the finest Scottish produce, perfectly prepared in dishes such as halibut with fried squid and mussel bisque, and roe deer venison with

Cafe Royal Circle Bar

celeriac, beetroot and kale. The two-course lunch for £14 is good value.

DRINKING & NIGHTLIFE

Edinburgh has always been a drinker's city. It has more than 700 pubs – more per square mile than any other UK city – and they are as varied and full of character as the people who drink in them.

Bow Bar Pub

(Map p240; www.thebowbar.co.uk; 80 West Bow, EH1 2HH; noon-midnight; ; 2, 23, 27, 41, 42) One of the city's best traditional-style pubs (it's not as old as it looks), serving a range of excellent real ales, Scottish craft gins and a vast selection of malt whiskies, the Bow Bar is often standing-room only on Friday and Saturday evenings.

Cafe Royal Circle Bar Pub

(Map p243; 0131-556 1884; www.caferoyaledinburgh.com; 17 W Register St, EH2 2AA; 11am-11pm Mon-Wed, to midnight Thu, to 1am Fri & Sat, to 10pm Sun; ; Princes St) The Cafe Royal is perhaps *the* classic Edinburgh pub; its main claims to fame are its magnificent oval bar and its Doulton tile portraits of famous Victorian inventors. Sit at the bar or claim one of the cosy leather booths beneath the stained-glass windows, and choose from the seven real ales on tap.

Royal Dick Microbrewery

(Map p240; 0131-560 1572; www.summerhall.co.uk/the-royal-dick; 1 Summerhall, EH9 1PL; 2-10pm; ; 41, 42) The decor at the Royal Dick alludes to its past as the home of Edinburgh University's veterinary school: there are shelves of laboratory glassware and walls covered with animal bones, even an old operating table. But rather than being creepy, it's a warm, welcoming place for a drink, serving artisan ales and craft gins produced by its own microbrewery and distillery.

Cabaret Voltaire Club

(Map p240; www.thecabaretvoltaire.com; 36-38 Blair St, EH1 1QR; 5pm-3am Tue-Sat, 8pm-1am

Sun; ; all South Bridge buses) An atmospheric warren of stone-lined vaults houses this self-consciously 'alternative' club, which eschews huge dance floors and egotistical DJ worship in favour of a 'creative crucible' hosting an eclectic mix of DJs, live acts, comedy, theatre, visual arts and the spoken word. Well worth a look.

ENTERTAINMENT

Sandy Bell's Traditional Music

(Map p240; 0131-225 2751; 25 Forrest Rd, EH1 2QH; noon-1am Mon-Sat, 12.30pm-midnight Sun; 2, 23, 27, 35, 41, 42, 45) This unassuming pub has been a stalwart of the traditional-music scene since the 1960s (the founder's wife sang with The Corries). There's music every weekday evening at 9pm, and from 2pm Saturday and 4pm Sunday, plus lots of impromptu sessions.

Summerhall Theatre

(Map p240; 0131-560 1580; www.summerhall.co.uk; 1 Summerhall, EH9 1PL; box office 10am-6pm; 41, 42) Formerly Edinburgh University's veterinary school, the Summerhall complex is a major cultural centre and entertainment venue, with old halls and lecture theatres (including an original anatomy lecture theatre) now serving as venues for drama, dance, cinema and comedy. It's also one of the main venues for events during the Edinburgh International Festival (p225).

Caves Live Music

(Map p240; www.unusualvenuesedinburgh.com/venues/the-caves-venue-edinburgh; 8-12 Niddry St S, EH1 1NS; 35) A spectacular subterranean venue set in the ancient stone vaults beneath the South Bridge, the Caves stages a series of one-off club nights and live-music gigs, as well as *ceilidh* (traditional music) nights during the Edinburgh Festival. Check the What's On link on the website for upcoming events.

Jazz Bar Jazz, Blues

(Map p240; www.thejazzbar.co.uk; 1a Chambers St, EH1 1HR; £3-7; 5pm-3am Sun-Fri, 1.30pm-3am Sat; ; 35, 45) This atmospheric cellar bar, with its polished parquet floors, bare stone walls, candlelit tables and stylish steel-framed chairs, is owned and operated by jazz musicians. There's live music every night from 9pm to 3am, and on Saturday from 3pm. As well as jazz, expect bands playing blues, funk, soul and fusion.

Best Whisky Bars

Bow Bar (p244) Busy Grassmarket-area pub with huge selection of malt whiskies.

Malt Shovel (0131-225 6843; www.maltshovelinn-edinburgh.co.uk; 11-15 Cockburn St, EH1 1BP; 11am-11pm Mon-Wed, to midnight Thu & Sun, to 1am Fri & Sat; ; 6) Old-school pub with more than 100 single malts behind the bar.

Cumberland Bar (Map p243; 0131-558 3134; www.cumberlandbar.co.uk; 1-3 Cumberland St, EH3 6RT; noon-midnight Mon-Wed, to 1am Thu-Sat, 11am-11pm Sun; ; 23, 27) Good summer choice; enjoy your malt while sitting in the garden.

T.W. VAN URK/SHUTTERSTOCK ©

INFORMATION

DANGERS & ANNOYANCES

Lothian Rd, Dalry Rd, Rose St and the western end of Princes St, at the junction with Shandwick Pl and Queensferry St, can get a bit rowdy late on Friday and Saturday nights after pub-closing time. Calton Hill offers good views during the day but is best avoided at night.

Be aware that the area between Salamander St and Leith Links in Leith is a red-light district – lone women here at any time of day might be approached by kerb crawlers.

EMERGENCY & IMPORTANT NUMBERS

UK's country code	☎44
International access code	☎00
Police (emergency)	☎999 or 112
Police (non-emergency)	☎101
Fire	☎999 or 112
Ambulance	☎999 or 112

USEFUL WEBSITES

Edinburgh Festival Guide (www.edinburghfestivalcity.com) Everything you need to know about Edinburgh's many festivals.

Lonely Planet (www.lonelyplanet.com/edinburgh) Destination information, hotel bookings, traveller forum and more.

VisitScotland Edinburgh (www.visitscotland.com/edinburgh) Official Scottish tourist board site.

The List (www.list.co.uk) Local listings and reviews for restaurants, bars, clubs and theatres.

TOURIST INFORMATION

Edinburgh Tourist Office (Map p240; Edinburgh iCentre; ☎0131-473 3820; www.visitscotland.com/info/services/edinburgh-icentre-p234441; 249 High St, Royal Mile, EH1 1YJ; ⏲10am-4.30pm Mon-Sat, to 4pm Sun Oct-Mar, longer hours Apr-Sep; 📶; 🚌23, 27, 41, 42) Accommodation-booking service, free city maps, gift shop and bookshop, and sales of tickets for CalMac ferries and CityLink and National Express buses.

GETTING THERE & AWAY

Edinburgh lies in east-central Scotland, and is well served by air, road and rail.

Air Edinburgh Airport (EDI; ☎0844 448 8833; www.edinburghairport.com), 8 miles west of the city, has numerous flights to other parts of Scotland and the UK, Ireland and mainland Europe. Flight time from London is around one hour.

Car Driving times are around one hour from Glasgow, two hours from Newcastle, and four to five hours from York. The drive from London can take anything from eight hours upwards and is not recommended.

Train The main rail terminus in Edinburgh is Waverley train station, located in the heart of the city. Trains arriving from, and departing for, the west also stop at Haymarket station, which is more convenient for the West End.

GETTING AROUND

CAR

Though useful for day trips beyond the city, a car in central Edinburgh is more of a liability than a convenience. There is restricted access on Princes St, George St and Charlotte Sq, many streets are one way, and finding a parking place in the city centre is like striking gold. Queen's Dr around Holyrood Park is closed to motorised traffic on Sunday.

PUBLIC TRANSPORT

For timetable information, contact **Traveline** (☎0871 200 22 33; www.traveline.info).

Bus Reasonably priced; extensive network. The main bus operators are Lothian Buses (www.lothianbuses.com) and First (www.firstgroup.com).

Taxi Local operators include **Central Taxis** (☎0131-229 2468; www.taxis-edinburgh.co.uk) and **City Cabs** (☎0131-228 1211; www.citycabs.co.uk).

Tram The tram line runs from the airport via Haymarket and Princes St to York Pl at the east end of the city centre and is operated by Edinburgh Trams (www.edinburghtrams.com).

Where to Stay

Edinburgh's accommodation options range from guesthouses set in Victorian villas and Georgian town houses to stylish boutique hotels. You can also choose between international chain hotels, and some exceptional hotels housed in beautiful historic buildings.

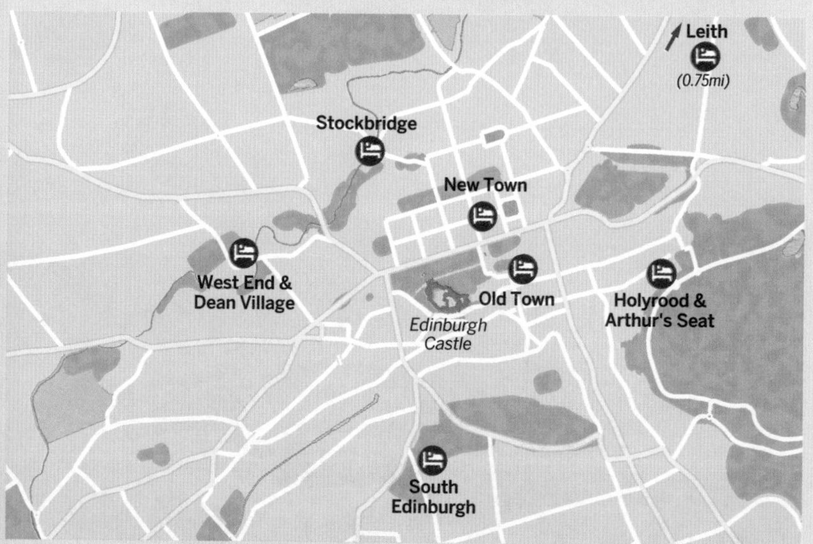

Neighbourhood	Atmosphere
Holyrood & Arthur's Seat	Mostly quiet and peaceful. Holyrood Park on your doorstep for morning and evening walks.
Leith	Lots of bars and restaurants. Handy for Royal Yacht *Britannia*. Good bus service.
New Town	Central, with good transport connections and a vast choice of eating places. Close to main train stations.
Old Town	Right in the thick of things, walking distance to the castle and Royal Mile.
South Edinburgh	Spacious rooms in Victorian villas and terraces, often on quiet backstreets. Good choice of restaurants and bars.
Stockbridge	Pleasant village atmosphere. Good local shops, cafes and restaurants.
West End & Dean Village	Close to the city centre, Haymarket train station and tram line. Hotels and B&Bs in attractive Georgian town houses.

THE SCOTTISH HIGHLANDS

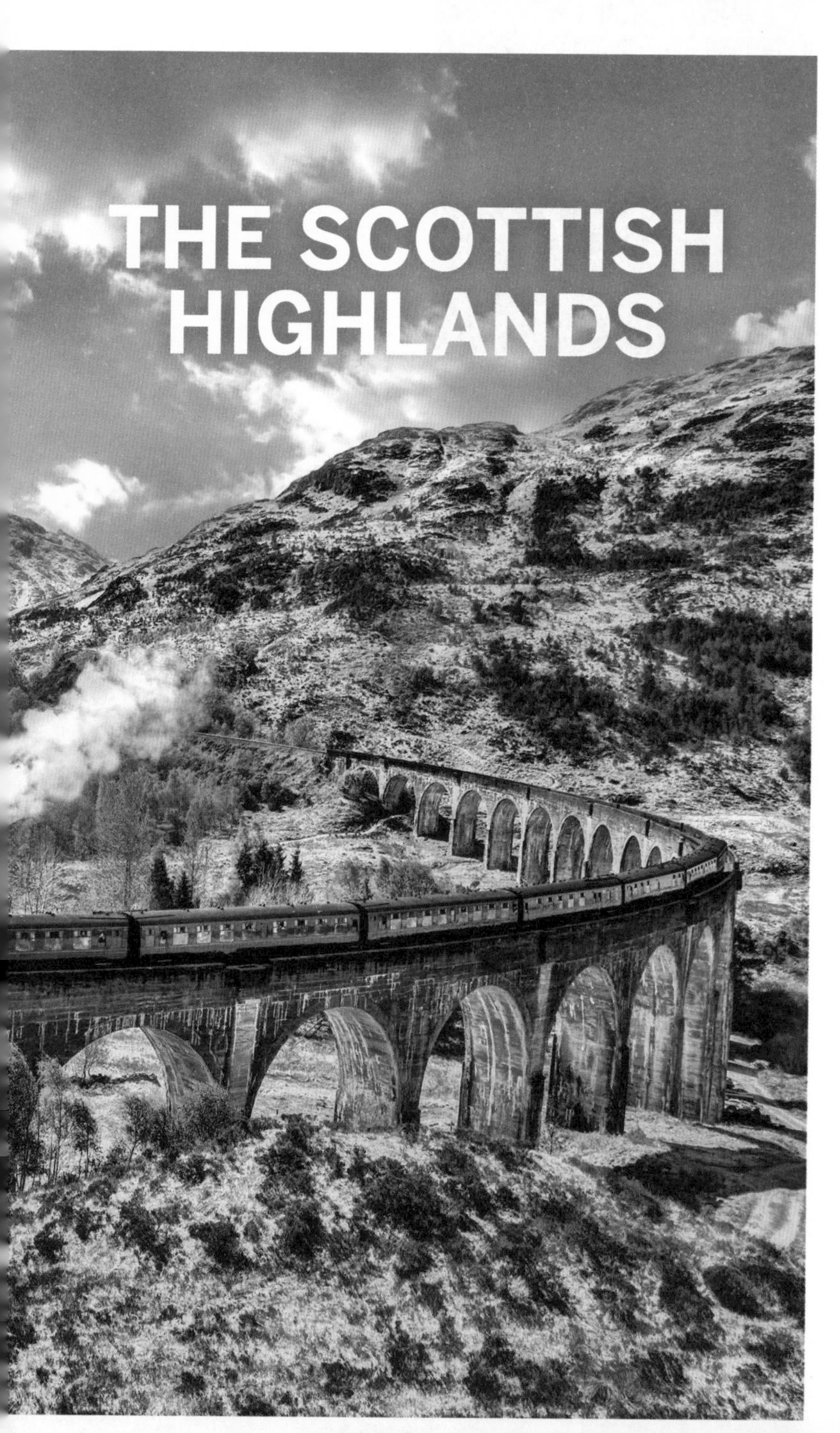

In this Chapter

The Scottish Highlands at a Glance...

With their sweeping lochs and brooding glens, the Highlands are a magnet for outdoors enthusiasts. Glen Coe and Fort William draw hikers and skiers; Royal Deeside offers a home to the Queen and magnificent castles; Inverness, the Highland capital, provides urban rest and relaxation; while nearby Loch Ness and its elusive monster add a hint of mystery. And then from Fort William the roads lead to the sea, where – waiting just offshore – lies the wildlife-rich Isle of Mull.

Two Days in the Scottish Highlands

Cruise Royal Deeside on day one, taking in the Queen's estate, **Balmoral** (p253), and nearby **Braemar Castle** (p253). The **Bothy** (p262) is a characterful place to refuel. On day two it's time to go Loch Ness Monster–hunting on a **boat trip** (p256). Next up, tour iconic **Urquhart Castle** (p256), before exploring the loch's quieter eastern shore. The **Dores Inn** (p257) is an idyllic spot to dine.

Four Days in the Scottish Highlands

On day three, head southwest to Fort William to dip into the **West Highland Museum** (p262), ride a **steam train** (p262) and admire **Ben Nevis** (p262). Feast on superb Scottish fare at **Lime Tree** (p263). On day four, travel to the Isle of Mull, and head out on a **whale-watching tour** (p260). Visit idyllic **Iona Abbey** (p261) and stop by **Duart Castle** (p261). Fill up on seafood at **Café Fish** (p261).

Previous page: Jacobite Steam Train over Glenfinnan Viaduct (p262)
SAMOT/SHUTTERSTOCK ©

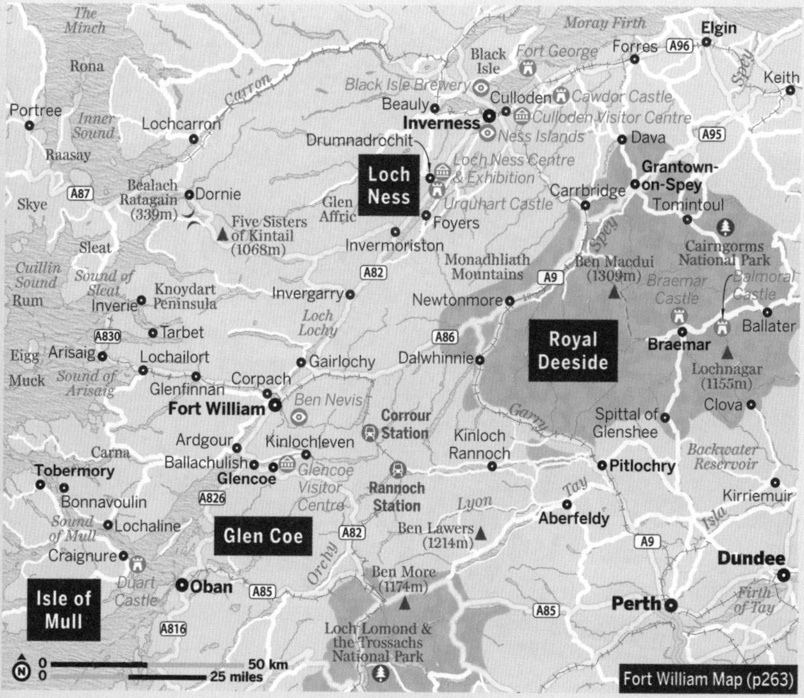

Fort William Map (p263)

Arriving in the Scottish Highlands

Bus Scottish Citylink (www.citylink.co.uk) runs buses connecting Inverness to Fort William along the Great Glen.

Car Braemar is around 100 miles (2½ hours) north of Edinburgh by car; Fort William is around a three-hour drive (150 miles) from Edinburgh.

Train Trains run roughly every two hours from Edinburgh to Inverness (£47, 3½ hours).

Where to Stay

Inverness and Fort William have the most options; in between, the Great Glen also has a wide range of possibilities (especially hikers' hostels). The Isle of Mull boasts everything from campsites to swish hotels, while Royal Deeside is rich with hotels and B&Bs. For all areas, and all price ranges, it pays to book ahead in spring and summer.

Ballater

IWETA0077/SHUTTERSTOCK ©

Royal Deeside

The picturesque upper valley of the River Dee takes in the settlements of Ballater and Braemar. Made famous by its long associations with the monarchy, the region is known as Royal Deeside.

Great For...

☑ **Don't Miss**

The hike to Balmoral Castle's Prince Albert's Cairn, erected by a heart-broken Queen Victoria.

Ballater

The attractive little village of Ballater owes its 18th-century origins to the curative waters of nearby Pannanich Springs (now bottled commercially as Deeside Natural Mineral Water), and its prosperity to nearby Balmoral Castle.

In the village, look out for the crests on the shopfronts along the main street proclaiming 'By Royal Appointment' – evidence that the village is a major supplier of provisions to Balmoral Castle.

Pleasant walks in the surrounding area include the steep one-hour woodland hike up Craigendarroch.

You can hire bikes from **CycleHighlands** (☎01339-755864; www.cyclehighlands.com; The Pavilion, Victoria Rd; Santa Cruz mountain bike hire per day £80; ⏲9am-5pm Mon-Thu & Sat, to 4pm Fri & Sun) and **Bike Station** (☎01339-

Balmoral Castle

PITSCH22/SHUTTERSTOCK ©

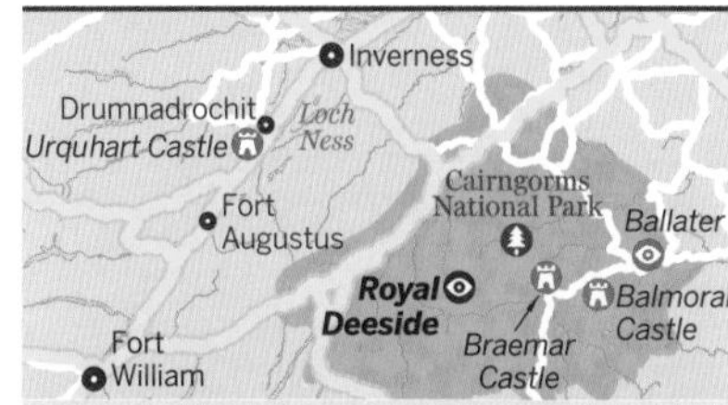

Need to Know

In winter Braemar is one of the coldest places in the country – temperatures as low as -27°C have been recorded – and during spells of severe cold, hungry deer wander the streets looking for a bite to eat.

Take a Break

Stop by the Bothy (p262) in Braemar for lunchtime treats.

★ Top Tip

Take outdoor kit for a visit to Balmoral Castle; the tour is largely outside.

754004; www.bikestationballater.co.uk; Station Sq; bicycle hire per day adult/child £20/10; 9am-6pm), both of which also offer guided bike rides and advice on local trails.

Balmoral Castle

Built for Queen Victoria in 1855 as a private residence for the royal family, **Balmoral** (01339-742534; www.balmoralcastle.com; Crathie; guided tour adult/child £15/6; 10am-5pm Apr-Jul, limited dates Oct-Dec; P) kicked off the revival of the Scottish Baronial style of architecture that characterises so many of Scotland's 19th-century country houses. In 2020 admission was by advance booking only for an hour-long guided tour of the grounds and the castle ballroom, which displays a collection of Landseer paintings and royal silver (don't expect to see the Queen's private quarters).

You can buy a booklet that details several waymarked walks within Balmoral Estate; the best is the climb to Prince Albert's Cairn, a huge granite pyramid that bears the inscription, 'To the beloved memory of Albert the great and good, Prince Consort. Erected by his broken hearted widow Victoria R. 21st August 1862'.

Braemar Castle

Just 9 miles west of Balmoral, turreted **Braemar Castle** (www.braemarcastle.co.uk; adult/child £10/4; 10am-5pm daily Jul & Aug, Wed-Sun Apr-Jun, Sep & Oct; P) dates from 1628 and served as a government garrison after the 1745 Jacobite rebellion. In 2007 it was taken over by the local community, which now offers guided tours of the historic castle apartments. There's a short walk from the car park to the castle.

Loch Ness

Deep, dark and narrow, the bitterly cold waters of Loch Ness have long drawn waves of people hunting Nessie, the elusive Loch Ness Monster. Despite the crowds, it's still possible to find tranquillity and gorgeous views. Add a highly photogenic castle and some superb hiking, and you have a loch with bags of appeal.

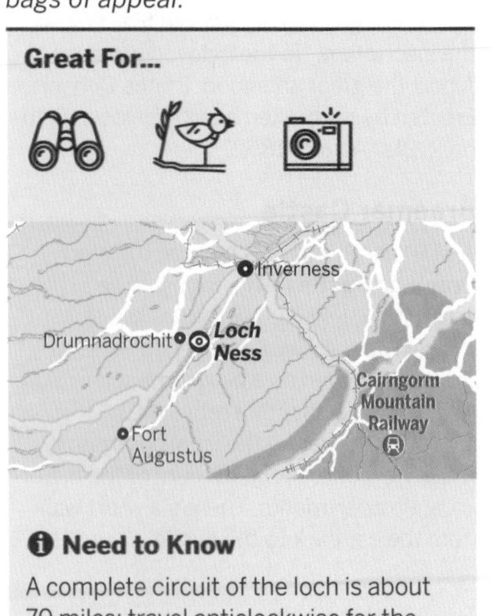

Great For...

Need to Know

A complete circuit of the loch is about 70 miles; travel anticlockwise for the best views.

★ Top Tip

Fancy a spot of Nessie hunting? Check out the latest at www.lochnesssightings.com.

ANDRE GONCALVES/SHUTTERSTOCK ©

Tales of the Loch Ness Monster truly took off in the 1930s, when reported sightings led to a press furore and a string of high-profile photographs. Reports have tailed off recently, but the bizarre mini-industry that's grown up around Nessie is a spectacle in itself.

Drumnadrochit

Seized by monster madness, its gift shops bulging with Nessie cuddly toys, Drumnadrochit is a hotbed of beastie fever, with Nessie attractions battling it out for the tourist dollar.

The **Loch Ness Centre & Exhibition** (☎01456-450573; www.lochness.com; adult/child £8.45/4.95; ⏰9.30am-6pm Jul & Aug, to 5pm Easter-Jun, Sep & Oct, 10am-4pm Nov-Easter; P 👪) adopts a scientific approach that allows you to weigh the evidence for yourself. Exhibits include those on hoaxes and optical illusions and some original equipment – sonar survey vessels, miniature submarines, cameras and sediment coring tools – used in various monster hunts, as well as original photographs and film footage of reported sightings.

To head out yourself, **Nessie Hunter** (☎01456-450395; www.lochness-cruises.com; adult/child £16/10; ⏰Apr-Oct) offers one-hour monster-hunting cruises, complete with sonar and underwater cameras. Cruises depart from Drumnadrochit hourly from 10am to 6pm daily.

Urquhart Castle

Commanding a superb location 1.5 miles east of Drumnadrochit, with outstanding views, **Urquhart Castle** (HES; ☎01456-450551; www.historicenvironment.scot; adult/

Urquhart Castle by Loch Ness

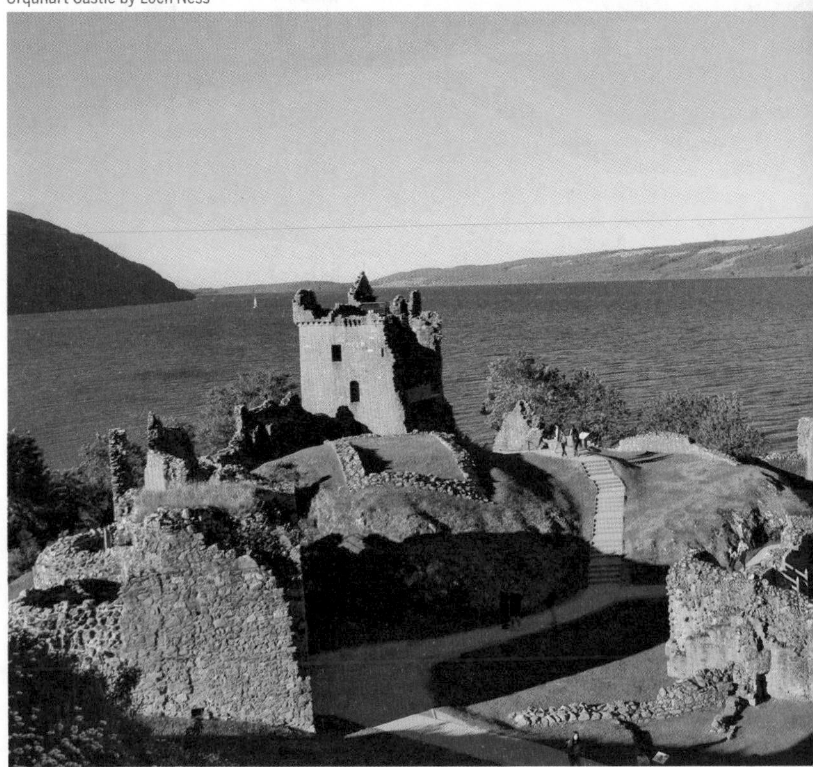

child £9.60/5.80; 9.30am-6pm Apr-Oct, to 4.30pm Nov-Mar; P) is a popular Nessie-hunting hotspot. A huge visitors centre (most of which is beneath ground level) includes a video theatre and displays of medieval items discovered in the castle.

The castle has been repeatedly sacked and rebuilt over the centuries; in 1692 it was blown up to prevent the Jacobites from using it. The five-storey tower house at the northern point is the most impressive remaining fragment and offers fine views across the water.

☑ Don't Miss

Climbing to the battlements of the iconic tower of Urquhart Castle, for grandstand views from the rocky headland, up and down Loch Ness.

KELSEYNY/SHUTTERSTOCK ©

Loch Ness' East Side

While tour coaches pour down the west side of Loch Ness to the hotspots of Drumnadrochit and Urquhart Castle, the narrow B862 road along the eastern shore is relatively peaceful. It leads to the village of Foyers, where you can enjoy a pleasant hike to the **Falls of Foyers**.

It's also worth making the trip just for the **Dores Inn** (01463-751203; www.thedoresinn.co.uk; Dores; mains £10-28; noon-9pm Wed-Sun; P), a beautifully restored country pub adorned with recycled furniture, local landscape paintings and fresh flowers. The menu specialises in quality Scottish produce, from haggis, neeps (turnips) and tatties (potatoes), and haddock and chips, to steaks, scallops and seafood platters. The pub garden has stunning Loch Ness views and a dedicated monster-spotting vantage point.

Hiking at Loch Ness

The **Loch Ness 360°** (www.lochness360.com) loops for 80 miles around the circumference of the loch from Inverness and back. The trail is divided into six day-long sections, with stops in Drumnadrochit, Invermoriston, Fort Augustus, Foyers and Dores. The 28 miles from Loch Tarff near Fort Augustus to Torbreck on the fringes of Inverness can be done on foot, by bike or on horseback.

The climb to the summit of **Meall Fuar-mhonaidh** (699m), on the northwestern shore of Loch Ness, makes an excellent short hill walk: the views along the Great Glen from the top are superb. It's a 6-mile round trip, so allow about three hours. Start from the car park at the end of the minor road leading south from Drumnadrochit to Bunloit.

✕ Take a Break

On the southern edge of Drumnadrochit, the **Loch Ness Inn** (01456-450991; www.staylochness.co.uk; Lewiston; inn s/d/f £120/140/170, bunkhouse q £135; P) is a good place for lunch or dinner.

The Lost Valley of Glen Coe

JONATHAN DOREY - SCOTLAND /ALAMY STOCK PHOTO ©

Glen Coe

Scotland's most famous glen is also one of its grandest. It was written into history in 1692 when the resident MacDonalds were murdered by Campbell soldiers in a notorious massacre.

Great For...

☑ Don't Miss

The cracking views from the Glencoe Mountain Resort. Ski lift provided.

The events of that one night in 1692 still seem to echo around Glen Coe. Soldiers largely from Campbell clan territory, on government orders, turned on their MacDonald hosts killing 38; another 40 MacDonalds perished having fled into snow-covered hills.

Arriving in Glen Coe

The approach to the glen from the east is guarded by the rocky pyramid of Buachaille Etive Mor and the lonely Kings House Hotel. The road leads over the Pass of Glencoe and into the narrow upper glen. The southern side is dominated by three massive, brooding spurs, known as the Three Sisters, while the northern side is enclosed by the continuous steep wall of the knife-edged Aonach Eagach ridge. The road threads its way past deep gorges and

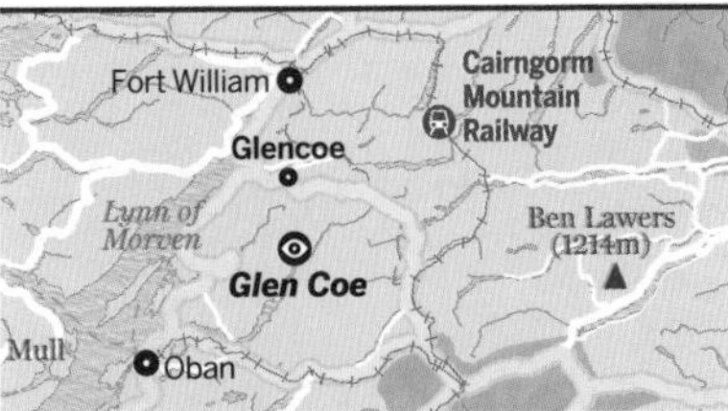

Need to Know

Glencoe Visitor Centre (NTS; 01855-811307; www.nts.org.uk; parking £4; 9.30am-4pm; P) FREE

Take a Break

Take a load off at the friendly **Glencoe Café** (01855-811168; www.glencoecafe.co.uk; Lorn Dr, Glencoe village; mains £4.50-10; 11am-5pm Fri-Wed May-Oct, to 4pm Nov-Apr; P wifi).

Top Tip

Learn all about Glen Coe's past at the visitors centre on the way into the village.

crashing waterfalls to the more pastoral lower reaches of the glen around Loch Achtriochtan and the only settlement here: Glencoe village.

Hiking at Glen Coe

There are several short, pleasant walks around **Glencoe Lochan**, near the village. To get there, turn left off the minor road to the youth hostel, just beyond the bridge over the River Coe. There are three walks (40 minutes to an hour), all detailed on a signboard at the car park.

The **Lost Valley** is a magical mountain sanctuary still rumoured to be haunted by the ghosts of MacDonalds who died here. It's only 2.5 miles round trip, but allow three hours. A rough path from the car park at Allt na Reigh (on the A82, 6 miles east of Glencoe village) bears left down to a footbridge over the river, then climbs up the wooded valley between Beinn Fhada and Gearr Aonach. The route leads steeply up through a maze of giant, jumbled, moss-coated boulders before emerging unexpectedly into a broad, open valley with a flat, 800m-long meadow.

The summits of Glen Coe's mountains are for experienced mountaineers only. Cicerone's *Ben Nevis & Glen Coe*, by Ronald Turnbull, details everything from short easy walks to challenging mountain climbs.

Other Activities

Scotland's oldest ski area, **Glencoe Mountain Resort** (01855-851226; www.glencoemountain.com; Kingshouse; chairlift adult/child £12/8; 9am-4.30pm), is also one of the best, with grand views across the wild expanse of Rannoch Moor. The chairlift continues to operate in summer providing access to mountain-biking trails.

Iona Abbey

MIKE CHARLES/SHUTTERSTOCK ©

Isle of Mull

With black basalt crags, blinding white sand and emerald waters, Mull has some of Scotland's finest scenery. A lovely waterfront 'capital', impressive castles, superb wildlife-watching and its proximity to idyllic Iona ensure it's an irresistible island escape.

Great For...

☑ Don't Miss

Taking the ferry from Fionnphort to the island of Iona, with its spectacular abbey.

Mull's main town, Tobermory, is a picturesque fishing port with brightly painted houses arranged around a sheltered quay.

Bird & Wildlife Watching

Four-hour whale-watching trips (adult/child £60/30) with **Sea Life Surveys** (☎01688-302916; www.sealifesurveys.com; Ledaig; ⊙Apr-Oct) head from Tobermory harbour to the waters north and west of Mull.

Britain's largest bird of prey, the white-tailed eagle, has been successfully reintroduced here. **Mull Eagle Watch** (☎01680-812556; www.mulleaglewatch.com; adult/child £10/5; ⊙Apr-Sep) has guided raptor experiences.

Turus Mara (☎01688-400242; www.turusmara.com; ⊙Apr–mid-Oct) offers trips from Ulva Ferry in central Mull to Staffa and the Treshnish Isles (adult/child £70/35, six

Tobermory

MARK CHRISTOPHER COOPER/SHUTTERSTOCK ©

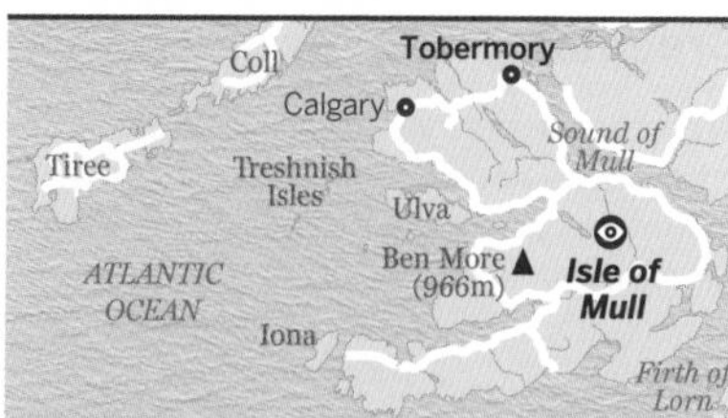

Need to Know

Explore Mull (01688-302875; www.isle-of-mull.net; Ledaig; 9am-5pm Easter-Jun & Sep–mid-Oct, to 7pm Jul & Aug;) has local info, books all manner of island tours, and hires out bikes.

Take a Break

Café Fish (01688-301253; www.thecafefish.com; The Pier; mains £12-26; noon-3pm & 5.30-11pm mid-Mar–Oct;) in Tobermory is superb.

Top Tip

Three CalMac car ferries link Mull with the mainland; check sailings at www.calmac.co.uk.

hours), with plenty of time ashore, where you can see seals, puffins, kittiwakes, razorbills and many other species of seabird.

Iona Abbey

Like an emerald teardrop off Mull's western shore, enchanting Iona, holy island and burial ground of kings, is a magical place that lives up to its lofty reputation. The ancient but heavily reconstructed **Iona Abbey** (01681-700512; www.historicenvironment.scot; adult/child £9/5.40; 9.30am-5.30pm Apr-Sep, 10am-4pm Oct-Mar) is the spiritual heart of the island. The spectacular nave, dominated by Romanesque and early Gothic vaults and columns, is a powerful space; a door on the left leads to the beautiful cloister, where medieval grave slabs sit alongside modern religious sculptures. The museum displays fabulous carved high crosses and other inscribed stones.

Duart Castle

The ancestral seat of the Maclean clan, **Duart Castle** (01680-812309; www.duartcastle.com; adult/child £8/4; 10.30am-5pm daily May–mid-Oct, 11am-4pm Sun-Thu Apr) enjoys a spectacular position on a rocky outcrop overlooking the Sound of Mull. Built in the 13th century, it was abandoned for 160 years before a 1912 restoration. Along with dungeons, courtyard and battlements, there's a lot of clan history, including the villainous Lachlan Cattanach, who took his wife out to an island in the strait, then left her to drown when the tide came in.

Walking on Mull

Standout walking includes the popular climb of Ben More and the spectacular trip to Carsaig Arches.

Braemar

Braemar is a pretty little village with a grand location on a broad plain ringed by mountains where the Dee valley and Glen Clunie meet. It's an excellent base for hill walking, and there's also skiing at nearby Glenshee.

ACTIVITIES

An easy walk from Braemar is up Creag Choinnich (538m), a hill to the east of the village above the A93. The 1-mile route is waymarked and takes about 1½ hours return. For a longer walk (4 miles; about three hours return) and superb views of the Cairngorms, head for the summit of Morrone (859m), southwest of Braemar.

You can rent bikes at **Braemar Mountain Sports** (☎01339-741242; www.braemarmountainsports.com; 5 Invercauld Rd; bike hire per 4hr/day £15/20; ⏰9am-6pm).

EATING

Bothy Cafe £

(☎01339-741019; Invercauld Rd; mains £4-10; ⏰9am-5.30pm Sun-Thu, to 6pm Fri & Sat; 📶👪) An appealing cafe for breakfast, lunch and cakes. It's tucked behind the Mountain Sports shop, with a sunny terrace out front and a balcony at the back overhanging the river.

GETTING THERE & AWAY

From Edinburgh, Braemar is a 2½-hour (100 mile) drive.

Fort William

Basking on Loch Linnhe's shores amid magnificent mountain scenery, Fort William has one of the most enviable settings in all of Scotland. It's an excellent base for exploring the surrounding mountains and glens.

SIGHTS

Jacobite Steam Train Heritage Railway

(☎0844 850 4685; www.westcoastrailways.co.uk; day return adult/child from £43/26; ⏰mid-May–Oct) The Jacobite Steam Train, hauled by a former LNER K1 or LMS Class 5MT locomotive, travels the scenic two-hour run between Fort William and Mallaig. Classed as one of the great railway journeys of the world, the route crosses the historic Glenfinnan Viaduct, made famous in the Harry Potter films – the Jacobite's owners supplied the steam locomotive and rolling stock used in the film.

Ben Nevis Mountain

Magical Glen Nevis begins near the northern end of Fort William and wraps itself around the southern flanks of Ben Nevis (1345m) – Britain's highest mountain and a magnet for hikers and climbers. The **Glen Nevis Tourist Office** (☎01349-781401; parking £4; ⏰8.30am-4pm, longer hours Jul & Aug) is situated 1.5 miles up the glen, and provides information on hiking, weather forecasts, and specific advice on climbing Ben Nevis.

West Highland Museum Museum

(☎01397-702169; www.westhighlandmuseum.org.uk; Cameron Sq; ⏰10am-2pm Tue-Fri) FREE This small but fascinating museum is packed with all manner of Highland memorabilia. Look out for the secret portrait of Bonnie Prince Charlie – after the Jacobite rebellions, all things Highland were banned, including pictures of the exiled leader, and this tiny painting looks like nothing more than a smear of paint until viewed in a cylindrical mirror, which reflects a credible likeness of the prince. In 2020 the museum operated with limited opening hours and an advance booking system.

ACTIVITIES

Nevis Range Outdoors

(☎01397-705825; www.nevisrange.co.uk; gondola day ticket adult/child £19.50/11; ⏰9.30am-4pm Thu-Mon) The Nevis Range ski

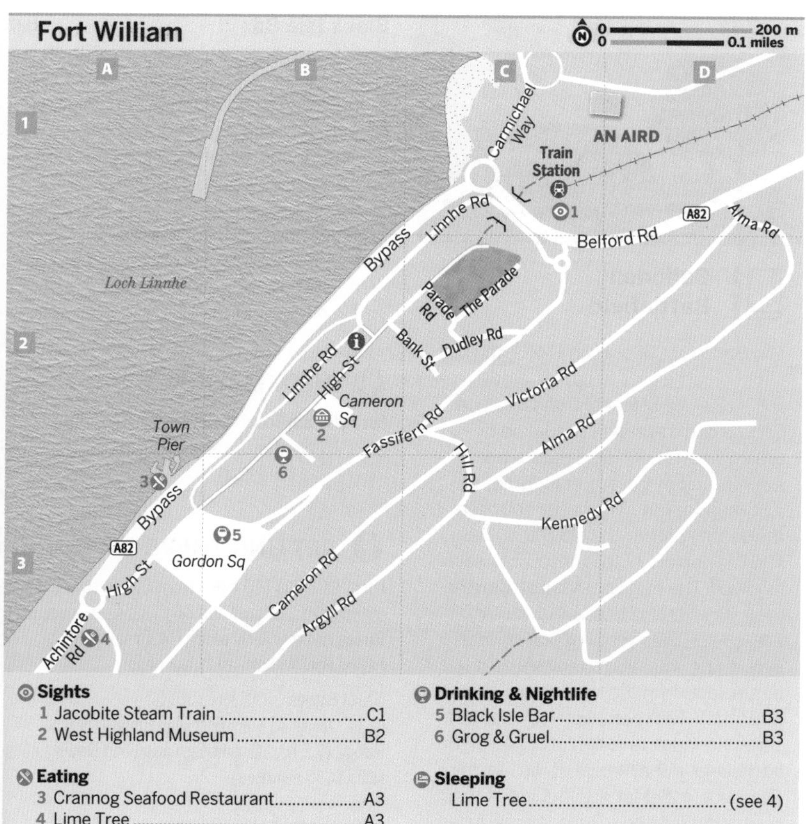

area, 6 miles north of Fort William, spreads across the northern slopes of Aonach Mor (1221m). The gondola that gives access to the bottom of the ski area at 655m operates year-round. At the top there's a restaurant and a couple of hiking trails through nearby Leanachan Forest, as well as excellent mountain-biking trails.

EATING

Lime Tree — Scottish ££

(☎01397-701806; www.limetreefortwilliam.co.uk; Achintore Rd; mains £19-22.50, set menu £30; ⏲6.30-9.30pm; P 📶) The restaurant at this small **hotel** (☎01397-701806; www.limetreefortwilliam.co.uk; Achintore Rd; d £155-175; P 📶) and art gallery has put the UK's Outdoor Capital on the gastronomic map. The chef turns out delicious dishes built around fresh Scottish produce, such as Loch Fyne oysters, Loch Awe trout and Ardnamurchan venison.

Crannog Seafood Restaurant — Seafood ££

(☎01397-705589; www.crannog.net; Town Pier; mains £10-22.50; ⏲noon-9pm) The Crannog wins the prize for the best location in town – perched on the Town Pier, giving window-table diners an uninterrupted view down Loch Linnhe. Informal and unfussy, it specialises in fresh local fish (there are three or four daily fish specials plus the

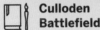

Culloden Battlefield

The Battle of Culloden in 1746 – the last pitched battle ever fought on British soil – saw the defeat of Bonnie Prince Charlie and the end of the Jacobite dream when 1200 Highlanders were slaughtered by government forces in a 68-minute rout. The battle sounded the death knell for the old clan system, and the horrors of the Clearances soon followed. The excellent **Visitor Centre** (NTS; www.nts.org.uk/culloden; adult/child £11/9.50; 10am-4pm Wed-Sun; P) has everything you need to know about the battle, including the lead-up and the aftermath, with perspectives from both sides. An innovative film puts you on the battlefield in the middle of the mayhem. Pick up a leaflet for a self-guided tour of the battlefield itself. Culloden is 6 miles east of Inverness.

MATTHI/SHUTTERSTOCK ©

main menu) though there are lamb, venison and vegetarian dishes, too.

DRINKING & NIGHTLIFE

Grog & Gruel Pub

(01397-705078; www.grogandgruel.co.uk; 66 High St; noon-midnight;) The Grog & Gruel is a traditional-style, wood-panelled pub with an excellent range of cask ales from regional Scottish and English microbreweries.

Black Isle Bar Bar

(www.blackislebrewery.com; Gordon Sq; bar noon-11pm, food noon-9pm;) In a grand granite building that was once a church, this pub serves craft beers from the **Black Isle Brewery** (01463-811871; www.blackislebrewery.com; Old Allangrange; 10am-5pm Mon-Sat) FREE as well as organic wine and local whisky. There are also wood-fired pizzas (£11.50 to £13) with Scottish toppings such as haggis and venison salami.

INFORMATION

Fort William Tourist Office (01397-701801; www.visithighlands.com; 15 High St; 9am-4pm, longer hours Jun-Aug)

GETTING THERE & AROUND

Fort William is 146 miles from Edinburgh, 104 miles from Glasgow and 66 miles from Inverness. Buses run regularly along the Great Glen between Fort William and Inverness.

Shiel Buses (01397-700700; www.shielbuses.co.uk) route 41 links Fort William with Nevis Range (£2.70, 20 minutes) and Glen Nevis (£2.20, 15 minutes).

Inverness

Inverness has a great location astride the River Ness at the northern end of the Great Glen. In summer it overflows with visitors intent on monster hunting at nearby Loch Ness, but it's worth a visit in its own right for a stroll along the picturesque River Ness, a cruise on Loch Ness, and a meal in one of the city's excellent restaurants.

SIGHTS

Ness Islands Park

The main attraction in Inverness is a stroll along the river to the Ness Islands. Planted with mature Scots pine, fir, beech and sycamore, and linked to the riverbanks and each other by elegant Victorian footbridges, the islands make an appealing picnic spot. They're a 20-minute walk south of the castle – head upstream on either side of the river and return on the opposite bank. The path on the eastern bank is the start of the Great Glen Way.

Fort George Fortress

(HES; ☎01667-462777; www.historicenvironment.scot; adult/child £9/5.40; ⏰10am-4pm; Ⓟ) One of the finest artillery fortifications in Europe, Fort George was established in 1748 in the aftermath of the Battle of Culloden, as a base for George II's army of occupation in the Highlands. By the time of its completion in 1769, it had cost the modern equivalent of around £1 billion. It still functions as a military barracks; public areas have exhibitions on 18th-century soldiery.

Cawdor Castle Castle

(☎01667-404615; www.cawdorcastle.com; Cawdor; gardens & grounds adult/child £8/4; ⏰10am-5pm May-Sep; Ⓟ) This castle, 5 miles southwest of Nairn, was once the seat of the Thane of Cawdor, one of the titles bestowed on Shakespeare's Macbeth. The real Macbeth – an ancient Scottish king – couldn't have lived here though, since he died in 1057, 300 years before the castle was begun. Nevertheless the castle tour (not available in 2020) gives a fascinating insight into the lives of the Scottish aristocracy.

Even if the castle interior is closed, as it was in 2020, the walled gardens, maze and woodland trails through the grounds are worth a visit, and the courtyard cafe and shop provide a glimpse inside the castle walls. To get here, take bus 2 from Eastgate shopping centre in Inverness to Cawdor village (50 minutes, hourly except Sunday), from where it's a 1-mile walk to the castle.

ACTIVITIES

Dolphin Spirit Wildlife Watching

(☎07544 800620; www.dolphinspirit.co.uk; Inverness Marina, Stadium Rd; adult/child £19.50/12; ⏰Easter-Oct) This outfit runs recommended cruises from Inverness into the Moray Firth to spot the UK's largest pod of bottlenose dolphins. The dolphins feed on salmon heading for the rivers at the head of the firth, and can often be seen leaping and bow surfing.

EATING

Café 1 Bistro **££**

(☎01463-226200; www.cafe1.net; 75 Castle St; mains lunch £9-11, dinner £12-30; ⏰noon-2.30pm & 5-9.30pm Mon-Fri, 12.30-2.45pm & 5.30-9.30pm Sat; 👪) Café 1 is a friendly, appealing bistro with candlelit tables amid elegant blond-wood and wrought-iron decor. There's an international menu based on quality Scottish produce, from Aberdeen Angus steaks to crisp pan-fried sea bass and pappardelle pasta with local wild chantarelles.

Cawdor Tavern Pub Food **££**

(www.cawdortavern.co.uk; Cawdor; mains lunch £7-20, dinner £15-24; ⏰noon-10pm Mon-Thu, noon-11pm Fri & Sat, 12.30-10pm Sun; Ⓟ📶👪) Cawdor Tavern, in the pretty village close to Cawdor Castle, is a cosy pub with wood panelling, open fires and an impressive whisky selection. There's also excellent pub food, including tempting daily specials.

INFORMATION

Inverness Tourist Office (☎01463-252401; www.visitscotland.com; 36 High St; ⏰9am-5pm; 📶) Accommodation booking service; also sells tickets for tours and cruises.

GETTING THERE & AWAY

Inverness is connected by train to Edinburgh (£47.40, 3½ hours, eight daily) and by bus to Fort William (£11.60, two hours, eight daily).

SKYE

In This Chapter

Skye at a Glance

In a country famous for stunning scenery, the Isle of Skye takes top prize. From the craggy peaks of the Cuillins and the bizarre pinnacles of the Old Man of Storr and the Quiraing to spectacular sea cliffs, there's a photo opportunity at almost every turn. Walkers, sea kayakers and climbers share this wilderness with red deer and golden eagles, and can refuel at the end of the day in convivial pubs and top seafood restaurants.

Two Days in Skye

On day one, tour the **Trotternish peninsula** (p270) marvelling at extraordinary rock formations and exploring fairy glens. Peel off to **Dunvegan Castle** (p277), then dine in style at **Three Chimneys** (p276). Day two, and its time to hike. Depending on the weather, and your capabilities, it might be to **Coire Lagan or Loch Coruisk** (p271) – it's spectacular either way. Hungry now? Feast on Skye produce at **Dulse & Brose** (p275).

Four Days in Skye

Day three: hills done, water next – **Whitewave Outdoor Centre** (p273) can get you eking out inaccessible coves. Keep it aquatic with dinner at **Loch Bay** (p276) and shellfish straight from the boat. Relax on day four with a voyage aboard **MV Stardust** (p274), a trip to **Talisker Distillery** (p275) and then souvenir-shopping at **Skye Batiks** (p274). End your island adventure in style at cosy **Scorrybreac** (p275).

Previous page: The Old Man of Storr (p270)

JAROSLAV SEKERES/SHUTTERSTOCK ©

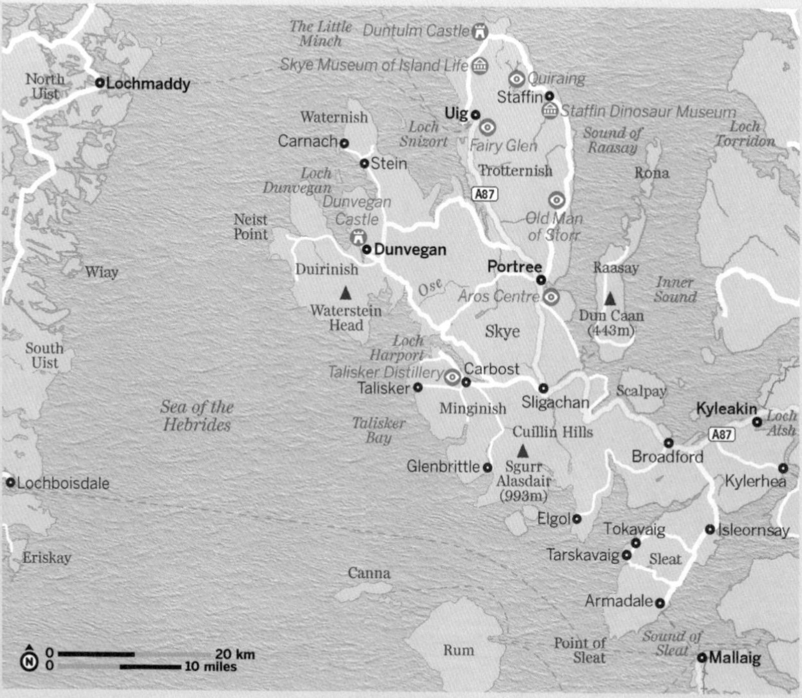

Arriving in Skye

Bus There are buses from Glasgow to Portree (£47, seven hours, three daily), and Uig (£47, 7½ hours, two daily) via Crianlarich, Fort William and Kyle of Lochalsh, plus a service from Inverness to Portree (£28, 3¼ hours, two daily).

Car The Skye Bridge opened in 1995, linking the island to the mainland by road; the crossing is now free.

Where to Stay

Skye is one of Scotland's most popular tourist areas, and offers a wide range of accommodation from basic campsites and hostels to luxury hotels. The latest trend is glamping (luxurious camping) and in the last few years many places have installed distinctive timber camping 'pods'. The island's popularity means that it's always best to book ahead.

Sea kayaker along the Skye coast

ELGOL/GETTY IMAGES ©

Exploring Skye's Wild Side

With its spectacular scenery, Skye offers some of the finest – and, in places, most challenging – outdoor experiences in Scotland. From splashing through streams or kayaking hidden coves to sleeping under the stars, this is a place to test your outdoor mettle.

Great For...

☑ Don't Miss

The impressive landslides, pointed rocks and eroding cliffs at Staffin Bay.

Skye's main town, Portree, is an ideal place to orientate yourself before exploring the island's wild spaces.

Trotternish Peninsula

The Trotternish peninsula to the north of Portree has some of Skye's most beautiful – and bizarre – scenery. A loop road allows a circular driving tour of the peninsula from Portree, passing on return through the village of Uig.

The 50m-high, pot-bellied pinnacle of crumbling basalt known as the **Old Man of Storr** is prominent above the road 6 miles north of Portree. Walk up to its foot from the car park at the northern end of Loch Leathan (2-mile round trip). This seemingly unclimbable pinnacle was first scaled in 1955 by English mountaineer Don Whillans, a feat that has been repeated only a handful of times since.

Fairy Glen on Skye

JONATAN ALEJANDRO PEREZ/SHUTTERSTOCK ©

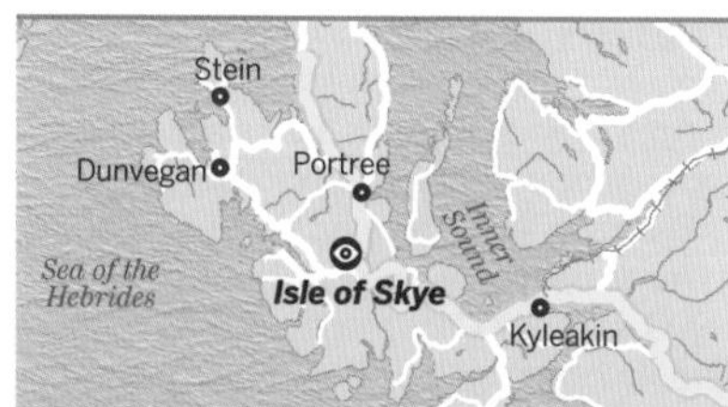

Need to Know

Portree Tourist Office (p276) is the island's only tourist office.

Take a Break

Flodigarry Hotel (01470-552203; www.hotelintheskye.co.uk; Flodigarry; r £215-450, ste £640-730; Easter-Oct; P) , on the Trotternish peninsula, has a good bar and restaurant.

★ Top Tip

Skye's hills can be challenging; don't attempt the longer walks in bad weather or in winter.

The occasional dinosaur bone has been turning up in the Jurassic rocks of the Trotternish peninsula since 1982 – intriguing, but nothing very exciting. Then, following a storm in 2002, a set of fossilised dinosaur footprints was exposed at An Corran in **Staffin Bay**. Geologists began taking a closer interest in the Trotternish rocks and, in 2015, a major discovery was made near Duntulm Castle – a 170-million-year-old trackway of footprints left by a group of sauropods. Skye is now a major focus for research into dinosaur evolution.

Staffin Bay is dominated by the dramatic basalt escarpment of the **Quiraing**: its impressive land-slipped cliffs and pinnacles constitute one of Skye's most remarkable landscapes. From a parking area at the highest point of the minor road between Staffin and Uig you can walk north to the Quiraing in half an hour.

Just south of Uig, a minor road (signposted 'Sheader and Balnaknock') leads in a mile or so to the **Fairy Glen**, a strange and enchanting natural landscape of miniature conical hills, rocky towers, ruined cottages and a tiny roadside lochan.

Cuillin Hills

The Cuillin Hills are Britain's most spectacular mountain range (the name comes from the Old Norse *kjöllen,* meaning 'keel-shaped'). Though small in stature – Sgurr Alasdair, the highest summit, is only 993m – the peaks are near-alpine in character, with knife-edge ridges, jagged pinnacles, scree-filled gullies and hectares of naked rock. While they are a paradise for experienced mountaineers, the higher reaches of the Cuillin are off limits to most hikers.

The good news is that there are also plenty of fantastic low-level hikes within the ability of most walkers. One of the best (on a fine day) is the steep climb from Glenbrittle campsite to **Coire Lagan** (6 miles round trip; allow at least three hours). The impressive upper corrie contains a lochan for bathing (for the hardy!), and the surrounding cliffs are a playground for rock climbers – bring your binoculars.

Even more spectacular, but much harder to reach on foot, is **Loch Coruisk** (from the Gaelic Coir'Uisg, the Water Corrie), a remote loch ringed by the highest peaks of the Cuillin. Accessible by **boat trip** (☎0800 731 3089; www.bellajane.co.uk; Elgol Pier; adult/child £28/16; ⊙Apr-Oct) from Elgol, or via an arduous 5.5-mile hike from Kilmarie, Coruisk was popularised by Sir Walter Scott in his 1815 poem 'Lord of the Isles'. Crowds of Victorian tourists and landscape artists followed in Scott's footsteps, including JMW Turner, whose watercolours were used to illustrate Scott's works.

There are two main bases for exploring the Cuillin – Sligachan to the north (on the Kyle of Lochalsh–Portree bus route), and Glenbrittle to the south (no public transport).

Kilmarie to Coruisk

The walk from Kilmarie to Coruisk and back via Camasunary and the 'Bad Step' is superb, but shouldn't be underestimated (11 miles round trip; allow at least six hours). The Bad Step is a rocky slab poised above the sea that you have to scramble across; it's easy in fine, dry weather, but some walkers find it intimidating.

Duirinish & Waternish

The sparsely populated Duirinish peninsula is dominated by the distinctive flat-topped peaks of Helabhal Mhor (469m) and Helabhal Bheag (488m), known locally as **MacLeod's Tables**. There are some fine walks from Orbost, including the summit of

Quiraing, Trotternish

Helabhal Bheag (allow 3½ hours return) and the 5-mile trail from Orbost to **MacLeod's Maidens**, a series of pointed sea stacks at the southern tip of the peninsula.

It's worth making the long drive beyond Dunvegan to the western side of the Duirinish peninsula to see the spectacular sea cliffs of **Waterstein Head** and to walk down to **Neist Point lighthouse** with its views to the Outer Hebrides.

Walking Tours

Skye Wilderness Safaris (☎01470-542229; www.skye-wilderness-safaris.com; per person £95-120, group of 4 from £250; ⊙May-Sep) runs one-day guided hiking trips for small groups (four to six people) through the Cuillin Hills, into the Quiraing or along the Trotternish ridge; transport to/from Portree is included.

★ **Top Tip**

Come prepared for changeable weather: when it's fine it's very fine indeed, but all too often it isn't.

CHRIS DAY/500PX ©

Sea Kayaking

The sheltered coves and sea lochs around the coast of Skye provide enthusiasts with magnificent sea-kayaking opportunities.

Whitewave Outdoor Centre (☎01470-542414; www.white-wave.co.uk; 19 Linicro, Kilmuir, IV51 9YN; half-day kayak session per person £40-50; ⊙Mar-Oct) offers sea-kayaking instruction and guiding for both beginners and experts; prices include equipment hire. Other activities include mountain boarding, bushcraft and rock climbing.

Climbing

The Cuillin Hills are a playground for rock climbers, and the two-day traverse of the Cuillin Ridge is the finest mountaineering expedition in the British Isles. There are several mountain guides in the area who can provide instruction and safely introduce inexperienced climbers to the more difficult routes.

Skye Guides (☎01471-822116; www.skyeguides.co.uk) offers a one-day introduction-to-rock-climbing course at around £285, or hire a private mountain guide for £295 a day (rates are for two clients).

Maps & Books

Detailed guidebooks include a series of four walking guides by Charles Rhodes, available from the Aros Centre (p274) and the tourist office (p276) in Portree. You'll need Ordnance Survey (OS) 1:50,000 maps 23 and 32, or Harvey's 1:25,000 *Superwalker – The Cuillin*.

✕ **Take a Break**

There are quite a few places to eat in the Duirinish peninsula, including some of the best restaurants and cafes on the island (see p276).

Portree

Portree is Skye's largest and liveliest town. It has a pretty harbour lined with brightly painted houses, and there are great views of the surrounding hills.

SIGHTS

Aros Centre Cultural Centre

(01478-613750; www.aros.co.uk; Viewfield Rd, IV51 9EU; 9am-5pm; P) FREE On the southern edge of Portree, the Aros Centre is a combined visitor centre, book and gift shop, restaurant, theatre and cinema. The 45-minute movie *Skye Story* is screened hourly from 10am to 4pm (per adult/child £8.50/free) and allows you to take a virtual tour of the island and its history. The centre has an indoor soft play area for children.

TOURS

MV Stardust Boating

(07795-385581; www.skyeboat-trips.co.uk; Portree Harbour; adult/child £20/10) MV *Stardust* offers 1½-hour boat trips around Portree Bay, with the chance to see seals, porpoises and – if you're lucky – white-tailed sea eagles. There are longer two-hour cruises to the Sound of Raasay (adult/child £25/15). You can also arrange fishing trips, or to be dropped off for a hike on the Isle of Raasay and picked up again later.

SHOPPING

Skye Batiks Gifts & Souvenirs

(www.skyebatiks.com; The Green, IV51 9BY; 9am-6pm May-Sep, to 9pm Jul & Aug, to 5pm Mon-Sat Oct-Apr) Skye Batiks is a cut above your average gift shop, selling a range of interesting crafts such as carved wood, jewellery and batik fabrics with Celtic designs.

Isle of Skye Crafts at Over the Rainbow Gifts & Souvenirs

(01478-612361; www.isleofskyecrafts.com; Quay Brae, IV51 9DB; 9am-5pm Mon-Sat) Crammed with colourful knitwear and cross-stitch kits, lambswool and cashmere scarves, plus all kinds of interesting gifts.

Portree

DANIEL BARQUERO/SHUTTERSTOCK ©

Isle of Skye Soap Co Cosmetics
(01478-611350; www.skye-soap.co.uk; Somerled Sq, IV51 9EH; 10am-5pm Mon-Sat) A sweet-smelling gift shop that specialises in handmade soaps and cosmetics made using natural ingredients and aromatherapy oils.

EATING & DRINKING

Isle of Skye Baking Co Cafe £
(www.facebook.com/IsleofSkyeBaking; Old Woollen Mill, Dunvegan Rd, IV51 9HF; mains £4-9; 9am-4pm Mon-Sat;) Famous for its 'lunch bread' – a small loaf baked with a filling inside, like cheese and leek, or beef stew – and platters of Scottish cheese and charcuterie, this cafe is also an art gallery and craft shop.

Café Arriba Cafe £
(01478-611830; www.cafearriba.co.uk; Quay Brae, IV51 9DB; mains £6-15; 8.30am-4.30pm Thu-Mon Apr-Oct;) Arriba is a funky little cafe, brightly decked out in primary colours and offering delicious flatbread melts (bacon, leek and cheese is a favourite), as well as the best choice of vegetarian grub on the island, ranging from a veggie breakfast fry-up to felafel wraps with hummus and chilli sauce. Also serves excellent coffee.

Dulse & Brose Modern Scottish ££
(01478-612846; www.bosvillehotel.co.uk; Bosville Hotel, 7 Bosville Tce, IV51 9DG; mains £9-17; noon-3pm & 6-10pm May-Sep, 6-8.15pm Oct-Apr;) This hotel restaurant sports a relaxed atmosphere, an award-winning chef and a menu that makes the most of Skye produce – including lamb, game, seafood, cheese, organic vegetables and berries – and adds a French or Asian twist to traditional dishes.

Scorrybreac Modern Scottish £££
(01478-612069; www.scorrybreac.com; 7 Bosville Tce, IV51 9DG; 4-course dinner £60; 5-9pm Tue-Sat Mar-Oct, limited opening Nov & Dec) Set in the front rooms of what was once a private house, and with just eight tables, Scorrybreac is snug and intimate, offering fine dining without the faff. Chef Calum Munro (son of Donnie Munro, of Gaelic rock band Runrig fame) sources as much produce as possible from Skye, including foraged herbs and mushrooms, and creates the most exquisite concoctions.

Isles Inn Pub
(01478-612129; Somerled Sq, IV51 9EH; 11am-11pm Mon-Thu, to midnight Fri & Sat, 12.30-11pm Sun;) Portree's pubs are nothing special, but the Isles Inn is more atmospheric than most. The Jacobean bar, with its flagstone floor and open fires, pulls in a lively mix of young locals, backpackers and tourists.

Talisker Distillery

Loch Harport, to the north of the Cuillin Hills, divides the Minginish peninsula from the rest of Skye. On its southern shore lies the village of Carbost, 18 miles drive southwest of Portree, home to Talisker malt whisky.

Skye's oldest **distillery** (01478-614308; www.malts.com/en-gb/brands/talisker; Carbost; tours from £15; 9am-5.30pm Mon-Sat, 10am-5.30pm Sun Apr-Oct, shorter hours Nov-Mar;), established in 1830, produces the smooth, sweet and smoky Talisker single malt. The guided tour includes a free dram (book in advance).

TYLER W. STIPP/SHUTTERSTOCK ©

The Duirinish Peninsula's Restaurants

There are quite a few places to eat in this corner of the islands, including some of the best restaurants and cafes on Skye. Some are seasonal (closed in winter) and it's always best to book ahead.

Loch Bay (01470-592235; www.lochbay-restaurant.co.uk; Stein, Waternish, IV55 8GA; 6-course dinner £95; 12.15-1.45pm Wed-Sun, 6.15-9pm Tue-Sat Apr-early Oct; P) One of Skye's most romantic restaurants and awarded a Michelin star in 2018. The menu includes most things that swim in the sea or live in a shell, but there are non-seafood choices too. Book ahead.

Three Chimneys (01470-511258; www.threechimneys.co.uk; Colbost, IV55 8ZT; mains £30-35; 12.15-1.45pm Mon-Sat mid-Mar–Oct, plus Sun Easter-Sep, 6.30-9.15pm daily year-round; P) Halfway between Dunvegan and Waterstein, this is a superb romantic retreat combining a gourmet restaurant in a candlelit crofter's cottage. Book ahead.

Cafe Lephin (01470-511465; www.cafelephin.co.uk; 2 Lephin, Glendale; mains £5-8; 11am-6pm Mon-Sat;) Cute little cafe in remote Glendale with great coffee and cakes, a comfy sofa and a menu that includes haggis panini.

Stein Inn (01470-592362; www.stein-inn.co.uk; Stein, Waternish, IV55 8GA; mains £9-17; kitchen noon-3pm & 6-9pm Easter-Oct, shorter hours Nov-Easter; P) Old country inn dating from 1790 with a lively little bar and a delightful beer garden beside the loch. The bar serves real ales from the Isle of Skye Brewery and excellent bar meals.

Three Chimneys

EDINBURGHCITYMOM/SHUTTERSTOCK ©

INFORMATION

Portree Tourist Office (01478-612992; www.visitscotland.com/destinations-maps/isle-skye; Bayfield Rd, IV51 9EL; 10am-4pm Mon-Sat year-round, longer hours Jun-Aug;) The only tourist office on the island.

GETTING AROUND

Much of the driving is on single-track roads – remember to use passing places to allow any traffic behind you to overtake. There are petrol stations at Broadford (open 24 hours), Armadale, Portree, Dunvegan and Uig.

Stagecoach (www.stagecoach.com) operates the main bus routes on the island, linking all the main villages and towns. Its Skye Dayrider/Megarider ticket gives unlimited bus travel for one/seven days for £9.50/35.50. For timetable info, call Traveline (p246).

You can order a taxi or hire a car (arrange for the car to be waiting at Kyle of Lochalsh train station) from **Kyle Taxi Company** (01599-534323; www.skyecarhire.co.uk; car hire per day/week from around £45/250).

Contact **Skye Bike Shack** (07826 842160; www.skyebikeshack.com; 6 Carbost, Skeabost Bridge IV51 9PD; bike hire per day from £30; 9am-1pm Tue-Sat) for bike hire.

Trotternish

Dramatic, otherworldly landscapes created by layered volcanic rocks characterise the Trotternish peninsula, Skye's northernmost extremity.

SIGHTS

Skye Museum of Island Life Museum

(01470-552206; www.skyemuseum.co.uk; Kilmuir; adult/child £4/50p; 9.30am-5pm Mon-Sat Easter-late Sep; P) The peat-reek of crofting life in the 18th and 19th centuries is preserved in the thatched cottages, croft houses, barns and farm implements of the Skye Museum of Island Life. Behind the museum is **Kilmuir Cemetery**, where a tall Celtic cross marks the grave of Flora

MacDonald – the cross was erected in 1955 to replace the original monument, of which 'every fragment was removed by tourists'.

Staffin Dinosaur Museum Museum

(☎01470-562321; www.staffindinosaurmuseum.com; 3 Ellishadder, Staffin, IV51 9JE; adult/child £2/1; ⏰9.30am-5pm; P) In an old stone barn by the roadside, this museum houses an interesting collection of dinosaur footprints, ammonites and other fossils discovered in the local Jurassic sandstones, which have become a focus for dinosaur research in recent years.

Duntulm Castle Castle

Near the tip of the Trotternish peninsula is the ruined MacDonald fortress of Duntulm Castle, which was abandoned in 1739, reputedly because it was haunted. From the red telephone box 800m east of the castle, a faint path leads north for 1.5 miles to **Rubha Hunish coastguard lookout**, now restored as a tiny but cosy bothy overlooking the northernmost point of Skye.

SHOPPING

Isle of Skye Brewery Food & Drinks

(☎01470-542477; www.skyeale.com; The Pier, Uig, IV51 9XP; ⏰10am-5pm Mon-Fri, to 4pm Sat & Sun) If you have time to kill while waiting for a ferry at Uig, the Isle of Skye Brewery shop sells locally brewed ales by the bottle, as well as gifts and souvenirs.

GETTING THERE & AWAY

Two or three daily buses (four on Saturday) follow a circular route (in both directions) from Portree around the Trotternish peninsula, taking in Flodigarry (£4.75, 40 minutes), Kilmuir (£5.60, 45 minutes) and Uig (£4.15, 30 minutes).

Car ferries run from Uig to Tarbert (Harris; car/pedestrian £32/6.50, 1½ hours) and Lochmaddy (North Uist; car/pedestrian £32/6.50, 1¾ hours) in the Outer Hebrides, with one or two crossings a day.

Dunvegan Castle

Skye's most famous historic building, and one of its most popular tourist attractions, **Dunvegan Castle** (☎01470-521206; www.dunvegancastle.com; adult/child £14/9; ⏰10am-5.30pm Easter–mid-Oct; P) is the seat of the chief of Clan MacLeod. Among artefacts are the Fairy Flag, a diaphanous silk banner that dates from some time between the 4th and 7th centuries, and Bonnie Prince Charlie's waistcoat and a lock of his hair, donated by Flora MacDonald's granddaughter.

Stagecoach bus 56 runs from Portree to Dunvegan (£5.60, 50 minutes), four times on Saturday year-round, and also Monday to Friday from May to September.

TARGN PLEIADES/SHUTTERSTOCK ©

A man in kilt and sporran with a dram of Scotch

GEORGE CLERK 17625I/GETTY IMAGES ©

In Focus

Hadrian's Wall (p200)

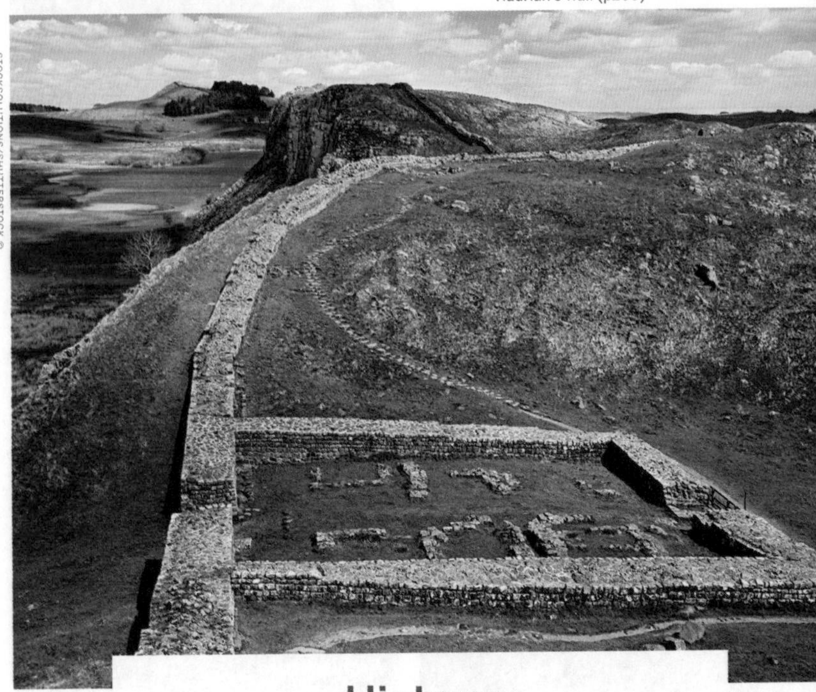

STOCKSOLUTIONS/SHUTTERSTOCK ©

History

Though a small country on the edge of Europe, Britain has rarely hugged the sidelines. For thousands of years, invaders and immigrants have arrived, settled and made their mark. The result is Britain's fascinating melange of landscape, culture, language and myth. That rich historic legacy – from Stonehenge to Culloden, via Hadrian's Wall and the Tower of London – is one of the country's most alluring and pervasive features.

4000 BCE
Neolithic peoples migrate from continental Europe and establish residences and farms.

43 CE
Emperor Claudius leads the first proper Roman invasion of England. The Romans control most of southern England by 50 CE.

c 410
After more than three centuries of relative peace and prosperity, Roman rule ends in Britain.

Churchill War Rooms (p67)

RIK HAMILTON/ALAMY STOCK PHOTO ©

First Arrivals

Around 4000 BCE a group of migrants arrived from Europe, but instead of hunting and moving on, they settled in one place and started farming. One of their most impressive legacies is the enigmatic stone circle at Stonehenge.

The Iron Age

During the Iron Age (from 800 BCE to 100 CE) the population expanded and began to divide into specific tribes. Forests were cleared as more land was used for farming. Territorial defence became important, so people built great earthwork 'castles' in southern England, stone forts in northern England and brochs (defensive towers) in Wales and Scotland.

850
Vikings, from today's Denmark, conquer east and northeast England. They establish their capital at Jorvik, today's city of York.

1066
The Battle of Hastings. Incumbent King Harold is defeated by the invading Normans. William the Conqueror is crowned.

1314
Robert the Bruce's army beats the English at Bannockburn; Scottish independence is consolidated for 400 years.

Enter (& Exit) the Romans

Emperor Claudius led a ruthless campaign resulting in the Romans controlling pretty much everywhere in southern England by 50 CE. Some locals fought back, including warrior-queen Boudica, who led an army as far as Londinium, the Roman port on the present site of London.

But by around 80 CE the new province of Britannia (much of today's England and Wales) was firmly under Roman rule – circumstances that lasted almost four centuries. The star of the Roman Empire eventually waned, however, and the Romans withdrew – the end of Roman power in Britain is generally dated at 410 CE.

The Emergence of England

Britain's post-Roman power vacuum didn't go unnoticed and once again invaders arrived from the European mainland. Angles and Saxons (Teutonic tribes from the land we now call Germany) advanced across the former Roman dominion.

The Waking of Wales & Scotland

While the Anglo-Saxons occupied eastern Britain, toward the end of the 5th century the Scotti (from today's Ireland) invaded what is today Wales and western Scotland. In response, by the 8th century the disparate tribes of Wales had started to band together and sow the seeds of nationhood. They called themselves *cymry* (fellow countrymen), and today Cymru is the Welsh word for Wales. The Picts were the dominant indigenous tribe in the north and east and named their kingdom Alba, which remains to this day the Gaelic word for Scotland.

The Viking Era

In the 9th century, Britain was yet again invaded – this time, by the Vikings from today's Scandinavia. The English Anglo-Saxon armies, led by Alfred the Great resisted and the battles that followed were seminal to the foundation of the nation-state of England; by 886 Alfred had gathered his strength and pushed the Vikings back to the north.

1066 & All That

The royal pendulum then swung between Saxon and Viking monarchs and by 1066, the crown had passed to Harold. But one of his relatives in Normandy (in the north of today's France), called William, harboured a claim to England's throne.

1455–85
The Wars of the Roses between the Houses of Lancaster and York. The Yorkists' King Edward IV eventually gains the throne.

1485
Henry Tudor defeats Richard III at the Battle of Bosworth, becoming King Henry VII.

1509–47
The reign of King Henry VIII sees the English Reformation – the founding of the Church of England.

The consequence was the Battle of Hastings in 1066 when William sailed from Normandy with an army of Norman soldiers, the Saxons were defeated and Harold was killed (as the story goes, by an arrow in the eye).

Magna Carta

In 1215 the barons found the rule of the then king, King John, erratic and forced him to sign a document called the Magna Carta (the Great Charter), limiting the monarch's power for the first time in British history. Although originally intended as a set of handy ground rules, the Magna Carta was a fledgling bill of human rights that eventually led to the creation of parliament – a body to rule the country, independent of the throne.

Henry VIII & the Break With Rome

In the mid-15th century, the Wars of the Roses raged between the House of Lancaster (emblem, a red rose) and the House of York (emblem, a white rose). By 1485, though, Henry VII (Henry Tudor) was in charge. But it's his son every school kid knows: Henry VIII. For him fathering a male heir was problematical, hence his famous six wives, but the pope's disapproval of divorce and remarriage led to a split with the Roman Catholic Church and Henry became the head of the Protestant Church of England.

The Elizabethan Age

Henry VIII's daughter, Elizabeth I, inherited a nasty mess of religious strife and divided loyalties, but after an uncertain start she gained confidence and turned the country around. Refusing marriage, she borrowed biblical imagery and became known as the Virgin Queen, making her perhaps the first British monarch to create a cult image.

It paid off. Her 45-year reign was a period of boundless optimism, characterised by the naval defeat of the Spanish Armada, the expansion of trade due to the global explorations of seafarers such as Walter Raleigh and Francis Drake, not to mention a cultural flourishing thanks to writers such as William Shakespeare and Christopher Marlowe.

United & Disunited Britain

Elizabeth I died in 1603 without an heir, and was succeeded by her closest relative, James, the safely Protestant son of the executed Mary Queen of Scots. He became James I of England and James VI of Scotland, the first English monarch of the House of Stuart. Most importantly, James united England, Wales and Scotland into one kingdom for the first time in history – another step towards British unity.

But the divide between king and parliament continued to smoulder. The power struggle worsened during the reign of the next king, Charles I, and eventually degenerated into

1558–1603
Queen Elizabeth I reigns. Enter stage right playwright William Shakespeare. Exit Walter Raleigh and Francis Drake.

1603
James VI of Scotland inherits the English throne, becoming James I of England, too.

1642–49
English Civil War between the king's Cavaliers and Oliver Cromwell's Roundheads establishes the Commonwealth of England.

the Civil War of 1642–49. The antiroyalist (or 'parliamentarian') forces were led by Oliver Cromwell, a Puritan who preached against the excesses of the monarchy and established Church. His army (known as the Roundheads) was pitched against the king's forces (the Cavaliers) in a conflict that tore England apart. It ended with victory for the Roundheads, with the king executed and England declared a republic.

The Return of the King

By 1653 Cromwell was finding parliament too restrictive and he assumed dictatorial powers, much to his supporters' dismay. On his death in 1658, he was followed half-heartedly by his son, but in 1660 parliament decided to re-establish the monarchy, as republican alternatives were proving far worse.

Charles II (the exiled son of Charles I) came to the throne, and his rule, known as 'the Restoration', saw scientific and cultural activity bursting forth. Exploration and expansion were also on the agenda. Backed by the army and navy (modernised, ironically, by Cromwell), British colonies stretched down the American coast, while the East India Company set up headquarters in Bombay (now Mumbai), laying foundations for the British Empire.

The next king, James II, had a harder time. Attempts to ease restrictive laws on Catholics ended with his defeat at the Battle of the Boyne by William III, the Protestant king of Holland, better known as William of Orange. William was married to James' own daughter Mary, but it didn't stop him having a bash at his father-in-law.

William and Mary came to the throne as King and Queen, each in their own right (Mary had more of a claim, but William would not agree to be a mere consort), and their joint accession in 1688 was known as the Glorious Revolution.

The Jacobite Rebellions

But in Scotland anti-English feeling refused to disappear. The Jacobite rebellions, most notably those of 1715 and 1745, were attempts to overthrow the Hanoverian monarchy and bring back the Stuarts. Although these are iconic events in Scottish history, in reality there was never much support for the Jacobite cause outside the Highlands: the people of the lowlands were mainly Protestant and feared a return to the Catholicism that the Stuarts represented.

The Empire Strikes Out

In the mid-18th century the British Empire continued to grow in America, Canada and India. The first claims were made on Australia after Captain James Cook's epic voyage of exploration in 1768.

The empire's first major reverse came when the American colonies won the War of Independence (1775–83). This setback forced Britain to withdraw from the world stage for

1775–83
The American War of Independence is the British Empire's first major reverse.

1799–1815
Emperor Napoleon threatens to invade; his efforts are curtailed by Nelson and Wellington.

1837–1901
In the reign of Queen Victoria the British Empire expands through Canada, Africa, India, Australia, Southeast Asia and New Zealand.

a while, a gap not missed by French ruler Napoleon. He threatened to invade Britain and hinder the power of the British overseas, before his ambitions were curtailed by naval hero Admiral Nelson and military hero the Duke of Wellington at the famous battles of Trafalgar (1805) and Waterloo (1815).

The Industrial Age

While the empire expanded abroad, at home Britain became the crucible of the Industrial Revolution. Steam power (patented by James Watt in 1781) and steam trains (launched by George Stephenson in 1830) transformed methods of production and transport, and the towns of the English Midlands became the first industrial cities.

From about 1750, much of the Scottish Highlands were emptied of people, as landowners casually expelled entire farms and villages to make way for more profitable sheep, a seminal event in Scotland's history known as the Clearances. Although many of the dispossessed left for the New World, others headed to the burgeoning cotton mills of Lanarkshire and the shipyards of Glasgow.

Age of Empire

Despite the social turmoil of the early 19th century, by the time Queen Victoria took the throne in 1837 Britain's factories dominated world trade and British fleets ruled the oceans. The rest of the 19th century was seen as Britain's Golden Age, a period of confidence not enjoyed since the days of the last great queen, Elizabeth I.

World War I

But in continental Europe four restless military powers (Russia, Austria-Hungary, Turkey and Germany) were sabre-rattling in the Balkan states. The assassination of Archduke Ferdinand in Sarajevo in 1914 finally sparked a clash that became the 'Great War' we now call WWI. Soldiers from Britain and Allied countries were drawn into a conflict of horrendous slaughter, most infamously on the killing fields of Flanders and the beaches of Gallipoli. By the war's weary end in 1918, over a million Britons were dead.

Disillusion & Depression

For the soldiers that did return from WWI, the war had created disillusion and a questioning of the social order. Many supported the ideals of a new political force, the Labour Party, to represent the working class.

Meanwhile, the bitter Anglo-Irish War (1919–21) saw most of Ireland achieving full independence from Britain. Six counties in the north remained British, creating a new political entity called the United Kingdom of Great Britain and Northern Ireland. But the decision

1939–45
WWII rages in Europe, Africa and Asia. Britain and the Allies eventually defeat the armies of Germany, Italy and Japan.

1948
Labour's Aneurin Bevan launches the National Health Service – the core of Britain as a 'welfare state'.

1952
Princess Elizabeth becomes Queen Elizabeth II. Her coronation takes place in Westminster Abbey in June 1953.

to partition the island of Ireland was to have long-term repercussions that still dominate political agendas in both the UK and the Republic of Ireland today.

The Labour Party formed its first government after winning the 1923 election, in coalition with the Liberals. James Ramsay MacDonald was the first Labour prime minister, but by the mid-1920s the Conservatives were back. The world economy was now in decline and in the 1930s the Great Depression arrived.

World War II

In 1933 Adolf Hitler came to power in Germany and in 1939 Germany invaded Poland, once again drawing Britain into war. The German army swept through Europe and pushed British forces to the beaches of Dunkirk (northern France) in June 1940. An extraordinary flotilla of rescue vessels turned total disaster into a brave defeat.

Between September 1940 and May 1941, the German air force launched the Blitz, a series of bombing raids on London and other cities. Despite this, morale in Britain remained strong, thanks partly to Churchill's regular radio broadcasts. In late 1941 the USA entered the war, and the tide began to turn.

By 1944 Germany was in retreat. Russia pushed back from the east, and Britain, the USA and other Allies were again on the beaches of France. The Normandy landings (D-Day) marked the start of the liberation of Europe's western side. By early May 1945 Hitler was dead, Germany was defeated and the war finally ended with the Japanese surrender in September.

Swinging & Sliding

Despite victory in WWII, there was an unexpected swing on the political front in 1945. An electorate tired of war and hungry for change turned to the Labour Party.

In 1952 George VI was succeeded by his daughter Elizabeth II and she has remained on the throne ever since, overseeing a period of dramatic change.

By the late 1950s, recovery was strong enough for Prime Minister Harold Macmillan to famously remind the British people they had 'never had it so good'.

Although the 1960s were swinging, the 1970s saw an economic slide thanks to a grim combination of inflation, the oil crisis and international competition. The rest of the decade was marked by strikes, disputes and gloom.

The British public had had enough, and in the elections of 1979 the Conservatives won a landslide victory, led by a little-known politician named Margaret Thatcher.

The Thatcher Years

Soon everyone had heard of Margaret Thatcher. Love her or hate her, no one could argue that her methods weren't dramatic. Looking back from a 21st-century vantage point, most

1960s
An era of African and Caribbean independence, including Nigeria (1960), Tanzania (1961), Jamaica (1962) and Kenya (1963).

1979
A Conservative government led by Margaret Thatcher wins power, ushering in a decade of dramatic political and social change.

1997
Tony Blair leads 'New' Labour to victory, with a record-breaking parliamentary majority, ending 18 years of Tory rule.

commentators agree that by economic measures the Thatcher government's policies were largely successful, but by social measures they were a failure and created a polarised Britain: on one side were the people who gained from the prosperous wave of opportunities in the 'new' industries, while on the other side were those left unemployed and dispossessed by the decline of the 'old' industries such as coal-mining and steel production.

Despite, or perhaps thanks to, policies that were frequently described as uncompromising, Margaret Thatcher was, by 1988, the longest-serving British prime minister of the 20th century.

New Labour, New Millennium, New Start

In 1997, however, 'New' Labour swept to power, with leader Tony Blair declared the new prime minister. The Labour Party enjoyed an extended honeymoon period, and the next election (in 2001) was another walkover. The Conservative Party continued to struggle, allowing Labour to win a historic third term in 2005.

In May 2010 Labour rule finally came to an end – to be replaced by a coalition government (the first in the UK since WWII) between the Conservatives and the Liberal Democrats.

Brexit, Boris & Covid-19

By 2015 the Tories had won sole power, which in turn led to the EU referendum of 2016 where the people of the UK voted, by 52% to 48%, to leave the EU.

Prime Minister David Cameron resigned almost immediately after the referendum, succeeded by Theresa May, whose premiership was marred by wrangling over the Brexit issue – as well as a misjudged decision to hold a snap general election in 2017, which resulted in her losing her majority in a hung parliament in the House of Commons.

May was forced from power in 2019 and replaced with populist, pro-Brexit, ex-London mayor Boris Johnson. The following months descended into fierce parliamentary division, as Johnson attempted to force through his hard-line Brexit strategy against the wishes of more moderate MPs.

Finally, to try to seize the agenda, Johnson called an unusual December election in 2019, running on a simple slogan of 'Get Brexit Done'. Unexpectedly, he won a 74 seat majority – the largest since Margaret Thatcher in 1987 – and, even more astonishingly, won many seats in the industrial heartlands of England and Wales, traditionally Labour strongholds. Crushed by defeat, Labour Party leader Jeremy Corbyn resigned, and was replaced by ex-Attorney General, Sir Keir Starmer.

Johnson's best-laid plans were, however, derailed in 2020 when the coronavirus pandemic swept across the country, forcing the nation into lockdown and recession with some of the worst infection and mortality rates in the EU.

2016
In the EU Referendum, 52% vote to Leave, 48% vote to Remain.

2018
Prince Harry weds American actress Meghan Markle, the first person identifying as biracial to marry into the royal family.

2020
Covid-19 sweeps the UK, plunging the country into the deepest recession since records began.

Natural History Museum (p75), London

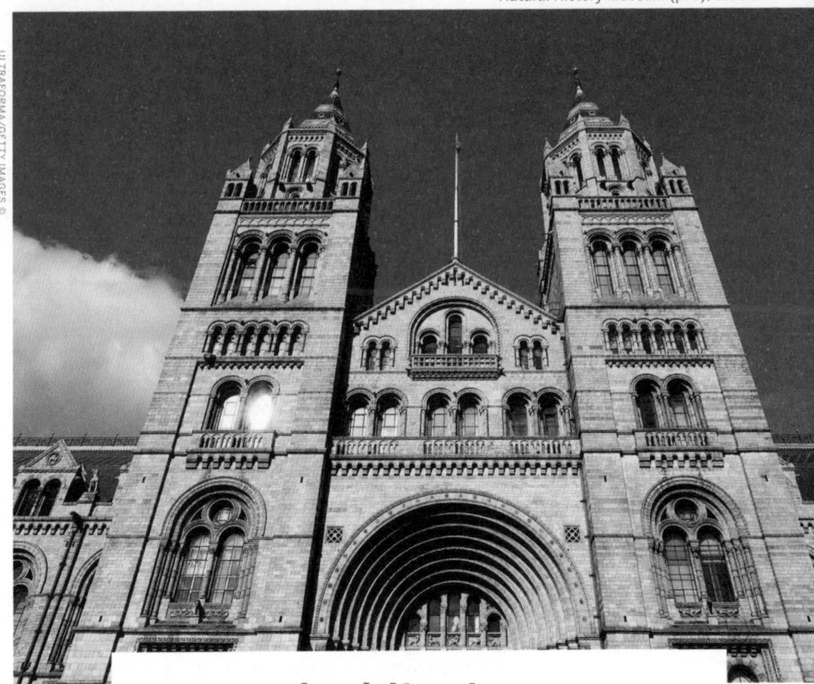

ULTRAFORMA/GETTY IMAGES ©

Architecture

The history of British architecture spans over four millennia, from the mysterious stone circles of Stonehenge to the shimmering skyscrapers of modern London. The country's built heritage includes Roman baths and parish churches, mighty castles and magnificent cathedrals, humble cottages and grand stately homes. Exploring it all is one of the great joys of a visit to Britain.

Early Foundations

The oldest surviving structures in Britain are the grass-covered mounds of earth called 'tumuli' or 'barrows', used as burial sites by the country's prehistoric residents. These mounds, measuring anything from a rough hemisphere just 2m high to oval domes around 5m high and 10m long, are dotted across the countryside and are especially common in areas of chalk downland such as Salisbury Plain in southern England.

Even more impressive than the giant tumuli are the most prominent legacies of the Neolithic era – such as the iconic stone circle at Stonehenge (p104) in Wiltshire. Again, its original purpose is a mystery, providing fertile ground for hypothesis and speculation.

The Roman Era

Remnants of the Roman Empire are distributed in many towns and cities (mostly through England and Wales, as the Romans didn't colonise Scotland). The bathhouse complex (p115) in the city of Bath is one of the most impressive sets of remains. Britain's largest Roman relic is the 73-mile-long sweep of Hadrian's Wall, built in the 2nd century as a defensive line stretching from coast to coast across the island.

London's New Landmarks

In the centre of the capital, the **Shard** – a giant, pointed glass skyscraper – dominates the South Bank; at 306m, it's one of Europe's tallest buildings.

On the other side of the Thames, two more giant new skyscrapers include **20 Fenchurch St** (nicknamed 'the Walkie-Talkie', thanks to its shape) and the slanting-walled **Leadenhall Building** (dubbed, inevitably, 'the Cheese Grater'). Once completed, **1 Undershaft**, Bishopsgate (labelled 'the Trellis' for its external crosshatch bracing) will be the City of London's tallest building.

Medieval Masterpieces

In the centuries following the Norman Conquest of 1066, an explosion of architecture in stone was inspired by the two most pressing concerns of the day: religion and defence. Early structures of timber and rubble were replaced with churches, abbeys and monasteries built in dressed stone. The round arches, squat towers and chevron decoration of the Norman or Romanesque style (11th to 12th centuries) slowly evolved into the tall pointed arches, ribbed vaults and soaring spires of the Gothic (13th to 16th centuries). These style transformations can often be seen all in the one church, as construction often took a couple of hundred years to complete. Many cathedrals remain modern landmarks, such as those at Salisbury (p108) and York (p178).

Stone was also put to good use in the building of elaborate defensive structures. Castles range from atmospheric ruins to stunning crag-top fortresses, such as Edinburgh Castle (p221). And then there's the most impressive of them all: the Tower of London (p43), guarding the capital for more than 900 years.

Stately Homes

The medieval period was tumultuous, but by the start of the 17th century life had become more settled and the nobility had less need for fortifications. While they were excellent for keeping out the riff-raff, castles were often too cold and draughty for comfortable aristocratic living.

Following the Civil War, the trend away from castles gathered pace, and throughout the 17th century the landed gentry developed a taste for fine 'country houses' designed by famous architects of the day. Many became the stately homes that are a major feature of the British landscape and a major attraction for visitors. Among the most extravagant are Castle Howard (p177) near York and Blenheim Palace (p137) near Oxford.

The great stately homes all display the proportion, symmetry and architectural harmony that was in vogue during the 17th and 18th centuries. These styles were later reflected in the fashionable town houses of the Georgian era, most notably in the city of Bath, where the stunning Royal Crescent (p116) is the ultimate example of the genre.

★ Best Castles & Stately Homes

Edinburgh Castle (p220), Edinburgh

Blenheim Palace (p136), near Oxford

Tower of London (p42), London

Castle Howard (p176), near York

Windsor Castle (p56), near London

Edinburgh Castle (p220)

Victoriana

The Victorian era was a very busy architectural period. A style called Victorian Gothic developed, imitating the tall, narrow windows and ornamented spires featured in the original Gothic cathedrals. The most famous example is London's Houses of Parliament (the Palace of Westminster; p66) and Elizabeth Tower (home to Big Ben). Another Victorian Gothic highlight in London is the Natural History Museum (p75).

Industrialisation

Through the late 19th and early 20th centuries, as Britain's cities grew in size and stature, the newly moneyed middle classes built smart town houses. Elsewhere, the first town planners oversaw the construction of endless terraces of 'back-to-back' and 'two-up-two-down' houses to accommodate the massive influx of workers required for the country's factories.

The 21st Century

During the first decade of this century, many areas of Britain placed new importance on having progressive, popular architecture as part of a wider regeneration. Edinburgh's Scottish Parliament Building (p233) is a fine example.

Britain's largest and highest-profile architectural project of recent years was the Olympic Park, the centrepiece of the 2012 Olympic Games. Situated in the London suburb of Stratford, it was renamed the Queen Elizabeth Olympic Park (p79) after the games. Alongside the main Olympic Stadium – now the home ground of West Ham United football club – there's the dramatic Velodrome and Aquatics Centre.

Elsewhere around the country, the most obvious examples of 21st-century architecture are the futuristic wind-farms that are appearing offshore. Less obvious, perhaps, but more impactful, are the large-scale housing developments that are currently underway in many areas to try to address Britain's chronic housing shortage. In 2019, more than 170,000 new homes were built – the highest figure in 11 years.

Shopping for vinyl in Notting Hill, London

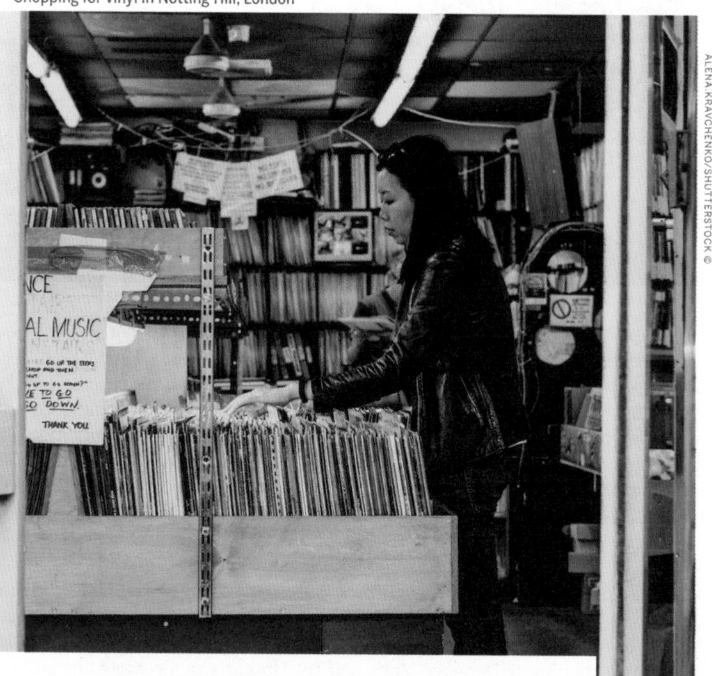

ALENA.KRAVCHENKO/SHUTTERSTOCK ©

Pop & Rock Music

Britain has been putting the world through its musical paces ever since a mop-haired four-piece from Liverpool tuned up their Rickenbackers and created The Beatles. And while some insist Elvis invented rock 'n' roll, it was the Fab Four who transformed it into a global phenomenon, backed by the other bands of the 1960s 'British Invasion' – The Rolling Stones, The Who, Cream, The Kinks and soul man Tom Jones.

Glam to Punk

Glam rock swaggered onto the stage at the start of the 1970s, led by the likes of Marc Bolan and David Bowie in their tight-fitting jumpsuits and chameleon guises, and was succeeded by early boy-band Bay City Rollers, art-rockers Roxy Music, outrageously costumed Elton John and anthemic popsters Queen. In the same era, Led Zeppelin, Deep Purple and Black Sabbath laid down the blueprint for heavy metal, while the psychedelia of the previous decade morphed into the spacey soundscapes of prog rock, epitomised by Pink Floyd, Genesis and Yes.

By the mid to late '70s, glam and prog bands were looking totally out of touch in a Britain wracked by rampant unemployment and industrial unrest, and punk rock exploded onto the scene, summing up the air of doom with nihilistic lyrics and three-chord tunes.

★ London Album-Cover Locations

Abbey Rd: *Abbey Road*, The Beatles

Battersea Power Station: *Animals*, Pink Floyd

Berwick St: *(What's the Story) Morning Glory?*, Oasis

Heddon St: *Ziggy Stardust*, David Bowie

Abbey Road

The Sex Pistols remain the best-known band of the era, while other punk pioneers included The Clash, The Damned, The Buzzcocks and The Stranglers.

Punk spawned New Wave, with acts such as The Jam and Elvis Costello blending spiky tunes and sharp lyrics into a more radio-friendly sound. Almost simultaneously, ska bands like The Specials and baggy-trousered rude boys Madness made dapper mod tailoring mainstream again. Meanwhile, a New-Wave-and-reggae-influenced band called The Police – fronted by consummate musician Sting – became one of the biggest names of the decade.

Mode, Metal & Miserabilism

The conspicuous consumption of Britain in the early 1980s was reflected in the decade's pop scene. Big hair and shoulder pads typified New Romantics such as Spandau Ballet, Duran Duran and Culture Club, while a growing penchant for synthesisers cultivated a new electronic sound with Depeche Mode and The Human League. More hits and highlights were supplied by Texas, Eurythmics, and Wham! – a boyish duo headed by the beautifully voiced George Michael.

Beyond the glitz, darker and gloomier corners of music were inhabited by The Cure, Bauhaus and Siouxsie & the Banshees, while Britain's heavy rock heritage inspired acts such as Iron Maiden. In a different tone entirely, the disaffection of mid-1980s Britain was summed up by the arch-priests of 'miserabilism', The Smiths, fronted by quiffed wordsmith Morrissey.

Raves, Indie & Britpop

The beats and bleeps of 1980s electronica fuelled the burgeoning dance-music scene of the early '90s. An eruption of ecstasy-saturated rave culture, centred on famous clubs such as Manchester's Haçienda and London's Ministry of Sound, overflowed into the mainstream through chart-topping acts such as The Prodigy and Fatboy Slim. Manchester was also a focus for the burgeoning British 'indie' scene, driven by guitar-based bands such as The Charlatans, The Stone Roses, James and Happy Mondays.

Indie grew up in the mid- to late-1990s, and the term 'Britpop' was coined, with Oasis at the forefront, but covering a wide range of bands including Blur, Elastica, Suede, Supergrass, Ocean Colour Scene, The Verve, Pulp, Travis, Feeder, Super Furry Animals, Stereophonics, Catatonia and the Manic Street Preachers.

Pop Today, Gone Tomorrow

The new millennium saw no let-up in the British music scene's shape-shifting reinvention. Jazz, soul, R&B and hip-hop fused into an 'urban' sound epitomised by artists such as Dizzee Rascal, Tinie Tempah and Stormzy.

The alternative and indie flame was kept alight thanks to Florence & the Machine, Muse, Kasabian, Radiohead, The Horrors and breakthrough grunge-pop band Wolf Alice. Meanwhile, Coldplay became possibly the hugest band in the world, with a repertoire of sing-along stadium anthems.

Folk and roots music, and folk-influenced acoustic music, enjoyed a revival with major names including Eliza Carthy, Mumford & Sons and Welsh band Allan Yn Y Fan. Another notable name is Michael Kiwanuka, whose third album *Kiwanuka* – a fusion of pop, soul and thoughtful songwriting – won the coveted Mercury Music Prize in 2020.

Boy bands continue to come and go, most notably One Direction, who clocked up the sales before going the way of all boy bands and splitting up in acrimonious fashion.

Meanwhile, the singer-songwriter, exemplified by Katie Melua, Ed Sheeran, the late Amy Winehouse, James Bay and the all-conquering Adele, has made a comeback. Ed Sheeran alone has sold more than 26 million albums and 100 million singles worldwide.

Pop on Film

If you want to combine British pop music with British cinema, try some of these films:

Yesterday (2019) A fantasy world in which The Beatles never existed.

Rocket Man (2019) Piano man Elton John biopic that hits all the right notes.

Bohemian Rhapsody (2018) Rami Malek channels Freddie Mercury.

24 Hour Party People (2002) A totally irreverent and suitably chaotic film about the 1990s Manchester music scene.

Gimme Shelter (1970) Classic rockumentary recording the final weeks of The Rolling Stones' US tour in 1969.

Control (2007) Biopic about Joy Division's lead singer Ian Curtis.

Nowhere Boy (2009) About John Lennon in his pre-Beatles days.

Amy (2015) Much praised documentary on the life of doomed singer Amy Winehouse.

A British Playlist

Get in the mood by loading up your music player with this Best of British play list featuring classic hits from the last 50 years of UK pop.

- 'Shape of You' by Ed Sheeran
- 'Stay with Me' by Sam Smith
- 'Safe from Harm' by Massive Attack
- 'Shape of my Heart' by Sting
- 'Sultans of Swing' by Dire Straits
- 'Patience of Angels' by Eddi Reader
- 'Love Me Like You Do' by Ellie Goulding
- 'Bonkers' by Dizzee Rascal
- 'An Endless Sky of Honey' by Kate Bush
- 'A Design for Life' by Manic Street Preachers
- 'Back to Black' by Amy Winehouse
- 'Common People' by Pulp
- 'Down By The Water' by PJ Harvey
- 'Breaking Glass' by David Bowie

Shakespeare's Globe (p74), London

PRES PANAYOTOV/SHUTTERSTOCK ©

Writers & Artists

Britain's artistic heritage is astoundingly rich and globally renowned, with deep literary roots reaching from Early English epics such as Beowulf through Chaucer, Shakespeare, Burns, Austen and Tolkien to today's best seller: JK Rowling. Artistic notables include Turner, Constable, Henry Moore and Damien Hirst. The nation's literary and artistic life can be discovered in countless cities, museums and galleries throughout the land.

Authors & Poets

Chaucer

The first big name in Britain's literary history is Geoffrey Chaucer. He is best known for *The Canterbury Tales*, a mammoth collection of fables, stories and morality tales, using travelling pilgrims (the Knight, the Wife of Bath, the Nun's Priest and so on) as a narrative hook.

Turner Contemporary Gallery, Margate

CBCK/SHUTTERSTOCK © ARCHITECT: DAVID CHIPPERFIELD

Shakespeare

For most visitors to Britain (and for many locals) drama means just one name: Shakespeare. Born in 1564 in the Midlands town of Stratford-upon-Avon, William Shakespeare made his name in London, where most of his plays were performed at the Globe Theatre.

He started writing plays around 1585, and his early theatrical works are grouped together as 'comedies' and 'histories', many of which are household names today – such as *All's Well that Ends Well, The Taming of the Shrew, A Midsummer Night's Dream*, *Richard II* and *Henry V*. Later in his career Shakespeare wrote the plays known collectively as the 'tragedies', including *Romeo and Juliet, Macbeth, Julius Caesar, Hamlet* and *King Lear*. His brilliant plots and spectacular use of language, plus the sheer size of his body of work, have turned him into a national – and international – icon.

Today, over 400 years after his death, the Bard's plays draw huge crowds; enjoy them at the rebuilt Shakespeare's Globe on London's South Bank and at the Royal Shakespeare Company's own theatre in his original hometown of Stratford-upon-Avon.

Burns

Familiar to pretty much everyone in Britain are the words of *Auld Lang Syne,* penned by Scotland's national poet Robert Burns, and traditionally sung at New Year. His more unusual *Address to a Haggis* is also still recited annually on Burns Night, a Scottish celebration held on 25 January (the poet's birthday).

★ Literary Locations

Stratford-upon-Avon (p147): Shakespeare

The Lake District (p193): Wordsworth

Edinburgh (p217): Burns, Scott, Stevenson, JK Rowling

Oxford (p125): Tolkien, Lewis Carroll, CS Lewis

Bath (p111): Jane Austen

Jane Austen Centre, Bath

Wordsworth & the Romantics

As industrialisation began to take hold in Britain during the late 18th and early 19th century, a new generation of writers, including William Blake, John Keats, Percy Bysshe Shelley, Lord Byron and Samuel Taylor Coleridge, drew inspiration from human imagination and the natural world (in some cases aided by a healthy dose of laudanum). Known as the 'Romantics', the best known of all was William Wordsworth; his famous line from the poem commonly known as 'Daffodils' – 'I wandered lonely as a cloud' – was inspired by a walk along the shores of Ullswater in the Lake District.

Dickens, Elliot, Hardy & Scott

During the reign of Queen Victoria (1837–1901), key novels of the time explored social themes. Charles Dickens' *Oliver Twist* is a tale of child pickpockets surviving in the London slums, while *Hard Times* is a critique of the excesses of capitalism.

At around the same time, but in a rural setting, George Eliot (the pen name of Mary Anne Evans) wrote *The Mill on the Floss*, whose central character, Maggie Tulliver, searches for true love and struggles against society's expectations.

Thomas Hardy's classic *Tess of the D'Urbervilles* deals with the peasantry's decline, and *The Trumpet Major* paints a picture of idyllic English country life interrupted by war and encroaching modernity.

Waverley by Scotland's greatest historical novelist, Sir Walter Scott, was written in the early 19th century and set in the mountains and glens of Scotland during the time of the Jacobite rebellion. It is usually regarded as the first historical novel in the English language.

Modern Authors

Britain – and its literature – changed forever following WWI and the social disruption of the period. This fed into the modernist movement, with DH Lawrence perhaps its finest exponent. *Sons and Lovers* follows the lives and loves of generations in the English Midlands as the country changes from rural idyll to industrial landscape, while his controversial exploration of sexuality in *Lady Chatterley's Lover* was banned until 1960 because of its 'obscenity'.

Other highlights of this period included Daphne du Maurier's romantic suspense novel *Rebecca*; Evelyn Waugh's *Brideshead Revisited*, an exploration of moral and social disintegration among the English aristocracy in the 1920s and '30s; and Richard Llewellyn's Welsh classic *How Green Was My Valley*. In the 1950s, the poet Dylan Thomas found fame with the radio play *Under Milk Wood*, exposing the social tensions of small-town Wales.

Some of the post-1970s writers of note include include Martin Amis *(London Fields)*; Ian McEwan (*Atonement* and *On Chesil Beach*); Kate Roberts *(Feet in Chains)*; Bruce Chatwin *(On the Black Hill)* and Irvine Welsh *(Trainspotting)*.

The most successful literary British novelist of recent years has been Hilary Mantel, whose bestselling trilogy of Tudor intrigue (*Wolf Hall*, *Bring Up the Bodies* and *The Mirror and the Light*) became historical blockbusters (the first two instalments also won the Booker Prize).

Children's Literary Favourites

Britain's greatest literary phenomenon of the 21st century is JK Rowling's *Harry Potter* series, a set of otherworldly adventures that have entertained millions of children (and many grown-ups, too) from the publication of the first book – *Harry Potter and the Philosopher's Stone* – in 1997, to *Harry Potter and the Deathly Hallows* (2007). The magical tales, brought vividly to life in the Harry Potter movies, are the latest in a long line of British children's classics that are also enjoyed by adults. The pedigree stretches back to the works of Lewis Carroll *(Alice's Adventures in Wonderland)*, E Nesbit *(The Railway Children)*, AA Milne *(Winnie-the-Pooh)*, CS Lewis *(The Chronicles of Narnia)* and Roald Dahl *(Charlie and the Chocolate Factory)*.

British Art

Portraits & Landscapes

In the 19th century, leading painters favoured the landscape. John Constable's best-known works include *Salisbury Cathedral* and *The Hay Wain*, depicting a mill in Suffolk (and now on show in the National Gallery, London), while JMW Turner was fascinated by the effects of light and colour, with his works becoming almost entirely abstract by the 1840s – vilified at the time but prefiguring the Impressionist movement that was to follow 50 years later.

Victorian Art

In the mid- to late-19th century, the Pre-Raphaelite movement harked back to the figurative style of classical Italian and Flemish art, tying in with the prevailing Victorian taste for fables, myths and fairy tales. An iconic work is Sir John Everett Millais' *Ophelia*, showing the damsel picturesquely drowned in a river; it can be seen at the Tate Britain.

William Morris saw late-19th-century furniture and interior design as increasingly vulgar, and with Dante Gabriel Rossetti and Edward Burne-Jones founded the Arts and Crafts movement to encourage the revival of a decorative approach to features such as wallpaper, tapestries and windows.

North of the border, Charles Rennie Mackintosh, fresh from the Glasgow School of Art, fast became a renowned artist, designer and architect. He is still Scotland's greatest art nouveau exponent.

Pop Art & Brit Art

The mid-1950s and early '60s saw an explosion of British artists plundering TV, music, advertising and popular culture for inspiration. Leaders of this 'pop art' movement included David Hockney and Peter Blake.

A new wave of British artists, dubbed 'Britart', came to the fore in the 1990s. Its leading members included Damien Hirst, initially famous (or infamous) for works involving pickled sharks, semi-dissected human figures and a diamond-encrusted skull entitled *For the Love of God*.

The Turner Prize (named after JMW Turner) is a high-profile (and frequently controversial) annual award for British visual artists.

Several high-profile new art museums have opened in recent years, including a new extension to the Tate St Ives, the striking Turner Contemporary in Margate, the sculpture-focused Hepworth Wakefield and Plymouth's The Box.

Six Nations Rugby

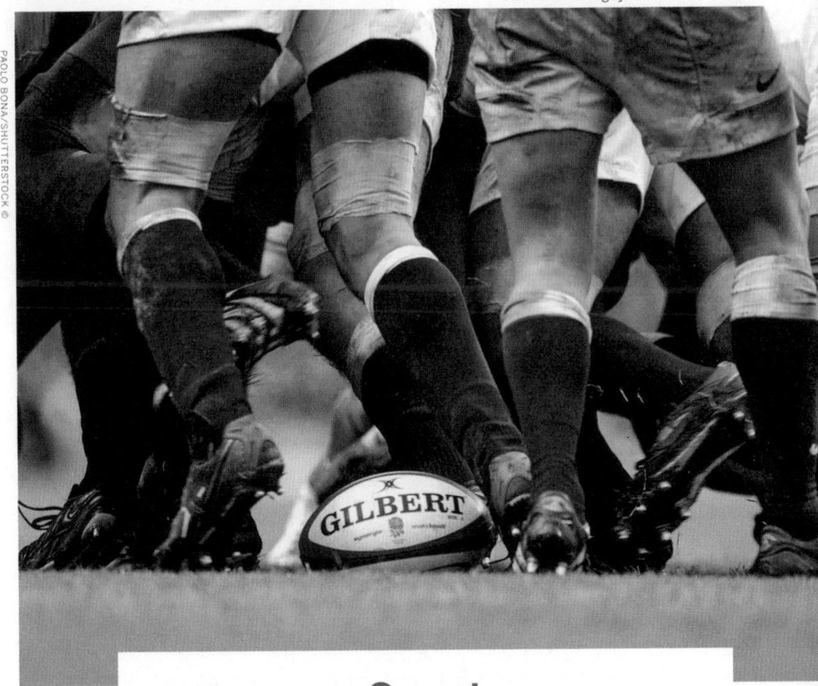

PAOLO BONA/SHUTTERSTOCK ©

Sport

If you want a shortcut straight to the heart of British culture, watch the British at play. They're passionate about their sport – as participants and spectators. Every weekend thousands of people turn out to cheer their favourite team, and sporting highlights such as Wimbledon keep the entire nation transfixed.

Playing & Watching the Game

The British invented many of the world's favourite team sports, or at least codified their modern rules, including cricket, tennis, rugby, golf and football (soccer). The men's national teams may not always be that successful internationally, but at the 2018 World Cup a young England football team reached the semi-finals. Unfortunately, Scotland, Wales and Northern Ireland failed to even qualify. The women's national teams do well: the England women's football team took third place in the FIFA Women's World Cup in 2015, and fourth in 2019.

Britain punches way above its weight in athletics, when the nation comes together to field a GB-wide team to huge success, especially at the Olympic Games in 2012 (third place) and in 2016, when Britain achieved a staggering second place.

Football (Soccer)

The English Premier League has some of the strongest teams in the world, dominated in recent years by Manchester City, Manchester United, Liverpool, Chelsea, Arsenal and Tottenham Hotspur. But there's still room for upsets such as in 2016, when unfancied Leicester City stunned pundits and delighted neutrals by winning the league. Liverpool have found top form again in recent seasons, finally winning the title in 2020, their first title in 30 years (and their first time as Premier League Champions) and winning the Champions League in 2019.

Seventy-two other teams play in the English divisions called the Championship, League One and League Two. In Scotland the game has long been dominated by Glasgow teams Celtic and Rangers, while in Wales football is less popular (rugby is the national sport) and the main Welsh sides such as Swansea, Cardiff and Wrexham play in the English leagues.

The football season runs from August to May. Tickets for Premier League matches are like gold dust; you're better off trying for lower-division games. You can often buy these tickets on the spot at stadiums. Otherwise go to club websites or online agencies such as www.ticketmaster.co.uk and www.myticketmarket.com.

Football or Soccer?

The word 'soccer', often used outside Britain, derives from the sport's official name Association Football (as opposed to rugby football), or possibly from 'sock' – a leather foot-cover worn in medieval times, ideal for kicking a pig's bladder around the park on a Saturday afternoon.

Rugby

A wit once said that football was a gentlemen's game played by hooligans, while rugby was a hooligans' game played by gentlemen. Whatever the truth, it's worth catching a game; tickets cost around £15 to £50.

There are two versions of the British game: rugby union (www.englandrugby.com) is played more in southern England, Wales and Scotland, while rugby league (www.rugby-league.com) is played predominantly in northern England.

Both codes trace their roots back to a football match in 1823 at Rugby School, in Warwickshire. A player called William Webb Ellis, frustrated at the limitations of mere kicking, reputedly picked up the ball and ran with it towards the opponents' goal – and a whole new sport was born. The Rugby Football Union was formally inaugurated in 1871, while the Rugby World Cup is named the Webb Ellis trophy after this enterprising tearaway.

The highlight of rugby union's international calendar is the Six Nations Championship (www.sixnationsrugby.com), between England, Wales, Scotland, Ireland, France and Italy.

Cricket

While it is also played in Wales and Scotland, cricket is a quintessentially English sport. Dating from the 18th century – although its roots are much older – the sport spread throughout the Commonwealth during Britain's colonial era. Australia, the Caribbean and the Indian subcontinent took to the game with gusto, and today the former colonies delight in giving the old country a good spanking on the cricket pitch.

While many English people follow cricket like a cult, to the uninitiated it can be an impenetrable spectacle. Spread over one-day games or five-day test matches, progress can seem slow and dominated by arcane terminology such as innings, over, googly, out-swinger, leg-bye and silly-mid-off. At the very least, it's worth trying to understand the scoring system: teams score one run for every successful run between the wickets, four for hitting the ball

★ **Useful Websites**

British Open Golf www.theopen.com

Rugby Union www.englandrugby.com

English Cricket Board www.ecb.co.uk

Wimbledon Tennis www.wimbledon.com

Cricketers

along the ground to the edge of the oval (the 'boundary', marked by a rope), and six if the ball reaches the boundary without touching the ground (like a home run in baseball).

One-day games and internationals are played at grounds including Lord's in London, Edgbaston in Birmingham and Headingley in Leeds. Tickets range from £30 to more than £200. The County Championship features teams from around the country; tickets cost £5 to £25. See the English Cricket Board website (www.ecb.co.uk) for more information.

Tennis

Tennis is widely played in Britain, but the best-known tennis tournament for spectators is Wimbledon (officially the All England Championships; www.wimbledon.com), when tennis fever sweeps through Britain in the last week of June and first week of July. By far the most successful British player of recent years is Andy Murray, a Scotsman, who won the Wimbledon title in 2013 and 2016.

Demand for seats always outstrips supply, but about 6000 tickets are sold each day (excluding the final four days). You'll need to rise early: dedicated fans start queuing before dawn.

Golf

Millions take to the golf fairways in Britain each week. The main tournament is the Open Championship ('The Open' or 'British Open'; www.theopen.com). The oldest of professional golf's major championships, it dates back to 1860 and is the only one held outside the USA. It's held in different locations, usually over the third weekend in July.

There are around 2000 private and public golf courses in Britain. Most private clubs welcome visitors; public courses are open to anyone. A round costs around £10 to £30 on public courses, and up to £200 on famous championship courses.

Horse Racing

Horse racing in Britain stretches back centuries, and there's a 'race meeting' somewhere pretty much every day. Buy tickets from the British Horse Racing Authority's website (www.greatbritishracing.com).

The top event is Royal Ascot at Ascot Racecourse in mid-June, where the rich and famous come to see and be seen. Other highlights include the Grand National steeplechase at Aintree in early April and the Derby at Epsom on the first Saturday in June.

Full English breakfast

SLAWOMIR FAJER/SHUTTERSTOCK ©

The British Table

There's been nothing short of a revolution in British food over the last 20 years. Celebrity chefs, Michelin-starred restaurants, local markets and cool cafes abound these days, and you'll be able to find something good to eat – and drink – no matter where you travel. With organic, seasonal and sustainable dishes gracing many menus, London is a global gastronomic capital, but great food can be found Britain-wide.

The Full British Breakfast

Many people in Britain make do with toast or a bowl of cereal before dashing to work, but visitors staying in hotels and B&Bs will undoubtedly encounter a phenomenon called the 'full English breakfast' – or one of its regional equivalents. This usually consists of bacon, sausages, eggs, tomatoes, mushrooms, baked beans, fried bread (or toast) and perhaps black pudding. In Scotland the 'full Scottish breakfast' might include tattie scones (potato bread) instead of fried bread. In Wales you may be offered laver bread, which is not a bread at all, but seaweed – a tasty speciality often served with oatmeal and bacon on toast.

Britain's Most Popular Restaurant Dish

Britain's most popular restaurant dish is chicken tikka masala, an 'Indian' curry dish created specifically for the British palate and unheard of in India itself.

Chicken tikka masala

Lunch

One lunchtime classic is the ploughman's lunch. Basically bread and cheese, these days the meal usually includes butter, salad and pickled onion. Variations include a farmer's lunch (bread and chicken), stockman's lunch (bread and ham), Frenchman's lunch (brie and baguette) and fisherman's lunch (yes, with fish).

Or try Welsh rarebit – a sophisticated variation of cheese on toast, seasoned and flavoured with butter, milk and sometimes a little beer. For a takeaway lunch in Scotland, look out for Forfar bridies (pastry turnovers filled with minced beef and onion).

Dinner

For generations, a typical British dinner has been 'meat and two veg'. The meat is pork, beef or lamb, one of the vegetables is potatoes and the other inevitably carrots, cabbage or cauliflower.

Roast beef is synonymous with Britain; perhaps the most famous beef comes from Scotland's Aberdeen Angus cattle, while the best-known meat from Wales is lamb. Venison – usually from red deer – is readily available in Scotland, and in parts of Wales and England. Yorkshire pudding is another speciality. It's simply roast batter, but very tasty when cooked well. Perhaps the best-known British meal is fish and chips, often bought from the 'chippie' wrapped in paper to carry home.

Puddings & Desserts

A classic British pudding (ie dessert) is rhubarb crumble: the juicy stem of a large-leafed garden plant, stewed and sweetened, then topped with a crunchy mix of flour, butter and more sugar, and served with custard or ice cream.

Scotland's classic pudding is 'clootie dumpling' (a rich fruit pudding that is wrapped in a cotton cloth and steamed). Another sweet temptation is cranachan, whipped cream flavoured with whisky and mixed with toasted oatmeal and raspberries.

Tea & Coffee

Britain's best-known beverage is tea, usually made with dark tea leaves to produce a strong, brown drink. More bitter in taste than tea served in some other Western countries, it's usually served with a dash of milk and perhaps sugar.

But Brits also consume 95 million cups of coffee a day. When you're ordering and the server says 'white or black', it just means 'Do you want milk in it?'

Beer & Cider

British beer typically ranges from dark brown to amber in colour, and is often served at room temperature. Technically it's called ale and is more commonly called 'bitter' (or 'heavy' in Scotland). This is to distinguish it from lager – the drink that most of the rest of the word calls 'beer', which is generally yellow and served cold. Bitter that's brewed and served traditionally is called 'real ale' to distinguish it from mass-produced brands, and there are many regional varieties.

The increasing popularity of real ales saw a huge rise in the number of artisan brewers and microbreweries springing up all over Britain – by 2018 there were almost 1850, with around 100 in London alone. They take pride in using only natural ingredients, and many try to revive ancient recipes, such as heather- and seaweed-flavoured ales.

Another must-try is cider – available in sweet and dry varieties and, increasingly, as craft cider, often with various fruit or herbal flavours added.

'Nose to Tail' Cuisine

One of many trends in modern British cuisine is the revival of 'nose to tail' cooking – making use of the entire animal, not just the more obvious cuts. So as well as dishes involving liver, heart and chitterlings (intestines), traditional delights such as bone marrow on toast, or tripe (cow's stomach lining) with onions are once again gracing fashionable tables. The movement has been spearheaded by chef Fergus Henderson at his St John restaurant in London (p88), and through his influential book, *Nose to Tail Eating: A Kind of British Cooking* (1999) and its follow-up *Beyond Nose To Tail* (2007).

Whisky

The spirit most visitors associate with Britain – and especially Scotland – is whisky. There's a big difference between single-malt whisky, made purely from malted barley in a single distillery, and blended whisky, made from a mix of cheaper grain whisky and malt whiskies from several distilleries.

A single malt, like a fine wine, somehow captures the terroir or essence of the place where it was made and matured – a combination of the water, the barley, the peat smoke, the oak barrels in which it was aged and (in the case of certain coastal distilleries) the sea air and salt spray. Each distillation varies from the one before, like different vintages from the same vineyard.

Bars & Pubs

In Britain the difference between a bar and a pub is sometimes vague, but generally bars are smarter, larger and louder than pubs, possibly with a younger crowd. Drinks are more expensive, too, unless there's a drink promotion (there often is).

As well as beer, cider and wine, pubs and bars offer the usual choice of spirits, often with a 'mixer', producing British favourites such as gin and tonic, rum and coke, and vodka and lime. These drinks are served in measures called 'singles' and 'doubles'. A single can be either 25mL or 35mL (depending on the bar) – just over one US fluid ounce. A double is, of course, 50mL or 70mL.

Remember that drinks in British pubs are ordered and paid for at the bar, and that it's not usual to tip pub and bar staff.

Underground station at Regent Street, London

Survival Guide

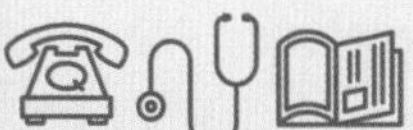

Directory A–Z

Accessible Travel

All new buildings have wheelchair access, and even hotels in grand old country houses often have lifts, ramps and other facilities. Hotels and B&Bs in historic buildings are often harder to adapt, so you'll have less choice here.

Modern city buses and trams have low floors for easy access, but few have conductors who can lend a hand when you're getting on or off. Many taxis take wheelchairs, or just have more room in the back.

For long-distance travel, coaches may present problems but the main operator, **National Express** (www.nationalexpress.com) has wheelchair-friendly coaches on many routes. For details, see the website or call the Disabled Passenger Travel Helpline (0371 781 8181).

On most intercity trains there's more room and better facilities, compared with travel by coach, and station staff are usually around; just have a word and they'll be happy to help. A **Disabled Person's Railcard** (www.disabledpersons-railcard.co.uk) costs £20 and gets you 33% off most train fares.

Useful organisations:

Disability Rights UK (www.disabilityrightsuk.org) Published titles include a holiday guide. Other services include a key for 7000 public disabled toilets across the UK.

Good Access Guide (www.goodaccessguide.co.uk)

Tourism for All (www.tourismforall.org.uk)

Download Lonely Planet's free Accessible Travel guides from https://shop.lonelyplanet.com/categories/accessible-travel.

Accommodation

Booking your accommodation in advance is recommended, especially in popular holiday areas and on islands (where options are often limited). Summer and school holidays (including half-terms) are particularly busy. Book at least two months ahead for July and August.

Book Your Stay Online

For more accommodation reviews by Lonely Planet authors, check out http://hotels.lonelyplanet.com/great-britain. You'll find independent reviews, as well as recommendations on the best places to stay. Best of all, you can book online.

B&Bs

The B&B (bed and breakfast) is a great British institution. At smaller places it's pretty much a room in somebody's house; larger places may be called a 'guesthouse' (halfway between a B&B and a full hotel). Prices start from around £40 per person for a simple bedroom and shared bathroom; for around £45 to £55 per person you get a private bathroom, either down the hall or en suite.

Prices Usually quoted per person, based on two people sharing a room. Single rooms for solo travellers are harder to find, and attract a 20% to 50% premium.

Booking Advance reservations are preferred at B&Bs and are essential during popular periods. You can book many B&Bs via online agencies, but rates may be cheaper if you book directly. Many B&Bs require a minimum two-night stay at weekends. Some places reduce rates for longer stays (two or three nights) mid-week.

Food Most B&Bs serve enormous breakfasts; some offer packed lunches (around £6) and evening meals (around £15 to £20).

Bed & Breakfast Nationwide (www.bedandbreakfastnationwide.com)

Hostels & Camping

There are two types of hostel in Britain: those run by the **Youth Hostels Association** (www.yha.org.uk) and **Hostelling Scotland** (www.hostellingscotland.org.uk); and independent hostels, most listed in the **Independent Hostel Guide** (www.independenthostelguide.co.uk).

Campsites range from farmers' fields with a tap and basic toilet, costing from £6 per person per night, to smarter affairs with hot showers and many other facilities, charging up to £15, sometimes more.

Hotels

There's a massive choice of hotels in Britain, from small town houses to grand country mansions, from no-frills locations to boutique hideaways. At the bargain end, single/double rooms cost from £50/60. Move up the scale and you'll pay £100/150 or beyond.

Chain hotels can be a good, affordable and functional option, though most are lacking in ambience. Some options:

Ibis Hotels (www.ibis.com)

Premier Inn (www.premierinn.com)

Travelodge (www.travelodge.co.uk)

Pubs & Inns

As well as selling drinks, many pubs and inns offer lodging, particularly in country areas. For bed and breakfast, you'll pay around £35 per person for a basic room, around £45 to £50 per person for something better.

Rental Accommodation

If you want to stay in one place, renting for a week can be ideal. Choose from neat apartments in cities or quaint old houses (always called 'cottages', whatever the size) in country areas. Rates fall at quieter times and you may be able to rent for a long weekend. Some handy websites include the following:

Cottages & Castles (www.cottages-and-castles.co.uk)

Cottages4you (www.cottages4you.co.uk)

Hoseasons (www.hoseasons.co.uk)

National Trust (www.nationaltrust.org.uk/holidays)

Stilwell's (www.stilwell.co.uk)

Climate

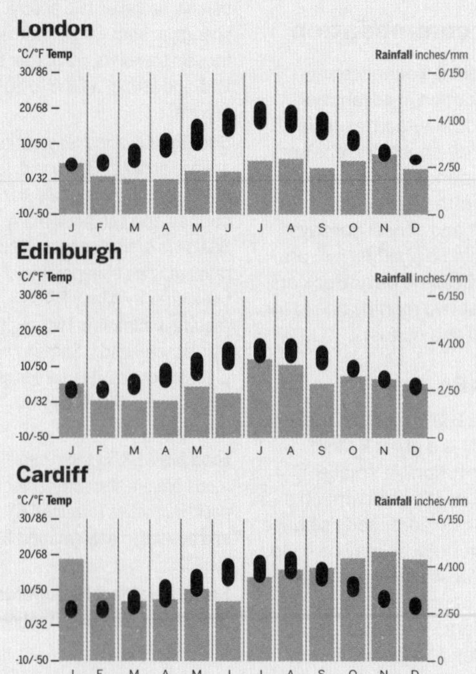

Customs Regulations

Travellers arriving in the UK from EU countries don't have to pay tax or duty on goods for personal use, and can bring in as much EU duty-paid alcohol and tobacco as they like. However, if you bring in more than the following, you'll probably be asked some questions:

- 800 cigarettes
- 1kg of tobacco
- 10L of spirits
- 90L of wine
- 110L of beer

Travellers from outside the EU can bring in, duty-free:

- 200 cigarettes *or* 100 cigarillos *or* 50 cigars *or* 250g of tobacco
- 16L of beer
- 4L of non-sparkling wine
- 1L of spirits *or* 2L of fortified wine or sparkling wine
- £390 worth of all other goods, including perfume, gifts and souvenirs

Anything over this limit must be declared to customs officers on arrival.

For further details, and for information on reclaiming VAT on items purchased in the UK by non-EU residents, go to www.gov.uk and search for 'Bringing goods into the UK'.

Food

The following price ranges refer to the cost of a main dish.

Category	London	Elsewhere
£	less than £15	less than £12
££	£15–25	£12–22
£££	more than £25	more than £22

Electricity

Type G
230V/50Hz

Health

- One of the most unwelcome aspects of Britain leaving the EU is the likely loss of reciprocal healthcare, as provided by the EHIC (European Health Insurance Card). From 1 January 2021, travellers from the EU and all other nations will require private travel insurance to cover medical care.
- Citizens from other countries should find out if there is a reciprocal arrangement for free medical care between their country and the UK.
- If you do need health insurance, make sure you get a policy that covers you for the worst possible scenarios, including emergency flights home.
- For medical advice that is not an emergency you can call the NHS 111 service (phone 111).

Internet Access

- 3G and 4G mobile broadband coverage is good in urban areas, but limited or sometimes nonexistent in rural areas. 5G is on its way but is currently not widespread.
- EU citizens can currently use their own mobile/cellphone data roaming allowance in the UK for no charge. This may change after Brexit, however, so check before you travel.

- Travellers from non-EU countries will usually incur high roaming charges – so buy a local SIM card or stick to wi-fi networks.
- Most hotels, B&Bs, hostels, stations, libraries and coffee shops (even some trains and buses) offer wi-fi access.
- Internet cafes are now very few and far between. If you're stuck, public libraries often have computers with free internet access.

Legal Matters

- Police have the power to detain, for up to six hours, anyone suspected of having committed an offence punishable by imprisonment (including drugs offences). Police have the right to search anyone they suspect of possessing drugs.
- Illegal drugs are widely available, especially in clubs. Cannabis possession is a criminal offence; punishment for carrying a small amount may be a warning, a fine or imprisonment. Dealers face much stiffer penalties, as do people caught with other drugs (especially 'Class A' drugs including cocaine, LSD, ecstasy and heroin).
- On buses and trains (including the London Underground), people without a valid ticket are fined on the spot (£80, reduced to £40 if you pay within 21 days).

LGBTIQ+ Travellers

Britain is generally a tolerant place. London, Manchester and Brighton have flourishing gay scenes, and in other sizeable cities (even some small towns), you'll find communities not entirely in the closet. That said, you'll still find pockets of homophobic hostility in some areas. Resources include the following:

Diva (www.divamag.co.uk)

Gay Times (www.gaytimes.co.uk)

Switchboard LGBT+ Helpline (www.switchboard.lgbt; 0300 330 0630)

Money

Currency

The currency of Britain is the pound sterling (£). Paper money ('notes') comes in £5, £10, £20 and £50 denominations.

Scottish banks issue their own sterling banknotes. They are interchangeable with Bank of England notes, but you'll sometimes run into problems outside Scotland – shops in the south of England may refuse to accept them. They are also harder to exchange once you get outside the UK, though British banks will always exchange them.

ATMs

ATMs (usually called 'cash machines' in Britain) are common in cities and even small towns. Cash withdrawals from some ATMs may be subject to a small charge, but most are free. If you're not from the UK, your home bank will likely charge you for withdrawing money overseas.

Credit & Debit Cards

Visa and Mastercard credit and debit cards are widely accepted in Britain. Other credit cards, including Amex, are not so widely accepted. Most businesses will assume your card is 'Chip and PIN' enabled (using a PIN instead of signing).

'Contactless' payment, where you wave your card over the reader rather than typing in a PIN, is very common (you can even use it instead of a ticket on the London Underground).

Moneychangers

Cities and larger towns have banks and exchange bureaux for changing your money into pounds. Check rates first; some bureaux offer poor rates or levy outrageous commissions. You can also change money at most post offices.

Tipping

Restaurants Not obligatory, but around 10% in restaurants and cafes is the norm. Tips may be added to your bill as a 'service charge'.

Pubs & Bars Unless you're eating and receive table service, you don't usually need to tip staff in bars or pubs.

Taxis Around 10%, or round up to the nearest pound, especially in London.

Opening Hours

Opening hours may vary throughout the year, especially in rural areas where many places have shorter hours or close completely from October or November to March or April.

Banks 9.30am–4pm or 5pm Monday to Friday; some open 9.30am–1pm Saturday

Pubs and bars Noon–11pm Monday to Saturday (many till midnight or 1am Friday and Saturday, especially in Scotland) and 12.30–11pm Sunday

Restaurants Lunch noon–3pm, dinner 6–9pm or 10pm (or later in cities)

Shops 9am–5.30pm (or to 6pm in cities) Monday to Saturday, and often 11am–5pm Sunday; big-city convenience stores open 24/7

Public Holidays

New Year's Day 1 January (plus 2 January in Scotland)

Easter March/April (Good Friday to Easter Monday inclusive)

May Day First Monday in May

Spring Bank Holiday Last Monday in May

Summer Bank Holiday Last Monday in August

Christmas Day 25 December

Boxing Day 26 December

Practicalities

- **Newspapers** Tabloids include the *Sun* and *Mirror,* and *Daily Record* (in Scotland); quality 'broadsheets' include (from right to left, politically) the *Telegraph, Times, Independent* and *Guardian*.
- **TV** All TV in the UK is digital. Leading broadcasters include BBC, ITV and Channel 4. Satellite and cable TV providers include Sky and Virgin Media.
- **Radio** The main BBC stations and wavelengths are Radio 1 (98–99.6MHz FM), Radio 2 (88–92MHz FM), Radio 3 (90–92.2 MHz FM), Radio 4 (92–94.4MHz FM) and Radio 5 Live (909 or 693 AM). National commercial stations include Virgin Radio (1215Hz MW) and non-highbrow classical specialist Classic FM (100–102MHz FM). All are available digitally.
- **DVD** PAL format (incompatible with NTSC and Secam).
- **Weights & Measures** Britain uses a mix of metric and imperial measures (eg petrol is sold by the litre but beer by the pint; mountain heights are in metres but road distances are in miles).

Safe Travel

Britain is a remarkably safe country, but crime is not unknown – especially in London and other cities.

- Watch out for pickpockets and hustlers in crowded areas popular with tourists, such as around Westminster Bridge in London.
- When travelling by tube, tram or urban train services at night, choose a carriage containing other people.
- Many town centres can be rowdy on Friday and Saturday nights when the pubs and clubs are emptying.
- Unlicensed minicabs – a driver with a car earning money on the side – operate in large cities, and are worth avoiding unless you know what you're doing.

Telephone

The UK uses the GSM 900/1800 network, which covers the rest of Europe, Australia and New Zealand, but isn't compatible with the North American GSM 1900. Most modern mobiles can function on both networks,

Emergency & Important Numbers

Britain (& UK) country code	☎44
International access code	☎00
Emergency (police, fire, ambulance, mountain rescue, coastguard)	☎112 or ☎999

but check before you leave home.

EU mobile users can currently use their home calls and data package in the UK for no extra charge, although this may change after Brexit.

Roaming charges for non-EU citizens can be prohibitively high, so it's generally worth getting a local number by buying a SIM card (widely available from shops, convenience stores and supermarkets). Pay-as-you-go SIMs start from £5 including some call credit, and can be 'topped up' with vouchers available from the same locations where you bought the card.

Your phone may be locked to your home network, however, so you'll have to either get it unlocked, or buy a cheap pay-as-you-go phone along with your SIM card (from £10).

Phone Codes

Dialling into the UK Dial your country's international access code then 44 (the UK country code), then the area code (dropping the first 0) followed by the telephone number.

Dialling out of the UK The international access code is 00; dial this, then add the code of the country you wish to dial.

Making a reverse-charge (collect) international call Dial 155 for the operator. It's an expensive option, but not for the caller.

Area codes in the UK Do not have a standard format or length, eg Edinburgh 0131, London 020, Ambleside 015394.

Directory Assistance A host of agencies offer this service – numbers include 118 118, 118 500 and 118 811 – but fees are extortionate (around £6 for a 45-second call); search online for free at www.thephonebook.bt.com.

Mobile phones Codes usually begin with 07.

Free calls Numbers starting with 0800 or 0808 are free.

National operator 100

International operator 155

Time

Britain is on GMT/UTC. The clocks go forward one hour for 'summer time' at the end of March, and go back at the end of October.

Tourist Information

Most British cities and towns, and some villages, have a tourist information centre or visitor information centre (for ease of reference Lonely Planet calls them 'tourist offices'). Some can assist with booking accommodation.

Before leaving home, check the comprehensive website of Britain's official tourist board, **Visit Britain** (www.visitbritain.com).

Visas

Visa regulations are always subject to change, and immigration restriction is currently big news in Britain, so it's essential to check with your local British embassy, high commission or consulate before leaving home.

- Due to the uncertainty surrounding the Brexit negotiations, double-check the latest rules before you travel.
- If you're a citizen of the EEA (European Economic Area) nations or Switzerland, you don't need a visa to enter or work in Britain – you can enter using your national identity card.
- Currently, if you're a citizen of Australia, Canada,

New Zealand, Japan, Israel, the USA and several other countries, you can stay for up to six months (no visa required), but are not allowed to work.

- Nationals of many countries, including South Africa, will need to obtain a visa: for more info, see www.gov.uk/check-uk-visa.
- British immigration authorities are tough; you may be required to demonstrate proof of onward travel or an outbound departure date, and possibly evidence that you have sufficient funds to support yourself while in Britain.

Transport

Getting There & Away

Air

Visitors to the UK arriving by air generally do so at one of London's two largest airports, Heathrow and Gatwick, which have a huge range of international flights to pretty much all corners of the globe. International flights also serve the capital's three other airports (Stansted, Luton and London City) and regional hubs such as Manchester, Bristol and Edinburgh.

London Airports

The national carrier is **British Airways** (www.britishairways.com).

The main airports are as follows:

Heathrow (www.heathrowairport.com) Britain's main airport for international flights; often chaotic and crowded. About 15 miles west of central London.

Gatwick (www.gatwickairport.com) Britain's number-two airport, mainly for international flights, 30 miles south of central London.

Stansted (www.stanstedairport.com) About 35 miles northeast of central London, mainly handling charter and budget European flights.

Luton (www.london-luton.co.uk) Some 35 miles north of central London, well known as a holiday-flight airport.

London City (www.londoncityairport.com) A few miles east of central London, specialising in flights to/from European and other UK airports.

Bus & Coach

You can easily get between Britain and other European countries via long-distance bus or coach. The international network **Eurolines** (www.eurolines.com) connects a huge number of destinations; you can buy tickets online via one of the national operators.

Services to/from Britain are operated by **National Express** (www.nationalexpress.com). Sample journeys and times to/from London include Amsterdam (12 hours), Barcelona (24 hours), Dublin (12 hours) and Paris (eight hours).

Ferry

The main ferry routes between Great Britain and other European countries are as follows:

- Dover–Calais (France)
- Dover–Boulogne (France)
- Newhaven–Dieppe (France)
- Liverpool–Dublin (Ireland)
- Holyhead–Dublin (Ireland)
- Fishguard–Rosslare (Ireland)
- Pembroke Dock–Rosslare (Ireland)
- Newcastle–Amsterdam (Netherlands)
- Harwich–Hook of Holland (Netherlands)
- Hull–Rotterdam (Netherlands)
- Hull–Zeebrugge (Belgium)
- Portsmouth–Santander (Spain)
- Portsmouth–Bilbao (Spain)

Fares

Most ferry operators offer flexible fares, meaning great bargains at quiet times of day or year. For example, short cross-channel routes such as Dover to Calais or Boulogne can be as low as £50 for a car plus two passengers, although around £75 to £120 is more likely. If you're a foot passenger, or cycling, there's less need to book ahead; fares on short crossings cost about £30 to £50 each way.

Bookings

Book direct with one of the operators listed here, or use the very handy www.directferries.co.uk – a single site covering all sea-ferry routes, plus **Eurotunnel** (www.eurotunnel.com).

Brittany Ferries (www.brittany-ferries.com)

DFDS Seaways (www.dfdsseaways.co.uk)

Irish Ferries (www.irishferries.com)

P&O Ferries (www.poferries.com)

Stena Line (www.stenaline.com)

Train

Channel Tunnel Passenger Service

High-speed **Eurostar** (www.eurostar.com) passenger services shuttle at least 10 times daily between London and Paris (2½ hours) or Brussels (two hours). There are three classes: Standard, Standard Premier (which includes wifi and a meal) and Business Premier. Buy tickets from travel agencies, major train stations or the Eurostar website.

The normal one-way fare between London and Paris/Brussels costs around £160; advance booking and off-peak travel gets cheaper fares, as low as £46 one way.

Channel Tunnel Car Service

Drivers use **Eurotunnel** (www.eurotunnel.com). At Folkestone in England or Calais in France, you drive onto a train, get carried through the tunnel and drive off at the other end.

Trains run about four times an hour from 6am to 10pm, then hourly through the night. Loading and unloading takes an hour; the journey lasts 35 minutes.

Book in advance online or pay on the spot. Standard one-way fares for a car and passengers start from about £60, but expect to pay substantially more during busy times.

Train & Ferry Connections

As well as Eurostar, many 'normal' trains run between Britain and mainland Europe. You buy one ticket, but get off the train at the port, walk onto a ferry, then get another train on the other side. Routes include Amsterdam–London (via Hook of Holland and Harwich). Travelling between Ireland and Britain, the main train-ferry-train route is Dublin–London, via Dún Laoghaire and Holyhead. Ferries also run between Rosslare and Fishguard or Pembroke (Wales), with train connections on either side.

Climate Change & Travel

Every form of transport that relies on carbon-based fuel generates CO_2, the main cause of human-induced climate change. Modern travel is dependent on aeroplanes, which might use less fuel per kilometre per person than most cars but travel much greater distances. The altitude at which aircraft emit gases (including CO_2) and particles also contributes to their climate change impact. Many websites offer 'carbon calculators' that allow people to estimate the carbon emissions generated by their journey and, for those who wish to do so, to offset the impact of the greenhouse gases emitted with contributions to portfolios of climate-friendly initiatives throughout the world. Lonely Planet offsets the carbon footprint of all staff and author travel.

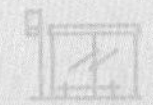

Getting Around

Air

A number of regional airlines operate in Britain, but unless you're travelling a really long way, there's rarely a huge time saving once you factor in travel to/from the airport and waiting for the plane. Short-haul air travel is also hard to defend from an environmental point of view.

The only exception is flying to some of the Scottish islands, when small planes are sometimes the only way to reach them. As always, booking early secures the best fares.

Britain's domestic airline companies include the following:

British Airways (www.british airways.com)

EasyJet (www.easyjet.com)

Loganair (www.loganair.co.uk)

Ryanair (www.ryanair.com)

Bicycle

Britain is a compact region, and hiring a bike – for an hour or two, or a week or longer – is a great way to really see the country if you've got time to spare.

Rental in London

London is famous for its **Santander Cycles** (☎0343 222 6666; www.tfl.gov.uk/modes/cycling/santander-cycles), known as 'Boris bikes' after the mayor that introduced them to the city. Bikes can be hired on the spot from automatic docking stations. For more information visit the website. Other rental options in the capital are listed at www.lcc.org.uk (under Advice/Bike Shops).

Rental Elsewhere

The **nextbike** (www.nextbike.co.uk) bike-sharing scheme has stations in Exeter, Oxford, Coventry, Glasgow, Stirling and Bath as at the time of research, while tourist towns such as York and Cambridge have plentiful bike-rental options.

Bikes on Trains

Bicycles can be taken free of charge on most local urban trains (although they may not be allowed at peak times when the trains are crowded with commuters) and on shorter trips in rural areas, on a first-come, first-served basis – though there may be space limits.

Bikes can be carried on long-distance train journeys free of charge, but advance booking is required for most conventional bikes. (Folding bikes can be carried on pretty much any train at any time.)

The PlusBike scheme provides information for travelling by train with a bike. Leaflets are available at major stations, or downloadable from www.nationalrail.co.uk/118390.aspx.

Boat

There are around 90 inhabited islands off the western and northern coasts of Scotland, which are linked to the mainland by a network of car and passenger ferries. There are two main ferry operators.

Caledonian MacBrayne (CalMac; ☎0800 066 5000; www.calmac.co.uk) Operates car ferry services to the Inner and Outer Hebrides and the islands in the Firth of Clyde.

Northlink Ferries (☎0845 6000 449; www.northlinkferries.co.uk) Operates car ferry services from Aberdeen and Scrabster to the Orkney and Shetland Islands.

Bus

If you're on a tight budget, long-distance buses (called coaches in Britain) are nearly always the cheapest way to get around, although they're also the slowest – sometimes by a considerable margin.

Long-Distance Buses

National Express (www.nationalexpress.com) Main coach operator, with a wide network and frequent services between main centres.

Scottish Citylink (www.citylink.co.uk) Scotland's leading coach company. Services link with National Express.

Megabus (www.megabus.com) Operates a budget coach service between about 30 destinations around the country.

Passes & Discounts

National Express offers discount passes to full-time students and under-26s, called Young Persons Coachcards. They cost £12.50 and give you 30% off standard adult fares. Also available are coachcards for people over 60, families, and travellers with disabilities.

Car & Motorcycle

Travelling by car or motorbike around Britain means you can be independent and flexible, and reach remote places. Downsides for drivers include traffic jams, the high price of fuel and high parking costs (and fines) in cities. Most rental cars have manual gears (stick shift).

Car Rental

Compared with many countries (especially the USA), hire rates can be expensive in Britain: the smallest cars start at about £120 per week, and it's around £190 and upwards per week for a medium car. You will require a credit card and a copy of your driving licence; drivers from some countries may also need an IDP (International Drivers' Permit).

Using a rental-broker or comparison site such as **Auto Europe** (www.autoeurope.co.uk), **UK Car Hire** (www.ukcarhire.net) or **Kayak** (www.kayak.com) can also help find bargains, but beware of cheap agencies that often have hidden terms and/or limited mileages.

Occasionally, local car hire firms can offer more competitive prices.

Basic third-party insurance is included, which covers liability to other drivers should you have an accident. Standard rental contracts usually have an excess payable in the event of damage to the vehicle, which can be £1000 or more depending on the vehicle you're driving. All car-hire firms will offer you the option of paying extra to waive this excess – but this is usually an expensive option.

Check whether your own car insurance covers you for excess on hire cars, or consider a standalone policy that covers you specifically for the excess (try comparing prices at www.moneymaxim.co.uk). If you damage the car, you will generally have to pay the excess when you return it, and then reclaim it later from your insurance company.

The main players:

Avis (www.avis.co.uk)

Budget (www.budget.co.uk)

Europcar (www.europcar.co.uk)

Sixt (www.sixt.co.uk)

Thrifty (www.thrifty.co.uk)

Motorhome Rental

Hiring a motorhome or camper van (£650 to £1200 a week) is more expensive than hiring a car, but saves on accommodation costs and gives almost unlimited freedom. Sites to check include:

Just Go (www.justgo.uk.com)

Wild Horizon (www.wildhorizon.co.uk)

Insurance

It's illegal to drive a car or motorbike in Britain without (at least) third-party insurance. This will be included with all rental cars. If you're bringing a car from Europe, you'll need to arrange it.

Parking

Many cities have short-stay and long-stay car parks; the latter are cheaper though may be less convenient. 'Park & Ride' systems allow you to park on the edge of the city then ride to the centre on frequent non-stop buses for an all-in-one price.

Yellow lines (single or double) along the edge of the road indicate parking restrictions. Nearby signs will spell out when you can and can't park. In London and other big cities, traffic wardens operate with efficiency; if you park on the yellow lines at the wrong time, your car will be clamped or towed away, and it'll cost you £130 or more to get driving again. In some cities there are also red lines, which mean no stopping at any time.

Also beware of other areas that may be restricted in some other way (eg for local residents or pass-holders only).

Road Rules

A foreign driving licence is valid in Britain for up to 12 months.

Drink-driving is taken very seriously; you're allowed a maximum blood-alcohol level of 80mg/100mL (0.08%) in England and Wales, and 50mg/100mL (0.05%) in Scotland.

Some other important rules:

- drive on the left (!)
- wear fitted seatbelts in cars
- wear helmets on motorcycles
- give way to your right at junctions and roundabouts
- always use the left lane on motorways and dual carriageways unless overtaking (although so many people ignore this rule, you'd think it didn't exist)
- don't use a mobile phone while driving unless it's fully hands-free (another rule frequently flouted)

Local Transport

Local Buses

There are good local bus networks year-round in cities and towns. Buses also run in some rural areas year-round, although timetables are designed to serve schools and businesses.

Local Bus Passes

If you're taking a few local bus rides in one area, day passes (with names like Day Rover, Wayfarer or Explorer) are cheaper than buying several single tickets. Often they can be bought on your first bus, and may include local rail services. It's always worth asking ticket clerks or bus drivers about your options.

Taxi

Officially there are two sorts of taxi in Britain: those with meters that can be hailed in the street; and minicabs, which are cheaper but can only be called by phone. More recently, in many locations these have been usurped by ride-hailing services like **Uber** (www.uber.com) and **Kabbee** (www.kabbee.com), which now operate in many British cities (including, at the time of writing, London).

In London, most taxis are the famous 'black cabs' (some with advertising livery in other colours), which charge by distance and time: they may be an institution, but be aware that they are also expensive. Depending on the time of day, a 1-mile journey takes five to 10 minutes and costs £7 to £10. Longer journeys are proportionally cheaper. Black cabs also operate in some other large cities around Britain, with rates usually lower than in London.

In London, taxis are best flagged down in the street; a 'for hire' light on the roof indicates availability. In other cities, you can flag down a cab if you see one, but it's usually easier to go to a taxi rank.

In rural areas, taxis need to be called by phone; the best place to find the local taxi's phone number is the local pub. Fares are £3 to £5 per mile.

Traintaxi (www.traintaxi.co.uk) is a portal site for journeys between the train station and your hotel or other final destination.

Train

For long-distance travel around Britain, trains are generally faster and more comfortable than coaches, but can be substantially more expensive – especially if you're used to cheap, subsidised fares in other European countries. In fact, per mile, train travel in Britain is among the most expensive in Europe.

Having said that, trains are usually by far the most convenient way to travel around – and there's a station in most sizeable towns and cities. Services aren't as punctual as they probably should be given the cost, but in general most services tend to run on time.

Information

Your first stop should be **National Rail Enquiries** (www.nationalrail.co.uk), the nationwide timetable and fare information service. Its website advertises special offers and has real-time links to station departure boards and downloadable maps of the rail network.

Operators

About 20 different companies operate train services in Britain, while Network Rail operates track and stations.

Tickets & Reservations

Once you've found the journey you need on the National Rail Enquiries website, links take you to the relevant train operator to buy the ticket. This can be mailed to you (UK addresses only) or collected at the station on the day of travel from automatic machines. There's usually no booking fee on top of the ticket price.

You can also use a centralised ticketing service to buy your train ticket. These cover all train services in a single site, but they may charge a booking fee on top of every ticket price. The main players include:

QJump (www.qjump.co.uk)
Rail Easy (www.raileasy.co.uk)
Trainline (www.thetrainline.com)

You can also buy train tickets on the spot at stations, which is fine for short journeys (under about 50 miles), but discount tickets for longer trips are usually not available and must be bought in advance by phone or online.

One tip that's worth considering is whether splitting your journey may result in a cheaper fare: services like **TrainPal** (mytrainpal.com) and TrainTickets.com can help you check. Cheap day returns are often not much more expensive than buying single tickets.

Costs

For longer journeys, on-the-spot fares are always available, but tickets are much cheaper if bought in advance, and if you're happy to specify the train on which you travel (which also means you get a reserved seat). The earlier you book, the cheaper it gets. Travelling off-peak (ie outside popular commuter hours) is cheaper.

One major drawback is that the cheapest fares (eg Advance) are usually non-refundable, so if you miss your train you'll have to buy a new ticket.

Whichever operator you travel with and wherever you buy tickets, these are the three main fare types:

Anytime Buy anytime, travel anytime – usually the most expensive option.

Off-peak Buy ticket any time, travel off-peak (what is off-peak depends on the journey).

Advance Buy ticket in advance, travel only on specific trains – usually the cheapest option.

Onward Travel

If the train doesn't get you all the way to your destination, you can add a **PlusBus** (www.plusbus.info) supplement when making your reservation to validate your train ticket for onward travel by bus. This is more convenient, and usually cheaper, than buying a separate bus ticket.

Train Passes

Discount Passes

If you're staying in Britain for a while, passes known as **Railcards** (www.railcard.co.uk) are worth considering:

16-25 Railcard For those aged 16 to 25, or full-time UK students.

Two Together Railcard For two specified people travelling together.

Senior Railcard For anyone over 60.

Family & Friends Railcard Covers up to four adults and four children travelling together.

Railcards cost £30 (valid for one year, available from major stations or online) and give a 33% discount on most train fares, except those already heavily discounted. With the Family card, adults get 33% and children get 60% discounts, so the fee is easily recouped in a couple of journeys.

Local & Regional Passes

Local train passes usually cover rail networks around a city (many include bus travel too). If you're concentrating your travels on southeast England (eg London to Dover, Weymouth, Cambridge or Oxford), a **Network Railcard** (per year £30) covers up to four adults and up to four children travelling together outside peak times.

National Passes

For country-wide travel, **BritRail** (www.britrail.net) passes are available for visitors from overseas. They must be bought in your country of origin (not in Britain) from a specialist travel agency. They're available in seven different versions (eg England only; Scotland only; all of Britain; UK and Ireland) for periods from four to 30 days.

Behind the Scenes

Acknowledgements

Climate map data adapted from Peel MC, Finlayson BL & McMahon TA (2007) 'Updated World Map of the Köppen-Geiger Climate Classification', *Hydrology and Earth System Sciences*, 11, 1633–44.

Cover photograph: Footbridge and cottage in Lower Slaughter, Gloucestershire, Adam Burton/Alamy Stock Photo ©

Illustrations pp44-5, pp202-3, pp228-9, pp234-5 by Javier Zarracina

This Book

This 3rd edition of Lonely Planet's *Best of Great Britain* guidebook was researched and written by Damian Harper, Isabel Albiston, Oliver Berry, Joe Bindloss, Fionn Davenport, Belinda Dixon, Anna Kaminski, Catherine Le Nevez, Tasmin Waby and Neil Wilson. The previous two editions were also written by Oliver, Fionn, Marc Di Duca, Belinda, Peter Dragicevich, Damian, Catherine, Sophie McGrath, Hugh McNaughtan, Lorna Parkes, Andy Symington, Greg Ward and Neil. This guidebook was produced by the following:

Senior Product Editor Sandie Kestell

Cartographer Alison Lyall

Product Editor Daniel Bolger

Book Designer Gwen Cotter

Assisting Editors Andrew Bain, Nigel Chin, Andrea Dobbin, Carly Hall, Kellie Langdon, Kate Morgan, Kirsten Rawlings, Brana Vladisavljevic

Cover Researcher Fergal Condon

Thanks to Genna Patterson, Karen Henderson, Amy Lynch, James Appleton, Bruce Evans, Katie Connolly, Angela Tinson

Send Us Your Feedback

We love to hear from travellers – your comments keep us on our toes and help make our books better. Our well-travelled team reads every word on what you loved or loathed about this book. Although we cannot reply individually to postal submissions, we always guarantee that your feedback goes straight to the appropriate authors, in time for the next edition. Each person who sends us information is thanked in the next edition, the most useful submissions are rewarded with a selection of digital PDF chapters.

Visit lonelyplanet.com/contact to submit your updates and suggestions or to ask for help. Our award-winning website also features inspirational travel stories, news and discussions.

Note: We may edit, reproduce and incorporate your comments in Lonely Planet products such as guidebooks, websites and digital products, so let us know if you don't want your comments reproduced or your name acknowledged. For a copy of our privacy policy visit lonelyplanet.com/privacy.

Index

000 Map pages

Symbols & Map Key

Look for these symbols to quickly identify listings:

- Sights
- Activities
- Courses
- Tours
- Festivals & Events
- Eating
- Drinking
- Entertainment
- Shopping
- Information & Transport

These symbols and abbreviations give vital information for each listing:

- Sustainable or green recommendation
- FREE No payment required
- Telephone number
- Opening hours
- Parking
- Nonsmoking
- Air-conditioning
- Internet access
- Wi-fi access
- Swimming pool
- Bus
- Ferry
- Tram
- Train
- English-language menu
- Vegetarian selection
- Family-friendly

Find your best experiences with these Great For... icons.

Art & Culture

Beaches

Budget

Cafe/Coffee

Cycling

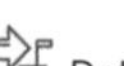
Detour

Drinking

Entertainment

Events

Family Travel

Food & Drink

History

Local Life

Nature & Wildlife

Photo Op

Scenery

Shopping

Short Trip

Sport

Walking

Winter Travel

Sights

- Beach
- Bird Sanctuary
- Buddhist
- Castle/Palace
- Christian
- Confucian
- Hindu
- Islamic
- Jain
- Jewish
- Monument
- Museum/Gallery/ Historic Building
- Ruin
- Shinto
- Sikh
- Taoist
- Winery/Vineyard
- Zoo/Wildlife Sanctuary
- Other Sight

Points of Interest

- Bodysurfing
- Camping
- Cafe
- Canoeing/Kayaking
- Course/Tour
- Diving
- Drinking & Nightlife
- Eating
- Entertainment
- Sento Hot Baths/ Onsen
- Shopping
- Skiing
- Sleeping
- Snorkelling
- Surfing
- Swimming/Pool
- Walking
- Windsurfing
- Other Activity

Information

- Bank
- Embassy/Consulate
- Hospital/Medical
- Internet
- Police
- Post Office
- Telephone
- Toilet
- Tourist Information
- Other Information

Geographic

- Beach
- Gate
- Hut/Shelter
- Lighthouse
- Lookout
- Mountain/Volcano
- Oasis
- Park
- Pass
- Picnic Area
- Waterfall

Transport

- Airport
- BART station
- Border crossing
- Boston T station
- Bus
- Cable car/Funicular
- Cycling
- Ferry
- Metro/MRT station
- Monorail
- Parking
- Petrol station
- Subway/S-Bahn/ Skytrain station
- Taxi
- Train station/Railway
- Tram
- Underground/ U-Bahn station
- Other Transport

Joe Bindloss

Joe Bindloss first got the travel bug from trips around the Med in the family camper van, and he's been travelling ever since, writing more than 100 guidebooks and reference titles for Lonely Planet and other publishers, covering everywhere from India and Nepal to Australia and England. For many years, Joe was Lonely Planet's Destination Editor for the Indian Subcontinent. He also writes regularly for newspapers, websites and magazines.

Fionn Davenport

Irish by birth and conviction, Fionn has spent the last two decades focusing on the country of his birth and its nearest neighbour, England, which he has written about extensively for Lonely Planet and others. In between writing gigs he's lived in Paris and New York, where he was an editor, actor, bartender and whatever else paid the rent; when he returned to Ireland in the late 1990s he tried his hand at radio, which landed him a series of presenting gigs, most recently as host of Inside Culture and regular travel contributor to the mid-morning Sean O'Rourke Show, both on RTE Radio 1. He moved to Manchester a few years ago where he lives with his wife, Laura, but he commutes back and forth to Dublin, only 40 minutes away. He posts his travel shots on instagram @ fionndavenport.

Belinda Dixon

Only happy when her feet are suitably sandy, Belinda has been (gleefully) travelling, researching and writing for Lonely Planet since 2006. It's seen her navigating mountain passes and soaking in hot-pots in Iceland's Westfjords, marvelling at Stonehenge at sunrise; scrambling up Italian mountain paths; horse riding across Donegal's golden sands; gazing at Verona's frescoes; and fossil hunting on Dorset's Jurassic Coast. Then there's the food and drink: truffled mushroom pasta in Salo; whisky in Aberdeen, Balti in Birmingham, grilled fish in Dartmouth; wine in Bardolino. And all in the name of research. Belinda is also a podcaster and adventure writer and helps lead wilderness expeditions. Something that's resulted in her clattering around on Himalayan glaciers, paddling Canadian canoes down Yukon rivers, climbing Dartmoor crags, surfing and swimming in England's winter seas and sleeping out under the stars. See her blog posts at belindadixon.com.

Anna Kaminski

Originally from the Soviet Union, Anna grew up in Cambridge, UK. She graduated from the University of Warwick with a degree in Comparative American Studies, a background in the history, culture and literature of the Americas and the Caribbean, and an enduring love of Latin America. Her restless wanderings led her to settle briefly in Oaxaca and Bangkok and her flirtation with criminal law saw her volunteering as a lawyer's assistant in the courts, ghettos and prisons of Kingston, Jamaica. Anna has contributed to almost 30 Lonely Planet titles. When not on the road, Anna calls London home.

Catherine Le Nevez

Catherine's wanderlust kicked in when she roadtripped across Europe from her Parisian base aged four, and she's been hitting the road at every opportunity since, travelling to some 60 countries and completing her Doctorate of Creative Arts in Writing, Masters in Professional Writing, and post-grad qualifications in Editing and Publishing along the way. Over the past decade-and-a-half she's written scores of Lonely Planet guides and articles covering Paris, France, Europe and far beyond. Her work has also appeared in numerous online and print publications. Topping Catherine's list of travel tips is to travel without any expectations.

Tasmin Waby

A London-born writer, Tasmin was raised on the traditional lands of Aboriginal Australians, for which she will always be grateful. As well as reading, writing and editing, she's madly in love with cartography, deserts, and starry skies. When not on assignment she lives on a narrowboat in the UK, raising two hilariously funny school-aged children.

Neil Wilson

Neil was born in Scotland and has lived there most of his life. Based in Perthshire, he has been a full-time writer since 1988, working on more than 80 guidebooks for various publishers, including the Lonely Planet guides to Scotland, England, Ireland and Prague. An outdoors enthusiast since childhood, Neil is an active hill-walker, mountain-biker, sailor, snowboarder and rock-climber, and a qualified fly-fishing guide and instructor. He has climbed and tramped in four continents, including ascents of Jebel Toubkal in Morocco, Mount Kinabalu in Borneo, the Old Man of Hoy in Scotland's Orkney Islands and the Northwest Face of Half Dome in California's Yosemite Valley.

Our Story

A beat-up old car, a few dollars in the pocket and a sense of adventure. In 1972 that's all Tony and Maureen Wheeler needed for the trip of a lifetime – across Europe and Asia overland to Australia. It took several months, and at the end – broke but inspired – they sat at their kitchen table writing and stapling together their first travel guide, *Across Asia on the Cheap*. Within a week they'd sold 1500 copies. Lonely Planet was born. Today, Lonely Planet has offices in Tennessee, Dublin, Beijing and Delhi, with a network of over 2000 contributors in every corner of the globe. We share Tony's belief that 'a great guidebook should do three things: inform, educate and amuse'.

Our Writers

Damian Harper

With two degrees (one in modern and classical Chinese from SOAS), Damian has been writing for Lonely Planet for over two decades, contributing to titles as diverse as *Vietnam*, *Thailand*, *Ireland*, *London*, *Mallorca*, *Malaysia*, *Singapore & Brunei*, China's Southwest and the UK. A seasoned guidebook writer, Damian has penned articles for numerous newspapers and magazines, including *The Guardian* and *The Daily Telegraph*, and currently makes Surrey, England, his home. A self-taught trumpet novice, his other hobbies include collecting modern first editions, photography and Taekwondo. Follow Damian on Instagram (damian.harper).

Isabel Albiston

After six years working for *The Daily Telegraph* in London, Isabel left to spend more time on the road. A job as writer for a magazine in Sydney, Australia was followed by a four-month overland trip across Asia and five years living and working in Buenos Aires, Argentina. Isabel started writing for Lonely Planet in 2014 and has contributed to 15 guidebooks. She's currently based in Ireland.

Oliver Berry

Oliver Berry is a writer and photographer from Cornwall. He has worked for Lonely Planet for more than a decade, covering destinations from Cornwall to the Cook Islands, and has worked on more than 30 guidebooks. He is also a regular contributor to many newspapers and magazines, including Lonely Planet Traveller. His writing has won several awards, including The Guardian Young Travel Writer of the Year and the TNT Magazine People's Choice Award. His latest work is published at www.oliverberry.com.

More Writers

STAY IN TOUCH LONELYPLANET.COM/CONTACT

Digital Depot, Roe Lane (off Thomas St),
Digital Hub, Dublin 8, D08 TCV4, Ireland

Although the authors and Lonely Planet have taken all reasonable care in preparing this book, we make no warranty about the accuracy or completeness of its content and, to the maximum extent permitted, disclaim all liability arising from its use.

All rights reserved. No part of this publication may be copied, stored in a retrieval system, or transmitted in any form by any means, electronic, mechanical, recording or otherwise, except brief extracts for the purpose of review, and no part of this publication may be sold or hired, without the written permission of the publisher. Lonely Planet and the Lonely Planet logo are trademarks of Lonely Planet and are registered in the US Patent and Trademark Office and in other countries. Lonely Planet does not allow its name or logo to be appropriated by commercial establishments, such as retailers, restaurants or hotels. Please let us know of any misuses: lonelyplanet.com/ip.

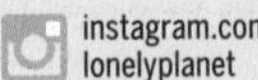

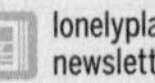